EC

ECO-WARRIORS

UNDERSTANDING ᵀᴴᴱ RADICAL ENVIRONMENTAL MOVEMENT

UPDATED EDITION

RIK SCARCE

FOREWORD BY DAVID BROWER

Left Coast Press Inc.   Walnut Creek, California

Left Coast Press, Inc.
1630 North Main Street, #400
Walnut Creek, California 94596
http://www.LCoastPress.com

ISBN: 1-59874-028-8

Library of Congress Control Number 2005928675

05 06 07 08 5 4 3 2 1

Printed in the United States of America

This title is printed on Perfection Antique Recycled paper containing a minimum 30% recycled waste. The balance contains virgin fiber. The paper is acid free and meets the minimum requirements of ANSI/NISCO Z 39.48-1992 (R 1997) (Permanence of Paper).

Grateful acknowledgment is made for permission to reprint excerpts from the following:

Pages 244: "Beauty of Things", copyright © 1951 by Robinson Jeffers, "Vulture", copyright © 1963 by Garth Jeffers and Donnan Jeffers, from *Selected Poetry of Robinson Jeffers* by Robinson Jeffers. Used by permission of Random House, Inc.
244–245: "Hurt Hawks", copyright © 1928 and renewed 1956 by Robinson Jeffers, from *Selected Poetry of Robinson Jeffers* by Robinson Jeffers. Used by permission of Random House, Inc. 246: "Bear," copyright © 2005 by Gary Snyder from *Left Out in the Rain*. Reprinted by permission of Shoemaker & Hoard Publishers. 247–248: "Holy Cow" by Kathy Minott, reprinted with permission of Kathy Minott. 248: "The Dying Mouse in the North Cascades" by Michael Robinson, reprinted with permission of Michael Robinson. 250: "Bad Wolf" by B. N. Koehler, reprinted with permission of B. N. Koehler. 252–253: "You Can't Clearcut Your Way to Heaven" by Darryl Cherney, reprinted with permission of Darryl Cherney.

For Petra and Alexander

CONTENTS

PART FOUR
INSPIRATION AND THE FUTURE

FOREWORD

David Brower

More than a quarter-century ago I wrote, "We still need conservationists who will attempt the impossible, achieving it because they aren't aware of how impossible it is." Today, some people within the environmental movement possess a firm grasp of the impossibility of their task, yet they persevere. They are the conscience of the movement, although some people who are silent as they watch environmental destruction prefer to label them as environmental "radicals." An ecological reading of recent history, however, shows that the truly radical actions are perpetrated by those who have given us acid rain, the greenhouse effect, decimation of species, and who pillage ancient forest, mountain, and ocean treasures without considering their incalculable damage to the Earth and the future.

Those who lay waste to wild places and wild beings increasingly face the ire of the new environmentalists. For the most part the old guard of the environmental movement stand still, waiting for just what, I do not know, having left it long ago. Meanwhile the new guard generate the *motion* within the movement. They provide the constant new breath people are craving, the freshness of innovative tactics, strategies, demands, and resolutions. Such is the energy behind any movement. If we close off ourselves from creatively confronting challenges and refuse to learn anew, how can we expect to engage others? Nothing is stirring, not even a mouse, in the stagnant pool of Conventional Wisdom. We need new ideas coming into light upstream, from the springs of fresh water.

The new guard do share some traits with the old: up to a point they beg to be heard and plead with regulators and lawmakers for something better than just a charade. But unlike their predecessors, they abhor the next step, compromise. This is by choice. They much prefer to sit down in front of bulldozers, sit up in trees, break out of the polite conservationist mold, and intervene to expose a cruelty to living things that is hidden behind a cloak of product safety and progress. They are determined to protect and restore the Earth.

The new guard place Earth first and immoderate human wants far down the list. They recognize the intricacy of the web of life and the challenges of living as part of it rather than apart from it. They are too late and too few to reverse past destruction, but these people spend little time

wringing their hands about it. Those who call them Cassandras forget that
Cassandra told the truth.They do not qualify for worse epithets: coward,
unbeliever, unhopeful, doubter, negativist, or realist ("We march toward
annihilation under the banner of realism"—Richard Barnet). They are optimistic enough to think something can be done. They do not want to be
like the practical man "who has made all his decisions, but lost the ability
to listen, and is determined to perpetuate the errors of his ancestors."

Someone calls me a pessimist in this book because I once was fond of
quoting Allen Morgan's prediction, "What we save in the next few years is
all that will ever be saved." The optimists in the environmental movement
note the nearly three decades of dust on that statement. Millions of acres
of unspoiled land have been dedicated to preservation in the last quarter-
century, but millions more have been released for development, and the
attack on wilderness boundaries continues. There are still some fair ladies,
but too many faint hearts, to succeed in winning them. Those fair places
and the legitimate denizens are being lost at an ever-increasing rate to
clear-cuts, over-grazing, dams, condominiums, pipelines, pavement, oil
spills, acid rain, ozone holes, and complacency.

Yesterday's warriors smugly lean back in their chairs and insist that
only a slow, deliberate course of action for the protection of the environment is satisfactory. Ninety million acres of wilderness saved, they say,
and good work is being done to protect more; the bald eagle and buffalo
were brought back from the bring of extinction; whaling is on the decline.
Such successes take time, they say, time and compromise. Direct action—
when the new guard go to the source of an environmnetal ill and attempt
immediately to end the travesties being perpetrated there—only hinders
compromise. Those who protest by carrying placards, sitting in trees, or
vitiating the implements of destruction are ideologues in the eyes of the
moderationists.

My half-century-plus of involvement with the movement prevents my
being convinced by the cool rhetoric of the over-confident. I do not suspect that I ever will be. The white noise behind their words sounds like a
materialistic mantra. "More, more, more," it spiritlessly drones on, "more
money, more comfort, more microwaves. We can have more, more more
while saving more and more wilderness."

We can't. Something is seriously askew in the optimists' equation, and
I think it has its basis in ecology, specifically in the rate of change that the
Earth's ecosystem can absorb and still maintain itself. Natural change in
nature happens slowly, with rare and usually local exceptions, like surprise crashes of asteroids. Human-caused changes, as we now know, can
occur with devastating rapidity. It takes millions of years to turn the plants
of bygone eras into pools of petroleum and clumps of coal. However, in
perhaps two desert tortoise life spans we humans made our own deadly

fossil brew, spewing the poisons into the air and spreading them over our seas and shores. That more, more, more depends upon non-sustainable energy supplies, depleted and un-repletable stocks of rare and precious minerals, farmed-out croplands, and air and water that is no longer fit for human consumption: more environmental sacrifices for more stuff. They make unattainable the sustainable society we like to talk about.

If we cannot agree with the optimists within the environmental community, what then is our choice? First of all, do not give up on them. Join the mainstream organizations, the ones discussed in this book and the others. Encourage them to make a difference. Send them your dues, write letters, and nudge them in the right direction. Meanwhile, they can help coax along the system within which they operate.

Secondly, embrace the new guard alternative. As Rik Scarce shows, these activists are not addicted to pessimism. They want to eradicate its source. From my experience, they like a good time as much as anyone. They are not dour, groaning doomsayers. They do not think that constantly haranguing their fellow humans will make a difference. They get involved and make things happen. They laugh hard, work hard, and don't mind a beer or two. Toast them! They long to go smiling into the promised land, an Earthly place where the highest human ideals are embraced by all. They fight unselfishly and with deeply held committment for community, kinship, freedom, beauty, love, and justice for all—humans, other animals, land, air, water, plants, and probably a few planets as well. The green wolf-fire in their eyes manifests a ferocity unmatched in the hundred-fifty-year popular struggle for protection of other beings, here now, or scheduled to arrive in decades and eons to come.

The time is ripe for embarking on new ways of living that will bring into balance the lopsided man-over-nature relationship. Today's industrialized society is addicted to Strength Through Exhaustion. It substitutes irreplaceables for renewables. Like the Forty-niners in their haste to gain wealth and live for today, we too often extirpate the riches that could sustain us, leaving a wasted landscape behind. Renewing their source will be monstrously expensive, but let our kids pay for it. Our challenge, and this gets to the heart of the environmental movement's message, is to live in the flow and yet refrain from mining, milling, and driving our successors and most of the rest of the world's species into oblivion.

These lifestyle changes cannot wait. If it takes creative mechanics on a bulldozer in the middle of an ancient forest to push society toward more healthful, ecologically sane ways of living, then so be it. The same goes for confiscating forty-mile-long driftnets that are stripmining the ocean. A liberated chimp will perish in your home town. End the practice of abusing them. Ecological grand larceny is what must stop, for no amount of creative mechanics can get an ancient forest back.

The time for compromise by the environmental movement has long since passed. A pluralistic society must compromise but the compromise must be between advocates, not compromisers. The public has grown tired of the lethargic responses by government and business to the eco-catastrophes now here. From Love Canal to the Grand Canyon, from the redwood forests to the Everglades, people are taking their planet's survival into their own hands in peaceful direct action. You and I need to be the eco-rescuers. The place to rescue is the Earth—all of it. Awaiting the outcome are trees, waterfalls, grains of sand, and generations of humans and other delightful living things yet to come aboard, but whose genes are here now, needing our protection.

It is important for the old guard—contemporaries and those a decade or two younger—to realize where the new environmentalists are coming from and what drives them. The new guard have watched while the gentle attempts to accommodate larcenous attacks on the Earth and on the rights of the future fail to slow those attacks. They have remembered, from Nuremberg, that those who watch such attacks and remain silent and inactive are considered to be co-conspirators. The new guard have become impatient as those who execute laws turn the process of preserving everyone's freedom in the protection of a few peoples's property. They have seen the appeals process become a charade, decisions already having been made behind closed doors before the formal hearing opens.

If the new environmentalists' frustration and exasperation erodes their sense of humor now and then—and if they forget to add wit to ther protests—they deserve to be forgiven and reminded that wit is their greatest asset. If exasperation should lead to desperation—and their protests are the early warning that desperation is not far away—those who refuse to forfend that desperation unwittingly become a dangerous driving force. They are co-conspirators in the violence that history tells us will follow. In a real sense, reckless prudence is co-conspiratorial.

A comparatively small group is now fighting in the hope that the eco-rescue effort is not already too late. That spirit of hope pervades this movement. Ordinary people feel it and rise to the occasion. Unlike nearly all revolutionaries of the past, these activists embrace life-affirming strategies and tactics that are inherently benign to all living things. Their cause isn't noble. It's essential. And if seeing love, compassion, beauty, and a bit of joy prevail makes you feel good, the cause is rewarding—and not impossible.

David R. Brower
Yosemite Valley
May 13, 1990

PREFACE TO THE UPDATED EDITION

With few exceptions, the book you hold is the same as the 1990 edition. What has changed is the final chapter, which I completely rewrote to be an update of the years 1990–2005; the index reflects those updates; the "Getting Involved" listing is longer and includes web addresses; and an "Errata" page notes mistakes that made it into the original edition.

Fifteen years on, I marvel at the radical environmental movement's continued relevance and its growing prevalence. Its relevance emerges from Western societies' unchecked destruction of ecosystems. Where would we be, environmentally, if the loudest voices on behalf of the planet were the whispers that emanate from the corporate-like boardrooms of the environmental organizations headquartered in Washington, D.C.? The radicals' warning screams from wilderness treetops and laboratory torture chambers call us to issues that otherwise would go unnoticed.

The movement's prevalence can be seen from coast to coast and continent to continent. Since 1990 environmental activism has grown dramatically. In recent years there have been more eco-warriors sitting in ancient trees, blockading roadways into wilderness, sailing the high seas in protection of marine life, freeing animals, and assaulting the forces of development than ever before.

And now they are joining with activists from diverse movements who live in every corner of the planet. We are, I think, witnessing a global, last-ditch struggle by those protestors for people and planet—for cultures, species, and ecosystems that are endangered by the same phenomenon: corporate globalization. It is a dangerous yet exciting time to be alive.

RS
Saratoga Springs, New York
October, 2005

PREFACE TO THE FIRST EDITION

Radical environmentalists present us with much to dislike. Loud, pushy, morally superior, they tend to answer somewhere between "everything" and "almost everything" when asked what bothers them about society. It seems they don't speak the same language as the rest of us; clearly they don't see the world in the same way. They talk about tribalism, anarchy, ecology, and other such subversive topics like the rest of us chat about our neighborhoods, the latest political scandal, and flower gardens. While the rest of us rally against the Earth's destruction one day in every twenty years, they set out to stop the pillaging—or at least to neutralize it—at its source day in and day out.

At first blush nothing seems sacred to these warriors for the environment. In truth, however, they believe in the highest ideals of Western society—the very ideals that are being put out of reach because of our civilization's overwhelming urge to control and manipulate everything, human and non-human alike. Perhaps the best label for them is *culturalists*. They believe, as someone once wrote, that culture is what lasts in a civilization—the best of the books, music, art, and ideas that survive the test of time. Eco-warriors might add "nature" to that list. It is a measure of the power of our tools that we can even begin to consider nature as something human-created. Yet in our time, extensive and nearly absolute control and manipulation of the non-human world is a given. We have achieved what our forebears spent untold generations attempting to accomplish: Nature is ours. Now radical environmentalists want to give it back.

In their own words and deeds, radical environmentalists challenge us to reorient our individual lives and our society. They ask, or demand, that we seek a steady-state relationship with all of nature's creations, wherein human attitudes and actions dominate no one and no thing. Their alternative seeks to guarantee life, liberty, evolution, and happiness for humans and non-humans alike. How they go about espousing their new world view may not be to our liking, and their actions often get in the way of their message. But by allowing these activists to speak for themselves, I hope their ends will become clearer and their reasons for choosing their means better understood. Only then can we fairly judge them—and ourselves.

Rik Scarce
Turner Creek Camp
Ventana Wilderness, California
April 1990

ACKNOWLEDGMENTS

Many people played important roles in the creation and development of this book. My mother, Jane Carr, imbued me with a librarian's love of the written word. More recently, Syndee Brinkman was of great help in introducing me to the Animal Liberation movement, and dozens of activists and critics of the radical environmental movement generously gave of their time to be interviewed. For their contributions in reading and commenting on chapters in draft form, Rod Coronado, Marti Goddard, Chris Jones, Madeline von Lau, Sue Rodrigues-Pastor, Myra Finkelstein, and Renee Grandi deserve considerable thanks. Marti Kheel applied straightforward criticism and a deft pen to the philosophy and Animal Liberation chapters. Of all my reviewers, Michael Robinson deserves special notice. He thoroughly examined each chapter and was something of a second editor; the final product reflects his insights and criticisms throughout. Despite all of these helpful hands, however, I remain solely responsible for the book's factual and conceptual accuracy.

It must be rare for a first-time author to have the pleasure and challenge of working with a redactor who, going into the project, is his or her closest friend. My guess is that it is rarer still that, as the effort continues, the two maintain their friendship. Somehow, that has been the case here. Mark Harris's sensitivity (to any outsider he would appear coarse and crass, but such is the nature of our good-humored friendship) to my ego and my anxieties, not to mention his unfaltering enthusiasm, helped me feel this effort was worthwhile and accomplishable. His insight into the strengths and shortcomings of the text were of the sort that one would expect from someone with many more years of experience in the field. The next one, S'kopf, is on me.

Lastly, my life partner, Petra Uhrig, was always there when I needed support and begged for patience. Somehow she almost singlehandedly held together the fragile web of our lives during the last year.

For the Updated Edition: I greatly appreciate the faith in this book that Mitch Allen, the publisher at Left Coast Press, has shown. In addition, Jennifer Collier, editor, and Detta Penna, copy editor, were consummate professionals. Finally, sociologist Douglas Bevington and an activist who shall remain nameless were of great help in suggesting changes to the final chapter.

PART ONE

TOWARDS AN UNDERSTANDING

CHAPTER 1

GANDHI MEETS THE LUDDITES

Three parachutists, commandoes outfitted for cold weather combat, floated down through the February cold of central British Columbia toward a snowy, city-block square clearing. Their mission, oddly, was not to destroy but to protect; their bodies were their only weapons. The three—Myra Finkelstein, Renee Grandi, and Randy Riebin—were from Friends of the Wolf, a non-profit group established to fight the extermination of wolves wherever they are threatened. The primary aim of their sensational stunt was to draw the media's attention by dropping into the middle of a government-sponsored wolf hunt and stopping the annual carnage dead in its tracks. Between 1982 and 1987 British Columbia had spent more than $2,400,000 to kill 800 *Canis lupus*, native wolves that annually killed thousands of elk, moose, and caribou, which were normally the targets of hunters. The government had organized the wolf hunt to placate angry hunters and recoup revenue lost from the drop in the hunting trade. Like the Friends, the wolf hunters also came by air. The government's hired guns baited the wolves with mounds of caribou meat. Later, as the wolves gorged themselves or lay relaxing nearby after their feast, the hunters would return in helicopters to swoop down on them, blasting away with their 12-gauge semiautomatic shotguns, turning the ice crimson with wolf blood. Ultimately, the government hoped to wipe the Muskwa River Valley clean of wolves, effectively killing one-half of British Columbia's wolf population.

Wolves, long portrayed in folklore as fearsome beasts, are in fact formidable predators, but ones loathe to have contact with humans. Because of ignorance about wolves' habits, and because they and other powerful mammals—like mountain lions and grizzly bears—kill the same "game" animals to live that humans kill for sport (and attack the livestock animals that humans attempt to raise in their former habitat), wolves have been hunted relentlessly. They have been poisoned, trapped, and shot, and their habitat has been so thoroughly obliterated by human incursions that fewer than an estimated 1,300 wolves exist in the U.S., a land in which they once roamed and flourished. These highly social animals co-existed with their prey for tens of thousands of years, playing out the rituals of birth, life, death, and rebirth. In British Columbia, however, the wolves were referred to as "shop lifters," says Finkelstein, adding, "They'd say the deer were at a devastatingly low populations and that they had to kill the wolves to compensate. But they never once talked about cutting back on the amount they were hunting. In fact, they upped the quota of native elk and stone sheep" that hunters could kill.[1] Driven by outrage at the human arrogance that would extirpate wolves and break the ages-old ecological chain, Friends of the Wolf set about their dangerous, daring task.

Finkelstein and her fellow eco-warrior skydivers landed in the soft snow on that February morning in 1988, gathered their parachutes, and disappeared into the dense woods. They were prepared to stay for a week. Along with a third woman, Sue Rodriguez-Pastor, Finkelstein and Grandi had spent eighteen months preparing for the action. Rodriguez-Pastor took the entire time off from school to plan and coordinate the campaign, and the others dropped out for several quarters as the time for the hunt drew near. They each made more than thirty parachute jumps, scrounged for equipment, and raised thousands of dollars in donations—$14,000 in material and money in all. About a month before the women left for the subarctic, they enlisted the assistance of Riebin, a jump master and wilderness survival expert. Because of the cost of the operation and the need for someone intimately familiar with it to handle the crush of media interest, the women decided that one of them would not make the jump. Rodriguez-Pastor drew the short straw and assumed the role of media coordinator.

Even with Riebin there to help with the jump and the hunt sabotage, in every way the action was the women's doing. They had met one another as students at the University of California at Davis, and as a group they became increasingly involved in environmental issues. In 1985 Finkelstein and Rodriguez-Pastor heard Paul Watson speak in Berkeley, and it was through his influence that they came to join the struggle for the wolves. Watson was a Greenpeace "mutineer" who left the organization in 1977 and founded the radical Sea Shepherd Conservation Society, a group devoted to the protection of whales, dolphins, and other marine mammals through means that have included ramming a pirate whaling ship. Watson led ambitious efforts to stop the British Columbia wolf hunt in 1984 and 1985, but he found the area of the hunt too large to cover by land alone.[2] His solution was a coordinated air and ground assault by hunt saboteurs. All three of the women from Davis had served as crew members in 1987 on a Sea Shepherd vessel that successfully chased Japanese drift net fishing boats from North Pacific waters. As they talked among themselves about Watson's plan for disrupting the wolf hunt, they became increasingly intrigued. When they announced during the drift net campaign that they would like to give it a try, Watson pledged his assistance whenever they needed it and sent them on their way.

The air assault was complemented by a group of Earth First!ers, radical wilderness advocates for whom the wolf is a totem, who intended to ski into the area as Watson had suggested. Earth First!ers had long opposed the wolf hunts, picketing British Columbia tourism offices and promoting a visitors' boycott of B.C., an effective target since tourism is the province's second-largest industry. John Lilburn, now an Earth First! organizer in Montana, said he had never done an Earth First! action until he and some friends read a plea by Watson for help in fighting the B.C. wolf hunt through direct action. Lilburn's group raised $2,500 in one month and took off for Canada posing as downhill skiing enthusiasts traveling to the Calgary Olympics. Their real plans were to ski into the hunt area and occupy a lake as "a symbolic act."[3] Lilburn's crew was unable to get to the hunt area—another group actually made it, although they did not encounter any hunters or any wolves—but they protested in front of the throngs at the Olympics. In so doing they reaped substantial publicity for their cause, as did other Earth First!ers, like those who pitched a tent in the office of the B.C. Minister of Environment, Bruce Strachan, on the opening day of Parliament and held a press conference on the spot.

The activists also had another front on which they were fighting for the wolves. During their fund raising, an unnamed individual approached the women and offered to pay up to $10,000 in legal fees if Friends of the Wolf would attempt to stop the hunt on legal grounds. He refused to give to the "direct action" campaign, saying that he was certain the suit would prove to the jaded activists that the system which they felt had consistently failed the wolves could work. Although the Americans had no legal standing to challenge the B.C. authorities in Canadian court, a Vancouver environmental group, the Western Canada Wilderness Committee (WCWC), eventually agreed to file suit. "You've got to use every tool that you can," Finkelstein says, explaining the rationale the group used to accept the proposal. "We did not put much faith in the lawsuit at first, just about none. But it turned out that our case was looking better and better, and we were trying to stall until it got into court."[4]

In the end, timing was everything. "If one thing had fallen apart," acknowledges Rodriguez-Pastor, "the whole thing would have fallen through."[5] She and the others were juggling three uncertainties: precisely when the wolf hunt would be announced, when the court case would be heard, and how long their money would hold out before they would be forced to go into the wild strictly for show or quit the campaign altogether. Things worked out perfectly. On Monday, February 22, Environment Minister Strachan announced that the hunt had begun—trackers were in the forest looking for the wolves. Finkelstein and Grandi left for B.C. immediately following Strachan's announcement; the Earth First!ers had already been there for ten days. Rodriguez-Pastor joined her comrades on the twenty-fifth. The actual killing, however, was delayed because of a warm spell that kept new snow from falling, making it impossible for the trackers to do their job since they needed fresh wolf tracks in the snow in order to follow and locate the wolves. Finally, after spending three days scouting possible locations for their jump and after spotting a freshly-baited lake and eight wolves happily devouring the easy pickings, the commandos decided to go in on February 25. Apparently, lack of fresh snow had not stopped the hunt after all. The women knew the wolves would soon be spotted and killed. As much as they wanted to delay their jump because of the lawsuit, the activists could wait no longer. Compounding their anxiety over the timing of the jump was the uncertainty of how they would get out—at the time, the group did not have the $1,000 that was needed to hire a helicopter to pluck them out following their planned week-long stay. They jumped anyway. But as soon as the media reported that the eco-warriors were on the ground, Strachan suspended the hunt to avoid a confrontation.

Press coordinator Rodriguez-Pastor was continually besieged with telephone calls from the media asking for updates. What a story! Two young women and a man trying to save hungry wolves—wolves that doubtless would eat their saviors if given half a chance, or so the press thought. In truth, there was little that Rodriguez-Pastor could tell the press. No hunters meant no action. With no hunt to disrupt, the trio in the bush, whose drop zone was near the baited lake where they spotted the wolves, spent their time hiking through the forest and warding off the canines from the hunt area. The battle looked more promising on the legal front, however. The lawsuit was filed on Friday, the day after the jump. The court denied an injunction that would have completely halted the hunt until the case could be heard in full, but it warned Strachan not to allow hunting over the weekend. The case would be heard the following Monday. It became clear that the hunt would not go on so long as the case was in court, so Rodriguez-Pastor managed to scrape together the funds to have a helicopter airlift the commandoes out of the wild. Little more than a week later, Justice Carol Huddart handed down her ruling: the permit allowing the hunt was invalid because Strachan had improperly delegated decision-making authority to a lower-ranking bureaucrat. Friends of the Wolf had won. The mysterious benefactor was right, on a technicality. Technicality or not, the hunt has never been resumed.

Who are the Radical Environmentalists?

The Friends of the Wolf action parallels hundreds of similar radical environmental struggles, and as such it provides clues as to what is unique about radical environmentalists. Foremost is their emphasis on confronting problems head-on through "direct action." This often entails picketing a lawmaker's office, the headquarters of a National Forest, or a laboratory that conducts cruel experiments on animals. It may also mean breaking the law. Some radicals use civil disobedience to get their point across, like the Earth First!ers who pitched a tent in Strachan's office and as Friends of the Wolf were prepared to do by interfering with the hunt. Others go a step farther, destroying machinery and other property used to build roads, dig mines, harvest trees, and kill animals. It is this willingness by some to sabotage the tools of "progress" which sets radical environmentalists apart from all of their predecessors in the environmental movement.

Secondly, the point of radical environmentalists' protests and actions is the preservation of *biological diversity*. A term from the science of ecology, the biological diversity of a place is, in a nutshell, its resemblance to what it looked like before people interfered with it. (Natural causes, such as massive volcanic explosions like the one on Krakatoa, may reduce biodiversity, too. Humans, however, have replaced natural causes as the primary force driving biodiversity reduction worldwide.) Biodiversity might be more properly called *ecological* diversity, because, as radical environmentalists use the term, it refers not only to plants and animals but to mountains, rivers, oceans as well—the non-living *and* living aspects of an ecosystem. Some places are not very diverse biologically or ecologically to begin with, like the regions near the polar ice caps where few animals or plants have ever lived. In other areas biodiversity is tremendous. A small section of a tropical rainforest, for example, may be home to thousands of species of insects and a multitude of other plants and animals, all of which are connected in intricate relationships that have come to be called the "web of life."

Human interference tends to lessen this biodiversity. When a rainforest is wiped out or a city is built on former marshland, few if any of the original inhabitants remain, and the physical character of the place is permanently changed. With too much human tampering, biologically diverse places become biological wastelands. By fighting for the wolves, the Friends were emphasizing the importance of biodiversity. Without a natural range of animals, including predatory animals, biodiversity in the subarctic would suffer. If the wolves were exterminated, a semblance of biological diversity could only be maintained through artificial agents, like humans. But humans are no substitutes for wolves. When the caribou, elk, and moose migrate out of the wolves' territory, will humans take to hunting mice, as do the wolves? Probably not.

Third, most eco-warriors act largely on their own and without direction from an organizational hierarchy. They get together in small groups, like the three women from Davis or John Lilburn's band from Montana, to take direct action on issues of concern to them, usually environmental problems in their own backyards. At the time of the B.C. wolf hunt, Montana environmentalists were arguing for the development of a meaningful wolf reintroduction plan for Glacier National Park. The well-being of wolves in British Columbia was important for its own sake and also because success in B.C. helped to extend the wolves' range southward into Montana, thereby restoring a level of biodiversity Big Sky country has not known for decades.

Fourth, many radical environmental activists are poor to the point of destitution. This is by choice. They possess an array of talents, and most have at least some college education. But their commitment to ending humanity's unrelenting abuse of the Earth is what motivates eco-warriors, and they often work in low-paying jobs for the environment or work only part of the year, saving enough money to get them to the next action. Finkelstein, Grandi, and Rodriguez-Pastor, for example, came home from Canada several thousands of dollars in debt (the huge donation for the court case was exclusively for that use). Radical environmentalists also choose lifestyles that have minimal impact on the environment. Some do not own cars, many are vegetarians, and nearly all eschew occupations that directly involve environmental destruction.

A fifth distinguishing attribute of radical environmentalists is that they usually have but minimal hope of actually ending on their own the practices against which they protest. The three pro-wolf commandos knew they could stay in the wild no longer than a week and that the hunt might well go on after they left. Rather than fighting to "win" themselves, which they could not afford to do, they did what they could with the resources they had. To get the most out of their efforts, their activities were designed to draw media attention to the plight of British Columbia's wolves in the hope that public sentiment against the hunt would increase to the point where it would be cancelled. In fact, nearly everything environmental extremists do takes place with an eye toward how it will play in the media, their strongest weapon in the fight for the Earth.

In addition, the radicals often act in ways that support the activities of more mainstream groups, such as the lawsuit filed by WCWC (although it is rare that the ties between the two are as clear as they were in British Columbia, where Friends of the Wolf gave WCWC the money it needed for the suit). In the big timber country of California, Oregon, and Washington, for instance, radical activists have repeatedly occupied redwood and Douglas fir trees after being told that a mainstream group like the Sierra Club Legal Defense Fund was seeking an injunction that would stop a forest from being felled. The tree sitters' presence, like that of the wolf activists, sometimes delays cutting until a judge can hear a request for an injunction. In other instances, the radicals offer extreme proposals for wilderness areas and the like that make those of mainstream environmental groups, such as the Sierra Club, Wilderness Society, and the National Wildlife Federation, look more reasonable. This so-called "niche theory" of environmental groups was an instrumental reason behind the formation of Earth First!. Initially, the founders adopted the role of the extremists as a tactic to allow the mainstream groups to look less radical and achieve more protection for the environment.

Some of the radicals' characteristics are shared at least partially by the mainstream. Increasingly, biodiversity is a concern for the environmental elites, which often depend on public pressure to help create the changes for which they agitate. However, as the next chapter shows, mainstream environmentalists are loathe to take direct action to press their points; they are highly bureaucratic, anything but poor, and expect to win when they do battle, although their definition of winning almost always entails losing something for the environment.

Battling the Eco-Wall

Several other factors are also essential to an understanding of this movement. Chief among them is that radical environmentalists are driven by an intuitive *ecological consciousness* which serves as the movement's soul force, compelling activists to sit in trees and in front of bulldozers, to sink whaling boats, and to liberate animals used for laboratory experiments. They are not the sole possessors of strong feelings for the environment or of a sense of connectedness to nature. What distinguishes their awareness of ecological issues is a belief that humans are not the measure of all things. Eco-warriors feel that humanity's role in nature would be no more or less important than the part played by any other species except that we may be the only ones who can repair the damage to the planet we have devastated. This humbling worldview (discussed further in Chapter Three) leads radical environmentalists to assert that only by drastically changing the way industrialized societies operate will *Homo sapiens* and other species be able to survive and thrive beyond the next few decades.

For centuries some humans, especially those who spread their brand of civilization from the Mediterranean outward, have seen themselves as somehow separated from nature. In its first lines the Bible tells us that God told Adam and Eve, "Be fruitful and increase, fill the earth and subdue it, rule over the fish in the sea, the birds of heaven, and every living thing that moves upon the earth."[6] According to this intellectual and religious tradition, nature was something to fight against, to conquer, and to dominate. Supported by this ethic, or perhaps propelled by it, humans for hundreds of generations have built a wall against the ecological reality of our lives, an *Eco-Wall* to keep out the alien force of nature both without and within us.

But we went too far. Acid rain, the greenhouse effect, ozone depletion, rainforest destruction, species extinction—the byproducts of our attempts to control and manipulate the non-human world—now are slowly strangling humans and all else on the planet. We deceived ourselves into believing we were winning a war over nature when in fact we were fighting ourselves.

The Eco-Wall is an environmental version of the crumbled Berlin Wall. Like it, the Eco-Wall was built unilaterally, though its builders were not only communists but capitalists, not only Eastern but Western. Even with today's "environmental protection" laws (in the few places where they exist), the interests of nature, *non-human* nature, are rarely considered. The British Columbian wolves' essential requirements for food and habitat matter little to a provincial government promoting hunter-tourism; the snail darter, a tiny fish that threatened to halt construction of a huge dam in the 1970s, only delayed "progress" until Congress passed a law to get around its own Endangered Species Act. In truth, the supposed *needs* of humans in opposition to the wolves and the snail darters are actually human *wants*: we want to be able to kill as many animals as we care to for pleasure, we want to acquire more electricity and better flood control. We do not need to do these things for sustenance or survival, but we possess the power to do them. Even the *Bible* tells us it is okay to do these things, so why shouldn't we?

Nearly all of us are trapped behind this Eco-Wall, most out of ignorance or a lack of caring. Even those who espouse ecological consciousness and who want no part in the use and abuse of nature often find it difficult to divorce themselves from societies which seem to know no other way. They feel powerless against the onslaught of industrialized civilization. By trying to live with nature, they find themselves struggling to practice "alternative lifestyles," as if they are freaks in a circus. Barriers loom around every bend. It costs them less to purchase and operate a high-polluting used car than to use mass transportation. Zoning regulations stop people from installing solar water heating and electricity panels on their roofs, and tax laws that once encouraged people to go solar have long since been stripped from the books. Even the choice of the food they eat becomes a matter of sacrifice—in one of the great paradoxes of our times, people pay more when farmers leave out chemical pesticides and fertilizers that are dangerous to humans and the environment than when poisons are applied. Vegetarian restaurants are rare, and it is rare that vegans, who eat no animal products at all (and in so doing benefit the environment immensely), can find a restaurant that has a substantial menu to suit their dietary choices. These are just a few examples. The list goes on and on, each item another brick in the Eco-Wall, another way that society reinforces the us-versus-it mentality we have toward "the environment." It is this philosophical, psychological, and tangible barrier which radical environmentalists feel must be smashed if the war *for* the environment—for everything human and non-human—is to be won. If the tone of their rhetoric is strident, they say, perhaps it is justified.

The idea of a sharp separation between humans and the non-human world (to say nothing of the servitude of the latter to the former) is hardly a new revelation, dating back as it does to well before the Old Testament. Its opposite, the position that humans are an inextricable part of the natural world, has been suppressed for centuries. At times the dominant philosophical and legal systems of Greece and Rome took the "rights" of the non-human world into account. Much more deeply, a central tenet of Buddhism to this day is the inherent worth of all beings, the belief that nothing by its nature is more or less important than anything else. Taoism, which emerged in the sixth century B.C., held that all in nature "had a purpose, a potential, a significance for the universe....The notion of 'neighbor' in Judeo-Christianity begins and ends with people. In the Asian doctrines, this circle of community knows no bounds."[7] Western culture, as it spreads everything from religion to consumerism throughout the world, continuously extends the edict of superiority of humans over all else. But by using the non-human world for our own ends rather than nurturing it and ourselves, we put our own backs up against the wall, with tragic consequences. Only through an extraordinary willingness to break with thousands of years of indoctrination can we smash the Eco-Wall.

Radical environmentalists are among those who, like the Taoists and the rarest of Christians, St. Francis of Assisi, have managed to breach this wall within themselves. Their attainment of ecological consciousness makes a difference not only in the way they live their lives but in the way they define living. No longer do they perceive themselves as apart from some external nature; they are part of it. Driven by their heightened awareness of the ties between humans and all else in nature, radical environmentalists refuse to compromise, believing as they do that the survival of the tiniest rainforest insect or the preservation of the most sublime side-canyon is a personal responsibility, an assurance of continued life and evolution that they owe to themselves and to all who follow. But most of all, they owe it to the Earth.

The wolf commandos saw in the human-caused extermination of those canines an immeasurable loss. Indeed, a government's willingness to utterly destroy other beings is a profound statement of the enormity of the Eco-Wall. With industrialists and politicians no longer satisfied with killing off a species here and there, however, the tragedy grows to universal proportions. To the radicals, "every species lost is an irredeemable defeat."[8] Humans, they say, have absolutely no ground on which to stand when they seek to justify any action or inaction that leads to a reduction in biodiversity. If extinctions are comparable to Guernica, the defenseless Basque village bombed into oblivion by the Nazis during the Spanish Civil War, then the destruction of entire ecosystems, as is happening in the world's rainforests and in numerous other places, amounts to an ecological Holocaust. Only by confronting our environmental Guernicas, assert radical environmen-

talists, can we hope to avoid *ecocide*, the annihilation of our fellow pas-
sengers on the Earth.

Radicalism's Role

If one goes by dictionary definitions, the adjective "radical" is paradoxically
sensible, meaning both "fundamental" and "extreme." The logic of these
seemingly contradictory definitions becomes clear when considering eco-
warriors' fight for the planet. Nothing is more basic than the lifegiver,
Earth; however, most of society considers it a crime to destroy the very tools
and mindsets that work to ruin the Earth. The radical environmental
movement's basic, foundational aspect comes from its emphasis on ecological consciousness and biological diversity. To radical environmentalists, the
truly radical occurs when we break ecological bonds and destroy biodiversity
by hunting wolves, damming rivers, and razing forests. Earth First!er Jamie
Sayen is adamant: "We see this as a struggle for survival, not just a parlor
game. That's the only sense that I'll admit to being radical—as a radical
reaction to insanity."[9]

"Environmentalist" is a somewhat hazy term. At its rudimentary level it
seems to refer to someone who seeks to limit human destruction of the
environment. But being an environmentalist is in vogue. In 1988,
Americans elected as president an oil explorer and close friend of big
business who claimed to be one. Even among those who clearly possess
"environmentalist" credentials the term has different meanings. This is so
because the environmental movement has become highly compartmental-
ized. Organizations typically choose to protect one or another aspect of
nature: the Wilderness Society emphasizes public lands, the National
Wildlife Federation concerns itself with animals in the wild, Audubon
focuses on birds and their habitats, and in its early years Greenpeace
worked almost exclusively on marine mammal issues. Some groups, most
notably the Sierra Club and today's Greenpeace, take a broader view of
environmental problems, stressing topics such as toxics and nuclear issues
along with wilderness and the ocean. Excluded from most lists of "environmental" organizations, Animal Welfare groups like the Humane Society of
the United States sponsor campaigns to end the use of fur for clothing and
promote sustainable agricultural practices, both of which benefit the
broader environment as they better animals' lives.

Radical environmentalism reflects similar divisions, with its land-based
emphasis represented by Earth First!; the sea-going aspect found in the Sea
Shepherds; and a third branch, Animal Liberation. Animal Liberation is a
label for a diverse and diffuse group of activists who fight on a variety of
fronts related to environmentalism. They seek to end trophy hunting (or
to halt hunting altogether) and to end experimentation on animals, intensive farming of animals, and the use of animals for entertainment purposes.

They possess the same intuitive ecological consciousness as the Sea Shepherds and Earth First!ers, who concern themselves with animals, plants, and all else that is in the wild. Animal Liberationists take increasing notice of the ecological impacts related to their issues, such as the costs to the environment resulting from disposal of animal wastes, the uncertain impact of genetically-altered animals on the environment, and the importance to the biodiversity of some ecosystems of having mink and lynx running wild instead of draping over someone's shoulder. They and Earth First!ers find themselves on common ground on many issues. The hunt sabotage in British Columbia was an Animal Liberation action in that it was anti-hunting and was intended to save individual animals; the focus on the health of an ecosystem was, technically, an Earth First! concern. Such distinctions, however, are becoming meaningless as many radical environmentalists find themselves crossing freely between branches of the movement without a second thought.

Non-Violence and Sabotage

The radical environmental movement's seemingly contradictory use of both civil disobedience and sabotage to break down the Eco-Wall bears special mention. For Mahatma Gandhi the distinction was clear: "Sabotage is a form of violence. People have realized the futility of physical violence but some people apparently think that it may be successfully practiced in its modified form as sabotage."[10] Gandhi's was a radical cause. The use of non-cooperation and civil disobedience to break the bonds imposed by colonial Britain in order to gain independence for India fits comfortably within the definition of "radical" used here. For Gandhi, non-violence was a way of life. Today, civil disobedience actions of the sort he advocated are commonly practiced by radical environmentalists. An Earth First! tree sit in a redwood forest that is under attack, illegally parking a Sea Shepherd vessel at the mouth of a port to prevent the slaughter of harp seals, and occupying a crane used to construct an animal experimentation laboratory are among the variations used by eco-warriors.

Many radical environmentalists refuse to go beyond civil disobedience in their activities, some for moral reasons, others out of fear of the penalties should they be arrested and convicted. Unlike Gandhi and those within the movement who foreswear property destruction, however, substantial numbers of radical environmentalists see civil disobedience merely as a tactic. Their attitude resembles what Gandhi called "passive resistance," which "does not exclude the use [of unarmed violence] if, in the opinion of a passive resister, the occasion demands it." Gandhi cited the suffragettes as an example of passive resisters.[11] Earth First!er Roger Featherstone is one who supports such gradations in tactics. "I think it is important to realize that the possibility of something stronger than the use of non-violence is so much more powerful than non-violence as a way of life," he says. "If the authorities know that so-and-so is completely non-violent, and never would go beyond this, there is a lot less respect than if folks think that if non-violence no longer works, there's something else. Non-violence is what works best for us."[12]

Featherstone's "something else" is a reference to sabotage and property destruction. Although he and others refer to sabotage and vandalism as violent, for the purposes of this book *"violence" means inflicting harm on a living being or a non-living natural entity,* such as a mountainside. The practical implication of this definition is to exclude the destruction of human artifacts—machines and the like—from the realm of violence. Australian radical environmentalist John Seed goes even farther, saying that ruining a bulldozer to preserve the environment is "property *enhancement,"* the highest and best use of a place being to leave it in its natural state.[13]

Most radical environmentalists share a dislike for the preponderance of technology in our daily lives, seeing it as symptomatic of our cultural drive to control nature. They feel that destroying machinery is an effective and necessary part of their efforts to protect the environment; some within the Animal Liberation movement have even resorted to arson. In their technophobia, if not the destructive ways that they give vent to it, radical environmentalists are in good company. Stephen Fox, a historian of the environmental movement, includes in a list of anti-modernist thinkers some "of the most powerful and original minds in American history:" Thomas Jefferson, Ralph Waldo Emerson, Henry David Thoreau, Mark Twain, Robert Frost, and Lewis Mumford among them. Each viewed "modern progress—implying cities, technology, and human arrogance—as ambiguous at best, probably nothing more than a harmful illusion that exchanged sanity and wholeness for less important physical improvements."[14]

In their dislike of progress, eco-warriors find themselves kin not only to these lofty thinkers but to the working class, which has long objected to new technologies which fill their days with drudgery, often cost them their jobs, and sometimes put their lives at risk while benefiting them but little. These sorts of complaints boiled over in the early 1800s when stocking mill workers in Britain calling themselves followers of "General Ludd" or "Luddites" rose up against the machinery that was the tool of their oppressors. Legend obscures the true origin of "Luddite," although there is some evidence that it was adapted from the name "N. Ludlam," a Leicestershire youth who became enraged at his tiresome job one day and took a hammer to his needles.[15] "Luddite" has since come to mean a technophobe or saboteur. Ecological sabotage, or "ecotage," is the name environmental Luddites give to destruction of technology in defense of nature. It includes Paul Watson's use of his ship to ram whaling vessels, smashing laboratory equipment used by vivisectionists, and hammering nails into trees to thwart their cutting. Radical environmentalists who take this course see themselves as having little other choice. They insist that they are non-violent in that they take precautions to avoid injuring others: tree spikers warn loggers of what they have done long before the trees are cut, and arsonists have only struck unoccupied buildings. This may not make what they do ethically or morally justifiable by traditional standards, but it does separate them from terrorists who could care less about the lives that they place in danger.

"A Matter of War"

While some urge "understanding" and "patience" in trying to control the environmental "genies" that humans have let out of the bottle, for radical environmentalists the time for such considerate behavior has long since passed. "I see this as a matter of war," says Darryl Cherney, an Earth First! organizer who once spent ten days in jail for sitting in a tree that belonged to a lumber company. The radical environmental movement "is not the aggressor—we are in the role of defenders of the environment. We are being attacked and we are engaging in as non-violent a manner of self-defense as we can possibly manage."[16] Cherney and others ask what the so-called "rational" course of action is when confronting such utterly irrational phenomena as governments which subsidize the torture of millions of animals a year and refuse to halt the destruction of rainforests. At a time of increasingly illuminating research into the Earth's natural processes, what sense is there in the perpetuation of lifestyles that only exacerbate ecological damage? The time has come, eco-warriors say, for the underground in this war to rise, to fight back against the onslaught of technomania sweeping every corner of the world from Silicon Valley to the Amazon River Valley, from the high seas to the highest mountain that holds an ounce of silver or gold.

That underground has the potential for being far more powerful than any resistance in any prior war, for it is comprised of each of us, the grassroots. Radical environmentalists feel that only by acting in our individual lives and in our communities can we effectively overcome the Eco-Wall. Their efforts are organized in precisely that way, not from the top down. Others outside of the movement proper have decided that they, too, have had enough, and their anger and anxiety are manifested in numerous ways. Michael Herz, fed up with the lack of enforcement of anti-pollution laws on San Francisco Bay, raised $200,000 to purchase a boat, coaxed manufacturers to donate the necessary equipment, and he now snoops harbors and inlets doing the government's job.[17] In New Hampshire, people in the small town of Sanbornton rose to fight herbicide spraying on utility rights-of-way.[18] Tens of thousands of others have done

the same thing, effectively protesting against nuclear waste dumps, garbage incinerators, subdivisions, and scores of other projects that threatened
themselves and the environment. Similar struggles are occurring with
more frequency worldwide. Bulgaria's first mass demonstration in forty
years of authoritarian rule was organized by a group calling itself "Eco-glasnost" that demanded attention be given to environmental problems.[19] In
Malaysia, members of the Penan tribe incessantly blockade logging roads
to stop the destruction of rainforests on their tribal lands by multinational
corporations. In Kenya and India, women have broken with tradition to
lead the fight to reforest their native lands.

What motivates these people? Near the end of his sobering book *The End
of Nature*, Bill McKibben asks, "If nature were about to end, we might muster
endless energy to stave it off; but if nature has already ended, what are we
fighting for?"[20] If THE END has already slipped by us unnoticed and we
are merely players in the Earth's denouement, why bother tearing down
the Eco-Wall at all? Why fight for the environment, risking one's freedom
and even one's life as eco-warriors do, when it is probably too late anyway?
While being interviewed for this book, activist after activist answered that
question in the same way: "Because we have to." Resignation is not in their
blood. A fiery, feisty spirit is. Their stories provide the best means to
understanding this drive that propels them to fight with such vigor against
the seemingly insurmountable Eco-Wall.

CHAPTER 2

A QUESTION OF COMPROMISE

"Muddling through." That's how the old guard of environmentalism's wilderness and wildlife-focused branch has approached its job for years, according to Sierra Club Chairman Michael McCloskey. National parks, anti-pollution laws, endangered species listings, hundreds of environmental brushfires and battles successfully fought—all by *muddling through*? "You do better not having grand plans and rigid ideologies," McCloskey explains. "Instead, you constantly redefine your approach as you go along," depending on the issue and the opponent, making deals as needed. "We come out of a mountaineering tradition where you first decide that you're going to climb the mountain. You have a notion of a general route, but you find the handholds and the footholds as you go along and you have to adapt and keep changing. It's a fairly loose, pragmatic approach."[1]

Pragmatism and "realism" about what can be acomplished are hallmarks of the environmentalism that emerged late in the 19th century. The approach and perspective of today's radical environmentalists contrast sharply with the practices of such traditional, mainstream organizations as McCloskey's Sierra Club, the Wilderness Society, the Audubon Society, and others. The radicals, driven by an ecological consciousness unfettered by conventionality, take a bold, "no compromise" attitude to environmental issues, while the elites of the environmental movement are almost genteel in their approach. Although the ways that the mainstream groups press for better environmental laws have become more sophisticated of late, they are slow to break with a century-old method of operation which relies entirely on a narrowly defined political process to win environmental preservation.

NOTE: This examination of the differences between the mainstream environmentalists and the radical environmental movement only considers groups that emphasize wilderness and wildlife issues, excluding Animal Welfare organizations and those involved in marine mammal protection. This enables more thorough consideration of the "land-based" groups, which consistently have fought the most visible battles in the environmental movement. Chapter Six discusses the contrasts between Greenpeace and the Sea Shepherds, and Chapter Seven looks at the Animal Welfare movement and its more radical offshoot, the Animal Liberationists.

The first fights over public lands in the U.S. gave rise to groups advocating minimal development of wild places, limiting it to what was necessary to the building of a constituency to protect those places. The Sierra Club and the Audubon Society were among the first of these. They recognized that in order to affect decision makers they needed to adopt the lobbying and advocacy tactics of the big business interests they opposed—in short, they had to play a role in the politics of compromise. The same is true today. "We try to get certain areas designated as wilderness," says the Wilderness Society's Ben Beach, summing up his organization's approach to issues. "For those areas not designated wilderness, we try to see that they are managed in the most sensible way they can be. That doesn't mean that we oppose logging or mining. We just want them done in the appropriate places and the appropriate ways with a fair payoff to the U.S. Treasury."[2]

The Sierra Club and the Wilderness Society are two members of the so-called "Group of Ten," large, powerful mainstream environmental organizations. Their counterparts in the Group of Ten include the Audubon Society, Natural Resources Defense Council, National Wildlife Federation, Izaak Walton League, Defenders of Wildlife, Environmental Defense Fund, National Parks and Conservation Association, and the Environmental Policy Institute. Although grouped together, these organizations vary somewhat in emphasis and approach. The Sierra Club and Wilderness Society stress large park and wilderness proposals more than most of the others. Traditionally, the Izaak Walton League and the National Wildlife Federation have had a strong constituency among hunters and have aimed at preserving wildlife and habitat so that their members would have places to pursue these activities. The Natural Resources Defense Council and the Environmental Defense Fund use the legal system to force compliance with environmental laws, and their emphasis is increasingly on toxics and other issues that are of more immediate importance to humans than to the non-human world. As for their approaches, the Izaak Walton League, Sierra Club, and Audubon Society have a history of grassroots organization; the others are largely without a grassroots emphasis that encourages members to get actively involved in environmental work.

What unites the Group of Ten (and numerous other national, state, and local environmental groups as well) today is their willingness to muddle through—in essence, to compromise—on environmental issues and their unquestioned participation in legal means of achieving environmental preservation. This approach has resulted in some impressive achievements: the establishment of some of the first national parks and the successful shepherding of numerous later park bills through Congress and past presidents; the Wilderness Act of 1964, which barred certain types of development from some of the nation's most important scenic and ecological treasures; and the Clean Air and Clean Water acts, to list but a few of their major achievements. Successful compromises allowed them to branch out into other areas less directly related to natural resources, such as law and education. At one time during the Reagan presidency the Sierra Club Legal Defense Fund and the Natural Resources Defense Council had more enforcement actions pending against polluters than did the federal government. Through their programs and publications, mainstream environmental groups have taught millions the importance of environmental preservation and the need to walk as softly on the Earth as industrial civilization allows.

From Conservation to Environmentalism

Serious, organized political activity in the U.S. on behalf of wilderness and wildlife dates back to the late 1800s with the foundation of the Appalachian Mountain Club. Near the close of the century, wilderness prophet John Muir and others established the Sierra Club in San Francisco, and since then it has gone on to become the leader among mainstream groups in visibility and prestige. Almost immediately upon its founding, the Club's members took up the task of advocating the need for wilderness, as Muir had done on his own for a quarter-century. The Club's first major struggle for environmental preservation began in 1901, a losing battle against a dam in Yosemite National Park that dragged on for twelve years and is still remembered as one of the great defeats in American environmental history. San Francisco was growing rapidly at the turn of the century, and its leaders knew they had to come up with a large, reliable source of drinking water or their dream of a new Babylon would wither in the rainless California summer. They looked to the mighty Sierra Nevada mountains and spied the perfect location for a reservoir: the Hetch Hetchy Valley, several miles north of the famed Yosemite Valley. Hetch Hetchy was a victim of its glacier-carved topography: the Tuolumne River tumbled from the Sierra crest to the narrow, two mile-long Valley, which had been scoured out by sheets of ice tens of thousands of years ago. Best of all for San Francisco, Hetch Hetchy narrowed to a canyon at its foot—the perfect place for a dam.

Muir thought of Hetch Hetchy as "one of nature's rarest and most precious mountain temples," comparable in many ways to Yosemite Valley.[3] The proposal to dam it was, in his eyes, inexcusable, indefensible, and needless. "These temple destroyers," he bitterly wrote of his opponents in this grand battle for water, rocks, flowers, and the soul of the Valley, "devotees of ravaging commercialism, seem to have a perfect contempt for Nature, and, instead of lifting their eyes to the God of the mountains, lift them to the Almighty Dollar. Dam the Hetch Hetchy! As well dam for water-tanks the people's cathedrals and churches, for no holier temple has ever been consecrated by the heart of man."[4] Alas, the infidels won. Muir tried muddling through, suggesting other sites for the dam, some even inside the park, but San Francisco would have none of his compromises. Its persistence paid off when, after two other presidents dismissed the city's pleadings, Woodrow Wilson signed legislation approving the dam late in 1913.

Within a year after the Hetch Hetchy defeat, Muir died of pneumonia. With the death of its inspirational leader the Sierra Club lost a large part of its spirit as well. For a time the heretics held sway, "wise use" advocates in the Club who promoted the doctrine of Muir's arch rival, Gifford Pinchot. Instead of locking away resources, they argued, it was in everyone's best interest that they be used to benefit humans. For a time the Club took an active interest in forestry, not to fight it but to promote the profession of cutting trees.

Regardless of its philosophy, however, the Club remained decidedly western and small; its first chapter outside of California was not formed until 1950, and at that time its membership totalled only about 7,000.[5] But it was geographically well-situated to take on the tidal wave of industrial development that followed World War II. After the war, the Club and other members of the conservation community, as it was then called, began to seriously reconsider their approach to issues. The massive economic apparatus that had been directed toward the war effort overseas shifted back home. The returning troops went to college and started families on a scale never before seen in the U.S. Americans created and moved to the suburbs, where they settled down to materialistically rich lives. Their refrigerators, automobiles, hula hoops, frozen foods, and fluoridated water replaced tanks, planes, bullets, and bandages as the drawdown of the nation's immense stock of natural resources continued unabated.

But the consumer ethic was not as inviolate as the war effort had been. The depletion of resources needed to fuel the nation's inexorable march of "progress" alarmed the conservation community, and their alarm began a true conservation *movement* which looked to preserve rivers and forests, especially in the West. Regaining Muir's spirit, the three-score-year-old Sierra Club led the fight, succeeding where its founder had failed: they stopped dams, dams in the people's parks. The circumstances surrounding the first of these struggles—for Echo Park Dam in Dinosaur National Monument—eerily paralleled Hetch Hetchy. Both places were remote, little known, of exceptional beauty, and were ostensibly untouchable, secure as they were in protected areas. The Echo Park Dam debate dragged on for five years before unprecedented efforts by conservationists on Capitol Hill defeated the proposal. In January 1963 another dam battle erupted over an even more audacious proposal. The federal Bureau of Reclamation introduced the Southwest Water Plan, which would plug the Colorado River in the Grand Canyon in two places. The Sierra Club prevailed only after it placed full-page advertisements in some of the nation's major newspapers calling on citizens to put a stop to the plan by writing to President Johnson and other officials. It was a major step in the conservation movement. Similar ads had run before, but the pressure brought to bear by four ads in the space of ten months proved crucial to staving off the Grand Canyon dams. The effort was also helped by the backlash from a politically-motivated Internal Revenue Service crackdown on the non-profit Club, which, according to the IRS, had violated the terms of its tax-deductible status through its supposed lobbying activity (non-profit organizations are tax exempt only if they refrain from engaging in political activity). The little conservation group versus the big bad government: Club membership doubled in three years to 78,000. As David Brower, the Sierra Club's first executive director, writes in his autobiography, "The American public, it turned out, did not wish the tax man to jeopardize the world's only Grand Canyon."[6]

The Bureau of Reclamation did get a dam out of the Grand Canyon fight, however. A compromise by the Sierra Club allowed for a location up the Colorado, just south of the Utah border. The dam filled a little known area called Glen Canyon. Hundreds of miles of dramatic, steep, slickrock side channels carved over millennia by coursing water, with walls beautifully painted by light on rock, now lie in darkness, covered by the Glen Canyon Dam's flood waters. Brower let that dam be built, to hear him tell of it. "I became a wimp, somehow, and let the Board compromise on Glen Canyon," he says. "The decision makers put the dam there, and we could have stopped them had we refused to compromise and simply stood up for our own Club policy. Instead we pleased the decision makers."[7]

Many call Brower "John Muir reincarnate." As with Muir, Brower's vision, energy, and creativity have attracted thousands of new wilderness advocates to the movement; the radicals have found validation for their approach in his uncompromising attitude. A mountaineer hewn in Muir's image, Brower was a native Californian, a Club member since 1933, a long-time volunteer, and editor of the *Sierra Club Bulletin* (now *Sierra* magazine) before he assumed his leadership position. By the time he made his first trip to Glen Canyon, its fate had been sealed, and in 1963 water started backing up behind it into Lake Powell, which, ironically is named after explorer John Wesley Powell, leader of the first expedition to navigate the Colorado.

After a few more years of leading the Club in environmental wars and fighting more and more battles within his own organization, Brower and the Club parted ways. The full-page ads and the magnificent exhibit-format books he produced to bolster the cause required capital, which the Sierra Club had but which some directors were unwilling to spend. Brower also found himself at odds with his old friend, photographer and Club director Ansel Adams, over the issue of nuclear power. Adams and a majority of the other directors supported siting the Diablo Canyon nuclear power plant north of Santa Barbara, California. To them, Diablo Canyon was a compromise—it was either the nuclear plant or several coal-fired ones. Brower, having experienced firsthand the dangers of compromise, ardently campaigned against Diablo Canyon and refused to yield. The two issues, books and nukes, drove a wedge between Brower and the Club's leadership, and the executive director was forced out in 1969. He moved on to found his own organization, Friends of the Earth, through which Brower freely and actively pursued environmental causes with tremendous energy and a sharp tongue. "Nice Nellie will never make it...," he said upon leaving the Sierra Club. "We cannot go on fiddling while the earth's wild places burn in the fires of our undisciplined technology.'"[8] He has since moved on from Friends of the Earth to establish the activistic Earth Island Institute.

Today, David Brower, white-haired, sharp-eyed, and still keen-witted in his late 70s, is the elder statesman of the world's environmental community. He was made an honorary vice president of the Sierra Club in 1972, and he still rides herd on the organization, fervently believing that it and other mainstream groups are indispensable to the cause of environmental protection while also exhorting them not to back down before those who would lay waste to the land. Never a lover of compromise, Brower has joined the eco-warriors in condemning the Group of Ten's almost exclusive use of the pragmatic approach in its attempts to halt environmental destruction. In a letter written in 1989 to the Sierra Club's conservation director, Brower put his feelings plainly. His sense is "that compromise is often necessary but that it ought not originate with the Sierra Club," as has happened with increasing frequency in recent years. The environment will be better served, and more of it preserved, if mainstream environmentalists "hold fast to what we believe is right, fight for it, and find allies and adduce all possible arguments for our cause," Brower says. "If we cannot find enough vigor in us or them to win, then let someone else propose the compromise. We thereupon work hard to coax it our way. We become a nucleus around which the strongest force can build and function."[9]

The environmental movement must stir people up, Brower urges, not just do the expected. With "the end of nature" ever closer, creativity in environmental battles is what's called for, not compromise. Besides, "the rules" so essential to the muddling-through process are there to defeat the little player: don't make scenes; don't make too many waves; remember that your opponent today may be the friend you need tomorrow. "There is a great deal of effort by some to duck confrontation," Brower says. "We're trying to be insiders, to negotiate. We're in a position of being Bambi to industry's Godzilla, as Ray Dasmann says. We're being taken out to lunch by high-level executives. As I see it that's one of their functions, to make us feel good while mid-level management goes on with mayhem as usual. My feeling is that the true radicals go by the name 'Earth Last!' They're also known as the Fortune 500." Brower adds, "You're not going to make these changes by going to lunch. You're going to make them by developing a power relation from the grassroots and in all of the professions you can, trying to build ecological consciousness into all spheres of human activity, including shopping and investing." His years of fighting environmental battles have led Brower to take a position as firm as any radical environmentalist. He shares their vision and their philosophy about the kind of action needed to awaken the slumbering green giant in the grassroots. "We have the first opportunity on Earth to build a sustainable society," Brower says with a gleam in his eye. "Let's do it! Make that the exciting chant. To get things going, we've got to be confrontational. I'm criticized for that, but that's what we have to do....People pay attention when there is confrontation. That is the best opportunity there is for immediate conservation education. You get a big battle going and people take sides. Somehow the truth comes out of it. Our side will win!" he says, chuckling self-consciously at his environmental cheerleading.[10]

The insider attitude of the big players also rankles him. "Little inner circles" and "quiet little meetings" miss the point of environmental activism's needs. "I don't think we have any business doing that in environmental organizations," Brower says. Grassroots involvement in environmental issues is an essential political reality. Without it the Eco-Wall will never crumble. As is, mainstream groups' ballooning membership rolls are going to waste. "We need to have them be part of the power relation with which we then try to get our way in Congress or wherever we're trying to get it," Brower states firmly. "But you have to have a power relation. Here are these millions of people organized in the environmental movement and we're not developing their relationship."[11]

The Sagebrush and Other Rebellions

As environmentally-conscious Americans watched in horror, James Watt's so-called "Sagebrush Rebellion" roared into Washington at the top of the 1980s on Ronald Reagan's coattails. Many of the millions that Brower mentioned reacted by flocking to the nation's top environmental organizations as never before, doubling their numbers within a few short years. This was but one result of the most important phenomenon since the grassroots *environmental* movement got its start around the first Earth Day: the betrayal of the environment by the federal government. In part, Reagan's contemptuous attitude toward the environment signaled the end of the old pragmatism. No longer was muddling-through certain to get something for the environment. When the president was unwilling to even sit down at the same table with members of the Group of Ten, compromise was out of the question. The Eco-Wall, which for a decade had been built higher in places but lowered here and there, suddenly took on a new, ominous character. Property rightists wooed the disenchanted electorate with promises of lower taxes and less government. Let's sell the federal lands, parks included, back to the people who can "manage" them best, they cried. Good management for them meant making a profit and little else. As Secretary of the Interior, Watt could not go as far as his Sagebrush buddies would have liked, at least not immediately. However, he did promise to halt the purchase of wild lands, to sell some back to private interests, and to "invest in the parks" by developing them. Americans, Watt believed, did not want more parks; they wanted "better" ones. That meant not having to get out of their cars to escape into the backcountry; Watt figured people preferred to drive there. And when they arrived they needed plenty of parking spaces and clean rest rooms and motels and gift shops. People should have to pay to play in the public's parks, held devotees of this grossly utilitarian philosophy. Entrance fees were established or increased throughout the park system in the 1980s, much of the money not going back into park programs but straight to the federal government's "general fund" and thence for Reagan's multi-trillion dollar defense buildup.

The Sierra Club's McCloskey admits that mainstream environmental organizations were caught off guard by the federal onslaught, resulting in a void in environmental leadership. "We have to think of the ideas," the graying, bespeckeled McCloskey says, seemingly bewildered by the change in events. "The pipeline has pretty much run dry in terms of the federal government. It is no longer innovative....The pragmatic wing of the movement is still adjusting to the fact that the source of leadership has shifted."[12] Despite the ominous signs preceding Reagan's election, mainstream groups were ill-equipped to take charge. And although their membership skyrocketed—the Sierra Club, for example, grew from about 147,000 members in the mid-70s to 550,000 in 1989 and the Wilderness Society went from less than 100,000 just before Reagan's election to 335,000 ten years later—the mainstream was slow to act. The lack of vigilance by the mainstream and their slowness in taking advantage of the power relation that Brower sees as so essential rankles radical activists like Earth First! co-founder Mike Roselle. "When Watt came to power we saw huge increases in the membership of the major groups," Roselle says. "But did we see an increase in their advocacy, a strengthening of their position? Did we see any new analysis or any new initiatives? No! All we saw was more $25 checks going to their post office boxes."[13]

Under Reagan and Watt, scenery, recreation, and spiritual re-creation— the values espoused by the mainstream environmental groups—were no longer of paramount concern when the government turned its mind to wild places. Suddenly, all federal lands were put to the same bottom-line test as any private company would use. The impact of this change in governmental philosophy, when mainstream groups began to catch up with it, resulted in an about-face in their approach. Ben Beach explains that in the 1980s the Wilderness Society decided that emotional arguments could no longer carry the day for environmentalists. Pragmatism, wilting beneath Reagan's money-green glare needed some spicing up. "We believe in the 'land ethic,'" Beach says, referring to the philosophy of Wilderness Society co-founder Aldo Leopold. "But we want to supplement those traditional arguments with these newer economic arguments."[14] Such a statement appears to border on heresy, for, as Leopold wrote, "One basic weakness in a conservation system based wholly on economic motives is that most members of the land community have no economic value."[15] Wolves are worse than valueless to a rancher; deserts are not worth much to any but the cactus and tortoise; a standing dead redwood is valueless except to the northern spotted owl living there; and a snail darter is nothing but a nuisance to a dam builder. Times have changed, Beach says. When you're muddling through, you have to dance to whatever tune is the rage, not what your conscience or your ethics tells you is right. If that was the way Reagan wanted to play, the pragmatists figured they had to answer with dollar signs themselves. The Wilderness Society and others issued numerous reports about the costs of the government's policies. After long-term ecological concerns were repeatedly shoved aside, environmentalists started groping to find the economic costs of ecological destruction. They discovered timber sales in the national forests were tantamount to a raid on Fort Knox and federal land was sold to private interests for a pittance.

Environmentalists adopted a new attitude out of necessity. The mainstream scurried for a way to spend its new riches and still appear effective in the face of an intransigent administration. But to the radicals, pragmatism was the problem. Indeed, it was the results—or, more correctly, the lack of results—from decades of muddling through that was more responsible than any other factor for the emergence of the radical environmental movement. The straw that broke the camel's back, and which gave Earth First! its start, was the U.S. Forest Service's Roadless Area Review and Evaluation II (RARE II) analysis of the large wilderness areas within the national forests. Conducted during 1978 and 1979, RARE II's mission was to categorize which of the large roadless areas in the national forests should be included as wilderness, studied for their potential as wilderness, or excluded and thus handed over for exploitation. Executives from the timber, mining, grazing, and oil industries slavered over the riches laying beneath the bear's belly and the eagle's wings. To win the RARE II battle against such foes, the Wilderness Society, Sierra Club, Audubon, and most of the rest of the Group of Ten, as well as many state and local organizations, felt they had to put up a unified front. In short, the environmentalists reasoned that the only way to beat the behemoths was to become one. But that entailed accepting the lowest common denominator, the weakest positions of the bunch, to keep everyone together.

The compromising was to come internally, and there had to be a lot of it. This, says Earth First! co-founder Howie Wolke, was a fatal weakness. Wolke disgustedly growls that out of eighty million acres of roadless areas in National Forests nationwide "only fifteen million acres of rock and ice" was recommended for wilderness in the final RARE II recommendations. The industry played on emotions, arguing that more trees would have to be cut in coming years for jobs and houses. But it never supplied the numbers to back up its assertions, says Wolke, who had spent many months mapping Wyoming's roadless regions prior to RARE II. "We played the game, played by the rules," he says. "We were moderate, reasonable, professional. We had data, statistics, maps, graphs. And we got fucked. That's when I started thinking, 'Something's missing, here. Something isn't working.' That's what led to Earth First! more than anything else."[16]

The radicals cite hundreds of more recent examples of the failure of compromise, like the Defenders of Wildlife's practice of paying ranchers when they kill a wolf which has attacked their cattle near Glacier National Park. Defenders feels that lessening the economic burden on ranchers caused by the area's few remaining wolves is vital if a full-blown wolf reintroduction program is ever to be attempted. But the self-contradictory nature of "defending" wolves by paying for their lifeless pelts leaves the radicals incredulous. They, too, acknowledge the economic realities of raising cattle in prime wolf habitat. Their answers, however, are sharply at odds with the mainstream's. Wild Rockies Earth First!er John Lilburn and others have proposed wolf leases and wolf easements, where the federal government would pay ranchers to allow wolves to roam un- threatened on their lands. Not only would this "no compromise" approach benefit the wolves, but Lilburn speculates that fewer head of livestock would be killed because the wolves would chase off coyotes. A wolf pack might kill one steer in 1,000, Lilburn says, but coyotes are known to be much heavier livestock predators.[17] In another example of the "no compromise" ethic in action, Arizona Earth First! proposed that every acre eligible for wilderness designation, all nineteen million acres identified by RARE II, be included in the state's wilderness legislation. The mainstream groups got together and proposed wilderness areas totalling 4.2 million acres, while the state's congressional delegation was split, with the largest of their bills equal to about half of the coalition's proposal.

Muddling through would not make it, insisted the radicals in the early 1980s. If the president was going to change the tune, somebody had to bring their own music. Earth First! did just that. It took "No Compromise in Defense of Mother Earth!" as its motto, pointedly displaying its anger at the mainstream approach. With wilderness as the bottom line, the radicals embraced as a fundamental truth Brower's oft-quoted observation that compromise would always fail since huge amounts of wilderness were being sacrificed and none new was being created. Once the deals were done, there was no turning back. Mike Roselle cites the example of the Tongass National Forest in Alaska. There, environmentalists (led by fellow Earth First! co-founder Bart Koehler) have tried to end logging operations that are the most heavily subsidized of any in the nation, costing taxpayers $350 million during the 1980s. "One problem with locking something up (through the compromise system) is that they're going to ask you to release something else," namely for development, Roselle says. "When you come back later and say, 'I don't want you logging in the Tongass,' they'll say, 'But when we wrote the Alaska Lands Act, you said this was released for life.' It doesn't do any good to say, 'Well, we didn't mean *that* kind of life.' You relinquish a little moral ground" through the compromise process.[18] Peter Steinhart, contributing editor for *Audubon* magazine, quotes Michael McCloskey as battling exactly that perspective: he once said that "'the problem with compromise is that people think you have lost your emotional engagement to the issue once you have compromised. They think that you aren't spiritually pure anymore.'"[19] Realism means relinquishing not only place but honor as well.

Finding a Niche

The 1960s and early 1970s saw the development of the precursor of the radical environmental movement, the "lifestyle" version of environmentalism. These back-to-the-land advocates possessed a strong ecological consciousness. By living simply they were making a political statement. Like the eco-warriors, they rubbed the mainstream the wrong way with their anti-industrialism talk and their ever-present ethics. But McCloskey says that "even though there were tensions between the lifestyle wing and the pragmatists, we didn't speak ill of one another. We realized we had different perceptions about which was the best way to go and what our priorities were. What is different now, since 1984 or 1985, is that the new radicals established their position by attacking the mainstream pragmatists. They only look good if we look bad. They have to attack us."[20] Yet McCloskey has been slow to recognize a new reality in the environmental movement. As Earth First! co-founder Dave Foreman points out, "Earth First! has made those groups more effective, and I think we have opened up more issues. We have been able to redefine the parameters of the debate, but it is so easy for radicals to get this holier than thou attitude and to not appreciate the hard work that the more mainstream groups do."[21] Surprisingly, Foreman places more importance in the mainstream than in the radical aspect of the movement which he so strongly embraces. "If we had to choose, are we going to have the mainstream groups and not Earth First! or Earth First! and none of the mainstream groups, I don't see any real choice," says Foreman, out-pragmatizing the arch-pragmatist. The power and prestige of the Group of Ten and others is more important in the abstract than the fringe that tries to pull them along.

Foreman and others point out that there are, in fact, frequent and mutually fruitful interactions between mainstream and radical activists. For some in the mainstream, the radicals have become part of the muddling through process by making the muddling a bit easier. Foreman often speaks of a "spectrum" of environmental groups. Jim Norton, the Wilderness Society's Southwest Regional Director, uses a more appropriate metaphor. "In the biological community, each organism has its own ecological niche," he says. "Similarly, each environmental group has evolved to have its own little ecological niche. I think that is appropriate and effective. Those niches cover a very broad spectrum of environmentalism. Earth First! would be the extreme on one end and the Nature Conservancy would be the extreme on the other end. The Wilderness Society is in the middle."[22] McCloskey demurs, despite his belief that there are "wings" to the movement. "I wouldn't accept that as a very useful argument," he says, "but I do accept that the radical groups have played some useful roles in pointing to the deficiencies of the mainstream groups, of experimenting with other techniques, certainly of intellectualizing about a lot of these questions. I think they are contributions, even if one is not always persuaded. I draw a line that I don't condone or approve violence. I don't think that is ever a contribution."[23]

But other mainstream environmentalists see more direct benefits coming from the radicals. Norton says he senses "that by Earth First! being out there with much larger wilderness proposals—and that is true in both Arizona and New Mexico, where Earth First! has proposals that are maybe twice the size of our coalition's proposals—it makes the coalition proposal look more moderate and reasonable. And it is. We don't include every piece of land that possibly could be wilderness, nor do we propose closing down major roads and other kinds of developments. Earth First! does. It definitely does make the coalition proposals look more mainstream and moderate and reasonable. If Earth First! wasn't there, then the coalition proposal would be on the extreme."[24] Foreman adds perspective to the tactical importance of the niche theory. "Ten years ago the horrible things that are now being said about Earth First! in small newspapers in the West and by politicians were being said about the Sierra Club....By pushing that edge out there, we have given the mainstream groups a lot more room in which to operate. We make them look credible without them having to compromise more,"[25] he says, noting a primary purpose behind Earth First!'s founding. The radicals take the heat, opening the way for the mainstream.

Nevertheless, it is difficult for McCloskey, Norton, and others to watch the upstarts rant and rave without feeling queasy. Although Norton does not sense that there have been any negative repercussions for mainstream groups, he says he fears "the backlash. I know that decision makers who ultimately will decide whether a given piece of land is given lasting protection or not are not going to respond to illegal activities or threats of illegal activities. In their view it is like responding to terrorism."[26] In some sensitive areas the damage is easily done, McCloskey says. In Utah, for example, they can't tell the difference between Earth First! and the Sierra Club, or at least they aren't interested in such distinctions. Any radical presence at all in such places is a setback for the embryonic inroads of the mainstream.[27] Often, though, these are locales for the most flagrant, ecologically unconscionable acts of destruction, the places where radicals feel their work is most important due to the shortness of time and the extent of environmental devastation.

A Challenge for the New Environmentalism

In the twilight months of Reagan's presidency, people awoke to the need of getting personally involved in environmental struggles, says Mike Roselle. After years of growing sensitivity to local and worldwide ecological catastrophes and a lack of leadership from mainstream environmental groups, some of the disaffected decided to take matters into their own hands. Roselle explains, "This is a very different kind of activism....There is a lot more solidarity, unity, cooperation, communication, and coordination—all of it. People say, 'What's the Green movement?' It isn't the [Green Party's] Committee of Correspondence, it certainly isn't the established political parties with their environmental planks, and I don't think it's the combined leadership and staff of the major environmental organizations. The Green movement in this country is the combined grassroots movement of people who are pushing from the bottom to make changes happen."[28]

Such sentiments mirror McCloskey's fears of the "radicalization of the grassroots" and its "sense of alienation" from national organizations. He warns, however, that any new groups which emerge to take leadership had better be prepared to deliver. "I think to the extent that the more radical groups start growing and attracting resources, they're going to be held accountable for results," McCloskey says. "Large followings are not going to be satisfied with the merely ideological answer that 'we stand for right things.' They're going to be asking 'What are you doing to make the world in which we're living better?'" An example of the pull of the mainstream on a semi-radical group can be seen with Greenpeace. McCloskey notes, "I think it is very interesting that Greenpeace, as they are growing huge, is moving more and more of its operations into the pragmatic theater of activity. We, in turn, are beginning to redefine the pragmatic boundary line to include some direct action."[29]

Although mainstream groups have not been as effective as they could have been in programs requiring fast implementation, such as the development of acceptable standards for toxic contaminants, McCloskey says, "I do not think there is yet much evidence that the radical camp has demonstrated that it can clean up pollution through local protests and marches around plants. But I think it's an open question....I don't think it is out of the question that that might get some results." With their emphasis on wilderness and wildlife, radical environmentalists have not waged many anti-pollution campaigns. But the question remains: can the radicals do just as well on their own issues and in their own ways? In August 1989, Earth First!'s National Tree Sit Week garnered nationwide media attention for the plight of publicly-held forests; a year later its Redwood Summer campaign drew thousands of protestors who engaged in months of sustained civil disobedience. Annual anti-fur campaigns and demonstrations at animal testing laboratories by animal rights activists and Animal Liberators have done the same, as have Sea Shepherd Conservation Society protests over captive dolphin programs and the slaughter of baby harp seals. Brower's somewhat tamer Earth Island Institute boycott of all tuna products to oppose the killing of dolphins by tuna fishing fleets proved successful. In April 1990, three major tuna canners announced that they would only purchase "dolphin-safe" tuna. McCloskey doubts the long-term effectiveness of these approaches, however. "I don't think the direct action techniques will work forever," he says, "but they will work for a while. That's a part of pragmatism: to keep trying things, seeing what works. As long as it works, you pursue it. When it stops, you go on to something else."[30]

Now that they have begun to fill the void in environmental leadership left by the retreating federal government, mainstream groups' self confidence is on the increase, McCloskey says. The time for action is at hand. Still, though, there is a level of uncertainty. "Whether pragmatists can do the job and do the job fast enough is something we'll never know," McCloskey says. "All we can do is keep trying and do the best we can." Confident that the pragmatic approach is the best way available, he puts the matter directly to the radicals: "There is no switch you can turn," he says. "Or I'll put it to them: If they know of a switch, why aren't they turning it?"[31] The radicals don't believe in such magic any more than McCloskey. At root, the two "niches" are separated by dramatically different ideologies. The radicals feel compelled to reach out to and to teach the public through dramatic action, to stop whatever environmental abuses they can by whatever non-violent means are available, including destruction of property. They assert that any time lost and any further compromise invites future disaster. The answer is to quickly and drastically reduce humans' impact on the environment. Further, it is much less a matter of what *they* can do to make the world a better place, as McCloskey posed the challenge, than it is a matter of how *we*, each of us, can act to effect a sane, sustainable world.

For McCloskey, refusing to compromise and calling for huge wilderness areas are unrealistic positions; he also sees them as unfair methods of claiming the moral high ground in the environmental debate. Those peaks, climbed so arduously and assiduously by those in the mountaineering tradition, are every bit as much the mainstream's as they are the radicals'. The Sierra Club puts Earth first, too, McCloskey says. Besides, a hard-line stance never gets you a seat at the bargaining table—where would saying no to every trash burning plant and every new oil well leave mainstream groups? The political system forces compromise. In order to maintain the lifestyles to which we in the West have grown accustomed, some level of environmental destruction is inevitable and acceptable.

It was fear of the unchecked destruction of wild places that prompted John Muir to establish the Sierra Club; fear that the vast, undeveloped forests and deserts would be obliterated drove Aldo Leopold, Bob Marshall, and Benton MacKaye to form the Wilderness Society. The radicals are naturally fearful because of the cumulative damage that they see adding up every day. Time is running out on the environment, they say. When that fear for the whole and for the long-term is absent, so too is a primary motivating force behind the movement. In this, at least, eco-warriors have more in common with the mainstream's founding fathers than do the mainstream groups themselves.

CHAPTER 3

ECOLOGY MEETS PHILOSOPHY

Most eco-warriors have no interest in a well-conceived philosophy or in any other explicit guideposts to tell them how to live their lives. Activist after activist, when asked to consider the events, ideas, and inspirations which led them to adopt their uncommon principles, acknowledge that it is intuition which spurs them to act, not some clear, rational, deductive thought process. Radical environmentalism emerges out of an ecological consciousness that comes from the heart—not the head—that has experienced the natural world. Earth First! activist Darryl Cherney, for example, longed to move to the Redwoods from his home in Manhattan. When he got there, he was shocked. "The day I arrived in Garberville, California, Humboldt County, I found that it was still legal to cut down redwoods and to clear cut—concepts that had never occurred to me before," Cherney says, recalling his first spark of ecological awareness. "No one really did those things, or so I thought. On that day I became an environmental activist."[1]

Cherney says he expected the Redwoods to be inviolate, pure—and expensive. "I grew up in New York City, where rents were astronomical—the nicer the neighborhood, the higher the rent. So I put off moving to the Redwoods for years because I assumed that such a magnificent place must have rents in the thousands of dollars per month. I think there are probably a lot of people who apply their own limited space, their parochial visions, to other areas of the world, not realizing the destruction and lack of appreciation that occurs there."[2] In May 1990 Cherney's struggle for the Redwoods nearly cost him his life. He was riding in a car driven by fellow activist Judi Bari when a pipe bomb exploded, severely injuring Bari and wounding Cherney.

Animal Liberationist Nancy Burnet's ecological intuition grew as she saw development around Los Angeles wiping out more and more wild habitat. It really took hold, however, when she began investigating the use of animals in the entertainment industry and realized the fundamental devaluation that occurs when a living creature is removed from its environment. "For example," Burnet says, "porpoises or whales or any other animal should be free to live in the ocean without being trapped and taken to Sea World or some other aquatic park....Any animal that is meant to live in the jungles of Africa or South America should be left to live there. That's where they were born. I don't believe animals should be kept in zoos. They should never be imprisoned for any reason. Everything needs to be left alone."[3] For her trouble, Burnet has been slapped with a lawsuit by an Animal Welfare organization that claims she has made unfair allegations about the group's poor record in protecting animals used in the movies.

No philosophy beyond what they intuit as the right course of action is necessary for Cherney, Burnet, and many others. For those new to this movement, however, ecological philosophy does help explain activists' beliefs and their actions, actions which can lead to attempts on their lives or can wipe out their life savings fighting a lawsuit. It is a philosophy not only of thought but of action as well—of *praxis*, the union of philosophy and activism. Nor is ecological philosophy an entirely new phenomenon. Philosophers, naturalists, and poets through the ages have espoused the importance of including animals, plants, rocks, and rivers within value systems. As Roderick Nash notes in his detailed history of environmental ethics, as long ago as pre-Socratic Greece, and later in third-century Rome, humans have sought to give animals a place in ethics and law.[4]

Some have argued that development of this line of thinking was blocked by the advent of a Christianity intent on dominating nature. Construction of the philosophical and conceptual bases for the Eco-Wall moved along rapidly with Christianity's increasing prominence. There were occasional setbacks—a thirteenth-century Italian friar, St. Francis of Assisi, managed to promote a love of both living and non-living nature in the cold climate fostered by the early Roman Catholic Church. But it was not until recently that environmental ethics, and the more radical ecological philosophy, found a voice. In many respects, eco-philosophy resembles the philosophies of the past. Its exponents speak of ontology, epistemology, and moral communities, and seem to split hairs over the smallest point of debate. But their perspective is challenging, and eco-philosophers have successfully carved out a new, controversial niche in the philosophical world. At least two new philosophies, "deep ecology" and "eco-feminism," have emerged in the last twenty years which promote ways of living that are consistent with radical environmentalists' objectives.

The "Subversive Science"

It is important to begin with a brief look at the science of ecology, central as it is to ecological philosophy, before examining two of these philosophies. Ecology is the study of how plants and animals, both as individuals and together as communities, relate to their environments. It differs from most other sciences because rather than break apart the world, chopping it up into ever-finer pieces so that the big picture is entirely lost, ecology puts all those pieces together.

Ecologists study ecosystems, webs of interacting biological and nonliving components. An instructive example of the principles of ecology at work and of the tenuous nature of these "webs of life," comes from the Amazonian rainforest. The Brazilian government requires farmers and cattle ranchers to leave one-half of their land as "intact" rainforest—trees in that area may not be cut. Ecologists theorized that when farmers create islands of forest isolated by meadow, as often happens, the result would be a reduction of species on those islands—a loss of biodiversity. Subsequent research confirmed their hypotheses. The researchers found that unbroken forest was essential to the survival of the ecosystem. The food chain deteriorates when animals which have evolved for millennia to be perfectly suited to their niches within these climax communities are displaced by the islandization of the forest.* Ecologist Robert Bieregaard found that army ants are a "keystone" species without which the rainforest ecosystem falls apart. A colony of army ants needs a minimum forest area of fifty acres to survive. At half that size the ants can no longer survive and disaster strikes the remnant wood. Antbirds, which feed on the insects fleeing from approaching hordes of army ants, die or seek other, complete habitats. Butterflies that eat the feces of the antbirds go the same way, as do wasps which must lay their eggs on the fleeing insects. The wasps pollinate plants upon which other species depend; the plants are doomed without the wasps and, indirectly, so are those other species. Habitat destruction causes the forest ecosystem to crumble niche by niche. "If a key species in this chain dies out," Bieregaard says, "an entire web of living things, each dependent on the other, inevitably rips apart."[5]

Bieregaard's observation is reminiscent of an oft-quoted statement by John Muir: "When we try to pick out anything by itself, we find it hitched to everything else in the universe."[6] This is ecology's lesson. It applies to the rainforests of the Northwestern U.S. as well. There the timber industry ravages hundreds of acres of forest at a time, stripping the land of all of its vegetable matter and utterly destroying the habitat essential to other plants and animals, in a process called clear cutting. In nationwide advertising the industry proclaims its concern for the "renewable resource," trees, and claims that there are more trees in the ground today than ever before. Yet quantity is not all that matters in nature; *quality* may be of equal or greater

---

NOTE: The food chain represents the flow of nutrients through the plants and animals in an ecosystem; niches are the roles that particular plants and animals assume in an ecosystem; and a climax community exists when there is a sustainable cycle of energy, nutrients, and other components in an ecosystem and where the plant and animal species are of the sort most able to withstand changes brought on by phenomena like fires and floods.

importance. An entire old growth forest extirpated and replanted with hybrid seedlings stands little chance of ever again harboring a climax ecosystem to match the complexity of the one that came before it. During the last century there has been a marked worldwide increase in this sort of destructiveness. The effects can be seen in phenomena such as the greenhouse effect and depletion of the ozone layer which threaten the future of all life on the planet.

As unique and illuminating as ecology may be, the fact that we have had to resort to such a rationalistic approach to learn about the world around us tells us just how formidable the Eco-Wall really is. Other cultures, including those of the Native Americans, knew the plants, animals, and landscapes of their worlds intimately; they were consciously a part of the ecological system around them, aware that what they did affected all of it. Some developed taxonomies for the flora and fauna of their regions similar to science's detailed listings of orders, families, genera, species, and subspecies. Ironically, most societies which lived with these close ties to the world around them have been obliterated or assimilated, their ecological wisdom blotted out by the same forces that have constructed the Eco-Wall. Today, such ecological consciousness like theirs has almost been forgotten, and to the extent that it exists, it competes for attention in a complex world in which consciousness or awareness is far more likely to be focused on the evening's television schedule than on living in harmony with the rest of nature.

Ours is a world of nonbelievers—not of religious nonbelievers, but of people who no longer trust their senses and feelings, their intuitions. What we do trust are the mediators in our lives, the authorities who tell us when the air is polluted, when a species is near extinction, or when there are "too many" wolves in a place and that they need to be killed. Science is today's oracle. Perhaps ecology, which has been called the "subversive science," can enable us to overcome the disasters created by other sciences and the mindset that exalts them. But it will do so only with a healthy infusion of intuition from a re-sensitized public unafraid to follow its heart when making major decisions.

Ecology's subversive side can help us to see beyond the myopia of conventional limits—short-term considerations of time and near-term considerations of space—by lengthening the time span and the physical territory of concern. It invites us to ponder the effects of today's actions on generations to come and in lands far removed from our own. The result opens our eyes to potentials and pitfalls. The materialistic, energy-gobbling, resource-wasting Western way of life cannot be extended to other areas of the globe to any great extent; an ecological understanding of recent history makes this clear.

There is something intuitively correct about ecology. "Correct" is not meant to imply that ecology presents some sort of scientifically created or verifiable "truth." Indeed, even in its quest for knowledge, ecology hammers away at the dominant Western worldview that all is knowable, that truth is verifiable and permanent. There are too many threads to the web of life, too many variables in too many ecosystems all connected to the world-wide ecosystem, for the whole of nature ever to be perfectly understood.

And what is understood is threatening to many. As eco-philosophers Bill Devall and George Sessions observe, "Ecology undermines not only the growth addict and the chronic developer, but science itself."[7] Ecology is a painful study. "One of the penalties of an ecological education is that one lives alone in a world of wounds," wrote Aldo Leopold, considered by many to be the originator of ecological philosophy.[8] By pointing out the endless connections between *everything*, ecology subverts the dominant paradigm, showing the weaknesses in the Eco-Wall from the other side, from the rest of nature's point of view.

Deep Ecology and the End of Boundaries

Self-Realization and Biocentric Equality

In 1972 Norwegian philosopher Arne Naess delivered a lecture outlining what has since come to be called "deep ecology." Deep ecology is one of the most recent expressions of the centuries-old minority tradition in Western philosophy that holds that humans are not the measure of all things but merely a part of all that is. While more popular in Eastern philosophies, including Buddhism, a core concept in this line of thinking is the barrier-less nature of reality. Australian philosopher Warwick Fox writes, "'[T]o the extent that we perceive boundaries, we fall short of deep ecological consciousness,'" a statement that expresses "the central intuition of deep ecology."[9]

Two core values guide deep ecology praxis. The first, *self-realization*, extends the environmentally conscious individual's perception beyond the traditionally accepted aspects of the "self"—that person and his or her family and loved ones—to include the environment as a whole. The absence of boundaries of which Fox writes is the experience of unity with all else, a release of the small, individual self to the larger Self through heightened environmental consciousness. This is a selfless Self committed to the flourishing of the natural world on its own terms and apart from excessive human intervention. The practical effects of self-realization are wide-ranging. For example, Naess says that self-realization can only come about through the creation of "nondominating societies" that treat all members fairly, human and non-human alike.[10] The aspect of deep ecology that advocates radical, social change emerges here. As Bill Devall and George Sessions write in their book *Deep Ecology*, "Change in persons requires a change in culture and vice versa. We cannot ignore the personal arena nor the social, for our project is to enhance harmony with each other, the planet, and ourselves."[11]

Deep ecology's second primary value is *ecocentrism*, the ethical stance that everything in nature possesses inherent or intrinsic worth or value. (Most deep ecologists use the term "biocentrism." "Ecocentrism" was developed later as a synonymous label to dispel any connotation that biocentrism was limited exclusively to living beings, which it is not. *As used here, ecocentrism includes not only the whole, but individuals as well*, a point that becomes especially important in the discussion of eco-feminism.) Gone are the crass economic, scenic, recreational, spiritual, or similar labels that humans use to appraise the non-human world. Deep ecologists argue that human-centered, or "anthropocentric," worldviews grant people a privileged status not unlike the belief of old that the sun and stars evolved around the Earth. Ecology teaches that no individual or species warrants such a special status. For ethical purposes ecocentrism places humans on par with trees, blades of grass, mountain lions, and roaches. The concept is so foreign to us Westerners that it is difficult to believe that some of the world's great religions espouse ecocentrically-based ethics. Buddhism teaches reverence and respect for the environment, emphasizing the continuum of life, its fluid, dynamic nature. Alive but for a short time, we die to be returned to the Earth and to re-emerge as a new being. This is a cosmological way of saying that we are a part of the food chain (or that we would be were it not for bronze caskets and concrete vaults!). A Chinese proverb gives guidance for ecocentric living: "There are four rules for living in the mountains: let there be no formation in trees, no arrangement in rocks, no sumptuousness in the dining house, and no contrivance in the human heart."[12]

Deep Ecology's Vision

With self-realization and ecocentrism as its primary forces, deep ecology differs sharply with the Western philosophical paradigm, focused as it is on humans as the exclusive species with "moral considerability," the only group in nature deserving of ethical treatment. Devall asserts the importance of deep ecology, while tacitly acknowledging the lengthy history which flows through it and compels its proponents to challenge traditional philosophy, saying, "I sense that we have crossed a watershed in Western philosophy. Deep ecology is one of the most powerful post-modern movements."[13] This "power" results in a thoroughgoing critique of the "dominant world view" as lived by Americans and most of the Western and industrialized world. Devall and Sessions summarized some of the key differences as follows:

DOMINANT WORLD VIEW	DEEP ECOLOGY
Dominance over Nature	Harmony with Nature
Natural environment as resource for humans	All nature has intrinsic worth/biospecies equality
Material/economic growth for growing human population	Elegantly simple material needs (material goals serving the larger goal of self-realization)
Belief in ample resource reserves	Earth "supplies" limited
High technological progress and solutions	Appropriate technology; nondominating science
Consumerism	Doing with enough/recycling
National/centralized community	Minority tradition/bioregion[14]

While there is no single accepted vision of a deeply ecological future that embraces the values in this list, deep ecologists have developed some guidelines for living in ways that are "deeply ecological." Practicing an ecologically-centered lifestyle, for example, means simplifying one's life, living with minimal impact on the environment. In practical terms, this may mean growing a garden, using public transportation rather than a personal car, being aware of how our choices as consumers affect the environment, and ultimately consuming as little as possible. In essence, deep ecology tells us that we should limit what we take from the environment to that which is necessary to fulfill our "vital needs." The generic vital needs for humans are food, housing, warmth, and clothing. However, deep ecologists say that in today's Western cultures this list may be enlarged temporarily to include transportation systems, although not necessarily automobiles; telephones; plumbing; refrigeration; and electricity. Many radical activists find themselves using sophisticated technologies (like computers, which they use to produce newsletters, write reports, and to communicate with one another) as an ecologically painful yet expedient way of bringing about a societal transformation to less extractive, more environmentally benign societies.

Deep ecologists also call for reductions in the Earth's human population to lessen the strain on non-human nature. They emphasize the ecological effects of fewer humans not only in developing nations where resources (or "supplies," the preferred term of some radical environmentalists) are already strained and where populations are rapidly growing, but in developed nations as well. North Americans, Europeans, and Japanese consume disproportionately large amounts of energy, food, health services, and material goods. Deep ecologists recognize that only with a reduction in human population is the extensive human manipulation of nature going to end. They assert that the ongoing destruction of the environment cannot be morally or ecologically justified, nor do they believe that it is sustainable over the long term.

Of particular concern to deep ecologists is the destruction of the remaining wilderness areas in the world. In the U.S., "wilderness" usually refers to large tracts of roadless land, ideally at least 50,000 acres in the crowded East and 100,000 acres in the West.[15] The importance of wilderness lies in "the general ecological functions of these areas," according to Sessions and Naess, most notably the "continued evolutionary speciation of animals and plants."[16] In other words, wilderness serves as nature's gene bank. Edward Goldsmith, editor of the respected magazine *The Ecologist*, has written "'that the changes brought by [industrialization] are, in fact, reversing ecological succession, [and] that is why we must consider industrial development or 'progress' as an anti-evolutionary process....By reversing ecological succession it is giving rise to ever greater ecological instability.'"[17]

In order to end these human-caused abuses, political and economic policies and ideologies must be changed. One "basic social thrust of the deep, long-range ecology movement is transformation of the masses into a new kind of society," according to Devall. The aim is "to empower more and more ordinary people with their ecological self and to empower grassroots movements with solidarity and effectiveness when facing vast bureaucracies and hierarchical organizations."[18] The ideal political form for achieving these ends would be compatible with the environment and with deep ecology's ideals. Given this, deep ecologists fault both capitalist and communist societies, based as they are on huge industries producing goods for an ever-growing population.

Deep ecology's answer is to advocate communities based on Gandhi's maxim: "'The ideally nonviolent state will be an ordered anarchy.'"[19] Deep ecologists' anarchy is not chaotic, but is based instead on the model of many tribal cultures. Individuals would be restricted by certain ethical boundaries, yet within those they would have substantial amounts of freedom to live as they will. Earth First! co-founder Dave Foreman distinguishes between such close-knit communities and "anarchy," saying, "I consider myself a tribalist, not an anarchist. I think if you look at any primal society, individuals within that society had a great deal of personal freedom, but it was freedom in the context of the tribal culture. The details of that tribal culture and the customs are not important. What is important is that cultural matrix and that there are values and ethical guidelines that you operate within."[20]

"Bioregionalism" is suggested by deep ecologists as the ideal political organizing theory. A bioregion's boundaries can be fixed, albeit loosely, according to ecological, philosophical, and anthropological criteria like an area's watershed, the shared sense of identification with a place, and the cultural distinctiveness of an area. The actual political process deep ecologists envision would be highly decentralized and truly democratic, allowing everyone in a community to have a say in political decisions.

Spiritualism and Deep Ecology

Essential to deep ecology praxis, according to Arne Naess, is its "'religious component, fundamental intuitions that everyone must cultivate if he or she is to have a life based on values and not function like a computer.'"[21] Values may be important in and of themselves, but their development through some sort of spiritual discipline is essential. Devall comments that "the praxis of deep ecology comes from a religious and community basis. I think what is driving that is spiritual yearnings" that emerge from our aimless consumerist cultures. He adds, "If our interpretations of deep ecology have been too mystical for this country, it is because this country is so materialistic."[22] Deep ecology's spiritualism—and that of ecophilosophy in general—is eclectic, drawing extensively on Native American metaphysics and spiritual practice, and other traditions as well, including Zen Buddhism, Taoism, Hinduism, and Christianity.

Most radical environmentalists follow no spiritual "path" yet feel a strong bond between themselves and their place that reinforces their beliefs and their actions. Devall ascribes to eco-warriors Zen-like qualities: "The new warrior does not ask ultimate questions in daily practice because asking the question entangles the warrior in framing the question and interferes with the answer." They are "intense, centered, persistent, gentle, strong, sincere, attentive, and alert."[23]

Eco-feminism's Challenging Perspective

The French term *ecofeminisme* was introduced in 1974 "to bring attention to women's potential for bringing about an ecological revolution."[24] Since then, eco-feminism has grown to become a major eco-philosophy as well as a budding economic, political, and social theory. One exponent calls it "a movement to end all forms of oppression,"[25] oppression that has its roots in so-called "male" values and social constructs. Thus, *androcentrism*, or male-centeredness, is the root of environmental problems, not the "gender-neutral" human-centeredness asserted by deep ecologists. That deep ecology has overlooked "the masculine world view" responsible for the domination of nature—and the domination of women and other "minorities"—is a major shortcoming, say the eco-feminists. Some eco-feminists do find common ground with deep ecologists on several themes, including the role of intuition in the development of philosophy in general and in fostering an ethical orientation toward the environment in particular. Both hold that experiencing non-human nature is important to the flowering of ecological consciousness, and deep ecologists and eco-feminists also share an interest in the spiritual nature of the quest for that consciousness.

However, the root cause of humanity's subjugation of nature—human-centeredness versus male-centeredness—sharply divides deep ecologists and eco-feminists. Eco-feminists believe that industrial societies, like others dating back thousands of years, are male-dominated hierarchies embracing androcentric values instead of more "feminine" values like egalitarianism, connectedness, and non-aggression. They note that men, driven by rationalism, domination, competitiveness, individualism, and a need to control, are most often the culprits in the exploitation of animals and the environment. Still, as Ynestra King notes, "male" values are not exclusively possessed by men. "There is no reason to believe," writes King, "that women placed in positions of patriarchal power will act any different-ly from men;" she goes on to say that economics and politics will have to be changed as part of "a feminist revolution."[26] Like deep ecology, eco-feminism asserts that only through widespread social change will today's social and environmental shortcomings be remedied.

Woman as the "Other"

It is important that environmental activists adopt a feminist perspective, since "a central reason for woman's oppression is her association with the despised nature they are so concerned about," King writes. "The hatred of women and the hatred of nature are intimately connected and mutually reinforcing."[27] Unless both are released from the grip of domination and control, neither will be free. Eco-feminists attempt to explain men's "hatred" of women with the aid of psychological theory. Psychologists theorize that women and men establish their self-identities in different ways. Recall that "Self-realization"—the act of embracing a larger, organic whole that encom-passes everything in nature—is one of two central values within deep ecology. Although deep ecologists say that Self-realization is possible only within societies which do not dominate any of their members, human or non-human, eco-feminists criticize deep ecologists for promoting a "gender-neutral concept of self."[28] In so doing, the deep ecologists fail to make a critical distinction between male and female perceptions of the world.

In brief, psychologists who espouse "object relations theory" say that men define themselves in opposition to that which is seen as female. Women have traditionally been seen as sharing characteristics like menstruation, pregnancy, and birth with non-human animals. Because of these com-monalities, women and non-human nature have become linked as the "other" against which men must strive for identity. In contrast, girls are not raised to feel detached from the world around them; they possess "a basis for 'empathy' built into their primary definition of self in a way that boys do not."[29] Thus, writes eco-feminist Marti Kheel, "women's self-identity, unlike that of men, is not established through violent opposition to the natural world. The guiding motive in women's self-identity is not the attainment of an autonomous self, but rather the preservation of a sense of connection to other living beings."[30] In most cultures, men must destroy nature and/or control and dominate women in order to truly become male. Women, on the other hand, are aware of their closer ties to the human and non-human world around them and develop their sense of identity in continuity with nature.

In practice, the male oppression of women and nature often goes hand-in-hand. For example, throughout the world women are responsible for domestic work. In Kenya and India, as in many other places, women have borne the burden of extensive deforestation of the lands near their homes by male-controlled timber companies. Once the trees are cut, women must walk farther and farther to gather fire wood. Still, their husbands expect all at home to be "normal." In Kenya, women have begun to answer with their own "Green Belt" movement, which not only replants denuded forests but pays the women who do the replanting, thereby enabling them to be somewhat independent of their wage-earning husbands. Green Belt has also organized collectives of women, many of whom are victims of sexual and physical abuse, and has assisted some women in the construction of their own homes. In India, the "Chipko" (literally, "hug the trees") movement has halted the cutting of forests in sensitive watersheds. This largely female movement has set about restoring forests upon which women and their families depend. (The Green Belt and Chipko movements are examined in more detail in Chapter Eight.)

Some eco-feminists also feel that at the same time that women are developing a sense of self and no longer perceiving themselves as extensions of their fathers or husbands, the deep ecologists advocate stripping them of their selfhood through their sexist, gender-insensitive rhetoric. Ecofeminist Janet Biehl reacts angrily to what she sees as the implicit de-valuation of women inherent in deep ecologists' expanded Self. She writes that "women are now intensely striving for...selfhood in a new society. *This aspiration is the revolutionary heart of the feminist and ecofeminist movements.*" She adds, "Women and men alike are thus asked [by deep ecologists] to efface themselves before nature, to ignore their identity as a species in a surrender to boundaryless, cosmic 'oneness.' In reality, the fact is that women know from long experience that when they are asked to become 'one' with a man, as in marriage, that 'one' is usually the man. Eco-feminists should be equally suspicious of this 'ecological' oneness."[31] Ecofeminist Karen J. Warren appears to agree with Biehl that deep ecology's "boundarylessness" is suspect. She notes that the non-human world is "independent, different, perhaps even indifferent to humans."[32] Those differences should not be the source of contempt, as they are today. They should, instead, be respected; each entity in nature, each woman, man, doe, buck, canyon, and stream deserves to be acknowledged as unique, not lost in an attempt to create a universal selfhood.

From Rights to Responsibilities

Eco-feminism's emphasis on female values has led Marti Kheel to propose an eco-feminist philosophy based upon "the sentiments of caring and responsibility," emotions that researchers such as Carol Gilligan say are much more important in the formation of women's ethics than men's. As she states it, responsibility, in the literal sense of "ability for response," is especially important. We must take an anticipatory, preparatory attitude toward non-human nature, "to attend to nature in order to detect not what we might want from her, but rather what she might want from us."[33] This responsive, even foresightful attitude toward the rest of the natural world stands in opposition to the "rights-based" approaches which dominate environmental philosophy. For example, although Kheel is an Animal Liberationist, she finds fault with animal rights philosophy's assignment of a hierarchy of value to the members of the natural world. Although animal rightists hold that animals deserve basic rights, such as freedom to live in their native habitat, this highly rational, logical perspective directs that a line be drawn to distinguish between those beings which are deserving of rights and those which are not. For animal rights philosopher Peter Singer, the distinguishing characteristic is "sentience," the ability to feel pleasure and pain. Thus, a chicken deserves membership in the "moral community" because it can feel pain (and presumably pleasure). An oyster, in contrast, does not appear to be sentient, and thus is morally disenfranchised.

Deep ecologists, on the other hand, establish a framework of identification with the whole ecosystem. Kheel says that in so doing, they ignore the abusive conditions under which animals on factory farms and those used for experiments live. We humans do empathize with other beings in pain, but because environmental ethicists do not acknowledge the ties between domesticated animals and a larger ecosystem, they turn their backs on cruelty. This "holistic" viewpoint also allows for the hunting of animals in the wild. This is seen by animal rights philosophers as a violation of individual rights; Kheel goes further, portraying hunting as an ideal example of the complex psychological need that some men have to achieve their identity through subduing nature.

For Kheel, "ethics is an 'ethos,' or way of life. It is not a matter of making abstract moral statements about who is allowed entrance into the moral community and who is not. That is an elitist, very *male* way of viewing the world. The masculine world view (shared by both environmental ethics and animal rights) maintains that there is a moral community of certain individuals and the only way in which you can be accorded value is by being drawn into that community."[34] Kheel advocates a philosophy where the importance of both the whole and the individual are respected. She points out that the apparent conflicts between environmental ethics and animal rights dissolve as one steps back and looks at the single (patriarchal) system that promotes both wilderness destruction and animal suffering. "Ninety percent of soil erosion, eighty percent of consumptive use of water, and seventy percent of deforestation is the result of...livestock agriculture," Kheel notes.[35] Thus the "root cause" behind much of the wilderness destruction in the U.S. and the simultaneous suffering of livestock animals is "the mentality that has reduced living creatures to reproductive machines."[36] In keeping with radical environmentalists who are propelled to act by intuition and emotion, Kheel stresses that our *feelings*, rather than some rational, abstract ethics, should be the basis for the way humans interact with the rest of the natural world. Those feelings should be based on "concrete, loving actions," Kheel says, advocating praxis and not passivity in our relations with non-human nature.[37]

Living to Nurture Earth

Eco-feminists stress the need for individuals to live their lives in ways that promote women's Earth-nurturing values. Ethics needs to become a conscious part of our lives, not something that comes to mind when we are forced by circumstances to make a "moral" decision. With this in mind, eco-feminists have adopted a theme commonly used by non-ecological feminists: the "personal is political." For Kheel this means living a "cruelty-free" lifestyle not dependent on animal products or animal testing in any way. She advocates holistic health care, condemning Western allopathic medicine for its "warfare mentality." In contrast to such animal-based approaches to medicine, the use of holistic health care represents a form of "non-violent civil disobedience" against the medical establishment. Dietary choices, too, are of extreme importance. We need to understand where our food comes from, Kheel says. "When people sit down, we choose not to recognize that we're eating an animal. As Carol Adams points out, our very language shows that: we eat *meat* and meat is an 'it,' no longer a she or a he. We don't think of meat as the flesh of an animal." She adds, "If we want to be honest, we should say we're eating 'her' or 'him.' In her book *The Sexual Politics of Meat*, Carol Adams says that if everybody had to acknowledge that as they ate some chicken or beef or whatever—*I'm eating her* leg or *her* breast—I think we'd feel very differently about it."[38] Perhaps more than anything, it is this *honesty* that is of most importance to eco-feminists. When we face up to the realities of our lifestyles, Kheel and other eco-feminists say, the aggression and control upon which society is based becomes clear. From there we can work toward a true ecological consciousness and thence to removing the barriers that separate us from one another and from the non-human.

Living Eco-Logically

The praxis of ecophilosophy requires that people consciously act to bring about this honest, harmonious world, to break down the Eco-Wall. The millions who participated in Earth Day 1990 activities were evidence of the widely-accepted need to act now in our individual lives, locally, societally, and worldwide, to resolve the human-environment conflicts which confront the planet. The only logical way for humans to live is sustainably (eco-logically, one might say). No one knows what a human culture that lives in balance with its surroundings looks like. Some argue that true sustainability is impossible, that even the most ecologically benign societies of the past harmed the world around them and that any sustainable community in the future will do the same. Eco-feminists disagree, asserting that some matriarchal societies probably existed harmoniously with their surroundings but were destroyed or assimilated by other cultures. Regardless, the daily workings of a sustainable society are as yet unknown. Perhaps the science of ecology can be combined with our re-emerging intuitive ecological wisdom to help bring about such new worlds. Without activism bringing those visions alive, however, the science and philosophy will be little more than academic curiosities.

PART TWO

WHO WOULD DARE?

CHAPTER 4

GREENPEACE: BRIDGE TO RADICALISM

The environmental movement began in earnest in 1970 with the first Earth Day. Almost overnight, the environment was a popular cause and no longer the province of a few relatively small groups of outdoor enthusiasts. But as membership in mainstream organizations grew, few realized that another, more radical wing of the old conservation movement was underway as well. Within fifteen short years the first of those radical groups would grow to such a size and stature that they would stand alongside the establishment of the movement. Its founders, who embraced direct action as an environmental cure from the start, chose a paradoxically tranquil name: the Don't Make a Wave Committee. It was formed in 1969 by a small cadre of peace activists and Sierra Clubbers, including a number of expatriate Americans who had moved their families to Vancouver, British Columbia, so that their sons would not be drafted to fight in Vietnam. The Committee's aim was to protest the testing of nuclear weapons by the U.S. at Amchitka Island in the Aleutians.[1] Along with the threat of radioactive leakage into the environment, the Committee feared that a nuclear detonation of between fifty and 250 times the size of that which leveled Hiroshima would set off earthquakes, which in turn would cause tidal waves all around the Pacific Rim. They hatched the idea of sailing to Amchitka at the time of a test in hopes of getting close enough to a detonation to stop it, thus calling attention to the insanity of it all. Before its first voyage, the Committee renamed its rented boat the *Greenpeace*, a combination of "green" for ecology and "peace" for, well, *peace*.

Although it failed at its original goal to stop a test at Amchitka, the Committee played an important role in the permanent halting of nuclear bomb testing on the island. The group's first voyage in September of 1971 ended when the U.S. cancelled the explosion; the Wavers were more than 1,000 miles from the island when an actual test took place during their second trip. Just by making the effort, however, they created a sensation in the media. Shortly after the Committee's second voyage, the U.S. announced that it was returning Amchitka to its prior use as a bird and Sea otter refuge. Amazingly, the Committee had won despite never coming close to meeting its objectives. It was a phenomenon that the old conservation groups had rarely, if ever, experienced: victory through failure! The crucial differences were the Committee's use of both direct confrontation and the media. The two are essential qualities of today's radical environmentalism.

Soon the Committee renamed itself the Greenpeace Foundation and set out on its next mission—to halt above-ground nuclear testing by the French in the Mururoa Atoll, near Tahiti in the South Pacific. It was the start of a long, violent, and ultimately tragic relationship between the growing antinuclear group and the hubris-filled French government. In 1972 the French Navy rammed a Greenpeace vessel owned and commanded by former Canadian badminton champion David McTaggart. The next year French sailors savagely beat McTaggart and another Greenpeacer as they attempted to halt a bomb test. The protests were not in vain, however; using the formula that had proved successful in the Aleutian campaign, Greenpeace scored a victory through direct action and publicity, driving the French tests underground in 1973.

From Whales to Toxics

When one hears "Greenpeace," whales come to mind. The giant cetaceans were first an issue for the organization in 1973 when a minority of members held a concert to raise money for a whale education tour in Japan, the world's largest consumer of whale products. Within a year or so the whale faction had become the majority in the democratically-run group, and in April 1975 Greenpeace set sail on a historic journey to confront the Soviet whaling fleet in the North Pacific. The crew brought home dramatic photographs and film of activists steering outboard motor-driven rubber dinghies, called "Zodiacs," between harpoon-firing Soviet killer ships and huge, helpless whales. Soon, evening news audiences were watching in astonishment as the Greenpeace Zodiacs, seemingly directed by a higher force, zoomed and swooshed in front of the menacing harpoons, taunting the whalers and guarding the whales. Even the harpoons shot over their heads were not enough to deter the activists in a later battle against Icelandic whalers. Then, and again off the coast of Spain, it took naval vessels to stop the Greenpeacers' shenanigans. Whales and Greenpeace became synonymous. At considerable personal risk, Greenpeace agents uncovered illegal whaling activity in numerous nations, building a case against the bloody, ages-old whale hunts which, with modern technology, had become species-cidal slaughters. Finally, in 1986 the International Whaling Commission approved a ban on commercial whaling for all but "research" purposes.

Without question, Greenpeace's approach to environmental issues, from nuclear tests to whales to the seals it fought to protect, was unlike anything the mainstream of the movement had ever seen. Greenpeacers were *active* activists. They not only sailed, climbed, and hiked to the sources of environmental problems, but they became daredevils who constantly created new tactics. They bolted shut effluent pipes leading from chemical plants and skydived off power plant smokestacks to publicize pollution. These media stunts held no hope of stopping a particular environmental ill in and of themselves, much less of ending all poisoning of the water or air. Rather, hugging seals and hanging banners were screams for attention, the cries of individuals, and of a rapidly-growing organization, that disdained the suit-and-tie conventionality of the mainstream. The Earth was dying, and it was time to do something serious to stop it, time to go to the public in ways that even David Brower had not yet attempted; it was time to use television, especially, to captivate and anger the public to some sort of action. Increasingly, though, there were commonalities with the mainstream. Greenpeace was an organization, and in time it grew larger and larger. It depended on solicitations through the mail and door-to-door for fund raising. With the emergence of groups willing to vent their ecological rage against private property, even Greenpeace's direct action protests carried an air of pragmatism. Their civil disobedience actions took matters a step farther than "CD" (civil disobedience) prophets such as Mahatma Gandhi and Martin Luther King, but they clearly were not about to go as far as the Sea Shepherds or Earth First!.

Going International

As Greenpeace evolved in the late 1970s and the 1980s, its concerns were no longer limited to the monarchs of the deep or helpless seals on ice floes. With McTaggart at its helm, the organization rapidly grew and then went international, eventually establishing offices from London to East Lansing and from Seattle to Sydney. Because the web of life includes all ecosystems and all individuals, Greenpeace reasoned that only by making its presence felt throughout the world could it bring pressure to bear on environmental problems. In so doing it assumed the role of the most ambitious environmental protection organization in the world. Among its many international operations, Greenpeace has established beach patrols in French Guiana to protect sea turtle eggs; protested Japan's use of drift nets, forty mile-long curtains of death which indiscriminately kill sea life; hung the international sign for "radiation" from U.S. and Soviet warships; and investigated the flow of toxic wastes from developed nations to the Third World. Perhaps the most ambitious of its far-flung exploits is its research base in Antarctica. Several nations have such stations there, but Greenpeace's is unique in that it is a non-governmental organization. It has attracted media attention by revealing the extensive and literal "trashing" of the cold continent by the very researchers who are there studying it. Huge waste dumps litter the landscape, and untreated sewage is dumped directly into the ocean, threatening fragile ecosystems. This led to a Greenpeace proposal to declare all of Antarctica a "World Peace Park."

Its opposition to nuclear weapons testing has continued as well, with tragic consequences. In July 1985 the Greenpeace flagship *Rainbow Warrior* sat moored in the Aukland, New Zealand, harbor making final preparations prior to sailing once more for Mururoa Atoll where it would try to evade the French Navy and interrupt underground bomb tests, much as the Don't Make a Wave Committee had planned to do. Just before midnight on the tenth of the month, an explosion ripped open the hull. It came without warning. The crew rushed to the deck as the boat listed. But photographer Fernando Pereira decided to return to the ship's bowels to salvage what he could of his equipment. Suddenly, another massive explosion rocked the ship. Water poured in through a truck-sized hole. Two hours later divers recovered Pereira's lifeless body. The bombs, forty-four pounds of explosives in all, had been planted by seven French commandos acting on orders from the upper echelons of the French military. Two of the bombers were captured and convicted of manslaughter, only to serve less than a year in a New Zealand prison before the French government's economic blackmail forced New Zealand to hand over the agents to serve the remainder of their sentences in French custody.[2]

Greenpeace U.S.A.

Greenpeace U.S.A., the formal name of the American group, classifies its campaigns into four categories: nuclear, toxics, ocean ecology, and atmosphere and energy. Its nuclear program may be best known for its 1989 run-ins with the U.S. Navy. Greenpeace repeatedly attempted to halt testing of the submarine-launched Trident II nuclear missile by sailing a ship into an area off-limits to all vessels. Shades of McTaggart's first run-in with the French, the U.S. Navy rammed the boat to make clear its displeasure at the interference. Its toxics programs are likely the most grassroots based of Greenpeace's efforts—they have helped organize numerous neighborhoods fight garbage and hazardous waste incinerators which spew toxic pollutants and threaten human health. In its ocean ecology work, Greenpeace lists as among its accomplishments the 1987 ban on the disposal of plastics at sea by the U.S. and the federal government's requirements that shrimp fishing boats, which kill thousands of endangered sea turtles each year, be equipped with "Turtle Excluder Devices," reverse trap doors that let as many as ninety percent of the turtles caught in shrimp nests escape. And as part of their atmosphere and energy campaign, Greenpeacers have occupied metal boxes placed across train tracks leading into several Du Pont factories to protest that company's continued manufacture of ozone layer-depleting chlorofluorocarbons.

Having it Both Ways

Although it is far from the anarchist's dream that characterized its early years[3] or which is typical of today's radical environmental movement, just the same Greenpeace cannot be fairly labeled as "mainstream." More than anything, it is a tactical and philosophical bridge between straight-laced old line environmentalism and the no-holds-barred radicals. Its scope exceeds even the Sierra Club's, and its size is huge: Greenpeace has grown from a committed few activists to become the largest environmental organization in the world. It is a multinational corporation headquartered in Amsterdam with gross revenues of $100 million, half of that from Americans. Its 400-plus full-time employees work out of offices in twenty-three nations; in the U.S. alone there are thirty-five field offices. Greenpeace membership (the organization prefers to call dues payers "supporters") in the U.S. numbers two million, half the world total.

In 1987 Greenpeace U.S.A. spun off a lobbying arm called "Greenpeace Action." It takes its case door-to-door throughout the nation and sponsors three lobbyists who buttonhole members of Congress and haunt the halls of the bureaucracies, just like the Group of Ten and the rest of the pragmatists. But Greenpeace's approach is different, insists Executive Director Peter Bahouth. In fact, it encompasses everything that the separate mainstream organizations do on their own, and then some. "We are multimedia in the sense that we are not a lobbying group or a research organization or a litigation house or a grassroots activist movement, but we are a bit of all of those things," Bahouth observes. "So when we formulate campaigns or projects, we combine all those things in what we do." He says that the people developing and carrying out Greenpeace actions are committed to the cause and are not the sort "that want to someday get to be Under Secretary of the Interior,"[4] a quip prompted by Earth First! co-founder Dave Foreman's confession that as a lobbyist for the Wilderness Society he once dreamed of holding a high-level government job.

In most people's minds what sets Greenpeace apart from other mainstream environmental organizations is its direct action approach to issues. The tactical idea "is to go to the site of the problem," says Bahouth, "whether it's the middle of the Pacific Ocean with drift nets or the back end of a chemical company or Washington, D.C., where policy is being made, or Antarctica....We want to expose things that certain institutions want to keep secret. And we work internationally to break down boundaries that have been set up by institutions or political powers that limit our ability to relate to the environment." Bahouth feels that "people are motivated to support us because they are moved to action. We are rewarded because we create a bond with the public by virtue of doing something that they do not necessarily have the ability to do themselves." In its campaigns Greenpeace takes what he calls an "ecological approach" to environmentalism. "We see that things are connected to one another very directly," Bahouth explains, adding, "If you're going to talk about (declining) salmon stocks, for example, you can talk about the fact that salmon are being caught in drift nets, about deforestation, which is ruining the streams, agricultural runoff, toxic pollution into streams and rivers, and in some cases you could probably talk about oil production and spills. We see that as an organization that you can paint yourself into a corner [if you do not] draw these things together" and act on them.[5]

Like its more radical cousins, Greenpeace feels "that change comes from people acting on their ethical concerns and in response to their local needs," Bahouth says.[6] Greenpeace encourages this through assistance to local groups, helping them to organize and fight against some of the largest corporations. Still, its huge size is a key ingredient that separates Greenpeace from the new radicals; the organization belongs on the mainstream shore of the bridge to radicalism. Spokesperson Peter Dykstra admits that Greenpeace has "this instinctive distaste for a large organization, and we're getting to be a large organization. Not compared to chemical companies or armies or governments, but compared to other environmental groups. But goddammit, we want to take on General Motors and the Pentagon and Dow and Du Pont and Exxon. You cannot do that by being a rugged individualist that remains true to some mythical standard of purity but remains as tiny and impoverished as possible. You make a good romantic magazine piece when you're like that, but you really limit your results."[7]

But how long can Greenpeace straddle both sides of the gap that separates the old ways from the new? Something has to give, and as Michael McCloskey observed in Chapter Two, it appears that direct action and confrontation have been the side that has been neglected as the allure of prestige and power has worked its spell. Earth First!er Michael Robinson gives Greenpeace credit for fighting the good fight, saying, "They're willing to break the law and do civil disobedience, and they do have more of a deep ecology vision than most of the other mainstream environmental groups, but they're still very mainstream."[8] Greenpeace's size is a primary piece of evidence for this radical put-down, says Robinson. The radicals hold firm in their belief that no *organization*, replete with hierarchy and defined leadership, can be flexible and dynamic enough to act quickly and in the best interests of the environment. The radicals insist that when the fight is over a local issue, activists using their own resources and making their own decisions without any top-down direction is the way to go.

Contrary to Dykstra's inferences, smallness in size has nothing to do with romance and everything to do with living by the movement's ethics. While many local citizens' groups, especially those in the anti-toxics field, give

Greenpeace high marks for its assistance, some have complained that Greenpeace has marched in and taken over their fledgling operations. Impoverish^d, decentralized local movements following a more radical path are loosely allied with one another but fully in control of their individual destinies and beholden to no one—only to the animals, plants, and ecosystems for which they struggle. They pay minimal salaries, if any at all—r..ost activists do not even receive expense money—and they are so consumed by their issues and live on such a tight margin that they have no choice but to spend their time and money wisely.

Greenpeace, on the other hand, can generate hundreds of letters or telephone calls on a matter of national importance, such as drift nets or nuclear weapons testing. But spending hundreds of thousands of dollars each year on junk mail, even if the paper is recycled, is no way for an environmental organization to operate, especially when it is certain that ninety percent or more of the "direct mail solicitations" will go un-answered or even unopened, dumped into the trash and taken to a landfill. That, many say, is ecological heresy. Although some of the organizations supportive of the Animal Liberation movement raise money through the mail, no radical environmental group solicits in that way. Efficiency and simplicity are the watchwords. And for all of Greenpeace's millions, its actions still can go wrong, as Chapter Nine shows.

Radicals also question whether Greenpeace is actually fostering iden-tification with non-human nature—ecocentrism—or if it often is merely remedying human-caused problems for humans without urging people to make ecological, ethical connections with the broader environment. In effect, the radicals are asking, How dramatically are people altering their lifestyles once they join Greenpeace or come in contact with a Greenpeace campaign? How many have stopped eating shrimp so that they play no role in the killing of sea turtles? Once the trash burning plant or the toxic waste dump is defeated, are their lives changed? A related criticism is that Greenpeace's policy proposals do not go far enough toward creating a steady-state world, and some radicals feel that even a no-compromise stance by Greenpeace's lobbyists on Capitol Hill is unacceptable. Why expend energy there at all, they ask, where the power is so well entrenched and the hope for the needed fast changes is nothing but a pipe dream? Greenpeace's answer is simple: it works. "I think what you'll find in Greenpeace is not necessarily an adherence to direct action as a religion or a quasi-religion or, for that matter, lobbying as a religion," Dykstra says. "It's whatever works. Whatever works is what we're going to do."[9] Tactically, Greenpeace sounds willing to muddle-through along with the mainstream.

So Greenpeace shares much with the mainstream: a hierarchical and somewhat bureaucratic organization, a longing for political legitimacy, membership (by one name or another), a concern for human well-being while sometimes not emphasizing ecocentrism to the extent that its critics would like. Commonalities with the radicals stand out as well: direct action, support for grassroots activists, emphasis on attracting the news media's attention, and an adherence to an ecocentric philosophy on many issues.

But the Greenpeace "bridge" abruptly ends at a roadblock on the radical shore called *property destruction*. For Greenpeace, property destruction is violence, plain and simple. Even if the offending inanimate object is a whaling ship or other tool of immense destruction, there is no excuse for damaging it. Bahouth says that "what is happening to the environment is a violent act, so we are not going to take violent action ourselves to fight that. That's what the fundamental principle is. It's also a recognition that if you do take violent action against property, you're sort of drawing upon yourself a like response." Reminiscent of the radicals' attitude, he calls this non-violence edict "a political and philosophical strategy....It's an approach, and I think Greenpeace thinks it's the correct one."[10] The difference is that for Greenpeace non-violence is *strategy*, the overall and final approach to issues; for many of the radicals, non-destructive behavior is a *tactic* to be used as part of an arsenal which also includes property destruction.

Despite Greenpeace's studious avoidance of property destruction, the French still killed Fernando Pereira, and numerous other Greenpeace activists have been subjected to violent acts. No matter how non-destructive the direct action, opposition to power attracts a disproportionately greater violent reaction from that power. While non-destructive activism may place one in a morally superior position, for the radicals the bottom line is how much wilderness is being saved, how many lives are being preserved, be they human, plant, or animal. Times and tactics have passed Greenpeace by, the radicals say; Greenpeace, the radicals and terrorists of yore, are doing the same old stuff, although they undeniably continue to attract huge amounts of publicity to their cause and often are effective. But no longer are they considered quite so radical. As with the mainstream, Greenpeace's less-controversial appearance is in large part due to the emergence of the new radicals. Greenpeace built the bridge. It showed that theater could work for the environmental movement, parlaying the media attention from harpoon dodging and banner hangings to gain public support and thence to take its case to the powers that be. Yet that is not enough, the radicals say. Show, lobbying, legal actions, and even support for the grassroots don't do enough to stop those who would ravage the environment or even to raise the public's level of concern so that they demand the needed changes. Development and destruction will not be stopped by the "usual means." The heat under the debate will not be sufficiently raised.

In their assertions that the mainstream and Greenpeace are not doing enough, perhaps the radicals are merely playing versions of the "We save more whales than you do" game that Greenpeacers derisively accuse people like Paul Watson of engaging in. The radicals should spend more time saving the Earth and less time kicking around other groups, they say. But Watson, one of Greenpeace's earliest activists, a former director of the organization and today an outspoken critic, emphasizes that saving the environment is not a spectator sport. "If you leave conservation and environmental activities to the professionals," he says, "it's sort of like leaving medical stuff only to your doctor or legal stuff to your lawyer—you're going to be in the dark about what's going on. That's one of the problems about these big organizations. People send in their annual dues to appease their conscience and that's it. 'That's okay. I'm a member of Greenpeace. I'm a member of the Environmental Defense Fund. I'm doing my part.' Meanwhile they're working in a factory destroying the ozone."[11]

Radicals do not abide by the argument that people have too many other things happening in their lives to do more than send in their dues or write an occasional letter. At root it is a question of love, and of fear, for the environment, essential emotions driving people like John Muir and David Brower. The wild world of Muir's time, that Brower explored as a boy in the Sierra, even that the early Greenpeacers sailed to the Aleutians to preserve twenty years ago, no longer exists except in shrinking pockets. Eco-warriors are convinced that if we do not all act soon there will be little else in our lives but ecological catastrophe rooted in human action and inaction. Personal involvement is the key in this struggle. We can no longer pretend to be vicarious ecological activists, letting someone else save the world.

Loners

Greenpeacers were not the only "radical" environmentalists in the early 1970s. Individuals and small groups brought civil disobedience and even environmental sabotage to the environmental movement in their own ways. The best known of these early ecological saboteurs was the "Fox," who plagued polluting industries in Chicago during part of the 1970s and was never apprehended. The Fox once "diverted liquid toxic waste from a U.S. Steel plant to a location inside the chief executive's private office."[12] He equated his actions to stopping someone who was beating a dog or strangling another human to death. Around the same time, "Billboard Bandits" in Michigan took chainsaws to the obnoxious outdoor advertisements. And when a 400-kilovolt direct current power line was constructed across Minnesota, farmers calling themselves the "Bolt Weevils" literally took monkeywrenches to the steel towers, toppling at least fifteen girders in protest of the incursion after civil disobedience failed to halt construction. Their protests ended in 1978. Two years later a new, highly visible

radical environmental movement emerged with a "crack" out of the
Arizona desert.

CHAPTER 5

EARTH FIRST!:
CRACKING THE MOLD

It was the 1981 spring equinox, a bright, cool, cloudless day in the Arizona canyon country, a fine time for ritual and myth, for celebrating survival and rebirth. Those primal urges ran thick through the veins of four men and one woman as they marched out onto Glen Canyon dam, "the dam that David Brower built," intent on rending the offending structure and breathing new life into the waters of the once mighty Colorado River. They heaved something over the back side of the "invading alien," as Edward Abbey had labeled the monster in the midst of the desert. And then it happened. Without a sound a long, thin, black gash cut into the face of the massive dam. Three hundred feet long, the fracture rolled out as if the vernal waters of the Colorado really had risen in revolt. But no water flowed through. This was show, a concrete catharsis, vicarious vengeance in the form of a huge roll of plastic that, once unfurled, looked from afar like a tiny black gash.[1]

Truth be told, the Cracking of Glen Canyon Damn, as the action was called, was much more than mere show, though that certainly was an integral part of it. The crack was a wisecrack, a daring bit of humor in an environmental movement that had become glum and solemn, having witnessed the sacrifice of most of the very wildlands that Americans thought the movement was protecting. Moreover, it introduced Earth First! and Earth First! humor, a wit on level with that of Lenny Bruce—political, challenging, poignant, and hilarious to the thoughtful, irreverent or insulting to the rest. More importantly, though, the crack symbolized a break with environmentalism's past. Something called "Earth First!" had arrived. Stumbling from the intemperate minds of its founders, Earth First! was the antithesis of the mainstream. No more muddling through. No more compromise. Earth First! would be there to at least try to stop that which the mainstream had given up on or never paid attention to. After the crack the environmental movement would never again be the same.

To some the Cracking of Glen Canyon Damn even must have bordered on the religious in significance, calling forth as it did the cult heroes and heroine of Abbey's book *The Monkey Wrench Gang*. It invoked the spirit of a committed, comedic, rag-tag bunch that refused to sit by and watch the destruction of the desert southwest without fighting back. In the opening pages of the book a rumor spread that the Gang was going to bomb Glen Canyon Dam; now, in the real world, it had been cracked (and, according to one of the crackers, the FBI at the time of the action was in the dam's bowels awaiting a more destructive assault). Abbey the prophet was even on hand to see his vision made real. He stood near the Dam and decried "the domination of nature [that] leads to the domination of man." The big-beaked writer had no problem with such fun, nor with destructive expressions of disgust at American society's addiction to growth. "I think we're morally justified to resort to whatever means are necessary in order to defend our land from destruction, invasion," Abbey said. "I see this as an invasion." He clarified himself: "I would advocate sabotage, subversion, as a last resort when political means fail."[2]

Myths and Wilderness

Political means. Some say Earth First! was Abbey's brainchild, and, in truth, there can be no doubt that its fun-loving, monkey wrench-wielding spirit draws much inspiration from the writings of "Cactus Ed," as Abbey was called. But it was indeed the failure of the political system that gave rise to Earth First!. Dave Foreman, who had left his job as the Wilderness Society's Southwest regional representative nine months before, said at the rally following the Cracking, "The main reason for Earth First! is to create a broader spectrum within the environmental community....The people who started Earth First! felt there was a need for a radical wing to the environmental movement. Somebody has to say what needs to be said."[3]

The particular political defeat which spurred Foreman and four other activists to break away from the muddle-through crowd and form Earth First! was RARE II, the Forest Service's Roadless Area Review and Evaluation project that had seen the old-line environmental groups compromise so much internally that less than one-fourth of the eighty million acres under study was designated as wilderness. It was time for the creation of a new niche within the environmental community. The idea itself, however, was not new. Foreman recalls that Bill Mounsey, a Colorado wilderness guide and outfitter, established a group called "the Striders...for just that purpose, sort of an artificial spectrum."[4] Hard-core wilderness advocates and even high-level Washington, D.C., lobbyists tossed around the idea of something similar, a group that would ask for double the acreage of any wilderness proposal made by the mainstream organizations. In so doing, perhaps the mainstream would appear reasonable.

But nothing came of the talk until Foreman, ex-Yippie Mike Roselle, Wyoming Wilderness Society representative Bart Koehler, his sidekick Howie Wolke, and former Park Service seasonal ranger Ron Kezar took a trip to the Pinacate Desert in northern Mexico. "If Earth First! hadn't come along, somebody else would have come along with something like it," says Kezar. "It was an idea whose time had come."[5] When he and the others stumbled out of Foreman's Volkswagen van into the warm Mexican sun in April 1980, their primary intention was to have a good time, not to carve a new niche for themselves in the environmental movement. They wanted to drink cases of beer at a sitting, eat fulsome quantities of shrimp, and forget about what was happening in D.C. As they sat around the campfire, however, their love for wild places took over.

What to do? In ways these five were an ideal bunch to do something new in the environmental movement. They were white males, like most of the rest of the movement, so even if they decided to become "radicals" they would still be noticed. More important for the long run, however, was the connections, credentials, commitment, and individual talents they brought with them. Roselle was the green one of the bunch when it came to environmental issues; his strong suit was grassroots radical politics. "I think they realized that I had a lot of experience that would be necessary if we were to start a radical environmental group," Roselle says, "since I had a lot of experience in radical groups and knew the politics of confrontation, how to work with the media, and organizing techniques to help people develop a program that would be confrontational. The environmentalists at that time didn't know how to do any of that stuff."[6] Roselle was already a veteran of the anti-Vietnam War movement when he left home at sixteen. After time spent with Abbie Hoffman's anarchic, counter-culture Youth International Party, where he learned how to direct and motivate people and to manipulate the press, he took off across the country on a years-long journey that began in Washington, D.C., following Richard Nixon's second inaugural, and ended up in Wyoming. Although Roselle did not know it at the time, he was on a pilgrimage to the wilderness.

In Wyoming Roselle met a wilderness advocate named Howie Wolke. Wolke was the Wyoming representative for Friends of the Earth, earning a paltry $75 a month for thirty hours or more of environmental activism a week. He was the sort whose primary motivation for fighting against the war had been "because they were ruining the jungle....There was an underlying feeling that war is not healthy for the planet."[7] After graduating from the University of New Hampshire in 1975 with a degree in conservation, Wolke eventually met up with Bart Koehler, a respected Wyoming conservationist for the Wilderness Society. The two met in Jackson, got drunk, and hit it off. For two years Wolke meticulously inventoried roadless areas throughout Wyoming for Koehler, growing to know and love some of the most pristine wild country anywhere in the land. Through

Koehler's tutelage he began to comprehend the convoluted politics behind conservation.

There must be wilderness in Koehler's blood. His birthday was April 21, 1948: the very day Aldo Leopold, the uncompromising founder of environmental philosophy and co-founder of the Wilderness Society, died, and the one-hundred-tenth-year anniversary of John Muir's birthday. Koehler grew up in the still-wild Adirondaks, spending his summers hiking and canoeing. In high school he took the trees' side to argue with his father, who was bent on clearing the land around their home. Driven by this urge to "work for the underdog," after college Koehler went west and earned his Master's degree in Environmental and Regional Planning at the University of Wyoming—his 1972 thesis, arguing for protection of wildlands, is still cited in scholarly papers. The following year, he was hired by the Wilderness Society as one of its field staff, becoming one of the first members of a group that some consider the best single bunch of wilderness advocates ever assembled by one organization. He was also the first of the group to quit the Wilderness Society, which he did on his birthday in 1979; within months the entire brilliant bunch was fired or was run out by a dictatorial executive director.

Koehler became fast friends with Foreman, another of Wilderness' field staffers, soon after they met in the summer of 1973. Foreman was born in Alberquerque, New Mexico, in 1945, a direct descendant of American rebels, the ones who fought the Revolutionary War. An Air Force brat, Foreman grew up as something of a "Redneck for Wilderness," as one of the favorite Earth First! bumper stickers reads. He was an Eagle Scout who joined the Marines during the Vietnam War and was kicked out after two months for going AWOL. Freedom. The Marines guard it, but they don't tolerate it within their own ranks. And it is freedom, the call of the wild, that courses through Foreman's veins, an indelible nucleus in every corpuscle. (He often expounds on his theory of the "wilderness gene," which he says separates lovers of the wild from the rest; to demonstrate it he literally growls and howls when prowling the stage before an audience.) After graduating from the University of New Mexico, where he worked hard for the election of right-winger Barry Goldwater for president, the anthropology/history major bummed around, trying his hand at a variety of cowboy and outdoorsy pursuits. He finally found a home with the Wilderness Society. But between the backstabbing of the environmental movement by the government and the general nature of big-time environmentalism, Foreman realized he had to get out.

The fifth Earth First! founder, Ron Kezar, met Foreman when the Wilderness Society rep visited Kezar's local Sierra Club chapter in El Paso, Texas, to fill them in on the struggle for wilderness in the desert southwest. Kezar was born and raised in Stockton, California. Although the Sierra Nevada mountains were only a short drive away, and on a good day their white-capped purple form showed above the San Joaquin Valley farms, the wild held no allure for him. It was not until a friend from high school took him on a Sierra Club mountain climbing trip in his early twenties that Kezar's wilderness gene was tapped. Initially his activism was limited to writing letters to legislators. After his discharge from the Army he settled in El Paso and soon became the conservation chair for the local Sierra Club chapter. He worked for passage of various wilderness bills and helped with a successful effort to stop a tramway from being laid to the top of Guadalupe Peak, Texas' highest point. In 1977, he went in with Foreman to buy land near the Gila Wilderness in New Mexico, took a 125-mile backpack trip with Foreman and Wolke in 1979, and was a natural to join the Penacate party.

Earth First! mythology has it that Kezar and the others created Earth First! while in the desert or while reveling in a whorehouse. That mythology is vitally important, as essential to Earth First!ers as founders' resumes are to mainstream environmental organizations. Cynics might say that myths cover up lies or unpleasantness. But for Earth First!ers they are concentrated truths, mixtures of reality, fantasy, and wisdom. The Earth First! creation myths are flavorful, rich and evocative of the sort of image that the macho cowboys wanted to propagate.

Although portions of the "real" story behind the founding have been lost, enough remain to clarify that the true genesis of Earth First! did not come in a wild, romantic desert or a cheap, bawdy brothel. Quite simply, Earth First! got started in Foreman's VW bus on the road to Alberquerque. After leaving Mexico, Wolke says the group dropped off Koehler in Tucson "to have an affair with a lady lawyer" he had met earlier in the trip, then they deposited Kezar at his place in New Mexico. Emulating *The Monkeywrench Gang*'s wild-eyed leader, Wolke and Foreman were in the front seats polishing off a case of Budweiser, Roselle sprawled out in the rear, as they drove toward Alberquerque and Foreman's mother's famous chicken-fried steak. There was more ranting and raving about the emasculated mainstream and fantastic talk of a group that would fight to set aside multi-million acre ecological preserves in Ohio, South Texas, and other forsaken places across the nation. "We were closing roads in Yellowstone and re-uniting the Absaroka wildernesses" in Idaho, Wyoming, and Montana, says Wolke. "The next thing you know, we were setting up a massive system of ecological land preserves in every bioregion of the United States."[8]

Suddenly, Foreman called out "Earth first!" "The next thing you know," Wolke says, "Roselle drew a clenched-fist logo, passed it up to the front of the van, and there was Earth First."[9] The exclamation mark was added later that year. With a tremendous amount of enthusiasm and no money, the Founding Fathers began plotting. "We identified all the ecosystems in the U.S.," Roselle recalls. "Then we identified areas within each of those that would have to be protected in order to maintain biological diversity so that no matter what happened outside of those, there would still be genetic material to reconstruct the biota."[10] They put together a mailing list of seventy-five influential contacts, sent them the biodiversity listing, and wondered what to do next.

Round River Rendezvous and Respect

Beginning on the pagan new year of November 1, 1980, a mimeographed newsletter was sent to the Earth First! contacts. (The newsletter has gone through several name and format changes and is now a tabloid-sized newspaper. For simplicity's sake it will be referred to as the *Earth First! Journal*, or simply the *Journal*.) It passed from person to person, spreading the word about the Earth First! *movement*. The word "movement" was important, although it only began to take on a clear meaning in the year after the Glen Canyon Dam cracking. Earth First! was to be like a Plains Indian tribe, existing in autonomous groups which shared the same beliefs. There would be no bureaucracy, no lobbyists, no organizational spokespeople, just a force of devoted, unpaid, grassroots activists occupying a niche they had created for themselves in the environmental movement—in short, an anarchy. "Organization" was a term and a reality to be avoided in connection with anything larger than a local cell. Perhaps most telling, there was to be no membership. The closest things to membership cards are T-shirts with Roselle's clenched-fist logo and the motto, "No Compromise in Defense of Mother Earth."

Essential to Native American tribal life were its summer-long celebrations. All of the autonomous tribal groupings came together for weeks of dancing, hunting, and revelry. The Earth First! tribal fathers emulated that by inviting everyone interested to an Independence Day, 1980, party in Moab, Utah. Foreman wanted to call it a "rendezvous," like the get-togethers that the Indians and the mountain men of the Old West used to have; Koehler added "round river" from the allegorical river which flows into itself, symbolizing the constant flow of life that Aldo Leopold wrote of so eloquently. The first "Round River Rendezvous" was held that July Fourth, four days after Foreman left his Wilderness Society job. The 200 people at that first Rendezvous, many from mainstream groups, drank lots of beer, sang to Johnny Sagebrush (Koehler's stage name) songs, and complained about RARE II. The next day they held the first "Sagebrush Patriots' Rally" to make it clear to the newly-emerged Sagebrush Rebellion just who the real Americans were. The message of the Rally was that real cowboys love the range and all that goes with it. James Watt and his fellow impostors wanted to poison the coyote and dam the rivers. The Earth First!ers dared to speak for both and to tell the land grabbers to go to hell.

The umbilical cord to power is a difficult one to sever, and at the time Earth First!'s ties to the big environmental organizations seemed logical.

"We originally set Earth First! up to have a circle of thirteen people directing it," recalls Foreman. "But we also had a group called *La Manta Mojada*, which means 'the wet blanket,' which was our advisors within the mainstream groups." That did not last long. Foreman says that "when it became obvious that Earth First! was not going to be directed by the mainstream, that it was something independent calling the shots and creating the new agenda, I think that's when the criticism began to come in."[11]

Foreman and Koehler took off across the nation in the fall of 1981 in the inaugural Earth First! "Road Show" to publicize the start-up tribe. With Koehler/Johnny Sagebrush playing the guitar and Foreman, a riveting speaker, extolling the virtues of wilderness and the need for people to *fight* for it, not just talk about it, Earth First! slowly began to grow. Picketing, local organizing, a drunken sing-along instead of an orderly annual conference, free-lance wilderness plans—all this was new to the land-based environmental movement. Everyone knew of Greenpeace's exploits on behalf of whales and seals, but no one had translated those tactics to activities in forests and deserts. In an article in the October 1981 issue of *Progressive* magazine, Foreman proposed bursting the conceptual dams that held back the vanguard of the environmental movement. He argued for limiting the size of major cities, reclaiming wilderness areas lost to development, and tearing down dams. Earth First! stood for "a pure, no-compromise pro-Earth" position, and while it would remain "ostensibly law-abiding," it nevertheless existed to "inspire others to carry out activities straight from the pages of *The Monkey Wrench Gang*"—ecological sabotage or "monkeywrenching."[12] The overwhelming reception to the *Progressive* article was the first real indication that Earth First! might be a force to be reckoned with. Three hundred letters poured into the Earth First! post office box. In no time subscriptions to the *Journal* topped 1,000. By the time of the third Round River Rendezvous in 1982, Earth First! was rolling like the crack down Glen Canyon Dam.

Staking Out Little Granite Creek

The location for that year's Rendezvous was near and dear to Koehler, Wolke, and Roselle. No story of Earth First!'s early years better exhibits its love of wilderness, its critiques of the mainstream, its willingness to resort to ecological sabotage, and its faith that the grassroots can prevail, than the struggle over Little Granite Creek in Wyoming's Gros Ventre Wilderness. South of Yellowstone and east of Grand Tetons National Park, the Gros Ventre (French for "big belly") is a rugged offshoot of the Rocky Mountains that ranges from 6,000 to nearly 12,000 feet above sea level, encompassing ecosystems from sagebrush to alpine. It is home to elk, moose, bighorn sheep, mountain lions, and, deep underground, oil.

Getty Oil bought the right to explore the Gros Ventre after the Nixon administration opened huge sections of Wyoming's Bridger-Teton National Forest to oil exploration in the 1960s. In all about two million acres were leased without any public input. In the early 1980s Getty announced its intention to drill two exploratory wells in the Gros Ventre, one at Cache Creek, a popular and convenient place of escape just outside of Jackson, and a second at Little Granite Creek, far from anywhere. The Sierra Club, Wilderness Society, and local environmental groups were looking for a compromise, looking to give up something almost as soon as Getty's plans were announced. Little Granite Creek was the obvious choice, but Roselle and Wolke would have none of it. At one meeting of local environmentalists, Roselle recalls, "Howie stood up and gave a speech about how he didn't give a damn about Cache Creek, that Little Granite Creek was more important in terms of wildlife habitat, it was more important in terms of wilderness, in terms of providing a wildlife corridor from Yellowstone. After that, things got quiet for a minute. Then this old doctor, about eighty with a fake hip who had delivered half the people in the room, stands up. He tells them, 'Howie's right!' And slowly the whole room began to turn around. We left there with a feeling of solidarity. If there hadn't been one radical in that room, it wouldn't have happened."[13]

The Earth First!ers persuaded their mainstream counterparts to demand that the two sites be combined in a single environmental impact statement. No land-based drilling proposal in U.S. history had required such a complete assessment of ecological risk. Nevertheless, the proposal was approved—with the obligatory environmental "mitigation." Mitigation is deceptively simple: the idea is that a development project's harmful impacts can be compensated for by altering the project in some way or by making up for the damage elsewhere. Critics say that mitigation is an excuse for incursions into wild places that should be left alone to begin with. They assert that it is impossible to allow destruction in one area and make up for it by "improving" another. We are not wise enough to successfully mimic nature. At Little Granite Creek, the mitigation efforts called for special road construction procedures, minimizing the impact of drilling on nearby wildlife, siphoning-off of poisonous gases, and special handling of the sub-surface fluids resulting from the drilling. Getty even offered to restore the road to the drilling site to something resembling its natural condition. The forest supervisor at Bridger-Teton declined, apparently seeing the free road as easy access into a virgin forest.

After the spring thaws of 1982, Getty sent a survey team to stake out a road into the Little Granite Creek drainage area. Roselle, Foreman and two others discovered the work in progress, marked as it was by little wooden stakes flagged with brightly-colored plastic ribbon. Although a lawsuit had been filed to prevent work on the road, the mainstream groups had failed to win an injunction. It appeared that Earth First!'s annual "wilderness" bash would be ruined by a roadway cut straight through to the Rendezvous site. So as the two-man survey crew completed plotting the road's path, the four Earth First!ers began a leisurely hike up the mountain behind them. Emulating the Monkey Wrench Gang, they "un-surveyed" the entire road as they went. With survey tape headbands flapping in the breeze and beers in hand, the monkeywrenchers drove away from the soon-to-be roadhead in Foreman's infamous VW bus. When Roselle and the others were asked by the police to come in for questioning a few days later, they asked a local lawyer what they should do. "'I don't think you guys have anything to worry about,'" Roselle recalls the attorney saying confidently. "'Don't answer any questions, give them my card, and just remember this: there ain't a jury in Teton County that will convict you.'"[14] The road again was surveyed, but it didn't stay that way for long. When the Rendezvous crowd of 300 people arrived on the scene, they marched the length of the planned road, five miles or more, behind a "Getty Go Home" sign, shamelessly removing all the stakes. Roselle remembers seeing Edward Abbey "walking down the trail with a survey stake sticking out of his belt and doing an interview with the local paper. It was open warfare on the road at that point."[15]

Earth First! opened a second front in the battle for the Gros Ventre when Koehler drafted an appeal of the road construction decision on a cocktail napkin at the Cowboy Bar in Jackson. After typing it up more formally at home, he sent it to the U.S. Department of Agriculture, which oversees the Forest Service. He figured it was a shot in the dark, but every avenue had to be explored. Wyoming Governor Ed Herschler, astute politician that he was, also got in on the act. Having earlier denounced the un-surveying, Gov. Herschler bowed to the grassroots rebellion and withheld a state drilling permit for the well site, a first in Wyoming history. He also filed an appeal similar to Koehler's, and within a week and a half construction on the road was halted by the order of the Department of Agriculture, making drilling impossible. Notably, it was Koehler's appeal that the Forest Service upheld.

The Gros Ventre, including Little Granite Creek, is now designated wilderness. In time the lawsuit questioning the validity of the environmental impact assessment also succeeded, validating the Earth First! founders' theory of the need for a radical niche within the environmental movement. If the sabotage had not taken place, construction on the road would likely have been well under way before a court had heard the suit. "It wasn't just the direct action, the demonstrations, or us being confrontational," Roselle says. "It was a whole integrated strategy that came out of the fact that we weren't going to take 'no' for an answer. A lot of people were saying 'We've got *other* things to worry about here, not just the Granite Creek well or the Cache Creek well.' They were always willing to accept defeat here because the other battle coming up was more important." But not the Earth First!ers.

"To us it was, 'Hey, we're sick of it. Not anything more. We're going to fight all the way on everything from now on.'"[16]

Wilderness for Its Own Sake

In June 1983 Earth First! revealed its "Wilderness Preserve System," the fulfillment of the beer-induced vision at Earth First!'s genesis and a vital step in declaring just how radical the Earth First!ers would be. Under the plan, fifty reserves comprising 716 million acres would be "declared off-limits to industrial human civilization as preserves for the free-flow of natural processes," wrote Foreman, Wolke, and Koehler. "A large percentage of the United States should be returned to its natural condition. We should have large wilderness preserves for all our biological communities."[17] Underlying such radical concepts was an ecocentric world view, the fundamental intuition that wilderness should be preserved for its own sake, entirely apart from any human value placed upon it. Biological diversity, a characteristic of places not yet ruined by human intrusion, was the key, not a place's beauty or even its recreational value. "Diamondback," an ecologist who has been active in Earth First! since the mid-1980s, says that "landscape-level biological diversity," meaning diversity not only of species but of interrelated communities of plants, animals, climates, and the like, "is such a large-scale phenomenon that it can only be represented in something like wilderness."[18]

Like the mainstream organizations, Earth First! develops detailed wilderness proposals; unlike the pragmatists, however, Earth First!'s proposals are far larger. They have created the outlines for a 5,000-acre redwood preserve in Northern California; for the California desert (16.8 million acres); for state wilderness areas in Montana and Arizona that total 9.3 million acres and 19 million acres, respectively; and other ecosystem protection plans for Idaho and the tri-state area around Yellowstone National Park, and in Colorado, Washington, Wyoming, and other areas.

Typically, Earth First!'s wilderness proposals include every scrap of roadless area greater than a few thousand acres. For this reason, they are seen as unrealistic by mainstream environmental organizations. But as the Wilderness Society's Jim Norton has acknowledged, with Earth First! filling the ambitious, radical niche, mainstream groups can ask for much more than they would otherwise ever dare. New England Earth First!ers Jamie Sayen and Jeff Elliott suggested that the federal government purchase 10 million acres of second-growth forest from timber companies eager to leave the region, making the Wilderness Society's later 2.7 million-acre proposal look "reasonable." Similarly, after Earth First!'s massive California desert wilderness plan was drafted, the Sierra Club reportedly enlarged the areas to be included in a wilderness bill that Sen. Alan Cranston was asked to carry. Cranston raised eyebrows when he accepted the Club's 8 million acre proposal, which includes eighty-one wilderness areas and the new Mojave National Park.

In recent years, Earth First!ers have gone even farther, arguing for the re-creation of wilderness through rehabilitating damaged ecosystems. More than one thousand species in North America alone are in immediate danger due to human-caused impacts, and in the next twenty years three thousand more species are likely to be placed in danger of extinction.[19] Preserving ecosystems is no longer enough; to curb this tide, Earth First!ers argue for the necessity of a "restoration ethic." No simple tree-planting project, restoration includes both human and non-human aspects. People are involved to the extent that they are necessary to remove the barriers they have created to natural recovery (Earth First!ers suggest that out-of-work timber industry employees be hired to do the work). Such remedial action may include restoring ecosystems like salmon streams and forests, then introducing extirpated native plant and animal species. Once this bed is made, restoration directs that natural processes take over from there.

Strategy and Tactics

North Kalmiopsis: Eye of a Storm

Earth First! rapidly gained a reputation in the West for hard-core activism of the sort that the environmental movement had never before witnessed, much less attempted. Not even Greenpeace could match Earth First!'s "violent" tactics, such as pulling up survey stakes. Earth First! did not merely stand firm at Little Granite Creek; it actually pushed back the agents of destruction. When Earth First! pushed even harder the next year, it found what it was like to be pushed back, literally. The place was Bald Mountain in the North Kalmiopsis region of southwestern Oregon. The North Kalmiopsis lies adjacent to an already designated wilderness called the Kalmiopsis. Together these areas comprise "the most diverse coniferous forest on Earth," an area that some believe is "the center of conifer evolution."[20] It is here that the three hundred fifty-foot tall redwoods from California meet the Alaska cedar, Pacific silver fir, and twenty-five other species of cone-bearing trees from the north. In all of North America, only the Southern Appalachians in and around Great Smoky Mountains National Park are home to a more diverse flora than the Kalmiopsis. Ninety-two well-defined plant *communities* exist here, and the number of rare plants exceeds one hundred. The rivers and streams run pure and cold, just as the native salmon and trout like them. The northern spotted owl, the focus of so much controversy between environmentalists and loggers, may be found here, along with black bear, cougar, and a long list of other animal inhabitants, including, some say, Bigfoot. But the mythical Sasquatch's home is rapidly shrinking. As recently as 1934 an 830,000-acre Kalmiopsis wilderness existed intact, but by the early 1980s only 404,000 roadless acres remained. Of that, only a mere 167,000 acres were protected by formal wilderness designation.

Earth First!'s fight for protection of the North Kalmiopsis began on April 25, 1983, when four people, including Mike Roselle, blockaded a bulldozer that was making the first cuts on the Bald Mountain Road. The road was to split the de facto wilderness in half, opening the entire North Kalmiopsis to logging and ripping apart the region's delicate, unmatched web of life. The blockade was a delaying action so that a court injunction could be requested to halt the road because of a perceived violation of the RARE II regulations. For three months the struggle raged. By the time the injunction was granted, Dave Foreman had suffered permanent damage to his knee after being dragged beneath a truck that had attempted to run him over at a blockade. No charges were ever filed against the truck driver; forty-four Earth First!ers were arrested for peacefully blockading the Bald Mountain Road that year. The injunction against further road construction was effectively nullified by provisions in the Oregon Wilderness Act of 1984. In March 1986 the first timber sale in the North Kalmiopsis was held since the blockades began, signaling the Forest Service's determination to gut the forest.

By 1987 logging was underway at multiple sites. A fire that year gave the Forest Service even more of an excuse to rid the area of its valuable timber; they hoped to "salvage" what they could of the burned forest before rot and insects ruined the wood for human uses. That year the protests heated up once more and eventually led to a precedent-setting court case that has become the eye of a storm within Earth First!. More than twenty arrests took place in the Northern Kalmiopsis in 1987 before a twenty-eight-year-old woman named Karen Wood and five other Earth First!ers became the "Sapphire Six." Wood is a short, bright-eyed computer scientist who grew up in Virginia. She moved to Oregon on her honeymoon in the mid-1980s. Her husband was in graduate school, and Wood remembers a poster he had tacked on a wall. Beneath a bold, black fist it read, "Earth First!, the radical environmental group. Watch for Earth First! leaders coming to your town." Today Wood chuckles at the "leaders" phrase, representing as it does the early mentality of those in the ostensibly "anarchistic movement."[21] In time Wood volunteered with the Cathedral Forest Action Group, a "Gandhian affinity group" that exclusively used civil defense—"CD"—to protect the ancient conifers.

Wood had already made up her mind to become directly involved in the struggle for the Kalmiopsis when she was asked in July 1987 to participate in an all-women's action there. The site that Wood's group chose was a yarding area for the "Sapphire" timber sale (each sale is given a unique name). Wood remembers arguing with Mike Roselle, who was present to

lend his organizing expertise, over fine points in the "standard non-violence agreement":
—We will be open, honest, and respectful to all beings we encounter;
—We will not run;
—We will carry no weapons;
—We will carry no drugs or alcohol;
—We will use no violence, physical or verbal.

Eventually the differences were settled to everyone's satisfaction, and two groups were formed. Wood and four other women decided to occupy the yarder—a truck with a huge pole mounted on it. Cables and pulleys at the top of the pole drag cut logs up and down steep slopes so that they can be loaded onto trucks. The second group, comprised of five men, were to climb trees and sit on platforms for several days—a tree-sit. When activist James Jackson showed up and asked to be a part of the yarder group, the women reluctantly accepted him "because we didn't want to be ex-clusionist," Wood says. The yarder occupation, set for July 23, was to be straightforward. "What we were planning to do was to get up in the middle of the night and hike down in the dark and lock ourselves onto the yarder," Wood explains. "When the crew came in we would say, 'Hi, guys. Drink your coffee and take a break.' What happened was that we got up at three [a.m.] and were packing up our stuff...and we heard trucks."[22]

It turned out that the workers had left a load of logs on the loading deck the previous day, and they had to get them on trucks before they could yard more trees. The group hurriedly hiked down to the tree where the anchor cable for the yarder pole was attached, and Valerie Wade began crawling out on the cable toward the top of the pole. Still undetected by the loggers, the other five strode toward the loading deck. Suddenly, they heard the yarder engine start. They rushed toward the deck, screaming for the yarder operator to stop the engine for fear that Wade would be injured.

Once the engine was turned off, the occupation force quickly locked themselves onto various pieces of equipment, using chains and Kryptonite locks. The workers were furious. They pulled at Jackson, who was locked to the cab. Then two lumberjacks approached Wood, first taunting her and then threatening to rape her. They only stopped when she screamed that there were people in the woods with cameras. The tree sitters heard her and started yelling. Not long after, sheriff's deputies arrived. They used bolt cutters and an electric drill to unlock the protestors, who were arrested and taken to jail on the spot. Eventually, the Sapphire Six were tried and convicted. Each was sentenced to fifteen days in the Curry County jail and fined $250, except Wade, whose daring climb along the cable to the top of the yarder pole landed her an extra five days in jail and a $350 fine. In addition, they were made to pay a total of $1,761 in restitution to Huffman & Wright Logging Company, the owners of the yarder.

It is the results of a lawsuit filed by Huffman & Wright against the Six, however, which has given ammunition to Earth First!ers who question the value—or are anxious about the potential monetary costs—of civil disobedience. Huffman & Wright's suit was a "SLAPP," or Strategic Lawsuit Against Public Participation. In most instances where this decade-old phenomenon has occurred, citizen groups have been SLAPPed to prevent them from effectively challenging the plans of a developer or a corporation. Community organizations end up spending most or all of their funds and energies defending themselves in court rather than fighting for their neighborhoods. In the Sapphire Six case, Earth First!ers ascribe Huffman & Wright's motives in suing six essentially destitute activists as a warning against other such acts. Prior to the Sapphire Six suit no one had ever successfully sued protestors engaged in civil disobedience for punitive damages. Judges had usually prohibited consideration of such claims because of a clear conflict with the First Amendment's free speech guarantees. In November 1988, however, the Sapphire Six were victims of judicial history. Following a week-long trial, a timber country jury awarded Huffman & Wright $25,000 in punitive damages and $5,000 in actual damages.

Some in Earth First!, reacting to the specter of more punitive suits should the verdict be upheld on appeal, condemn the use of "excessive" civil disobedience. "I see civil disobedience as more conventional warfare, taking on the system head-on, getting enmeshed with the whole legal process," says Dave Foreman. "That's why, philosophically, I'm much more of a monkeywrencher." Eventually, he says, committed activists are forced to take their tactics to the limit to protect wilderness from the saw and the bulldozer. As with the Sapphire Six, there comes a time when "the system doesn't want to let you do civil disobedience," Foreman says. "Then what's the alternative? They force you into more and more radical actions."[23]

Wood remains unbent, however. "Civil disobedience doesn't work without failures," she says resolutely. "CD is a long-term strategy. If you want to keep a particular [timber] sale off, you should probably spike it." But it is civil disobedience that makes the indelible mark. "CD is lasting, will change the hearts and minds of people. The Sapphire Six case has scared some people off, but in a way that's good because those people weren't ready to do CD. To do CD you have to be ready to make sacrifices. Some people see it as a game, but it's not. You have to have people ready to make a commitment."[24]

Roselle, for one, admitted to a degree of ambivalence over the wisdom of monkeywrenching nearly a year before he signed onto a statement renouncing the use of tree-spiking in northern California in April 1990. "I think that non-violence is more powerful," Roselle said the previous summer. "I think when you can stand up and say why you did something, you make a tremendous sacrifice. You can speak directly to the public about why you did it. I think that is more powerful than sneaking around in the middle of the night." On the other hand, he says, "If we had been totally non-violent, we probably would have had more public support, but would we have been more successful in saving old growth [timber]? I think not."[25]

Public protests

As a result of the lawsuit against the Sapphire Six, the debate within Earth First! has intensified between advocates of civil disobedience and proponents of wide-scale environmental sabotage. Until recently, most press reports about Earth First!'s activities have largely ignored non-destructive protests like those of the Sapphire Six. An occasional tree-sit or banner hanging would make the news. But the media's primary interest was on activists' covert assaults on development using tactics such as spiking trees and destroying machinery. Regardless of the legality of the act, nearly everything that Earth First!ers do is considered "direct action," which may be defined as any action taken to improve the basic conditions of one's existence. The phrase is one of many things Earth First! has borrowed from the International Workers of the World, the radical labor union nicknamed the "Wobblies." (Along with Wobblie tactics like tree-spiking, Earth First! has adopted the use of "silent agitators," small stickers with messages such as "Boycott Coors" or "Stop Public Lands Grazing" that are placed in highly visible areas. The Wobblies' *Little Red Songbook* of protest ditties has been adapted into Earth First!'s *Little Green Songbook*, in which a staple Wobblie tune such as "Union Maid" is reworded to become "Earth First! Maid.")

Public protests like those of the Sapphire Six are the non-destructive subset of direct actions. As evidenced by the civil rights and anti-Vietnam War protests, public protests and civil disobedience are especially effective means of presenting alternatives to those who have never considered them or who refuse to do so. In the name of Earth First!—and anyone can act in the name of Earth First!—people sit in front of bulldozers; chain and lock themselves to doorways and gates of construction sites; and perch on door-sized platforms 150 feet up in trees for days and even weeks at a time. They have taken over legislators' offices; marched on Wall Street; picketed at hundreds of locations; and hung banners from the World Bank, the Lincoln Memorial, and over the Governor of Colorado as he marched the route of the Denver Stockmen's Show parade. A complete list of such actions would number in the range of one thousand. In each case, the target and the message are carefully chosen, given the importance of media exposure. At the World Bank the issue was the worldwide destruction of rainforests that results from the Bank's loans. The two annual Denver protests were aimed at "welfare ranching." Tree sitters attempt to halt or slow down timber cutting in ancient forests until remedies can be sought through the courts. (A nationwide week of tree-sitting in 1989 is discussed in Chapter Ten.)

The actual action may have several components. At a 1988 protest against the Forest Service on John Muir's birthday, twenty-five sign-carrying activists in San Francisco paraded in front of the Forest Service's regional headquarters during the lunch hour, some dressed in mountain lion and bear costumes. When the press arrived, several Earth First!ers presented a humorous play featuring a devious Forest Service ranger. Actor Lee Stetson, who performs a one-man Muir show in Yosemite Valley, and Bay Area Earth First! organizer Karen Pickett spoke to the media about the Forest Service's faults. Then Pickett and another protestor went inside the building and confronted the regional forester's top-ranking deputy to demand changes in Forest Service policy. After they gave their demands, they refused to leave the office. A long standoff ensued, with the Earth First!ers unmovable except by force. Finally, federal marshals were called in and the two were handcuffed; then, oddly, they were taken to a side door and released. Neither Pickett nor her fellow protestor were charged by the Forest Service.

Monkeywrenching

Mahatma Gandhi and Martin Luther King embraced "non-violence," including respect for property, as a way of life, the highest and purest form of living on the Earth and an emulation of heavenly existence. In contrast, Earth First!'s founders perceived non-violence as a tactic. In 1982 Dave Foreman wrote, "I am entirely pragmatic about violence/non-violence. We should use whichever we feel comfortable with and whichever is most appropriate to a particular situation....I believe there is room in Earth First! for ex-Marines like myself and for followers of Gandhi. There are many paths one can take to defend our Earth Mother."[26] If anything, Foreman's estimate of the value of CD has dwindled over the years. After being run over in the North Kalmiopsis, he knows better than most the risks inherent in civil disobedience. Although he continues to participate in CD whenever he feels it is appropriate, Foreman questions a central feature of civil disobedience, its publicity-generating capacity. "I've always been concerned about an over-reliance on civil disobedience," he explains. "It's news the first time you do a banner hanging or blockade a bulldozer or do a tree-sit. When does it cease being news? I think when you begin to hit that point you have to come up with more and more creative things. It's sort of a game."[27]

If this is so, then CD can be considered checkers and monkeywrenching the equivalent of chess. Although played on the same board, the pieces are entirely different and so are the rules. Civil disobedience entails directly confronting one's adversary; monkeywrenching—sabotage in the name of the environment, also called "ecotage"—demands stealth. One's body is the primary force used at a sit-in or when blocking a bulldozer; ecological saboteurs use drills, bolt cutters, and a host of other means to protect the environment. And until recently those practicing CD usually expected brief jail terms and light fines; "ecoteurs" attempt to avoid capture. When Howie Wolke was convicted in 1986 for removing survey stakes not far from Little Granite Creek, he was sentenced to six months in jail, fined $750, and had to pay more than $2,200 in restitution. (On a different level is "paper monkeywrenching." It includes filing appeals and similar legal maneuvering, and has proven effective as a method of forestalling or preventing environmental destruction. However, it involves none of the visible, energetic action of public protests or the illegal daring of ecotage.)

Monkeywrenching is usually a tactic of last resort, as was true at Little Granite Creek, although it may be an anticipatory, preventative means against harm to the environment. Earth First!ers see ruining a bulldozer or spiking a 2,000-year-old redwood tree to deter its "harvesting" as tantamount to taking the bullets out of the gun of Gandhi's assassin *before* the shots were fired. The mainstream's "pragmatic," less pro-active approaches permit the crime to be committed at an incalculable loss, say the radicals. According to Earth First! organizer Karen Pickett, monkeywrenching "is often something that just gets in the way, makes things a bit more difficult." She admits that individual acts may not have much of an effect, "but if it's done constantly, everywhere, it slows the wheels."[28] Greg King, a former journalist now working full-time to save the ancient forests on California's north coast, agrees with Picket but emphasizes the technophobic, Luddite side of monkeywrenching. "For the most part, monkeywrenching is sending a message to everyone that these machines and the use of them is bad enough that people are willing to destroy them, even though they are pretty much the deities these days," King says. "Plenty of people think it is cracked up, but the thought is out there."[29]

Phoenix Earth First! organizer Leslie Sellgrin acknowledges the uncertainty toward monkeywrenching even within the movement. "A lot of people who are involved in Earth First! would never monkeywrench for moral reasons, some would never take the risk, and some are too much in the public eye to take the risk—they're being watched or whatever," she says. "I have to say that some monkeywrenching is great and some I'm not real fond of."[30] Earth First!ers believe that any negative publicity that results from destructive methods of environmental preservation will be balanced by the increased awareness and tension over the issues and that in time their perspective will win out. In each case "it's the confrontation that creates the illumination," says Mike Roselle. "It brings these issues to light....Obviously, signing a petition for a wilderness area isn't going to get it, it doesn't create the illumination. But shutting down a logging area does do it."[31] And it is saving wilderness by shutting down destruction that many monkeywrenchers say is their primary concern. Concerns about publicity come in a distant second.

Any questions about Earth First!'s acceptance of monkeywrenching were dispensed with early in the tribe's existence. In 1982, *Journal* editor Pete Dustrud protested the increasingly "violent nature" of the "Dear Ned Ludd" column. In particular he found a piece detailing the construction and use of metal road spikes to disable trucks, which he called a "metal punji stake," exceptionally offensive.[32] He also claimed that the Circle of Thirteen advisors was guilty of censorship by prohibiting him to publish letters that took Foreman's advocacy of monkeywrenching in the *Progressive* article to task. Dear Ned Ludd has long-outlasted Dustrud's involvement with the *Journal*, a testament at least to Earth First!ers' interest in monkeywrenching and probably to its pervasiveness as well. In the first installment, the editors explained that they had "decided to run a regular column of 'eco-tactics,' which are on the unconventional side."[33] The choice of "unconventional" is more than an apt description; the military uses the same label to refer to guerrilla warfare.

Suggestions in the early days of the column included the best mixes for sticking posters to walls, various means to ruin dirt roads, and instructions on how to destroy helicopters (on the ground). Billboards, an object of the Monkey Wrench Gang's ire, received considerable attention. The volume of suggestions grew over the years to the point that Foreman was able to realize an early dream of Earth First!. In March 1985 he published a how-to book called *Ecodefense: A Field Guide to Monkeywrenching*. Now in its second edition, it is reminiscent of that fabled guide to chaos, *The Anarchist's Cookbook*. In *Ecodefense*'s 311 pages can be found detailed instructions for destroying just about anything used to ruin wild places, including heavy equipment, power and seismographic lines, and snowmobiles. Jamming locks, making smoke bombs, engaging in sabotage in an urban environment, and protecting oneself against discovery are among the other topics exhaustively discussed. Foreman says *Ecodefense* was intended to provide "an ethical context in which to operate, to give it a strategy."[34] The hows and whys are immensely important if one is attempting to win over the public through acts that are widely seen as needlessly destructive, violent, and in some instances potentially deadly. "If you are monkeywrenching in the context of the Boston Tea Party instead of the October 1917 [Russian] revolution, it comes off differently," he says. "I think monkeywrenching is a very honorable American tradition. If you couch it that way, then it comes off more acceptably."[35]

Tree spiking

Ecodefense has found a substantial cult audience, having sold several thousand copies. While its impact is impossible to measure, media reports of monkeywrenching do emerge periodically. For example, Earth First!ers took responsibility for sabotaging a cross-desert motorcycle race in California by barricading a tunnel; the race has since been banned because of the damage the dirt bikes cause to the ecosystem, including crushing desert tortoises and rupturing the eardrums of kangaroo rats. Activists also repeatedly ruined tests of a genetically-altered microbe designed to keep frost from forming on sensitive plants. Innumerable bulldozers and other pieces of heavy equipment at wilderness construction sites have been "de-commissioned" by burning, pouring grinding compound in the crankcase, or any of a dozen other methods. But the prevalence and prominence of monkeywrenching has Foreman worried that it could back-fire. He suspects that a fire at a livestock barn in California in 1988 that was attributed to Earth First! (and to Animal Liberators) may have been set by the owner for insurance purposes, and that an Idaho tree-spiking in 1989 done in Earth First!'s name could have been a deliberate effort by a timber company to defame the tribe.[36]

Tree-spiking, driving nails into trees to prevent them from being cut, has long been a hot topic among Earth First!ers. To many in the public, Earth First! and tree-spiking are synonymous. The initial monkeywrenching column in the *Journal* carried a letter promoting spiking as a way to save trees.[37] In recent years tree-spiking is said to have escalated considerably. Earth First!ers claim spiking is ubiquitous in the Pacific Northwest, especially in Washington state, where timber sales on public lands have been quietly canceled when heavily-spiked areas have been encountered. Other spikings have been more prominent. In January 1990 the "Raging Bull Avengers" served notice that they had spiked a timber sale bordering on the Bull Run watershed, Portland, Oregon's, primary source of drinking water. A communique from the Avengers alleged a U.S. Forest Service/City of Portland conspiracy "to allow logging in and around the watershed which would greatly degrade water quality through erosion and other impacts, as well as destroy some of the last old growth and mature second-growth forest Oregon has left."[38] At Meares Island, which is off the British Columbia coast in southwest Canada, more than 11,000 helix spikes were driven into spruce and hemlock trees in the winter of 1984-1985. Plans call for cutting ninety percent of the trees on the 21,000-acre island within twenty years.[39] And spiked trees at Bowen Gulch near Boulder, Colorado, "reportedly cost the [Forest Service] $16,000," wrote Earth First!er Michael Robinson. He went on to give a primary reason for spiking: "Since each Forest Service district is allocated a limited amount of dollars for wilderness destruction [that is, road construction and the like] per fiscal year, that $16,000 may well have prevented several miles of road from being built."[40]

In an official report, "Ecotage from Our Perspective," the Willamette National Forest supervisor condemned two well-publicized 1984 spikings. "Both spikings forced the Forest Service to commit much extra time and expense to locating and removing the spikes prior to harvest," said the report.[41] Earth First! co-founder Mike Roselle admits to being partially responsible for one of those incidents, the Pyramid Creek spiking. It was the first publicized tree-spiking by Earth First!ers, and it followed three years of civil disobedience at Cathedral Forest in the Willamette. Increasingly, the protestors had felt ignored by the press and abused by the authorities. Roselle and an accomplice spiked the grove as "a political act, a public event, a media stunt," he explains. Although the Cathedral Forest protestors had paid restitution for the delays they had caused by blockading logging roads, the logging companies and local officials persisted in cracking down on them. The spiking was intended as "a message....'All right, you guys: you're going to arrest us, sue us, drag us around, beat us up, scare people away from our site. Well, we can get tough, too.'"[42]

Roselle says only a few nails were hammered into each tree at Pyramid Creek. "It really hardly slowed them down, except that they were so freaked out about it because they didn't have a policy and they didn't know what was going on. They had twenty-two rangers out there for three days pulling these fucking nails out, and they still missed a bunch of them."[43] The spiking reaped some impressive publicity for Earth First!, although none of it favorable. The *Wall Street Journal* and the *New York Times* both viciously attacked Earth First! for the spiking, the first substantial press the group had received in major publications since a few introductory blurbs. The articles quoted Cathedral Forest Action Group members as distancing themselves from the action. But when ABC did a story on the incident, interest in Earth First!, as evidenced by subscriptions to the *Earth First! Journal*, picked up substantially.

Most tree "spikes," including the ones that Roselle used at Pyramid Creek, are actually common nails driven into trees with a heavy hammer. The nails do not harm trees but can easily ruin lumber mill saw blades. The "20 penny" length used at Pyramid Creek is at the short end, about four and a half inches long; spikes range up to six-inch 60 penny nails and beyond to eleven-inch bridge spikes. *Ecodefense* calls helix, or spiral, nails like those used at Meares Island "the ultimate in metallic spikes....The spiral makes the nail extremely difficult to remove, and removal is virtually impossible when the head of the nail is clipped off."[44] Steel welding rod and specially-cut hard rocks can be used for spiking by first drilling a hole into the tree. Rocks and ceramic spikes, made by rolling non-ferrous clay into inch-thick pieces and baking them at high temperatures in a kiln, are both touted as a means of avoiding discovery by forestry officials or loggers using metal detectors.

No Earth First!er has been arrested for tree spiking, nor has anyone been injured by trees spiked by radical environmentalists. Spikers following Foreman's ethics notify the relevant parties prior to the cutting of spiked trees. This is done to prevent injury to lumberjacks and millworkers and to keep trees standing. In the only confirmed injury from a tree spike, a California timber mill worker, George Alexander, was severely injured when his saw struck an eleven-inch spike at its full length.[45] The mill was never warned that the tree was spiked. *Audubon* magazine columnist Peter Steinhart reported that a sheriff's investigation "pointed not to environmental groups" as the attacker "but to a Los Angeles man who visited property next to the [site where the trees were cut] and had a reputation for right-wing military fantasies and weird behavior."[46] Charges against that suspect were never filed.

Steinhart also wrote, "It is probably only chance that the injuries to George Alexander were caused by a crank rather than an environmentalist."[47] There appears to be little basis for such a statement. Earth First!ers are struggling to save old-growth forests, areas that have never been cut, yet the tree containing the nail that caused Alexander's injuries came from a "second-growth" forest, one that had already been cut once. Spiking any but the oldest second-growth trees would be a waste of time, Earth First!ers say, given the large amount of pristine forest that is threatened. Moreover, Earth First!ers reason that standing trees are far more valuable to forest ecosystems than already cut trees like the one containing the spike that injured Alexander. And by notifying governmental agencies and timber mills of a spiking, Earth First!ers hope to push the cost of a sale over the brink of economic viability. The revenues that lumber companies lose by not cutting spiked trees for fear of damage to machinery may be substantial; however, at $3,000 per sawblade, prudence directs that in most cases spiked trees be left alone.

Roselle calls George Alexander's injury "tragic," and he agrees with critics who say that Earth First! should take some of the responsibility for his injuries simply because the group publicizes spiking. "But Ken Kesey wrote about spiking in *Sometimes a Great Notion*, so he should take some responsibility, too," Roselle says. "They passed a law in California in 1875 making spiking illegal. This was over 100 years ago, so we didn't start this whole thing. We'll take some of the responsibility, but let's be realistic. In reality, the George Alexander incident did not hurt the cause. In fact, it gave us a whole new profile. It allowed us to say, 'Sure we spike, but we don't do it that way. We're saving the old growth, and it's not going to help unless you do it the right way.'"[48]

Tree-spiking of any sort draws cries of "terrorism." Terrorism as terrorists do it directly threatens innocent lives. Using this definition, eco-warriors say that it is improper to label them as terrorists, given the precautions they take to avoid injuring others. Rather, the real danger comes from the timber company executives who throw trees and people into the mills as necessary ingredients for a money-making mix. "These guys are terrorists," Roselle says. "There are more people killed from logging accidents and log truck accidents than spiking accidents. And what about herbicides, all the miscarriages, cancers, and that stuff from logging? There's violence there. And we think there's violence in cutting down a thousand-year-old tree to make lawn furniture, too."[49]

Earth First! at the Grassroots

Monkeywrenchers usually work alone or in small numbers. Most Earth First! activities, however, take place in the context of local groups, the tribe's autonomous bands. By late 1981, after the first Road Show tour, the *Journal* listed Earth First! contacts in Maine, Virginia, New Jersey, Montana, Colorado, and Wyoming. Five years later when the Earth First! Foundation had been created as a non-profit educational corporation, there were international representatives in Australia and Japan, groups in forty-four cities, and thirty-two additional "local contacts." By 1990 ten special project groups had been formed emphasizing biodiversity, wolf preservation, direct action, and other topics. There are international representatives in nine nations, seventy-two local groups, and contacts in another thirty-five locales. Sixteen of the local groups produce their own newsletters.

Biodiversity in the Bay Area

Local Earth First! groups get started in any number of ways. One of the first and longest-lasting is Bay Area Earth First! in Berkeley, California, which is organized by Karen Pickett. When the brown-haired, business-like Pickett first arrived in the San Francisco area from Boston in 1971, she lived in a shack with a wood stove and no electricity. She made candles, baked bread, and "got by with no money....It was valuable for learning how to live," she says matter-of-factly. "And it was valuable for doing environmental work later on because I ceased to care about making money. I saw that I could get by on practically nothing and I could be resourceful enough, so I didn't need to worry about a career and a good-paying job. It made it a lot easier to do what I felt was important."[50]

In time she started working at the Ecology Center in Berkeley, which was founded a year before Earth Day 1970 prompted a wave of similar environmental education and small-scale recycling establishments across the nation. In January 1983, Dave Foreman walked into the Center with a stack of newsletters and some T-shirts under his arm, a copy of his *Progressive* article in hand. "I was just mind-blown when I read that," Pickett says, her voice breaking out of its usual monotone and growing animated. She had sensed that there had to be something more to environmental activism than recycling and Sierra Clubbing, and when Foreman returned that afternoon as promised, Pickett asked how she could get involved. Within six months she had helped form an affinity group for the Bald Mountain actions in the North Kalmiopsis; their blockade was the seventh and final of the year. The group was arrested, but their effort was not wasted—the day they got out of jail the injunction came down stopping the road. "It was an incredibly powerful experience in terms of convincing me that that kind of a tactic was effective," Pickett says.[51]

In the years since, she has nurtured an urban Earth First! group that is the largest and most active of its kind. Because it attracts a substantial number of employed activists, Bay Area Earth First! is something of a money tree, sending funds to other Earth First! groups as needed. And despite the destruction of more than eighty percent of San Francisco Bay's wetlands and encroaching urbanization throughout the area, Pickett says that the "local issues that we've gotten involved with here still have to do with biodiversity and habitat. Both San Bruno Mountain and Buckhorn Canyon are last remnant habitats."[52] San Bruno Mountain stands just south of San Francisco. Development already surrounds the two thousand foot-high peak, a bastion of wilderness in a sea of cement. The endangered mission blue butterfly and several other rare plant and animal species make their home on San Bruno Mountain, but that is too much space for them so far as the McKessen Corporation is concerned. Headquartered in San Francisco, McKessen wants to cover the mountain with condominiums. Numerous arrests have taken place at the site as Bay Area Earth First! activists have protested further development using civil disobedience. Buckhorn Canyon, east of San Francisco, is slated to become a reservoir, flooding 1,000 acres of vanishing streamside habitat that is home to another endangered species, the Alameda whipsnake. Earth First!ers have testified against the dam, picketed outside of meeting halls, and pledged direct action if the project is approved.

Pickett sees biologically crucial islands like San Bruno Mountain and Buckhorn Canyon as opportunities for educating city dwellers to the basics of ecocentrism, that undeveloped land is important for animals, plants, and the landscape itself. "That's what makes them important, not because they are open space or because they're a greenbelt for the city," Pickett says, "but because they are habitat for endangered species and because there is biodiversity within those little islands. I think that sometimes it's difficult for people to plug in in an urban area because they are so overwhelmed with concrete and car exhaust and everything."[53]

Phoenix—Up from the Ashes Again

Teachers tend to take an interest in education—it comes with the job. But when Leslie Sellgrin agreed to resurrect a Phoenix, Arizona, Earth First! group in February 1989 in part as a way of educating herself about the issues, she didn't know what a crash course she was in for. In a matter of weeks, she and a dozen others went from a somewhat casual interest in wilderness issues to well-tutored activists able to argue fine points in the proposed Arizona Wilderness bill. When the hearings on the proposed legislation were held in Phoenix, a dozen Phoenix Earth First!ers testified on behalf of their ambitious plan. The group was up from the ashes.

Sellgrin, a soft-voiced elementary school teacher who emphasizes ecology in her classes, grew up in the mountains of Idaho with an innate love of nature. She knew of Earth First! for years before she got actively involved. Initially, she was attracted by its novelty. But she says she came to recognize the importance of Earth First!'s no compromise stance. "I truly think that other groups are making far too many compromises and there simply is not the time....Most of the people that would belong to Sierra Club, are they really making a difference, can you actually do something? Unless you're a lawyer, there's not a heck of a lot you can do. Even then, there's a lot of compromises being made."[54]

Sellgrin and her Phoenix cohorts stepped up their activities following their experience with the wilderness bill. At Earth First!'s 1989 Round River Rendezvous in New Mexico, Sellgrin asked Northern California organizer and musician Darryl Cherney to help her organize a demonstration that drew twenty people against the nemesis of the redwoods, the Maxxam Corporation. The conglomerate also owns Horizon Corporation, a desert developer headquartered in Phoenix. Phoenix Earth First! has also picketed at Sen. Dennis Deconcini's office to express their displeasure at his support for the proposed telescopes at Mt. Graham, east of Tucson, which is home to the endangered Mt. Graham red squirrel. They regularly distribute information at Catholic churches before Sunday mass on the same subject—the Vatican is intending to build a telescope on the mountain. The group has marched at a national cattle ranching conference in Prescott and has protested the planned use of mahogany from endangered rainforests for panelling at the new state courthouse.

Sellgrin is convinced that Earth First! can make a difference as no other group can. "I think one of our biggest jobs or accomplishments is educating," she says. "That's what demonstrations are all about, really. 'Hey! Wake up, this is what's gong on.'...I can remember the first time I ever saw Earth First!. It was at one of the first demonstrations at Yellowstone," where Earth First!ers dressed up as grizzly bears to protest Park Service destruction of habitat for the threatened ursines. "I thought, 'Those people look *crazy*. They look like a bunch of fools out there.' But that attitude changed for me."[55]

Radicals and Lumberjacks

Timber industry executives would have their employees believe that their worst enemies are environmentalists, and the worst of the lot are the Earth First!ers, those "terrorists" who prefer to see a logger dead than a tree downed. Judi Bari has taken it onto her shoulders to prove the industry propaganda and the employees' stereotypes wrong. In so doing the forty-year-old University of Maryland drop-out has succeeded where most environmentalists would never dream of trying. She has also nearly gotten herself killed.

Bari cut her activistic teeth in union politics. In her three years in college during the Vietnam War, Bari "learned a lot, but not in class"—she cites as evidence a Chairman Mao clock in her kitchen that she built in 1970. Full of Marxist vigor but broke, she quit school and joined the proletariat, working in a grocery store's bakery. She was soon fired for decorating a cake with a hammer and sickle that read "U.S. Get out of the War." To her amazement, the union got her job back for her. When the union struck a couple of years later, she and others picketed peaceably by day and at night sealed locks with liquid steel and let the air out of management's tires. After an unsuccessful attempt to overthrow the same union that had gotten her job back for her—she insisted it was in cahoots with management—she went to work as a package handler at a U.S. Post Office bulk mail center. None of the three unions there did enough to protect their workers from long hours and dangerous conditions, Bari says. This time, instead of boring from within, she set up her own union, eventually winning out and becoming the leader of a single union at the massive complex.

Beginning early in 1988, Bari was again into the union fray. Bored with her success in the postal union, she had come west several years before to get married. It didn't work out, and she found herself with two young daughters and a strong urge to join the fight to save the redwoods on California's north coast. Chief among her adversaries was the Pacific Lumber Company, "Palco." For decades it had been a family-owned firm that cut trees at a sustainable rate, taking only as much wood as grew back each year. It was still the largest private holder of ancient redwood forests when, in 1985, it was taken over by the same Texas conglomerate, Maxxam, that Leslie Sellgrin's group protested against in Phoenix for razing the desert. In order to pay off the massive junk bond debt it had incurred in the purchase of Palco, Maxxam had to "liquidate" the only real "capital" Palco owned—the redwoods. That, Bari recognized, spelled doom not only for the forests but for the workers as well. There was forced overtime, meaning less time with family and more accidents, and the faster the trees were cut, the sooner the workers would lose their jobs.

At the same time, the northern spotted own controversy was reaching fever pitch. Scientists had been warning of a decline in the population of the beautifully camouflaged predator which spends its life in old growth timber stands. Environmentalists adopted the owl as a symbol of the decline of the ancient forests; to industry the bird became a scapegoat for its own self-destruction. The timber companies established groups such as the Yellow Ribbon Coalition to whip up an almost jingoistic fervor among employees. "Kill an Owl, Save a Logger," read the bumper stickers. T-shirts for sale throughout the Pacific Northwest picture a proud lumberjack beneath the declaration, "Endangered Species."

The crucial question for many was who was to blame for the rapid loss of jobs throughout the region. According to the Green Ribbon Coalition of environmental groups, 13,000 loggers were laid off from 1982 to 1988 in the Pacific Northwest. Industry denied anything more than minimal responsibility for the decline, pointing a finger instead at the environmentalists. In fact, some of those jobs were lost because of environmental successes, such as establishing wilderness areas and halting timber sales due to poor environmental impact assessments. But blaming environmentalists or the northern spotted owl for all of the job loss is nothing but a smokescreen, according to Bari and others. They point to the fact that twenty-five percent of the total "harvest" of timber from the Pacific Northwest was shipped to Japan and elsewhere in 1988, as compared to two percent in 1962. Most of those trees leave the U.S. as whole logs with the bark intact and only the branches missing; no American mill worker ever handles them.

In addition, most of the ancient forests have been cut, and the smaller trees that are left take fewer workers to handle. Further, the timber industry has embarked on a major automation campaign designed in large part to cut labor costs. In the meantime, timber companies reap enormous profits—Weyerhaeuser, for example, was in the black to the tune of $447 million in 1987.[56] When Louisiana-Pacific Corp. laid off 195 workers in California in March 1990, it blamed environmentalists for holding up a steady supply of lumber. At the same time, it was preparing to open a plant in Mexico to finish partially-cut logs—logs shipped from California. The machinery in Louisiana-Pacific's Mexico plant was moved from its Potter Valley, California, mill, which the company had closed a year earlier.

The first thing Bari did as an Earth First!er was attend the California Rendezvous in 1988 and conduct a seminar on the history of the International Workers of the World with Dakota Sid Clifford, an Earth First! musician and longtime Wobblie. It was the best attended workshop of the gathering. But Bari wasn't merely interested in Wobblie history or what sabotage tactics could be learned from the radical union. She set about her self-appointed task as an Earth First! field organizer—that idea, too, was borrowed from the Wobblies—determined to add a new twist. "I got most of my political experience in the factories," Bari says in her twangy "Bal'mer" accent. "I've never found anything as fun as that in my whole life.... When I started working in Earth First! it was the same, it had the same feeling to me, the same immediacy."[57] It all came together for the Marxist as a sub-conscious dialectic: thesis—the exploited timber workers; antithesis—the rabid radical environmentalists; synthesis—a radical timber worker's union working with Earth First!ers, of all people, to preserve both jobs and forest ecosystems. Thus was born IWW-Earth First! Local 1. Its symbol is the Wobblie's mangy black "Sab Cat" holding a monkey wrench.

Bari knew from her experiences that the mill workers were neither stupid, as many Earth First!ers thought they were, nor apathetic, as industry hoped. "All they need is to be shown a little victory here and there and they just come to life," Bari says from behind dark-ringed, reddened eyes. That victory, she felt certain, could come through the incredible union she co-founded. A key to making inroads with the workers was to understand the realities of their lives. "When I go to these workers, I'm not saying, 'Okay, I want you to support sustained-yield logging,'" Bari explains. "I'm saying, 'You're getting screwed: you're working overtime, you're getting in accidents—look, I had the same experience. This is the newsletter that we put out [at the bulk mail facility], this is how we beat it, and maybe we can try it here.'....I'm not approaching them on environmental issues. I initially approach them on workroom floor issues."[58]

For two years relations with the timber workers slowly improved. A few workers quietly made contact with Bari and her union organizing sidekick, Darryl Cherney. Surreptitious newsletters questioning management's point of view began appearing in two of the mills. In the main Palco mill in the company town of Scotia, the management's newsletter, "Timber Line," faced new competition from "Timber Lyin'," the workers' mouthpiece that noted safety problems and the dangers to employees' futures—job and health alike—from the stepped-up tree cutting. Then, at an annual environmental law conference in Oregon in March 1990, an unexpected new opportunity presented itself. Timber worker Gene Lawhorn, who had risked losing his job by appearing on a conference panel with Bari, told an audience that the only way that Bari's radical environmentalist-timber worker alliance could ever hope to work on a large scale was for Earth First! to renounce tree-spiking. The lumberjacks and millhands felt their lives were being placed in danger, despite Earth First!'s practice of warning when an area had been spiked. Lawhorn looked at Bari and waited for a response. Unprepared and on the spot, she simply said, "I hereby renounce tree-spiking." The room erupted in applause. Even the Earth First!ers in the audience supported her. After discussing her statement with them and with the activists she had worked to organize throughout the North Coast region, Bari's group and several others decided to formally renounce tree-spiking in their areas. Seven Northern California Earth First!ers, including Mike Roselle, issued a statement in mid-April saying their decision had been motivated by the emerging timber worker/radical environmentalist dialogue. Earth First!ers in Oregon did the same thing. But monkeywrenching was not denounced altogether; their statements tacitly encouraged equipment sabotage by mill workers to slow the industry's wheels.

In the spring of 1990, Bari turned her attention to organizing "Redwood Summer." It would be patterned after the "Mississippi Summer" of 1964, when hundreds of Freedom Riders descended on Mississippi to draw attention to the state's unyielding segregation. By calling on college students and others from across the nation to come.to Northern California, Bari and others hoped to bring a kind of pressure on the timber companies that they had never experienced: the intense scrutiny of the entire nation. But before the activists arrived for Redwood Summer, tragedy struck Bari and Darryl Cherney. In the late morning of May 24, the two were driving through Oakland toward the coastal college town of Santa Cruz, where they were to give a concert to round up support for Redwood Summer. Bari was at the wheel of her white Subaru station wagon with Cherney in the passenger seat. Without warning, a pipe bomb exploded beneath Bari's seat, ripping into her lower abdomen. Cherney's left eye was injured by flying debris. The twisted car careened off parked vehicles and came to rest against a van. Both Bari and Cherney were rushed to the hospital, where Bari underwent surgery to repair extensive "soft tissue" damage and a broken pelvis. She remained in full traction for six weeks.

Within hours after the bombing, Oakland police, FBI agents, and other law enforcement personnel announced that Bari and Cherney had made the bomb themselves and that it had accidentally exploded while they were carrying it to an unknown location. Judging by the bomb's apparent placement, authorities said the two "should have known" it was there. Officials said that nails and tape identical to that used to make the bomb were found in Cherney's van, which he had driven from his home north of San Francisco to Berkeley, where he had spent the previous night. Similar incriminating evidence was found at both activists' homes. Cherney was held by the police for questioning for four hours immediately following his release from the hospital. During none of that time was he allowed to see an attorney.

Every Earth First!er the press interviewed rejected the idea that any of them, and in particular Bari and Cherney, would have anything to do with the bomb. For weeks following their arrests, Bari and Cherney waited to be formally charged or freed. At an arraignment in mid-June, the Alameda County district attorney requested a continuation before charges were filed. In the meantime the police kept a steady stream of incriminating leaks flowing to the press. They revealed their list of "evidence" in the case and circulated a photograph of Bari holding an Uzi submachine gun, which Bari had had taken as a gag shot. On July 5 Oakland police said nails from the bomb matched those taken from Bari's home.

Then, on July 17, the district attorney announced that no charges would be filed. The evidence against Bari and Cherney, it turned out, was nonexistent. The bomb was in fact beneath Bari's seat and not easily visible to her. Although the nails in Bari's home and in the bomb were of the same type, they were of such a common type "that they were meaningless as evidence...."[59] Further, a special FBI evidence laboratory could not link items and tools from Bari's home that might have been used to make the bomb's components. Tried and convicted in the press, Bari and Cherney were set free.

As never before, the environmental community rallied to the defense of the radical environmentalists following the bombing, though some came around more quickly than others. Within days, Greenpeace had hired a private investigator to search for the real culprits—the authorities steadfastly refused to consider that there might be any suspects other than the victims. The day before the charges were dropped, the Sierra Club, the National Wildlife Federation, Friends of the Earth, and other mainstream groups requested that the House and Senate judiciary committees in Congress and the California attorney general's office investigate the investigative agencies probing the bombings. Congressmember Ron Dellums of Oakland condemned the FBI's trial-by-media tactics as well. Cherney was convinced that the true bombers were put up to the task by one or more timber companies. Bari, especially, was too dangerous, her wood worker-environmentalist union talk a chilling proposition for companies which operated effective monopolies over their workers' lives, secluded as they are from other sources of information and employment.

Trials and Tribulations of the Tribe

Undoubtedly the attempted murder of two of their best-known, most energetic organizers sent a tremor through the tribe. But it was not the first time tribal chieftains had been under the glare of suspicion. Almost exactly a year before the car bombing, Dave Foreman awoke one morning to find a cocked .357 magnum pointed at his head. At the other end was an FBI agent. It was the culmination of an investigation that lasted more than a year. The FBI accused Foreman and three others of plotting a mega-monkeywrench against power lines leading from nuclear power and weapons facilities in three states. If convicted of Conspiracy to Destroy an Energy Facility, Foreman could be sentenced to five years in prison and a $10,000 fine. The others each were charged with Destruction of an Energy Facility, Destruction of Government Property, Destruction of Property which Affects Interstate Commerce, and Conspiracy. They each face jail terms of as long as thirty-five years and fines of $80,000.[60]

In 1987 and 1988 several attacks took place in Arizona that became the basis for the FBI's investigation. Power lines leading to the Palo Verde nuclear power plant were shorted out, chairlift supports at a controversial ski resort built on sacred Indian land were twice sabotaged, and power line poles for uranium mines near the north rim of the Grand Canyon were toppled. At the 1988 Round River Rendezvous, FBI agent Mike Fain, posing as a carpenter who had trouble reading and writing because of a learning disability, was introduced to Peg Millett, a popular Earth First!er (it later came out that their mutual friend Ron Frazier was also an FBI informant). Fain spent long evenings trading stories with the energetic, outgoing Millett and confessed to her that he was an ardent tree-spiker. They discussed monkeywrenching methods at length, and the FBI alleges that Millett eventually told Fain of her involvement in the first downing of pylons at the Fairfield Snow Bowl. According to the FBI she also implicated Mark Davis, an anti-nuclear activist who did not consider himself an Earth First!er.[61] Eventually, the government says, Davis and Millett told Fain of their plan to knock out transmission lines leading from three nuclear facilities: Arizona's Palo Verde and California's Diablo Canyon power plants and the Rocky Flats nuclear weapons complex outside of Denver. Fain offered to help by contacting Earth First!ers in California and Denver who might be willing to help with the action.

At Fain's request, Foreman gave Davis $580 to support his activism, apparently without knowing exactly how the money would be spent. Two months later, in mid-May 1989, Fain asked Foreman for more money. He was given $100, all there was in the Earth First! office's petty cash box. Those transactions became the case against Foreman. On the night of May 30, Fain, Millett, and Davis picked up Marc Baker at his home. Fain barely knew Baker, a non-Earth First! environmentalist and a close friend of both Davis and Millett. As the sun set they drove into the desert for a trial run on a power line tower leading to a Central Arizona (Water) Project pump station. Over Fain's strenuous objections, Davis insisted on the test to see if the towers could be knocked down. Using a blowtorch, Davis had cut halfway through a pylon, when flares suddenly lit up the night and fifty FBI agents stormed the activists. Millett got away and was arrested the next morning, as was Foreman.

A Wide Net

Even before the arrest of the "Arizona Four," a home shared by several Missoula, Montana, Earth First!ers was raided by the FBI, following reports of a tree-spiking in Idaho's Clearwater National Forest. John Lilburn, the only one home at the time, was folding laundry when the FBI knocked. Agents in body armor swarmed through the house, taking diaries, computer disks, rock climbing gear, and photo albums.[62] Eventually, Lilburn and six others were subpoenaed by the FBI. Known for throwing a "wide net" in its investigations, the FBI questioned twenty-five or more Earth First!ers following the May raids. The Bureau compiled 575 tape recordings "from household bugs, phone taps, and conversations taped by" Fain in its investigation;[63] almost no one active in Earth First! believes his or her telephone is not tapped. The net was hauled in a bit more in December 1989, when Ilse Asplund, with whom Mark Davis was living prior to his arrest, was indicted by an Arizona grand jury on two charges relating to the downing of electrical lines leading to uranium mines.

Foreman's attorneys have alleged that the FBI's investigation of their client was politically motivated, another in a long line of assaults on dissenters that goes back to the Wobblies in the early years of this century, which includes Martin Luther King, the Black Panthers, anti-war protestors, the American Indian Movement, and the Central American peace movement. In Earth First!, however, the FBI has encountered a new, decentralized, leaderless movement, Foreman says, and it really does not know what to make of the tribe. "I don't think the FBI is mentally capable of understanding how Earth First! operates," he says. On the other hand, perhaps the FBI has a better handle on the tribe than anyone realizes. Foreman suspects that "the FBI has been exploiting some of the differences within Earth First!. I think some of the more anarchist, punk-type faction in Earth First! has been duped by underground agents and that they have been put up to certain things."[64] Although the anarchists deny any possible motivation other than their own feelings, Foreman and others insist otherwise.

Earth First!ers maintain that they cannot be split by FBI plots—they are too diffuse, decentralized, and disdainful of "leadership" to suffer, even if influential members like Foreman or Millett are taken out of the picture by a governmental scam. They can be hurt from within, however, by debates reminiscent of those which have proven so disruptive to mainstream environmental groups, the Sierra Club in particular. When Judi Bari, Darryl Cherney, Karen Wood, Mike Roselle, and others spoke for their local groups and renounced tree-spiking, it drew a prompt and furious reaction. Michael Robinson, a friend of Bari and Cherney, wrote prior to the bombing, "It will be hard to hold the middle ground [between accepting tree-spiking and denouncing it universally, not just in the Pacific Northwest], and at a certain point the question arises of what divisions our movement can withstand and still be one movement. This is hardly a new question, but the necessity to keep re-asking it is keeping us from focusing on our common battles." Sounding like David Brower chastising the mainstream, Robinson added that "equating the rights of victimized sawmill workers with the needs of ecosystems disempowers us from speaking clearly in the future about the ecosystems....Let someone else make those connections and alliances; it's not our job."[65] Despite this, Robinson and the rest of the tribe immediately came to Bari and Cherney's defense following the car bombing, partially mending a movement under siege from its own internal dissent.

Which Anarchy?

Tree spiking's role in Earth First! is only the most recent source of debate within the tribe. One deep split which has yet to be resolved is between the so-called "Old Guard" and socially activistic anarchists. Anarchy of a sort has always been a part of Earth First!. Most of the Old Guard, Sagebrush Patriot wing of Earth First! would likely subscribe to Edward Abbey's approving definition of anarchy as "the maximum possible dispersal of power: political power, economic power, and force—military power. An anarchistic society would consist of a voluntary association of self-reliant, self-supporting, autonomous communities."[66] This is hardly the definition that would leap to most people's minds; chaos and violence typify the common concept of the term.

About 1987, however, Earth First! began to attract youthful "Circle-A" anarchists who brought with them the idea that a chaotic anarchy could be a means to social change. Under the rallying cries of "Stumps Suck" and "Live Wild or Die," they opposed the Old Guard's anarchic vision as merely an end for which to strive. One of the central figures in the clash between the anarchists and the Old Guard was Mike Jakubal, a wandering activist who pioneered tree-sitting when he ascended an ancient Douglas fir in 1985. He gradually became disenchanted with Earth First!'s methods and frustrated with its "organization"—as represented by the *Journal* and the Old Guard, led by Foreman, which together set the tone for Earth First!. To express their contrasting ideal, Jakubal and others published the first issue of a newspaper, *Live Wild or Die*, in February 1989. Jakubal's editorial explains that *Live Wild or Die* eschews labels of any sort, including "radical environmentalist." Instead, people should act "out of our own true desires, our own wild subjectivity, our internal wilderness. Personally, what I dream of is a fuller, wilder way of life and living, not just a new set of slogans to suffer for."[67] "Chaco," Jakubal's co-editor, wrote that Earth First! "has become self-limiting in its scope. It's done this by trying so hard to *define* itself, and thereby draw boundaries which encircle some and eliminate others." Worst of all, Chaco felt that "there are lots of vital voices which are not being heard within the realm of Earth First!...."[68]

A tendency that Chaco and others decried was Earth First!'s reluctance to accept internal criticism and that from "would-be allies. If we can't allow ourselves to be criticized," she wrote, "then we can't change and grow. Our ideas become *doctrines....*" One writer in the first issue of Live Wild or Die observed that in contrast to the organizational side of Earth First!, "There is another Earth First!....The real movement is an anti-authoritarian, anti-industrial civilization, pro wilderness movement...."[69] Earth First! is but a catchy phrase for the press to latch onto, one that has come to be associated with "red-neck, macho, racist posturings of Abbey, Foreman, and others."[70]

In addition to criticisms of Earth First!, *Live Wild or Die* is a crazy quilt of ideas for bringing down industrial society. The first two issues included how-to articles on shoplifting, hoboing, spiking trees to thwart "longbutting" (a logging technique that leaves a tall stump to get above spikes), living semi-permanently in the wild, and making free long-distance telephone calls. The idea behind these schemes is to undercut the system in whatever way one can. Important as the anarchist phenomenon in Earth First! is in its own right, it is also the clearest indication that Earth First! is no longer the small, close-knit group it once was. Foreman observes that the "internal, informal, mutually agreed upon limits" of the early years "have broken down," adding that "maybe we're at the point where we need to say, 'Bye. Earth First! doesn't exist anymore.' I don't know. That's not for me to say."[71] Among the actions Foreman cites as evidence of the failure of the old commonly held checks are the anarchists' "consciously offensive" actions, like a "Puke-in" at a Seattle-area shopping mall in December 1988. There, members of the "Gross Action Group" shared an emetic, and as the drug took effect and they began vomiting, they unfurled signs and shouted anti-consumerism messages at the strolling holiday shoppers. Even more troublesome for Foreman was the anarchists' partial burning of an American flag at the 1989 Rendezvous, less than a month after the Arizona Four arrests. Judi Bari supported the flag burning, saying it "was a symbolic representation of a political struggle that had been going on the entire Rendezvous. It was between the old-line Earth First!ers—the old boy network (who wanted nothing to do with any of these social and political issues)—and a majority of the other people. They said that you can't talk about preserving wilderness without talking about the social and political system that is destroying it."[72]

Foreman, however, calls for a "no-fault divorce" between the anarchists and the Old Guard. He insists that he is "not saying [that flag burning and puke-ins] are *wrong*; I'm saying they're not my style and I'm uncomfortable with them. This doesn't mean that somebody shouldn't be doing them. I think that in general the diversity within Earth First! has probably gotten too big to be completely contained under one umbrella."[73] Each side in this struggle calls the other "ideologues," too inflexible to see the other's point of view (the same criticism outsiders like Michael McCloskey make of the radicals). Yet both arguments have their valid points. The Old Guard's emphasis on media "spin" is sensible. Public perception is a key to social change. Their wilderness-first emphasis seems logical as well. But holding to that while excluding all else fosters a narrow world view and ignores the political reality of Earth First!'s message, namely that the entire social system must change before there can be an assurance of permanent wilderness protection.

For their part, the anarchists' chosen role as internal critics is desperately needed. They draw out some important contradictions in Earth First!—for instance, how can anyone seriously imply that vomiting in a shopping mall looks worse to the public than potentially placing people's lives in danger with tree spikes? And complaints about an Earth First! "organization" of some sort appear well-founded: the *Earth First! Journal* has not published articles representative of the full spectrum of opinions and activities in the movement, and many feel that a portion of the tribe's elders have dictated by fiat what is and is not acceptable.

At root, however, are egos. Earth First! is putting itself through exactly the sort of turmoil that mainstream environmental organizations endure, the sort of tumult that Earth First!ers have long cited as impediments to those organizations' success. Perhaps internecine war is inevitable. But for so much energy to be expended on internal sniping by so many in a decentralized, anarchic/tribal "movement" appears utterly incongruous. Rick Bernardi, an Earth First!er and Animal Liberator, expresses disgust at the whole thing, saying, "Here's a hole in the sky and here are the clear cuts, and what are we talking about? Flag burning!"[74]

Cowboys and Women

Until recently, the image of Earth First! propagated by the press was of a loosely-knit bunch of macho-male hooligans. Nancy Zirenberg, who because of her position as merchandize manager for the *Earth First! Journal* in the tribe's Tucson, Arizona, office may be as close to the sources of that stereotype as any woman, observes, "There's a macho image. There's also a very feminist image that is not portrayed in the media. The women in Earth First! are not coming across in the media. We've talked about how we're going to remedy that, and in the end it has to come individually. We have to push ourselves to take the spotlight."[75] She notes that the press gravitates to men as spokespersons even at "all-women's events." When reporters arrived at the Sapphire Six action, they immediately looked to the lone male for comment, the unspoken assumption being that he must be the one "in charge," when in fact he had little to do with the planning of the action. While this reflects a bias in the press, it also shows the lasting imprint of Earth First!'s male-dominated origins.

Some women, however, complain of a reality behind the stereotype. Judi Bari says that prior to joining Earth First! her impression was that it was male-dominated. That, and a concern that it was "anti-worker," initially kept her out of the movement. Having been a part of it for two years now, she has seen her fears validated. Bari notes that her close friend, Darryl Cherney, received an award from Earth First! at the 1989 Rendezvous for his work with the press and for his efforts in organizing timber workers. As deserving of recognition as Cherney's media relations work in the fight for the redwoods is, Bari says he was much less involved with the efforts to unite Earth First! and the workers. The award, she says, should have been shared with her.[76] Bari also says that the grant she received in 1990 from the Earth First! Foundation to support her organizing efforts was only the second ever given to a woman. As a musician, too, she is disturbed by the under-representation of women. At the 1989 Round River Rendezvous, the "Wild Women's Caucus" was angered that most of the nightly campfire sing-alongs were dominated by men. Bari says that a group of female musicians decided to literally steal the show, and the resulting hours-long performance won them new respect. The flip side to all this, Bari says, is that at the grassroots level Earth First!ers treat women and men alike. She says she deals with higher-level male-female problems by ignoring them and staying focused on local organizing.

Karen Pickett agrees with Bari "that there are a few" chauvinistic males in Earth First!. "But," she adds, "there are fewer problems with women being able to go unimpeded to whatever heights they are capable of within this group than any other group of people that I've ever been involved with. I'm really glad for that."[77] While bothered by the media-created image of male domination in Earth First!, Pickett says she has not felt anti-female sentiments directed toward her. Even in her early days of organizing, when she was often the only woman working with a roomfull of men on an action, the group was focused on the issues. Problems simply did not arise over sex or sexism.

Anarchists and women are not the only ones struggling for a voice within Earth First!. Long-running debates with vegetarians and Animal Liberators, who argue that meat eating and hunting damage the environment, have only recently cooled down. There is also a "woo-woo" faction of highly spiritual devotees of Earth First! who prefer meditation to action. With all these pressures, it might be expected that the pipe bombing and the FBI's crackdown on Earth First! came at a perfect time to save it. Just when it appeared that tensions between factions were going to rend the tribe, something comes along to give everyone an enemy against which to rally. But that would not be very Earth First!-like. The Arizona Four arrests happened only days before the Rendezvous, and if anything they increased tensions, as evidenced by Foreman's insistence that the flag-burning was instigated by an FBI agent provocateur. As for the car bombing that injured Bari and Cherney, some in the movement who advocate widespread monkeywrenching note that the renunciation of tree-spiking did nothing to protect these most non-destructive of Earth First!ers from becoming victims of violence. The divisions remain.

AIDS, Starvation, Ending Immigration: Environmental Cure-Alls?

As is obvious in the debates over Earth First!'s wilderness-only and monkeywrenching values, there rarely, if ever, is complete agreement on *anything* within the tribe. Earth First!'s grassroots emphasis allows for any number of opinions to be openly expressed. To the extent that this freedom is not understood, however, it has caused a substantial image problem— not that any movement advocating tree-spiking and the destruction of machinery would find much public sympathy. Still, as Dave Foreman has said, within the context of a desperate fight against an unjust opponent, those who choose monkeywrenching may find a sympathetic audience.

Then there are those who see nature as its own best defender. In articles published in 1987 in the *Earth First! Journal*, a writer calling himself "Miss Ann Thropy" (read: misanthropy) speculated about how Acquired Immune Deficiency Syndrome (AIDS) could benefit the environment. Miss Ann Thropy's first article begins, "If radical environmentalists were to invent a disease to bring human population back to ecological sanity, it would probably be something like AIDS."[78] Seeing no other possibility for the preservation of biological diversity on the Earth than a drastic decline in the number of humans, Miss Ann Thropy says AIDS is ideal for the task primarily because "it only affects humans" and shows promise for wiping out large numbers of them.[79] The article concludes that the pain and suffering of AIDS victims should not be disregarded or discounted. However, as "radical environmentalists, we can see AIDS not as a problem, but a necessary solution."[80]

Miss Ann Thropy returned several months later to answer his critics. Emphasizing the inevitable massive die-off of humans by some means because of our environmentally abusive ways, Miss Ann Thropy wrote that such reductions "will mean the end to industrial tyranny which controls every aspect of our lives, which determines how we work and where we live and even what we think. It will disintegrate the central powers that make total war, toxic wastes, and human bondage possible." The hunter-gatherer world emerging in the aftermath of an AIDS pandemic will result in non-hierarchical communities where nature's resources are shared by all.[81]

Another schema for human die-off was proposed by Dave Foreman. In a 1986 interview with Bill Devall that was published in the Australian magazine *Simply Living*, Foreman said that "'the worst thing we could do in Ethiopia is to give aid—the best thing would be to just let nature seek its own balance, to let the people there just starve....The alternative is that you go in and save these half-dead children who never will live a whole life. Their development will be stunted. And what's going to happen in ten years' time is that twice as many people will suffer and die.'"[82] Foreman has also defended Edward Abbey's controversial statements about the need to halt immigration into the U.S. if we are to put an end to social and environmental ills from "mass unemployment" and "an overloaded welfare system" to "rotting cities and a poisoned environment."[83] Abbey foresaw a "social, political, and moral revolution which is both necessary and inevitable" in Latin American nations. He suggested that the U.S. encourage it by stopping "every *campesino* at our southern border, give him a handgun, a good rifle, and a case of ammunition, and send him home. He will know what to do with our gifts and good wishes."[84]

Some Earth First! sympathizers say that these statements are hyperbole, rhetoric to get the tribe noticed, and that their underlying message is a warning of the need to overcome some of the multiplicity of problems which comprise the Eco-Wall, including the exploding human population. Others feel these articles were a public relations nightmare. The shock value of a correctly-done tree-spiking (one that causes no harm) is one thing; the advocacy of a pox on all humanity is another. Both may cost Earth First! supporters, but at least people might be tempted to take the trees' side in the debate surrounding spiking; AIDS advocacy, however, cannot be explained fully in a sound bite or magazine article. As such, any hope of a deeper debate is sacrificed from the start.

Those in both right-wing and left-wing political circles fail to accept that a reduction in human population is essential to the maintenance of a healthy Earth. Along the current path lies certain, widespread suffering.[85] In the ecological terms used by environmental sociologist William Catton, we have overshot Earth's carrying capacity.[86] Without fossil fuels and huge dams, we cannot feed, house, and clothe the five billion of our kind. Even if we limited ourselves to extracting our "vital needs" and forsook our materialistic "wants," we would make the planet unlivable for our descendants and those of all other species.

In their dire warnings of ecological and social collapse, Miss Ann Thropy, Foreman, and Abbey were correct. What is troubling—in addition to wishing a plague or starvation on anyone—is the underlying cultural bias their statements reflect. Some say these social critics are "racists," which they are not. However, Foreman and the others seem to have ignored a basic fact of AIDS and crop failures: they afflict more pain on Third World peoples than on those living in developed nations. Foreman writes that, when taken on its own, his comment regarding Ethiopia "was insensitive and simplistic. The point I was trying to make, and which I think is made when the rest of the interview is taken into account, is that oftentimes a feel-good humanitarian response from the United States or Western Europe may not have the result we hope and may even have the opposite result."[87] This clarification ignores that we in the West have the luxury of being able to afford huge expenditures to halt or slow diseases and to ensure our food supply by massive, environmentally ruinous irrigation projects and applications of petroleum-derived fertilizers and pesticides. In fairness, Foreman (and Abbey, before his death) has fought these projects, which in themselves encourage population explosions and further environmental destruction, with a zeal unmatched by many.

The fact remains, though, that ecologically-sound misanthropic arguments would hold that the environment would be much better off if those in the over-developed nations of the West were starved to death or died en masse of a plague. For it is we who buy, spill, and burn the oil that fouls the air and the seas; purchase beef and wood from former rainforests (and support the development projects that destroy them); emit the caustic smoke and CFCs that cause acid rain and destroy the ozone layer; demand ivory trinkets that come from endangered elephants; and so-forth, *ad infinitum*. By doing so, we inflict many times more damage on the biosphere, person-for-person, than people living in Third-World nations. What is needed, however, are constructive suggestions, not death wishes.

We could start with contraception rather than with killing—only thirty percent of couples in developing countries outside of China use birth control.[88]

Where to Now?

Even as the FBI chips away, anarchists raise hell, and organizers renounce tree-spiking and join with timber workers, most Earth First!ers see a future for their movement, although one far different from the past. Others are not so sure. "I don't know if Earth First! is going to survive," says Foreman. He adds one of the few sentiments that he and anarchists could agree on: "I don't know if Earth First! *should* survive. Ten years ago when we started it, we joked about having a sunset clause: we said maybe we ought to do this for ten years and then say, 'It's over.' And we'd start up somewhere else so that we didn't form a bureaucracy. There are certain things in Earth First! that I'm not terribly comfortable with, certain directions, things that have gone on. But they're really irrelevant. What's important is that the work gets done."[89] It is ironic that it is an excess of anarchy, not bureaucracy, that threatens the founders' vision. Old Guarder Roger Featherstone insists that Earth First! should be re-oriented toward its original bearings. The anarchists will still belong, Featherstone says. "Everybody will always have a place within the movement. But the problem has been that folks have been trying to create the Earth First! movement in their own image."[90] Judi Bari's sentiments contrast sharply with Featherstone's. "If we're going to try and pretend that we can continue to espouse such revolutionary concepts [as ecocentrism]and still fly the flag and pretend that we're patriotic Americans, we're dooming ourselves to failure," Bari says. "I think we need to realize how revolutionary what we're saying really is."[91]

Mike Roselle, who at times has had open, bitter disagreements with Foreman over tactics and philosophy, is attempting to be something of a peacemaker in all this. He wants to see Earth First! move ahead, to take its "second step." Confident that it has accomplished its original goals of articulating the need for an ecological world view and for overcoming the Eco-Wall through action, now he wants more action, activity like the environmental movement has never before seen. The time is ripe. "We have the clout, we have the profile and the grassroots organization, now, to do other things," he says. "What we have to do now is to bring ourselves into direct confrontation with the most heinous aspects of this industrial monster that is devouring the planet." In order to prepare for this, everyone within Earth First! must "put everything on the table. We're going to have to deal with a lot of the contradictions within the organization. We'll have to not be afraid to be so divisive that some people are going to walk out of there."[92] But Roselle doesn't know what the result will be any more than he knew what would happen after he sketched the Earth First! logo from the back seat of Foreman's VW bus.

Charles Bowden, a friend of Foreman, Abbey, and others in the movement, has written, "Earth First! is guerrilla theater, not guerrilla war, and it can be a dull, hard life."[93] He was writing of the tribal chieftains, however. At the grassroots it is war, albeit of an unconventional type. Thus far it has been peaceful—destructive but non-violent. That may change, but it is doubtful. More likely is that events such as "Redwood Summer" will be the new Cracking of Glen Canyon Damns, only this time with a cast of thousands in communities from Asheville to Arcata. The only thing for sure is that if the next ten years are anything like Earth First!'s initial decade, environmentalism will never be the same again.

CHAPTER 6

THE SEA SHEPHERDS:
BRINGING JUSTICE TO THE HIGH SEAS

Paul Watson says he doesn't remember when he first heard of the *Sierra*, an infamous pirate whaling ship that prowled the waters of the Atlantic for nearly twenty years. It was like an archetypal specter that was always *out there*, menacing the waves in the collective consciousness of anti-whaling activists. In the summer of 1979, with little more than a "gut feeling" to go on, Watson set out to change all that by tracking down and destroying the 678-ton killer/factory ship that haunted him. His bond with whales was strong, having been cemented by a vision in an Oglala Sioux sweat lodge when he was initiated into the tribe following the Indian uprising at Wounded Knee in 1973. A bison appeared to Watson, who was made a member of the tribe after he snuck into the besieged encampment during the seventy-one day rebellion and worked as a medic. The buffalo told him that he should "concentrate on the mammals of the sea, especially whales."[1]

It was a profound visitation, Watson says, especially because of the messenger. "The Plains Indians were the first people to ever fight a war to save something other than themselves—the buffalo."[2]

In this parable of the high seas, the *Sierra* was a seagoing version of the rapacious foreigners who wiped out Indians and bison in their relentless drive to "conquer the west." Like Buffalo Bill, the *Sierra* was a terrorist practicing genocide, bound by no written or moral law. In one three-year period the *Sierra* slaughtered 1,676 whales, selling the meat to Japan for 138,000 yen per metric ton. At a time of increasing international pressure to halt all whaling, the *Sierra* operated with impunity toward the unenforceable strictures and quotas established by the International Whaling Commission (IWC).[3] Watson felt that such lawlessness could be stopped only by taking the fight to the high seas. Only months before, he had convinced Cleveland Amory, a philanthropist and president of the Fund for Animals, to put up the money for a ship that Watson re-christened the *Sea Shepherd*. Amory had an abiding love for all animals and a strong urge to protect them through whatever non-violent means were available. As he wrote in the introduction to Watson's book, *Sea Shepherd*, "I wanted a tough team able to take on—head-on, if need be—the major cruelties to which so many animals are regularly and ruthlessly subjected."[4] In Watson, Amory saw an ideal warrior for the animals of the sea. During a June 1979 meeting, Amory asked his captain to take the ship to the Aleutians and block a fur seal kill there. But the barrel-chested, baby-faced, blunt-spoken Watson felt the *Sierra* gnawing at his bones. His ship was ready to go. "'Give me a month,'" Watson pleaded with his benefactor. He wanted to search out the *Sierra* and send it to the depths to avenge the gentle leviathans who had met their end at the point of the pirate's harpoon. Amory relented, and the desperate chase soon was on.[5]

The *Sea Shepherd* began life in 1960 as a 779-ton, 206-foot-long deep-water trawler, a cod fishing ship that Watson purchased with Amory's money in December 1978 for $120,000. Its time on the ocean ended barely a year later at the bottom of the harbor at Leixoes, Portugal, scuttled by order of its own Captain Watson to avoid having it turned over to the pirate whalers. But that is the denouement to the hunt for the *Sierra*. The story begins on July 15, 1978, when Watson discovered the whaling vessel off the Portuguese coast. The twenty-eight-year-old commander found his adversary after a cross-ocean hunt lasting twelve days, guided only by some vague information that the *Sierra* would be somewhere off the Iberian peninsula. The excitement over the imminent end of the chase must have been tremendous, but the ships were too far from shore for Watson to act. His strict code of non-violence prevented him from smashing into his antagonist then and there, on a cold and frothy sea far from port, risking the lives of the *Sierra's* crew and his own. Watson figured he would soon enough have his opportunity.

The next day that chance came, but was nearly lost. After following the outlaw ship all night as it slowly made for shore, Watson was tricked into port by the Portuguese authorities around noon. They had him believe that the *Sierra* was heading in as well, when in reality it was soon to leave. Watson, more determined than ever to get the pirates, dashed the *Sea Shepherd* out of the harbor without permission. He had been docked for one hour, which was long enough to discharge nearly all of his twenty-person crew—only two chose to stand with him and risk the uncertain punishment that would befall them. Then it was onward after the *Sierra*.

Watson sailed out of the mouth of the port to find the pirate whaler sitting languidly at anchor a quarter-mile from shore, biding its time until the appointed hour to steam out and meet a Japanese cargo ship into which it would disgorge its whale flesh. Watson wasted no time in heading straight for the *Sierra*, whose crew was sunbathing on deck. On the first attack he used the *Sea Shepherd's* concrete-reinforced bow to smash into the *Sierra's* leading edge in the hope of severing the pendent harpoon platform; the collision left major damage to the whaler but failed to take off the executioner's stand. Watson banked his ship hard and took aim amidships of the *Sierra*. Its crew ran about frantically. They must have been trying to start the engines, but no wake could be seen. Sitting there idle, the *Sierra* was an easy target. "When you ram another ship and you can control it in calm waters," Watson explains, "it's not like two cars hitting each other. You've got 750 tons of metal hitting 680 tons of metal. That's a lot of steel to absorb the shock of the impact."[6] Gentle though it might have felt, the second charge was devastating, the combination of speed and mass as powerful as a bomb. The collision ripped open a hole in the hull six feet wide by eight feet long. Whale meat could be seen hanging inside. As Watson turned to administer the *coup de gras*, his adversary finally got underway and limped the short distance to the harbor.

Suddenly, it was Watson's turn to play the outlaw. He and his tiny crew ran the *Sea Shepherd* at full speed up the coast in hopes of reaching Spanish territorial waters, thereby avoiding any penalties which the Portuguese might levy. Their desperate dash ended eight miles short of the mark, when a Portuguese naval destroyer demanded that Watson turn his ship around or be fired upon. The *Sea Shepherd* was escorted back to Leixoes and docked at the far end of the harbor from the critically damaged, listing *Sierra*.

The *Sea Shepherd* sat there for four and a half months while the Portuguese debated what to do. Maritime law dictated that the ship, not the captain or the crew, was to blame for certain high seas crimes, so Watson was released. He spent much of his time on television and radio shows telling of his exploit. Then in December, Watson was finally given the terms, or term, under which the *Sea Shepherd* would be returned to him: pay $750,000 in damages and fines. Refusal to pay would mean the *Sea Shepherd* would be forfeited to the *Sierra*'s owners. Watson flew to Portugal to inspect his ship and found that many vital components had been stripped by thieves, including the port police, who had stolen the ship's radio.

Even if he had been able to raise three-quarters of a million dollars to get his $120,000 ship back, the repair expenses would be enormous. Giving up the ship to the whalers was out of the question. Watson's way was clear. As close to heartbroken as the tough merchant marine could ever be, Watson realized that his only choice was to scuttle his pride and joy, sending it to the bottom of the harbor and then running like hell.

Amidst the pandemonium of New Year's Eve, *Sea Shepherd* Chief Engineer Peter Woof crept aboard the vessel at night, stealing into the engine room. There he opened a valve that, when closed, kept sea water from entering the engine. Brine gushed into the ship. Woof escaped from the vessel before it sank. He immediately left the country; Watson, however, wanted one last look at his vessel. The day after the scuttling, he drove by the port. Police were everywhere; it was obvious the job was well-done. Watson avoided extraordinary security measures by the incensed Portuguese authorities and escaped to London.[7]

On February 6, 1980, a bomb tore open the hull of the fully-refitted *Sierra* as it sat in Lisbon's harbor, ready to sail and kill once more. It sank in 10 minutes. An anonymous caller to United Press International said, "The *Sierra* will kill no more whales! We did it for the *Sea Shepherd*." Within weeks, two of Spain's five whalers were sunk by the same three saboteurs who did-in the *Sierra*. Watson was an ocean away at the time of all three bombings. No one was injured, and the perpetrators were never caught.[8]

Greenpeace Mutineer

The Sea Shepherd story is very much Paul Watson's story. His deeply confident, clear vision of purpose guides the organization, his energy and knowledge of what makes news gets it noticed, and his combination of daring and absolute commitment to the cause at times places him and his crew in positions of danger that might be avoided by those with less devotion. For the Sea Shepherds, property destruction and radical tactics are a way of life, of getting noticed, of getting the word out, and most importantly, of saving life. But Watson's earliest foray into property destruction on behalf of animals, in 1977, did not impress those who called the shots, his fellow Greenpeace directors. Watson was there in 1972 at the formal establishment of the Greenpeace Foundation, but even then was pegged as "'too radical'" by those in control of the organization. For one thing, Watson had a habit of walking around in a jacket with a North Vietnamese flag stitched to it,[9] and although opposition to the Vietnam War played a major role in Greenpeace's formation, from the start it tried to keep its image "clean."

But Watson was big, strong, and enthusiastic, and an able seaman. In time he took an even more active role in the organization, serving with the first Greenpeace flotilla to confront a Soviet whaling fleet in 1975. He piloted one of the Zodiacs (the speedy, motor-driven, inflatable dinghies Greenpeace made famous) that rushed to the whales' side, and he watched from a scant few yards away as two sperm whales, a male and a female, were killed with harpoons capped with explosive charges. When the bull was struck while making a mad rush at the huge Soviet whaling ship, its dying moments were spent staring Watson in the eye, subliminally telling the young sailor that it was up to him to avenge the whales.

By 1977 Watson was on the Greenpeace board of directors and was entrusted with an expedition to protest the killing of baby harp seals, the defenseless, doe-eyed white furballs that had become almost as synonymous with Greenpeace as whales. The protest took place on the treacherous Labrador Front ice floes off Newfoundland. At one point Watson took a wooden club used to kill seals out of a sealer's grasp and threw it into the icy water. Watson then moved several harp seal pelts from one floe to another to make it harder for the sealers to do their job. His intent was to interfere as much as possible with the slaughter without hurting anyone. When he spied a cable used to haul pelts onto the nearby sealing ship, Watson, who had a pair of handcuffs attached to his belt, ran to the cable and cuffed himself to it. He was certain that this move would shut down the sealing.

But the winch operator, undeterred, turned on the motor to bring in the pelts—and Watson. As the cable was drawn in, Watson quickly lost his footing and was dragged through slush, then pulled ten feet above the water, slamming against the ship. The cable stopped, then suddenly slackened, dropping the Greenpeacer waist deep into the frigid water. Watson was lifted again, then dunked. And again, with blood-streaked sealers cheering all the while from the ship's railing. Suddenly, as he was being pulled out of the water yet again, Watson's belt broke. He plunged beneath the icy slush. Greenpeacers rushed to retrieve his half-frozen body, then negotiated for thirty minutes with the captain of the sealing ship before Watson, who was ebbing in and out of consciousness, was allowed to be brought on board. The numb-bodied activist was dragged across the blood-covered deck by the crazed, jeering seal killers, then dumped into a cabin to spend the night.[10]

When Watson returned to Greenpeace headquarters in Vancouver, Canada, after the campaign, his reward for nearly getting himself killed in defense of the seals was expulsion from the organization. Greenpeace, the only visible "radicals" in the environmental movement at the time, had their limits. As Watson's close friend Robert Hunter writes in his history of Greenpeace's early years, Watson "seemed possessed by *too* powerful a drive, too unrelenting a desire to push himself front and center, shouldering everyone else aside." Watson's action of throwing the club and pelts into the water, considered a crime under Canadian law, cost Greenpeace its tax-exempt status in the U.S. Moreover, Watson was a "mutineer," Hunter says, who fomented revolt against the organization's hierarchy wherever he went.[11] The tribal/anarchist had to go.

It must have been a terrible blow to Watson. His daring efforts on behalf of whales and seals were repaid with expulsion. Today he says he holds no bitterness toward Greenpeace, but his tone of voice in speaking of them belies that. Paul Watson is Greenpeace's most unrelenting critic. The organization got away from its founders because they were spending too much time in the field doing what Greenpeace was established to do, he says. Had they stopped to take stock of the direction Greenpeace was heading, the world's best-known environmental organization might today have an entirely different approach. "When we set up Greenpeace it was because we wanted a small group of action-oriented people who could get into the field and, using these McLuhanist principles (for attracting media attention), make an issue controversial and publicize it and get to the root of the problem. That was fine for the first seven years or so. We were successful at doing that. And then one day we woke up." Watson's awakening came too late, at the board of directors' meeting where he was kicked out. He recalls telling his fellow directors, "'I was the bloody expedition leader, I didn't hurt the guy, I could do what I wanted.' And one of the lawyers says to me, 'I don't think you understand what Greenpeace is all about.' And I said, 'Well shit, I'm one of the founders of this organization, and you, who I don't even know, a goddamned lawyer, is telling me I don't know what this organization is all about! Who needs this organization!?'"[12]

None of the Greenpeace founders remain as directors. Watson says that today the "Warriors of the Rainbow" are little more than money-grubbing, publicity-grabbing hypocrites self-victimized by size and inertia. "They're nothing but the Avon ladies of the environmental movement," he says, "knocking on every door asking for handouts. I find the whole thing rather demeaning. They're just an example of eco-corporations, eco-business." He complains that Greenpeace has raised "three or four million dollars to stop the killing of pilot whales in the Faroe islands, yet never goes there."[13] In 1985 and 1986, the Sea Shepherds sailed to the tiny Danish protectorate in the North Atlantic, which has one of the highest standards of living in the world. Both years the Sea Shepherds dropped anchor in the port of Torshavn, the capitol city. Their mere presence put a halt to a macabre massacre of the docile whales, during which islanders use small boats to encircle migrating schools of the pilots, which at adulthood grow to ten or fifteen feet in length. The Faroese whalers pound the water, driving the whales toward shore, where they become disoriented and beach themselves.

Then the islanders use machetes to cut the whales' spinal cords. For up to ten minutes the whales struggle fitfully, crying out in high-pitched voices before they succumb to the blows. The islanders, all men and boys, stand by and smile, joke, and drink as the water around them turns crimson with the carnage. Only a small portion of the meat from the whale kills is consumed by the Faroese. Watson asserts that the reason Greenpeace can't go there is Greenpeace Denmark supports it as an aboriginal hunt. This appears to be a misunderstanding. Greenpeace U.S.A. spokesperson Peter Dykstra replied to Watson's accusations by saying that Greenpeace Denmark has never considered the Faroese hunt aboriginal, and thus permissible. He says a newspaper report misconstrued the remarks of a Greenpeace representative in the Faroes, leading to the confusion regarding the organization's official position on the hunt.[14]

Greenpeace, Watson says, is a tidal wave in the environmental movement, so large that the Sea Shepherds are often swamped by it. He explains that "almost every time Sea Shepherd gets involved in a campaign, everybody and his dog is out there making money off of it. When we were out there protecting pilot whales, the Humane Society, Greenpeace, and about a dozen other organizations were sending out direct mail, making money....Now, it's the tuna/dolphin issue. We're the only organization to have confronted these guys out there, the only ones to have hunted them down, the only ones who even know where they are," yet Greenpeace and those who do not employ direct action get rich off of the issue. "Those people are just as bad as the whalers and sealers themselves. In fact, one sealer once referred to Greenpeace as the highest paid sealers of them all because they make a *business* of saving seals. So long as the seal hunt is going on, they're getting paid." Nor is there any turning back for Greenpeace. "It's gone now," Watson says. "They've got the 'Gang of Ten.' It should be the 'Gang of Eleven.' No. It's a corporation. As Bob Hunter said, 'Nothing could be done to stop it from growing. It'll keep growing and growing, a juggernaut that is out of control.'"[15]

For a time it appeared that a high seas rivalry would develop between the two marine environmental groups. In 1981 Sea Shepherd brought back evidence of illegal whaling activities from Siberia. No one was hurt in the dramatic action that entailed piloting a Zodiac within yards of Soviet soil. Despite a chase, the Red Navy was faced down by Captain Watson. The photos the Sea Shepherds brought back showed non-aboriginal Siberians skinning whales ostensibly killed in an aboriginal hunt. More telling were the rows of cages like those used to house minks or foxes that lined the background. The little village of Loren was a fur farm, not a native Siberian encampment. Inexplicably, except for the potential of publicity, Greenpeace "duplicated the campaign in 1983," Watson says, "ignoring the fact that we had already gotten the information. They went and had a couple of people with broken bones and seven people arrested." The arrests made newspapers worldwide.[16]

Another, albeit humorous, source of smoldering anger for Watson is "Operation Asshole," which Greenpeace rejected as soon as it was proposed. It seems that in 1977 Watson and Ross Thornwood, an eco-radical from Hawaii, cooked up the idea of purchasing a ship called the *Ohana Kai*, a "piece of crap" Watson calls it, from Greenpeace Hawaii. It had been used in only one Greenpeace campaign and was about to be sold at a tremendous loss after $350,000 was spent on repairs. Thornwood and Watson wanted to buy it for $1. Then, Watson says, they would "take the *Ohana Kai* out and ram it full speed right up the rear slipway of the *Dalniy Vostok*, the Soviet whale processing ship, and wedge it in there so tightly they would have to go back to Vladivostok and pull it out." Watson sighs. "It would have been a great campaign." Greenpeace dismissed the idea out of hand.[17]

Watson's criticism of Greenpeace is somewhat misplaced, ignoring as he does the organization's continuing impact on a widening range of environmental problems. There is little question, though, that as radical environmental philosophy and tactics have evolved, Greenpeace has been left behind. As such, conflicts between the Sea Shepherds and Greenpeace continue: Greenpeace led an ultimately successful boycott against Icelandic fish products to protest that nation's whaling policy, and some of its activists even stalled the off-loading of Icelandic fish from a freighter to publicize the issue; the Sea Shepherds' approach was to sink half of the Icelandic whaling fleet. The story is told in Chapter Eleven.

Message for the Media

One thing Watson has borrowed from Greenpeace is its flair for dramatic, news-catching actions. That is not the only reason for direct action, any more than an Earth First! tree-sit exists only to get air time. But no confrontation is planned without considering press play. The early Greenpeacers became masters at this game, deeply influenced as they were by fellow Canadian Marshall McLuhan's aphorism, "The medium is the message." They recognized that the mass media, especially television, held immense possibilities for reaching large numbers of people and for affecting them to degrees inconceivable a generation before. Watson quotes Bob Hunter, who masterminded the early Greenpeace media-based campaigns, as saying, "'When you do an action it goes through the camera and into the minds of millions of people. The things that were previously out of sight and out of mind now become commonplace. Therefore, you use the media as a weapon.'"[18] The media wants the sensational, so Watson figures why not give them what they want. "For instance, one of the things we do is dramatic confrontation," he says, echoing David Brower and Mike Roselle. "The more dramatic you can make it, the more controversial it is, the more publicity you will get. If you've got film of it, all the better. The drama translates into exposure. Then you tie the message into that exposure and fire it into the brains of millions of people in the process. Hunter said one time, 'If it's stupid tactics that are required to do it, then stupid tactics are what we're going to do, whether it's spraying seals with dye or whatever.' That's what they're going to pay attention to."[19]

No Compromise and Negotiating

Few in the environmental movement take the no compromise stance farther than the Sea Shepherds. Like their cousins in Earth First!, the Sea Shepherds stand firm for their principles when they go to sea. And like Earth First!, the Sea Shepherds acknowledge the value of having a spectrum of environmental groups. Sea Shepherd President Scott Trimingham says, "Our negotiating strategy is that you don't negotiate. When you don't negotiate you tend to get a little bit more than if you compromise. [It puts others] in a position of saying, 'Well, you can deal with these Sea Shepherd people who won't negotiate with you. But why don't you deal with us. We seem to be more reasonable.' That gives them a chance to get some other things accomplished."[20]

Although the Sea Shepherds are handicapped by being able to sail for only a short time each year, they command considerable respect among their adversaries because of their methods. For example, in 1987 the Sea Shepherds chased Japanese drift net fishing boats from Alaskan waters midway through the fishing season without ever seeing a Japanese vessel. The forty-mile-long gill nets used by drift netters kill uncounted sea creatures incidental to the intended species.

As confrontational as the Sea Shepherds are, however, they have shown that "no compromise" does not rule out negotiating. In 1982 Watson brought his version of gunboat diplomacy to bear on the problem of the annual killing of dolphins by fishermen at Iki Island in Japan. Wielding the club of intimidation (his ship) and the calm of a diplomat—is one really that much different from another?—Watson successfully ended the slaughter.

Intimidation was his weapon in 1985 and 1986 in the Faroe Islands as well. Rod Coronado, who sailed on both of those voyages, recalls that in 1985 the Greenpeace vessel *Sirius* was already in the Faroes when the Sea Shepherds arrived, but that there had been no halt to the whaling. "When we arrived, we immediately saw the police put the emphasis on the Sea Shepherds as far as fearing for the whaling," Coronado says. "They put a ban on the whaling while we were there. The ships did not leave port. There was a 24-hour guard on the whaling vessels and on our ship, and every day there were divers going down and checking for bombs under the hull" of each small whaling boat.[21] The first trip resulted in a written agreement that no more whales would be killed in 1985. Over the authorities' objections, the islanders took up the slaughter again within weeks. The following year the Sea Shepherds returned, prepared to put their bodies between the islanders and the whales. Several crew members were arrested when they went ashore, and the Faroese police later assaulted the ship in an unsuccessful attempt to chase the environmentalists from their waters.

Gandhi's High Seas Prophet

Watson was labeled a "one-man vigilante squad" for taking the wooden club out of the sealer's hand in 1977 and tossing it into the water off Newfoundland.[22] At that time it was a label he resented; today he accepts it. To Watson, the oceans are like the Old West: an amoral anarchy pervades even though laws exist. It is time for citizens of the planet to take the law into their own hands, Watson says, and the Sea Shepherds are ready to do the job. "We would welcome an enforcement agency" to uphold regulations intended to save the lives of whales, dolphins, and other marine mammals, Watson says, "but nobody is there and the law exists, so therefore *the law must be enforced*. And that's what Sea Shepherd is. We are a policing body, but because we are self-appointed I guess we could qualify as vigilantes."[23]

There is none of the chaos one might expect from such talk, however. Watson demands that all of his crew abide by five rules derived from Gandhi's principles of non-violence: "One is that we don't use firearms. Two, we don't utilize explosives. Three, we don't take any action where there is the possibility of injury to somebody. Four, we accept responsibility for what we do. And, five, we accept whatever moral or legal consequences will befall." This code has been put to the test on numerous occasions. Watson and members of his crew have been shot at, tear gassed, beaten, threatened, insulted, and called terrorists as they practice what Watson claims Mahatma Gandhi referred to as *negative ahisma*. "Positive ahisma," says Watson, "is non-violence which includes not attacking property. Negative ahisma, which [Gandhi] says is just as acceptable, is a form of the practice of non-violence that will include property destruction. Although he said that there might be hardship or suffering caused to the owner of that property, if the objective in destroying that property is to save lives, then it takes precedence over any hardship which the owner of that property would recognize."[24]

Watson's reading of Gandhi is unconventional, to say the least, given Gandhi's position that property destruction is sabotage and is therefore unacceptable as a means of nonviolent protest. *Negative ahisma*—or negative non-violence—is merely harmlessness toward an opponent. *Ahisma's* positive, or "active" side is based on love, Gandhi says.[25] Further, Watson differs from Gandhi in that the "lives" in question here are non-human. However, it is unlikely that Gandhi, an avid vegetarian and early disciple of animal rightist Henry Salt, would find offense in the ethical extension.[26] Watson obviously feels comfortable in using this moral basis for monkeywrenching, however strained it may be. "I think a lot of people misinterpret Gandhi. One time someone asked him if he were a pacifist. He said, 'I've never been a passive anything. I don't approve of pacifism.' He says non-violence is a tactic."[27]

The Sea Shepherds take more from Gandhi than just a commitment to non-violence (as they define it). They live his vow of poverty as well. Unlike Earth First!, the Sea Shepherd Conservation Society was originally incorporated, in Canada, and then in the U.S. Their formal membership numbers 15,000 and is slowly growing. For the first time their annual budget topped $500,000 in 1989, but in the same year they were forced to sell one of their two ships, the *Divine Wind* (the English translation of "kamikaze"), leaving only the *Sea Shepherd II*, the 185-foot, 657-ton vessel which replaced the ship scuttled in Portugal. All membership dues and other revenues go to support the campaigns, and nothing is left over. "For the first several years, and 1980 in particular, we existed on *nothing*," says Scott Trimingham. He adds that "Sea Shepherd is an experiment, like our strategies. We're pushing the limits on what we can do out there, how far we can go and the changes we can effect. Organizationally, too, we're an experiment. We're the largest [environmental] group that is still all volunteer and non-bureaucratic."[28] Trimingham holds down the Sea Shepherd office, located in the basement of his home, and operates the group's marine mammal hot line to assist seals and whales caught in nets or otherwise in trouble in Southern California. He, Watson, East Coast liaison Ben White, and Peter Brown comprise the board of directors and decide which campaigns should be undertaken.

On Board the Sea Shepherd

Perhaps the most glaring evidence of the Sea Shepherd's poverty is that Watson is, in effect, a captain without a ship for much of the year. There simply is not enough money coming into the Sea Shepherd coffers for non-stop, or even frequent, actions. This leaves Watson to fend for himself on the speech and lecture circuit for month after month to make ends meet before finally taking to the warpath once more. When the Sea Shepherds return to sea, their adventures rival the best of Conrad or London. Rod Coronado, Myra Finkelstein, and Sue Rodriguez-Pastor, among those who have sailed with Watson, have much to tell about life as shepherds of the sea. All three are in their early twenties. Finkelstein and Coronado grew up on opposite ends of the same California county, although they did not meet one another until they began crewing together on the *Sea Shepherd II*. Rodriguez-Pastor spent her childhood in Peru and met Finkelstein while both were attending the University of California at Davis. They soon became close friends and took an active role in an Earth First! campaign to halt mountain lion hunting in California. When the women saw Watson speak in 1986 they both felt attracted to the message of non-violent direct confrontation promoted by the Sea Shepherds.

All three sailed with Watson on the 1987 expedition that chased the Japanese drift netters from Alaskan waters; Coronado was already a veteran of several campaigns, including the commando raid on the Icelandic whaling fleet. Finkelstein says that when her parents heard she had volunteered to ship out as a cook with a group called the Sea Shepherds, they thought she had joined a cult. What she found, however, was a group of people who worked with a profound sense of purpose but with minimal control and direction, quite a feat for any sea-going vessel. Many crew members, including Coronado, consider themselves anarchists and resist authority. Their ideal vision of decision-making is through a consensus process, with everyone agreeing on a course of action. Such sentiments are quixotic, even on a boat captained by a tribalist. "As long as I've been on the ship, there has been the element of crew members that are disgusted with the lack of consensus," Coronado says. "I agree with them; I'd love to have consensus. But if we did, the ship would never leave port. There are a lot of people who come on the ship who feel they can make a worthwhile decision when in reality they haven't been on board long enough to know what's best. As much of an anarchist as I may be, when I went on the ship I realized that I had to work under a hierarchical structure. If I had ever had a problem, I would have left."[29]

Democracy does play an important role in the operation of the ship, however. From the outset the purpose behind each mission and the tactics that may be used are made clear, Finkelstein says. "Sea Shepherd doesn't hide anything from the crew members. They have a talk with everyone ahead of time and they say, 'This is what we're going to do, this is what it's going to be like and this is what you can expect. If we have a confrontation and we're going to get arrested, then you're going to get arrested. If you can't handle it, then you should get off the ship now.' No one is ever in the dark. You can always ask questions."[30]

To crew on a campaign those who are interested have to first earn their way on by chipping paint, raising funds, or taking care of other tasks. "We try to avoid having someone step on at the last minute," says Scott Trimingham. "Everybody is dirty and greasy and then this other person comes on who's going to share in the adventure but didn't share in any of the work."[31] The all-volunteer nature of their task lends a spirit to the crew that makes much of the preparation almost enjoyable, despite the spartan conditions. Some volunteers stay for six months or more, some only for a day, but all seek out the Sea Shepherds on their own. Because of the frequent turnover, training is on-the-job.

Finkelstein was impressed by the single-mindedness of the crew from the moment she stepped on board. "Everyone is there because they believe in it," she says. "People are always asking, 'What can I do, what can I do?' You never have the problem of people saying, 'Well, they *told* me I had to do this.'"[32] Finkelstein, Rodriguez-Pastor, and schoolmate Renee Grandi volunteered as cooks for the 1987 trip to Alaska. During the month or so that the ship was in port in Seattle prior to sailing, they were responsible for scrounging up food each day from sympathetic local grocery stores. At first, begging for handouts did not come easily. But the women soon found that the Sea Shepherds were widely known and that many stores were eager to contribute. It is not an uncommon phenomenon. Rodriguez-Pastor tells a story of asking for contributions in a Key West bar while the group was preparing for its 1989 voyage to the Pacific. Four college students began querying her, and when she told them that she was sailing on a ship that was going to attempt to stop the slaughter of dolphins by tuna fleets, they took her tin can and panhandled for her.

Life aboard ship is a microcosm of society, or perhaps of the society that many eco-warriors hope to bring about. Most of the crew is vegetarian, many are vegan, and all share a deep commitment to the cause. "You're with twenty-seven people who feel as strongly as you do," says Finkelstein. "It's a wonderful feeling, a powerful feeling, because at sea you don't have the influences of other society. You only have your crew members. A strong family develops."[33] Tensions arise between individuals, Coronado says, but they can be displaced by something as simple as the sighting of dolphins off the bow. "Everyone rushes to the railing to get a look," he says, "and whatever bad feelings there might have been between people disappear pretty quickly."[34] The crew will take advantage of a mid-ocean stop caused by a problem with the engines, a frequent occurrence, to leap overboard en masse and swim with migrating turtles. At other times they play "Take away the Fire Hose" to keep cool on a hot summer day. Capt. Watson, on most voyages the largest of the crew, usually manages to win the game and douse all comers.

Unlike Greenpeace vessels, which lavish their crews with air conditioning and beer-stocked refrigerators, the Sea Shepherds find few creature comforts. While everyone eats three hardy meals every day, food restrictions are sometimes applied to keep nibblers from raiding the cupboard. Little things like hiding away an orange for a later date can lead to good-hearted bickering, as happened during a fruit shortage in the middle of the ocean when Coronado discovered citrus peels in a trash can and accosted cabin-mate Rodriguez-Pastor for not sharing. On one occasion weevils got into the ship's store of flour and had to be sifted out; the water supply sometimes takes on an unpleasant tint after harsh seas stir-up sediment in the rusty old tanks; and whenever crew members use the head they must fetch their own bucket of seawater to flush. The adversity is taken in stride, however. It is the cause, not the comfort, that keeps the crew going.

When the time comes to actually confront "the enemy," as Coronado calls the objects of the Sea Shepherds' wrath, the crew is tested as a team and as individuals. Rodriguez-Pastor says she had heard of the eighteen who left the *Sea Shepherd* in Portugal rather than sail out to sink the *Sierra*. "I was terrified of being one of the people who would jump off," she says, "so I wouldn't go on a Sea Shepherd campaign until I knew I was one of the ones who would stay on...and I was certain that I was ready to make that commitment, whether it was jail or loss of life or whatever." From her experience, not enough of the crew confronts themselves with the grave potentialities at the outset. "For too many people it is an impulse thing, 'Yeah! I want to go save the whales.' But it is something that takes a lot of consideration. Are you ready to lose your life for something that you believe in?"[35]

Defending the Dolphins

It became obvious that some crew members had not submitted to that sort of introspection when Watson decided to stage something of a repeat of his *Sierra* performance against a tuna boat in the summer of 1989. Several of the crew left the ship to fly home. But most remained and took part in a dramatic, if not entirely successful, action that exemplifies the excitement and the occasional disappointments inherent in shoestring environmentalism.

The Sea Shepherds went to the Eastern Tropical Pacific off of the Central American coast to look for tuna fishing fleets responsible for the decimation of dolphins in that region. For days Watson was unable to track down any tuna boats, as most skeptics had predicted. Finally, he got a break when the *Sea Shepherd II* pulled into the harbor at Puntarenas, Costa Rica. They discovered two Panamanian tuna fishing boats, the *Pan Pacific* and the *Seoul '88*. The Costa Rican authorities were holding the *Pan Pacific* because of some vague legal problem. Rodriguez-Pastor, who speaks fluent Spanish, went ashore with Coronado and approached skeptical Panamanian fishermen who mistook the activists' ship for a Greenpeace vessel. The Sea Shepherd crew members calmed the Panamanians by claiming that they were merely recording whale sounds as they made their way up the coast. Rodriguez-Pastor and Coronado were promptly befriended by their unwary adversaries, who talked with considerable openness about fishing for tuna using dolphins.

The Sea Shepherds were fighting the practice of "setting" nets on dolphins. Eco-activist Sam LaBudde chronicled the carnage inherent in this process on film, and his shocking footage was aired throughout the nation. In an *Atlantic* magazine article that retells LaBudde's exploits, Kenneth Brower explained how the dolphins' fate became tied to that of yellowfin tuna. Several species of dolphins swim with yellowfin, and for millennia anglers who would catch the fish that swim below have used the cetaceans as markers. About thirty years ago the age-old and effective practice of fishing for tuna with rod, line, and an unbaited but shiny hook gave rise to technology more appropriate to the destructiveness of the twentieth century. This method, purse-seining, employs mile-long nets. One edge of the net is weighted to sink, the other has floats. A small, fast boat called a "panga" pulls out—or "sets"—net from the ship, arcing around to encircle the tuna-covering dolphins. "Seal bombs" are thrown from the panga boat to herd the dolphins (and the tuna) toward the center of the net; the explosions damage the dolphins' sensitive sonar in their foreheads to the point where they are essentially "blind." After the net is played out into a complete circle, the bottom edge is pulled closed, creating a massive cone through which no marketable yellowfin tuna can swim. Nor can any dolphin. The ship then draws in the net. Despite precautions and prohibitions meant to limit injury to dolphins, they frequently are caught in the net and dragged upward toward a "power block" through which the net is hauled. There the lucky ones are crushed to death; the unlucky fall to the deck of the ship twitching and are shoved down a slipway into the jaws of sharks that inevitably follow the death boats.[36] Between 250,000 and a half-million dolphins die this way each year. Purse-seining has reduced the numbers of some species to the verge of extinction.

When Rodriguez-Pastor and Coronado told Watson that the Panamanians were planning to sneak out of port, the Sea Shepherd crew held a meeting and agreed that the best course of action would be to detain the Panamanian vessel in their own vigilante style and then request a meeting to gather information on the location of other tuna boats. It was likely to be their best and only chance to find working tuna boats. At 5 p.m. on a July evening, Finkelstein and two other female crew members steered a Zodiac alongside the Panamanian ship and chained themselves to the anchor line. "We used women because we figured the Panamanian crew members would have less hostility toward women chained to their anchor," Finkelstein explained. "Some people might have a problem with that, but you have to figure that if you're going to get yourself in a situation, you try to make it as safe as possible. We had a Zodiac with our crew members and press people filming us the whole time, so it wasn't like they just left us there."[37] Still, the Panamanians cursed and threw things, including a seal bomb that landed twenty feet away from the women and made a deafening explosion the likes of which Finkelstein had never heard. The Panamanian crew soon realized, however, that hostility was not going to get their anchor out of the water, and they began offering the women hot coffee.

In the meantime, Watson, Rodriguez-Pastor, and Ben White asked to meet with the Panamanian ship's captain. Doubtless eager to rid himself of the albatross on his anchor chain, the captain graciously agreed and invited them aboard. Rodriguez-Pastor translated. The captain showed the environmentalists the records of his catches. He, like many others with whom the Sea Shepherds spoke, admitted that the unbridled killing of the dolphins troubled him. Whether he was merely humoring them was of little importance. What mattered was the information he was able to share regarding the location of tuna fleets off the Costa Rican coast. Late in the evening the protest was ended.

The *Sea Shepherd II* left the next day. Even with the tuna boat captain's information, the hunting was frustrating. For nine days they searched in vain for tuna boats. Then, as Watson was preparing to head the ship home, the crew came upon a lone Mexican boat floating as lifeless as the *Sierra* had been on that fateful day a decade before. His crew knew what they were in for; after Puntarenas it was clear Watson wanted to put the fear of the Sea Shepherds in the tuna industry's heart the best way he knew how. According to Rodriguez-Pastor, Watson wanted to set an example, not just stand back and watch as the carnage continued. "Any ramifications which might come from hitting a boat," she says, "would be offset by how much more we could do by letting them know we are serious and that there is not much they can do once we find them."[38] It was five in the morning, near dawn, and the *Sea Shepherd II* was quickly noticed by the *Gloria Hortensia*. Watson hailed the boat and chatted with its biologist, required by the Inter-Tropical Tuna Association to accompany the ship. He said he had recorded the deaths of 100 dolphins in the time they had been fishing. Watson was ill-impressed.

After circling and taking a few photographs of the still lounging ship, Watson took aim at the small panga boat tethered to the *Gloria Hortensia*. Without it, the tuna boat could no longer fish. The ships were in open waters, outside of any nation's jurisdiction, so property destruction was unlikely to pose much of a serious legal risk, not that that mattered much to Watson. "If he felt it was in the best interest of the dolphins," Rodriguez-Pastor says, Watson "would ram that ship even if he had a mutiny on his hands."[39] The *Sea Shepherd II* steamed closer and closer, until the Panamanians realized what was about to happen. Then a crewmember jumped into the panga boat seconds before its certain destruction. Watson threw the wheel around to avoid hitting the skiff and thereby injuring the sailor. By the time Watson was able to turn and prepare for another pass, the speedier fishing boat was under way.

Several frustrating, fruitless days followed that missed opportunity. But the word was out. Each time the Sea Shepherds got close, making nine or nine and a-half knots, the tuna boats would speed off almost twice as fast. The Sea Shepherd crew took this as a measure of the campaign's success. "We were the first boat to have ever gone out there and tried to confront the tuna fishing boats," Finkelstein says. "There has never been another marine mammal boat that has done that. I think that has an effect." In addition, the trip was something of a research effort. Finkelstein says, "We gathered a lot of information to go on" when Sea Shepherd returns to the tuna fishing grounds. "I think it was successful in the sense that anytime you go out there and do something it is successful. It is a shame, you wish your boat was faster. But you can't always look at it like, 'Well, I wish this was that way.' You have to say, 'This is what we did.' Everyone tried to do their best. It wasn't like we didn't try to chase them."[40]

Terror on the High Seas?

"Negative ahisma" is not the most common term for chasing down and ramming ships, of course. Governments, industries, and other environmental groups worldwide call the Sea Shepherds' tactics "terrorism." Watson scoffs at such accusations. "What is a 'terrorist?'" he asks. "Someone who disagrees with you, usually. Terrorism is a tactic applied by disenfranchised, under-equipped poor people against superior odds. When the Israeli Air Force bombs a Palestinian village in Jordan it's considered 'war,' but when the Palestinians blow up a school bus in Israel it's considered 'terrorism.' What's the difference? Children are dying!" Watson notes that when the Greenpeace ship *Rainbow Warrior* was sunk by French commandos, no one called it the work of terrorists. "Mrs. Thatcher said, when a Labor M.P. brought it up, 'It's none of our concern.' When the Member of Parliament said, 'Well, it's a British ship with a British flag and a British captain and a British crew in a British Commonwealth harbor sunk by the French government,' she said, *'It is none of our concern.'*[41] Such reactions exemplify the hypocrisy commonplace within the statist system, Watson says.

He turns the terrorism argument on its head, as do Earth First!ers and Animal Liberators. "I'm not too concerned about what those people have to say," Watson says. He admits to being "terra-istic. The Latin translation for that is *terra*, the Earth, -istic...of the Earth! Yeah, we'll agree with that. But the fact is that no other group, like the Palestinians or what have you, operates under the five [non-violence] guidelines that we operate under." Watson adds, "You can't be too concerned with what people call you and you can't be too concerned about people's attitudes. All you can do is be true to yourself: you don't kill anybody, you don't injure anybody, you do everything you can to save as many lives and as much habitat as you possibly can. If you do that, then you're doing the right thing."[42]

CHAPTER 7

ANIMAL LIBERATION: FROM LABS TO HUNT SABS

The first good storm of the 1989-1990 wet season had drenched the rugged Cache Creek wilderness west of Sacramento, California, making the hiking difficult for Rufus Cohen and his accomplice. They were hunting, but their quarry was not animal game. They were searching for signs of other hunters, specifically, the fifteen holders of permits for California's first Tule elk hunt. Cohen, a lanky, lightly-bearded Earth First!er whose progress toward an environmental studies degree had been slowed considerably by his activism, was operating in the grayest area between Earth First! and Animal Liberation—that of a hunt saboteur. Slipping and sliding up and down steep mountainsides to protect animals and to preserve the integrity of wilderness was not new to him. With other Earth First!ers and Animal Liberators, he had sabotaged many such hunts in actions appropriately called "hunt sabs." For two years now he had been attempting to stop trophy hunters from killing the rare Nelson bighorn sheep, which lived in the rugged desert mountains of Southern California.

State fish and game officials throughout the nation assert that only by hunting animals can their populations be balanced with the surrounding habitat. But Cohen did not accept the state's position regarding the Tule elk, nor did the ragtag group of fifteen punk culture Animal Liberators, anarchists, and others who were spread over the 300-square-mile hunt area. They found it difficult to believe that any benefit could come from killing members of a species whose numbers once ran in the millions, but which now was on the brink of the United Nations' definition of "endangered"— under 2,000 members. Cohen believed that the true purpose of the hunt was for the enjoyment of trophy hunters. He knew that the grizzly bear, which had been the primary natural predator of the stately brown deer for millennia, had been killed off nearly a century ago, and that the elks' favorite habitat, shallow marshland, was gone as well, drained and turned into farms and subdivisions. With the state unwilling to re-introduce the big bears or to find suitable habitat for the elk, trophy hunting was a handy way to keep the elk's population in check.

On that muddy day, Cohen and company never spotted a hunter. But by the end of the three week long hunt, fewer than half of those who had come to kill drove home with an elk head in the back seat. On several occasions the hunt saboteurs successfully evaded a bevy of federal and state game wardens, following hunters until they were prepared to fire on an elk. Then, with a shrieking blast from their Coast Guard-approved air horns, the saboteurs frightened away the hunters' target.

Like nearly all radical environmental protests, there was little hope that blaring air horns would solve the greater problem, which, as Cohen and the others saw it, was that in killing elk the hunters were in fact killing other living beings. When asked what good he hoped the hunt saboteurs would do, Cohen replied, "It's hard to let one of these things happen and not do something. It's a matter of conscience for me and a lot of other people, getting the practice and doing what we can for the animals."[1] But even then he acknowledged that the most he and the other hunt saboteurs could do was to act as "an irritant."

A Part of the Big Picture

Similarly, the best that most eco-warriors can realistically hope to accomplish is pricking society's conscience. Nowhere is this truer than in the area of Animal Liberation.*

Few of us give a second thought to using animals for food, clothing, and other purposes. Vast industries have built up around what Animal Liberators see as the "exploitation" of non-human animals. Experiments on animals for medical research, consumer products, and the like annually kill 100 million or more rabbits, rats, cats, dogs, monkeys, guinea pigs, horses, goats—almost any non-human animal that a researcher might want to use. And that number is small compared to the estimated *six billion* animals killed for human consumption every year.

Because of society's dependency on other animals, the actions of Animal Liberators challenge the Eco-Wall within each of us more directly than the other branches of the radical environmental movement. Hunting, for example, is one of America's favorite "recreational" pursuits. Moreover, Animal Liberators ask us to forego the animal-based mode of our medicine,

---

NOTE: A word about terminology: distinctions can be made within the animal activism movement between "Animal Welfare organizations," which advocate better treatment of animals that humans use; "Animal Rightists," which may be grassroots in orientation and involve a level of non-passive activism, such as picketing to protest human uses of animals; and "Animal Liberators," who may engage in legal and illegal protests against using animals for human ends. To simplify terminology, "Animal Liberators" and "Animal Liberation" are used exclusively here to refer to those who differ with Animal Welfare advocates in their methods and beliefs. This terminology also reflects a trend in the movement away from the use of "rights" language and toward "liberation."

without which, we have been told, treatments and cures for everything from smallpox to insomnia would have been impossible. Advocates for non-human animals also confront us with the environmental effects of eating meat and the suffering inherent in raising animals for food and clothing. And they call our attention to the lives of animals used for our entertainment in zoos, movies, rodeos, and elsewhere.

Although animal rights and animal liberation *philosophers* argue with other environmental philosophers about whether it is more important to save individual animals or entire species, *activists* within the radical environmental movement increasingly stress the commonalities between the two and the need to do both. For them, Animal Liberation is a vital part of a bigger environmental picture. Rick Bernardi, who participates in Earth First! activities and Animal Liberation protests, emphasizes the areas which overlap. "There are certain Animal Rights [Animal Liberation] issues that some Earth First!ers do not support—[not eating] meat, for example," Bernardi says. "But I don't see that there is any difference, really, between Earth First! and Animal Rights. I can't see them as different except that in general Animal Rights doesn't get into questions of preserving trees or rivers. Animal Rights is more focused on animals. If I have any critique of Animal Rights, it's just that. There is a whole world dying out there, [and] it's not just animals. I can say the same critique of Earth First! [that it does not address Animal Liberation issues]. . . .There is a perception that there are two different movements, and essentially there are. But I don't see them as separate."[2]

Activists in both the Animal Liberation and Earth First! movements share a concern for the integrity of wild places and of non-human beings. The philosophical assertion that only "sentient beings," animals somewhere above an oyster on some pain/pleasure scale, deserve any sort of "rights" matters little to Bernardi and most other Animal Liberation activists.[3] They emphasize what they see as the gross wrongs being perpetrated by humans on others, acts which violate the inherent worth of each animal. Radical animal activists speak of eliminating suffering and cruelty, but the ultimate reasons for their doing so are centered on respect for the integrity of other life forms, their inherent freedom to live their lives fully, unfettered by humans. Rufus Cohen speaks to this point, saying, "I see Animal Rights as a symbolic, urban manifestation of deep ecology. It is just as vital....They are recognizing a right to life of something other than humanity. Take an Animal Rights activist out into the wilderness and click, click, click, the connections start happening."[4]

Bernardi and Cohen are among the newest of the eco-warriors, young activists who easily move between movements that the mainstream—and even some of the early radicals—find difficult to bridge. They share a wholistic vision, not one that emphasizes only a single issue or a group of concerns. The ground they have to cover is thus far larger, a fact reflected by the partially-completed college degrees and the fully-depleted bank accounts common to young activists.

Making the Connections

While Earth First!ers and the Sea Shepherds venture to distant wilderness and the deepest oceans to protect the wild, Animal Liberators often wage their struggle in the places farthest from untrammeled deserts and unscathed seas. Animal Liberators' concerns fall into four categories: vivisection, animals in agriculture, hunting/trapping, and animals in entertainment. As such, they go to the stark concrete bunkers of animal testing laboratories, fur breeders' steel cages, and chicken warehouses, where the stench is overwhelming and the conditions utterly cruel. Profound ecological connections exist in Animal Liberators' efforts to end such cruelty and suffering.

This is especially true in regards to animal agriculture. In *Diet for a New America,* John Robbins notes that Americans' taste for animals—six billion are consumed in this country every year—has led to extensive environmental damage.[5] While the environmental community has focused the world's attention on the destruction of Amazonian rainforests to create pasture land, it fails to acknowledge that deforestation in North America continues for the same reasons, unabated since the first Europeans arrived here nearly three hundred years ago. In addition, the runoff from livestock excrement is polluting streams, causing irreparable environmental damage in the delicate biosphere of the Florida Everglades, and depleting the ozone through the release of methane.

Animal experimentation also causes many real and potential affronts to ecosystems. For example, chimpanzees and other animals threatened with extinction are taken from their native jungles for experiments. Animal Liberators are also concerned that genetically engineered laboratory animals might someday be released into the environment, affecting the gene pools of their "parent" species in unknown ways. Some also speak of the potential ripple effects caused by a genetically-engineered "monster" finding its way into the wild (the same may be said about plants which have been tampered with). Animals used in zoos, movies, and circus sideshows, never see their native habitat; ethically, say the Animal Liberators, humans have no basis for denying other animals a full life in the habitats where they have evolved. These connections between captive animals and environmental abuse go to the core of today's ecological ills and provide some of the best examples of the enormity and complexity of the Eco-Wall.

Animal Liberation Emergent

The Animal Liberation movement emerged in the U.S. in the mid-1970s. At that time, a New York activist named Henry Spira was attempting to build bridges between the traditional Animal Welfare movement and Animal Liberation philosophy. Animal Welfare organizations, such as the Humane Society of the United States, the Society for the Prevention of Cruelty to Animals, and the American Humane Society, had argued for a century or more in favor of animal protection laws and for more "humane" treatment of laboratory animals. Like today's Group of Ten mainstream environmental organizations, they worked exclusively within the parameters of the law and through the political process. But Spira felt that the Animal Welfare groups were not coming down hard enough on the vivisectors, scientists and others who conducted experiments with animals. What prompted him to action was Peter Singer's popular book, *Animal Liberation*.[6] Singer's utilitarian philosophy attracted Spira because it "did not depend on sentimentality, on the cuteness of the animals in question or their popularity as pets. To me he was saying simply that it is wrong to harm others, and as a matter of consistency we don't limit who the others are; if they can tell the difference between pain and pleasure, then they have the fundamental right not to be harmed."[7]

Spira wanted to do more than talk philosophy, however, and in 1976 he decided to act on his new found convictions that non-human animals have "rights" like the rest of us. His first target was New York City's American Museum of Natural History, which was conducting sex tests on deliberately brain-damaged cats. After male cats were operated on and their wounds allowed to heal, they were placed in a room with both a female cat and a female rabbit. The immediate object of the research was to see with which animal the male cat would attempt to copulate. When Spira informed Ed Koch about the experiments, the then-Congressman and future New York City Mayor demanded that the Museum explain the benefits society would reap from such government-funded tests; his answer was a blank stare.[8] Within a year the National Institutes of Health pulled funding from the Museum's research.

Having caught the public's attention, Spira went on to document the suffering and waste of life caused by the "Draize test" and "LD50" experiments. The Draize test was named for John H. Draize, who in 1944 invented a test to determine how different substances would affect humans' "skin and membranes."[9] The test, which was later adopted by the Food and Drug Administration, involves dripping the substance being tested into a rabbit's eyes, or even rubbing it onto male rabbits' penises. The rabbits are restrained so that they cannot rub their eyes or other body parts during the tests, which go on for days. The substance is repeatedly applied to see how severe the inflammation becomes. Although the Draize method has been used to test hundreds, even thousands, of products, including cosmetics, shampoos, and floor waxes, critics say the test tells little about how a substance will affect humans. They point out that rabbits' eyes and their penises differ substantially from humans'. Rabbits have a higher threshold of pain in their eyes, and thus are slower to wash away irritating substances. They also have three eyelids, which may further protect their eyes.

The LD50 test, which stands for "Lethal Dose, fifty percent," determines the dosage of a particular substance at which one-half of the animals tested die within a given time period. Neither the LD50 nor the Draize test is required by the federal government—others that do not involve the use of animals are acceptable. Companies use them only to protect themselves against lawsuits. And results from both the Draize test and the LD50 may produce misleading results because they are used on non-human animals. Spira successfully publicized these cruel and unnecessary experiments, and over a few short years his efforts informed the populace about the research establishment's abusive methods. However, his methods—thorough investigation of his target, picketing, and exposure through the mass media—were tame compared to what has followed since.

Liberating in the Land of Liberty

Someone once called Animal Liberation "mainstream," a timely and inevitable continuation of the civil rights and feminist movements.[10] It seems farfetched to put Animal Liberation on a level with those movements, however. "Mainstream" carries connotations of widespread acceptability and popularity, neither of which Animal Liberation has achieved, although it has attracted attention and support because it appears to be rapidly growing. The American Animal Liberation Front (ALF), closely patterned after a slightly older British movement of the same name, first surfaced three years after Spira brought the purposeless Museum of Natural History experiments to light. On March 14, 1979, activists emulating tactics that had been used successfully in Britain, and spirited away a cat, two dogs, and two guinea pigs used for research at the New York University Medical Center.

In scores of actions since then, the ALF and other Animal Liberation groups, such as the Band of Mercy, True Friends, Last Chance for Animals, and the Animal Rights Militia, have exposed and ended what they see as atrocities being perpetrated on animals ostensibly for human "benefit" or "enjoyment." *Animals' Agenda* and *PETA News* regularly document horrifying animal abuse. Cover photographs may picture cats with circuitry implanted in their skulls, one eye dilated, the other not; a live turkey being manhandled by its wings on its way to the slaughterhouse and then to someone's holiday dinner table; or a drawing of a helpless lobster about to be thrown into a pot of boiling water with the headline, "Caring Not Who Suffers, but How. . .Even Lobsters!" The inside stories reveal the shocking variety of ways by which humans inflict pain on other animals.

ALF is perhaps best known for its frequent "liberations" of animals from research facilities—although it also acts against factory farms—and for its participation in hunt sabotages. It is a highly secretive movement that is dependent on sympathetic, visible groups to do the talking for it in the same way British ALF activists use other animal rights organizations in that country. One such American group is People for the Ethical Treatment of Animals (PETA), which was established by Alex Pacheco and Ingrid Newkirk in 1980. The year following the group's founding, Pacheco, then twenty-three, infiltrated the Institute for Behavioral Research in Silver Spring, Maryland, in hopes of discovering what vivisection was all about. There the veteran of the Sea Shepherds' hunt for the *Sierra* gathered material for almost four months on sadistic tests on monkeys before taking the evidence to five respected experts. They confirmed that the experiments, such as the "acute noxious stimuli test," wherein a surgical clamp set to its highest tension was used to pinch a monkey's skin, had no scientific value. The case is now known as "Silver Spring Monkeys" for the seventeen primates Pacheco rescued.[11]

PETA's relationship with the ALF exemplifies the mutually-supportive mix of organization/bureaucracy and decentralization/anarchy within the Animal Liberation movement. PETA, with a membership that numbers 240,000 and is growing by 40,000 to 50,000 every year, reflects the growing interest in animal rights; an estimated two million people are involved in as many as 10,000 local Animal Liberation groups across the country. In 1987 PETA's budget was about $2 million; by 1989 it was nearly $7 million. Employment at its suburban Washington, D.C., headquarters over the same time was up from thirty to sixty, and two receptionists are needed to handle the hundreds of calls coming into the organization every day.

There is little doubt about the group's radicalism, tempered though it is with a huge helping of mainstream-like organization. That it is a mouthpiece for ALF is only one piece of the evidence. PETA also operates its own aggressive research and investigation unit that analyzes and publicizes the information gained from activists who infiltrate vivisectors' laboratories and obtain information substantiating allegations of abuse. Their "Animal Rights 101" course visits dozens of cities each year, instructing newcomers to the movement about the myriad cruelties inflicted upon animals and what they can do in their areas to stop vivisection, factory farming, and other sources of animal suffering. Most telling, however, are PETA's boycotts against companies involved in animal testing. Due to a PETA boycott of their products, Avon, Revlon, and clothing manufacturer Benetton quit testing their products on animals; the group is continuing its campaign against Gillette, Cosmair (parent company of L'Oreal and Lancome), Amway, Noxell, and Mary Kay.

In Defense of Animals (IDA) has also supported Animal Liberators, especially those in California. Established by veterinarian Elliot Katz in 1983, IDA's membership now exceeds 50,000. Katz had owned a large, lucrative veterinary practice in Brooklyn and on Long Island before moving to Big Sur, where he became a guerrilla veterinarian, treating animals without a license and receiving vegetables or other goods as payment. Eventually, his veterinary contacts led him to the University of California at Berkeley, where faculty members told him of the "extreme negligence and cruelty" in animal testing laboratories there.[12] Those abuses prompted Katz and IDA to file lawsuits and to appeal environmental impact reports, both of which were common tactics among mainstream "environmental" groups but were unheard of within the Animal Welfare community. Katz says that today "a major thorn in [the research establishment's] side is how animal advocates work with environmental laws and EIRs to slow down their projects and to cost them."[13]

Although IDA continues to use lawful tactics to slow the animal research machine, its members also undertake civil disobedience—Katz has been arrested a dozen or more times—and it has served as the primary support group for several highly visible actions, including the week-long occupation of a sixteen-story crane being used to construct an animal experimentation and germ warfare laboratory at Berkeley (see Chapter Twelve).

The Issues and the Actions

Vivisection

According to PETA, Animal Liberators have pursued their campaign against animal experimentation, the use of animals for food and clothing, hunting, and in entertainment in numerous ways. They have broken into laboratories, vandalized slaughterhouses, smashed furriers' storefront windows, and otherwise conducted at least eighty actions or groups of actions since 1979, not including hunt sabotages;[14] activists say that many more incidents have taken place than were reported to PETA. Most of the energy in these actions has been directed against vivisection.

Animal experimentation's history goes back hundreds, perhaps thousands of years. It was used early in the "Age of Reason" to study the workings of living bodies, and it was to renowned philosopher Rene' Descartes that the first modern vivisectors looked for justification of their research; he obliged them by stating confidently that animals felt no pain.[15] But it wasn't until the last half of the nineteenth century that anti-vivisection activism emerged in response to the growing use of animals for experimentation. Eco-feminist philosopher and Animal Liberation activist Marti Kheel comments on the construction of the Eco-Wall for purposes of vivisection, observing that "a century ago researchers brought the animals they experimented on into their homes and performed their experiments in basements." In those early days of modern vivisection, neighbors reacted in horror to the animals' cries of agony, as did many well-known literary figures of the time, who demanded a stop to the torture. "For many people it was a religious matter—harming God's creatures and desecrating the 'temples of science,'" Kheel adds. "Some considered it a form of black magic...In those days, there was a sense that science was a sacred activity. But the researchers themselves had not achieved the status of gods [as they have today], and they could be criticized for desecrating the temples of science. That's exactly how the people at that time talked about it."[16]

Women were in the vanguard of the earliest modern opponents of animal experimentation, including feminist Frances Cobbe and Anna Kingsford, who spoke out against vivisection in the late 1800s. Kingsford, a vegetarian, "was one of the first women to attend medical school," Kheel notes. "She went there with the intention of proving that humans didn't need to eat meat to be healthy, and in order to chronicle the atrocities that were being perpetrated against animals for the purposes of research....She referred to her experience of seeing what was being done to the animals as 'a descent into a living hell.'"[17]

Beginning with the work of early advocates like Cobbe, Kingsford, Henry Salt, and others, Animal Welfare groups have struggled for more than 100 years to get laws on the books which ensure that the animals being experimented upon were properly fed, housed, and anesthetized. Mere reforms, though, are not enough for the Animal Liberators, who justify their actions against vivisectors in a number of ways. One is the anti-Cartesian argument that animals do, in fact, feel pain. The struggle of Animal Welfare groups for better care of animals are inadequate, say Animal Liberators. They believe that no animal should have to suffer in our attempts to eliminate disease in humans or to ascertain the safety of a household cleanser or eye shadow. Many Animal Liberators are motivated to take this no-compromise stand on animal suffering because they intuitively rebel at the oppression of animals, which, they believe, also includes removing animals from their natural habitats. As such, increasing numbers of anti-vivisection Animal Liberators emphasize the importance of biodiversity. They note the direct links between removing animals from their native environment for research purposes, such as AIDS experiments on chimpanzees, and reducing the biological diversity of some ecosystems.

A related concern is expressed by Rod Coronado, who is active in the Sea Shepherds, Earth First!, and the Animal Liberation movement. One of the first things that struck Coronado after he began educating himself about Animal Liberation issues "was that the main goal behind vivisection is to eliminate all diseases and all sickness in the human animal, as if it was totally unnatural to be ill and sick and to die. If we were to achieve that, you would see an incredible amount of environmental destruction."[18]

Animal Liberators also question the value of vivisection in promoting health care. Those in the movement say that their reading of scientific studies shows that animal research benefits humans minimally, if at all. "In Western society the reasons why our health has improved so much is not because of vivisection-based curative medicine," says PETA's executive director, Kim Stallwood, raising the most common and potentially most effective counter-argument to vivisection outside of ethical considerations. "It has to do with improved sanitation, water supply, housing, working conditions, things of those ilk. It is that which has improved our health. And this isn't an anti-vivisection treatise. If you look at books that discuss the history of medicine they will tell you this. What we have today are diseases of affluence that are brought about because of our lifestyle and because of the environment. If you want to cure cancer or heart disease or if you want to prevent AIDS, what you need to look at is the way we conduct ourselves, the way we live our lives, the ways that we abuse the environment."[19] And if the scientific basis for vivisection is found lacking, then it behooves us to stop the practice by whatever means necessary, Animal Liberators argue. The simplest is urging people to live lives that do not involve animal cruelty. Such "cruelty-free lifestyles" (explained in more depth in the following section) is a major concern of PETA.

University researchers in particular have received a great deal of attention from Animal Liberators.[20] Some allegedly have been the targets of death threats—in February 1990, a nationwide police alert was issued after Knoxville, Tennessee, authorities heard "'thirdhand'" that "militant Animal Rights advocates might be planning to kill a veterinary school dean each month for a year." The alert was prompted by the murder of the dean of the University of Tennessee Veterinary School outside of his home earlier in the month by an unknown assailant.[21] However, there is no evidence that any researcher has ever been physically assaulted or injured in eleven years of Animal Liberation activities in the U.S. Animal Liberators say they emphasize saving lives, not threatening them or taking them. Threatening the researchers' work, however, is another matter. That position was demonstrated in January 1990 when activists raided the office of University of Pennsylvania researcher Adrian Morrison. The break-in "marked the first time in over forty raids on animal research labs that the ALF had singled out an individual experimenter," wrote Jack Rosenberger in the *Village Voice.* "The group had been waiting for almost ten years to attack Adrian Morrison," who had long served as an apologist for experiments targeted by the ALF.[22]

More commonly, however, laboratories are raided to save the animals, not to threaten their tormentors. On Independence Day, 1989, for example, members of the Animal Liberation Front entered a Texas Tech University laboratory and freed five cats that had survived a series of grotesque experiments. While inside the lab, the activists caused approximately $70,000 worth of damage to physiologist John Orem's electronic equipment. Over the course of twelve years, Orem had received nearly $1 million in taxpayer-funded grants to study phenomena such as sleep deprivation on animals. One of his experiments involved forcing "cats to balance for twelve or more hours in darkness on small pedestals in fifty-gallon drums of water, into which they would fall if they went to sleep. He then forced them to run for three hours on a treadmill."[23] He also implanted electrodes into cats' skulls and diaphragms to monitor the animals.

To pull off the Texas Tech break-in two of the people involved said they carried out extensive reconnaissance missions weeks in advance. They had nothing but contempt for Orem. "John Orem is what we call a career vivisector," said one of the ALF members in *PETA News*. "That means he's typical of animal experimenters who make a handsome living mutilating animals with government funds." The cats were taken to a veterinarian as soon as they were removed from the lab. One had a respiratory infection, another had "peculiar stumps instead of legs," and a third "had a traumatic hernia the size of a Texas grapefruit" which was promptly removed. There was "no point" in alerting authorities to Orem's experiments, the Animal Liberators commented. "No law's being broken. The stark truth is the [federal] Animal Welfare Act doesn't even cover animals during actual experiments. No law does. Not one! Experimenters don't even have to use anesthesia, and frequently they don't. When you complain to the funding agencies, they defend *everything*."[24]

Less typical of American ALF actions against vivisectors is the 1987 arson attack on the Animal Diagnostic Laboratory, an animal experimentation center under construction at the University of California at Davis. The action caused $4.6 million worth of damages—the most ever inflicted by a radical environmental group. (One of the activists who participated in the arson explains the reasons behind the attack and how it was carried out in Chapter Thirteen). Many Animal Liberators have no more qualms about destroying property used by vivisectors than do monkeywrenchers when it comes to defending the forests or the seas. And, as is also true of their Earth First! and Sea Shepherd counterparts, they abide by the radical environmental credo of eschewing all violence toward any living being. In the case of the Davis arson, the activists took extensive precautions to ensure that no one would be injured by the attack.

Opponents of the ALF argue that animal experimentation is necessary for advances in human health care and that Animal Liberators indirectly threaten lives by setting back experiments. This is the basis for one of the "terrorist" arguments used against Animal Liberators. An article in the September 1989 issue of *Animals' Agenda* examined "The 'Terrorist' Label: How to Neutralize It." It featured the opinions of representatives from five major Animal Rights organizations, groups which do not openly support Animal Liberation activities. The response of Donald J. Barnes of the National Anti-Vivisection Society shows the difficulty that many people in the less militant Animal Rights movement have with disavowing Animal Liberation's use of property destruction. Barnes wrote, "'Terrorism' is defined in my dictionary as 'the systematic use of terror, violence, and intimidation to achieve an end.' One would be hard pressed, indeed, to find anything systematic about the Animal Liberation movement, particularly in our use of terror, violence, and intimidation. Lacking substantive justification for their exploitation of non-human animals, however, our opponents have seized upon the public's fear and abhorrence of international terrorism as a weapon to discredit our motives and philosophies." Barnes' sentiments reflect those of activists in the other branches of the movement when he states that "the real terrorists are those who cause, pain, suffering, and death to billions of non-human animals each year in the U.S." and that "the day will come when the public will, in effect, become the Animal Liberation Front by demanding access to the laboratories and, eventually, the freedom of the animals within."[25] Barnes argues that destruction of property only hardens vivisectors and that they might be turned around through gentler treatment.

Elliot Katz holds out little hope for widespread enlightenment among animal experimenters. What matters to him is prompt action. "I know those animals don't belong in there....In terms of doing illegal acts that would bring out the animals, bring out information, and bring out some of the documentation that shows what the realities are, I think it's the morally correct thing to do."[26]

Just as the debate over the value of civil disobedience and property destruction continues in Earth First!, so too is it a lively topic of disagreement within the Animal Liberation community. Rick Bernardi acknowledges this mixed response, saying, "There are people within the movement that will say, 'Great, they got the animals out of the laboratory." But when activists go farther, "Then there are people who will say, 'They shouldn't have gone in there and busted the lab up and burned it down because it just turns public opinion against us and makes it harder for us to do our job.' There is some support for what they are doing and there is also some opposition. It's like Earth First!. There are differences of opinion about how to do things."[27]

Marti Kheel feels that civil disobedience "has become a bare minimum that you can do. There's a yearly World Day for Laboratory Animals [typically in the third week of April]. I think that many people feel that it is no longer enough to just get out there with your picket signs—the media may or may not come. If you do civil disobedience, however, the chances are that they will come." Kheel expresses disappointment at the feeling of sameness in the actions from year to year. "It's not as significant as I'd like it to be....But it is certainly important that people are doing it. It does attract attention and it does get people to think, 'Oh, people are willing to get arrested for this. I wonder what that's about?'"[28]

Animal Liberators involved in anti-vivisection protests say they have scored numerous major victories on behalf of the animals through illegal activities. The University of Pennsylvania's Head Injury Clinic was broken into in 1984 and sixty hours of videotapes were stolen by ALF. The tapes showed improperly anesthetized baboons and monkeys being used for brutal skull-smashing experiments. The Clinic's funding was taken away and the head of the Clinic reportedly has not conducted further experiments. Federal funds for the City of Hope National Medical Center in California were also cut after evidence from another 1984 raid showed numerous improprieties. An arson attack in 1989 against a University of Arizona animal research laboratory caused $100,000 in damage to two buildings, and activists freed nearly 1,100 mice, rats, rabbits, guinea pigs, and frogs. Subsequently, the University was reported by some to have given up research on primates.

Activists say that their continued success in gaining entrance to labs has indirect benefits as well. Break-ins often breed suspicion among researchers, who feel that colleagues who do not engage in vivisection may be assisting Animal Liberators. Extraordinary security procedures, including guards, frequently changed door locks, and sophisticated surveillance systems are commonplace today at the labs. Eco-warriors credit themselves with forcing laboratories to divert funds from research to security measures. In addition, Animal Liberators assert that the use of such extreme precautions, together with vivisectors' consistent unwillingness to open their laboratories to public inspection, may well be evidence of continued abuse of animal welfare laws.

Animal-based Agriculture

Animal Liberators in general strongly object to the use of animals for food and clothing. They feel that the most effective means of remedying animal suffering inherent in the poultry, livestock, leather, and fur industries is to adopt a cruelty-free way of life. "Cruelty-free, in my book, ultimately means adopting a vegan lifestyle," says Kim Stallwood. "A vegan lifestyle is one in which you do not use any animal products whatsoever." As a vegan, "You don't eat meat, you don't eat dairy products or some honey," he says. "You don't wear animal products: wool, leather, silk. And you don't consume products which have involved animal suffering, products that have been tested on animals or products which have animal products within them." Stallwood claims that it makes good economic and ecological sense to live such "a Green lifestyle which minimizes the amount of consumer products that you utilize in your life. We feel that it's the most logical, most ethical, most planetary-friendly lifestyle you can adopt."[29] Along with being the easiest way to have an impact on the use and abuse of animals in agriculture, veganism is one of the simplest yet most effective lifestyle options an individual can adopt to benefit the environment.

While less activistic Animal Liberators persevere with "meat-out" campaigns in the hope of ending the use of animals for human consumption, the approach of their more radical cousins is more direct and controversial. They have freed turkeys from poultry farms shortly before Thanksgiving and were allegedly responsible for burning down a livestock barn in Dixon, California (Earth First! was also implicated). They have also vandalized butcher shops and veal processing facilities. Indeed, the plight of veal calves is one of the longest-running battles between animal protectors and the livestock industry. New-born calves intended for slaughter are taken from their mothers almost immediately after birth and are locked in wooden crates twenty-two inches wide by fifty-four inches long until they are slaughtered. The calves' only food is government surplus milk, and in order to keep their meat the desired pink color, they are denied any iron in their diet. Even Animal Welfare groups find this treatment so disgusting that they have fought back with anti-veal campaigns, including what for many of them is a dramatic step—boycotts.[30]

Animal agriculture in the U.S. has resulted in extensive deforestation. A majority of our farmland is turned to pasture for grazing animals; another large section goes to growing feed that is only fed to cattle. There is nutritional inefficiency inherent in using animals for food. Ninety percent of the protein content of grain is lost when fed to livestock; ninety-six percent of its calories and all of its fiber and carbohydrates vanish out the tail ends of cows, hogs, and sheep. If Americans reduced their beef con-sumption by only *ten percent*, the left-over grain would feed all of the sixty million people who starve to death throughout the world each year.[31] Omnivorous humans also unwittingly bolster the arguments for damming free-flowing rivers and streams. John Robbins writes, "To produce a day's food for one meat-eater takes over 4,000 gallons [of water]; for a lacto-ovo [dairy product and egg-eating] vegetarian, only 1,200 gallons; for a pure vegetarian, only 300 gallons. It takes less water to produce a *year's* food for a pure vegetarian than to produce a *month's* food for a meat eater."[32] Much of that water, especially in the arid West, comes from rivers dammed to create reservoirs. And like animals in the world's research laboratories, many farm animals are denied the space they need to move about and experience the environment; indeed, these "factory farm" animals have no direct connection with any ecosystem at all. Moreover, their ancestors were removed from their natural environment long ago; with each passing generation their natural, "wild" genetic material withers, to be replaced with artificial characteristics appropriate only to packed warehouses and sterile laboratories.

Another aspect of animal agriculture is "fur farming," which is in a league by itself. Mink and foxes are the species most commonly raised on fur farms. Row upon row of cramped, wire-floored cages exposed to extreme weather conditions house neurotic, filthy animals. When it is time to kill the animals, "Minks are usually gassed," a *PETA News* article reported. "Farmers guide a small motorized vehicle with a large box alongside the cages and stuff the animals into the box through a small hole." The hole is covered, a hose from the tailpipe of the vehicle is attached to the box, and the animals die from breathing the carbon monoxide fumes. Foxes are electrocuted by being forced to bite down on a metal grip while a metal probe is inserted into their anuses. Then the current is turned on. "Even the ultra-conservative American Veterinary Medical Association does not include electrocution on its list of recommended methods of killing," says PETA. Yet anything goes "in this totally unregulated industry."[33]

In 1988 PETA learned of a bankrupt beaver farm in Montana where hundreds of animals were confined to "fifty concrete pens with stagnant water full of dead and dying beavers." PETA's director of investigations, Jeanne Roush, cared for the animals with the help of a veterinarian, a wildlife biologist, and volunteers. When the out-of-state owner of the farm threatened to reclaim his operation, Animal LIberators spirited the animals out of the ranch "under mysterious circumstances at about the same time as a PETA investigative team drove away." Roush was subsequently charged with felony theft and sued by the farm's owner. She was later found not guilty of the criminal charges, and the civil suit eventually was dropped.[34]

Animal Liberation activists may be best known for carrying their anti-fur campaigns to the consuming public each year at the start of the holiday buying season. Women and men affiliated with PETA, In Defense of Animals, the Animal Rights Coalition, and other groups line up outside of upscale department stores to implore people not to purchase fur coats. The actions have drawn as many as 2,500 protestors to Fifth Avenue in New York City, where shoppers dressed in mink, sable, raccoon, and beaver are sometimes forced to run a gauntlet of anti-fur activists wearing death masks and crying "Shame, shame, shame" and "Don't you know that fur is mur-der?" Emulating the tactics of the British ALF, radicals in the U.S. and Canada have smashed furriers' windows and doused the coats with red paint. Anti-fur protests clearly are paying off, although it is uncertain which tactics have the greater effect. In 1989 a Bloomingdale's fashion director said, "'I think there's a great emphasis on fake furs this season because the conservationists finally got their message across.'" As the *New York Times* wrote, "when Giorgio Armani, Claude Montana, and Christian Lacroix use fake fur, it becomes fashion." Italian designers have even created a special mixture of acrylic and cotton they call "ecological fur."[35]

However, not all of the anti-fur tactics can be expected to yield converts. The British ALF fell into disfavor following a series of incendiary attacks in the late 1980s. American Animal Liberators may be making the same mistake. Although the ALF did not take responsibility for the actions, several "incendiary devices" were left near the fur salons at San Francisco-area department stores during the 1989 holiday season; none were ignited or caused any damage. The devices used in Britain were designed not to burn down the store but only to create enough smoke to cause the sprinkler system to turn on and ruin merchandise. In some cases, however, the devices caused fires and extensive damage.

Trapping and Hunting

Fur-bearing species used for clothing but not raised on farms are trapped or shot, and thousands of other wild animals are killed each year by hunters for food, trophies, or mere "sport." Hunting and trapping are areas both of substantial overlap and conflict between Animal Liberators and Earth First!ers. While both activities affect ecosystems—Earth First! ground, so to speak—in unknown ways, trapping, especially, involves considerable pain and affects individual animals—common Animal Liberation concerns. Earth First! co-founders Howie Wolke and Dave Foreman, both avid hunters, classify trappers as "slob hunters." They write of trapping, "Not only is it cruel, but it is usually done from road or ATV [all-terrain vehicles, themselves the cause of substantial ecological damage]. Trapping targets bobcat, lynx, marten, mink, river otter, and other predators with low reproductive rates." Further, trapping "upsets the normal predator-prey balance" and nearly caused the extinction of beaver in many states.[36] Foreman quotes the following number of animals killed in Colorado during the 1982-1983 trapping season: 14,419 coyote, 7,516 beaver, 4,800 raccoon, 2,505 bobcat, 1,832 badger, and 1,735 red fox.

These numbers result from a "hobby" practiced largely by teenagers. One writer reports vividly of the cruelty of the commonly used leg-hold trap. After being caught and attempting unsuccessfully to flee, some animals "lay down and quietly await death....It is not unusual for a trapped animal to spend two or more days locked in the grip of a leghold trap [before dying]. When bad weather sets in, as it often does in the prime winter trapping season, the wait grows longer. Trapping authorities have often espoused the desirability of an animal who freezes to death while trapped, which eliminates the need for killing by gun or club and thereby insures an undamaged pelt for market." Other than working for legislative prohibitions, there is little visible evidence that activists are doing much to stop trapping. However, Foreman's book, *Ecodefense*, implies that some are ruining traplines using trained dogs and metal detectors, as well as their own wits and familiarity with trapping methods, to find and then destroy them.[37]

Foreman, Wolke, and a number of other Earth First!ers enjoy hunting some species, such as deer and duck. Hunting is integral to the hunter-gatherer future vision espoused by many Earth First!ers, and they argue that hunting also plays a role in maintaining healthy populations of animals in places where predators have been extirpated by humans. This is in conflict with Animal Liberators' views, and this issue is one of the primary points of divisiveness within the radical environmental movement. Yet even here the chasm is fairly narrow and shallow. Nearly all Earth First!ers object to trophy hunting, which has often been the object of hunt saboteurs. Foreman and Wolke have no sympathy for "sleazy trophy hunters," who kill important population-controlling species, eliminating from the food chain wolves, coyotes, mountain lions, grizzly bear, and other predators.

Animals in Entertainment

Since 1939, when horses were abused during the making of the film *Jesse James*, Animal Welfare groups have closely monitored the film industry's use of animals. Others concern themselves with zoos, circus animals, and the like. But Animal Liberators are not satisfied with better treatment of performing or caged animals; they want their use ended forever. No more panda bears behind bars, Shamu splashing around at Marine World, or grizzlies on "Grizzly Adams." Such hopes may seem at least as quixotic as ending trapping or animal testing or curbing our appetite for meat and leather. Yet Animal Liberators say inroads are being made here as well. Nancy Burnet is a leading advocate of ending what she sees as the exploitation of animals in show business. She joined with game show and beauty pageant emcee Bob Barker in 1987 to found United Activists for Animal Rights and a spin-off group, the Coalition to Protect Animals in Entertainment. After Barker was told of serious cases of animal abuse which took place during the making of the movie *Project X* (ironically, about animal experimentation), the two began investigating animal abuse within the motion picture industry.

"We learned that animals are frequently brutalized during the making of motion pictures, commercials, and any other mode of 'entertainment,'" Burnet says. "The more we got into it, the more we learned about the extent of the problem. For so long it had been trotted about in all this wonderful public relations that animals were treated like human stars. Nothing could be further from the truth."[38] Elephants in circuses are beaten with sledge hammers and axe handles or are hooked behind their ears and between their toes to keep them in line, Burnet says. Chimpanzees and other primates are sometimes made to wear remote-controlled devices concealed beneath their costumes that permit trainers to administer shocks following unwanted behavior. The list of abuses goes on and on, Burnet says. "It's the same with dogs and cats. They're drugged. Bears have their paws burned to keep them standing upright....Animals are starved. Food is withheld—not enough to affect their weight, because they have to look good, but to keep them 'in shape.' They are kept in tiny cages, sometimes in areas where they are cold in the winter and [where] they roast in the summer."[39] Reformed animal trainer Pat Derby has been quoted as saying, "'To get an animal to perform on cue requires cruelty, and I've personally done everything I'm criticizing....Animals can't speak for themselves. People have to speak for them."[40]

When their careers are over, many of the animals "are thrown away....They end up in roadside zoos, in research labs. They are locked up in cages for the rest of their lives," Burnet says.[41] Her information comes from eyewitnesses, people working on movie sets or elsewhere who risk being blackballed by the entertainment industry for speaking up. *PETA News* reported the secret backstage filming of a major Las Vegas animal act in July 1989 by Ottavio Gesmundo, a dancer at the Stardust casino. One expert said, "'In my professional opinion, the videotape depicts a clear case of gross abuse and cruelty via unprovoked, systematic physical beatings.'" The film prompted fifteen people to step forward and attest to having witnessed abuse heaped on the animals by showman Bobby Berosini and his trainers dating back for several years. Despite evidence to the contrary, the U.S. Department of Agriculture cleared Berosini of any wrongdoing.[42]

Zoo animals, too, face miserable lives—and not only in zoos. Many zookeepers like to think of themselves as modern-day Noahs and their zoos as arks for endangered species. Yet when zoos have more members of a particular species than they can handle, even if it is one that is near extinction, they often sell the "excess" animals to so-called "animal brokers." In many cases, these dealers resell the animals to the highest bidder at exotic animal auctions. Animal activist Jim Mason attended one such auction, purported to be the world's largest, at the Hale Brothers' 5-H Ranch in Cape Girardeau, Missouri. There he befriended a soft-hearted animal keeper whom he called "Katie." She told him that "zoos dump some animals here, but 'they don't like to be associated with us.' The zoos, it seems, have lofty ideas and a prestige that would be sullied by any direct involvement with private profiteers." The brokers are supposed to make everything clean. "Who wants these animals?" asks Mason. "People who run drive-through 'safari parks' and petting zoos," places not known for the quality of care they give animals.[43] A *60 Minutes* broadcast explored the connection between zoos, exotic animal auctions, and the burgeoning numbers of private hunting reserves catering to rich trophy hunters who like the ease of tracking prey in fenced-in enclosures. After passing through a broker, a zoo's endangered Oryx can become a French surgeon's easy kill.[44] There are no laws governing what zoos do with their extras. The *60 Minutes* report made it clear that zookeepers often make no attempt to follow the trails of the animals that they allow to slip off of their arks.

Animal Users Fight Back

People like Bobby Berosini, who have reputations and lucrative careers at stake, do not just sit back and allow even well-substantiated allegations to fester. He filed a $20 million lawsuit against PETA for publishing its allegations against him. Burnet and Barker became ensnared in a lawsuit of their own, which was filed against them by the American Humane Society, the organization which took on the responsibility for policing Hollywood after the *Jesse James* cruelties. The AHS is not doing its job, Burnet asserts. She sees the lawsuit as a SLAPP, "a way of shutting up those of us who are too active." Burnet says that AHS "is hoping, through this lawsuit, that we will stop our probe into what is going on within the film industry and the use of animals for entertainment purposes. The fact is that AHS has failed and is failing to fully protect them. AHS has said in some interviews that this is a power struggle, that United Activists would like to take over their job. That's not what we're about. We would like to see someone there adequately protecting animals until we can stop it. We want to stop it. Period." The suit alleges libel, slander, defamation, interference with contractual agreements, and other charges, as well as conspiracy— with the City of Los Angeles. "AHS says, 'This is the first lawsuit that we have ever filed,'" says Burnet. "It is very revealing that the people that they [the AHS] actually do file a suit against are people who are exposing the cruelty to animals in entertainment....We aren't interested in compromising or making deals with people or saying 'a little bit is okay,' because a little bit is not okay. We do not have a right to say how much suffering is okay for another species."[45]

Another form of counterattack is being waged by vivisectionists. Animal Liberation support organizations such as PETA and IDA have obtained confidential memoranda from the American Medical Association (AMA); the Cosmetic, Toiletry and Fragrance Association (CTFA); Proctor & Gamble; and the government-run National Institutes of Health (NIH) outlining detailed strategies they plan to take against Animal Liberators. The AMA's "Animal Research Action Plan," dated June 1989, claims that to "defeat the Animal Rights movement, one has to peel away the outermost layers of support and isolate the hardcore activists from the general public and shrink the size of the sympathizers." The hearts and minds of young people are especially important, according to the AMA. "The movement has succeeded in turning many children into sympathizers and the recruitment of children remains a primary goal of most animal activists," it asserts, without offering evidence to support its allegations. The Humane Society of the U.S. does publish a magazine for school teachers, but there does not appear to be a systematic effort on the part of Animal Liberators to inculcate children to the horrors of vivisection. Nevertheless, the AMA plans an extensive, expensive indoctrination program including development of a "teaching module, with video backup, for elementary, middle, and high schools," along with "articles and other informational materials...explaining the importance of animal research through publications like *Weekly Reader* and others." The AMA encourages the use of euphemisms such as implanting "'Advancing Biomedical Research'" in the vernacular in place of "'Animals in Research.'"It envisions "public forums"—sham "debates"—to discuss vivisection. They would "only [be] appropriate under 'controlled audience circumstances,'" presumably before a sympathetic group and without knowledgeable opposition.[46]

While the AMA memo does not mention costs, Proctor & Gamble has proposed spending $12.5 million over three years for an industry "animal testing coalition" to promote the benefits of vivisection.[47] Similarly, CTFA told its members "that a full-scale educational campaign in key states, targeted at legislators, the media, and public opinion makers, will cost one million dollars beyond that provided in the 1989 CTFA budget."[48] The existing budgeted amount was not specified.

In a 1987 memo, Frederick K. Goodwin, Director of Intramural Research for NIH's National Institute of Mental Health, warned that the "Animal Rights' (sic) movement threatens the very core of what the Public Health Service is all about." He wrote, "The health research community must participate in a more pro-active posture," including finding "some acceptable way to provide funding for some of these efforts and technical support for others," which funding and support would be paid with taxpayers' dollars. Goodwin's memo recommended, "The PHS should prepare a list of Senators and Congressmen who have a special interest in health research on a particular disease...and their support should be enlisted just as it is for budgetary matters." Such efforts could even be seen as "consistent with the [Reagan] Administration's wishes to contain costs and restrain excessive regulation." Less regulation, not more, of animal testing could be promoted through publicizing "the cost of regulations,"[49] wrote this official of the federal agency charged with ensuring that animal research dollars are spent on legitimate and worthwhile experiments.

The NIH and PETA have an intense adversarial relationship which got its start in the struggles over the fate of the Silver Spring Monkeys that Alex Pacheco saved in 1981. This conflict continues to drag on; rather than attempt to rehabilitate the eight monkeys that have not died, NIH now wants to conduct one last experiment on them and then kill them. More recently Pacheco and Carol Lyn Burnett were arrested and charged with assaulting a federal police officer at an April 1989 protest at NIH, but were later acquitted of the charges. For their part PETA has employed hyperbole against NIH, the federal government's primary medical research arm, calling it "the root of all evil." Kim Stallwood explains, "Its main approach is vivisection-based curative medicine. Dollar-for-dollar it is a waste of money. The emphasis should be on preventative medicine. Plus there's the fact that we have had case after case where we have submitted written critiques, substantiated by professional expert opinion, of a particular researcher or laboratory....When we have attacked those, NIH has always defended them. They even defended the University of Pennsylvania Head Injuries Clinic." Stallwood adds, "I'm sure that in some cases for some people [vivisection] is doing good. But if you wanted to take the broad picture and attempt to validate that they are having an impact on society as a whole and improving everyone's health, then I would say no....It is a scandal, and it's our taxpayers' money that is providing it all. It is wrong."[50]

In his memo Goodwin recommended a number of guidelines for dealing with Animal Rightists. Stallwood has seen those directives in action. Researchers whose labs have been attacked are unavailable to answer the media's questions about their work, for example, and persons whose lives will be "jeopardized" by delays in research are found and brought forth for the press. "It's just a racket," Stallwood says. "The animal abuse industry would like to paint us as 'Reds under the dog basket,' that here we are claiming to be compassionate and wanting to see rights for animals, but really we would kill a human any day to save a rat. That's rubbish! Our credo is *kill nothing*." Stallwood says of NIH, "They're the dinosaur, and someone has to push them over."[51]

Supplementing their lawsuits and public relations campaigns, the animal research industry has even gone undercover to entrap activists. U.S. Surgical Corporation, which demonstrates surgical staples on anesthetized dogs and has been the object of Animal Liberators' scorn for years, hired Perceptions International, a Stamford, Connecticut, private investigations firm, to infiltrate the Animal Liberation movement, ala the FBI and Earth First!. One of its agents, Mary Lou Sapone, befriended animal activist Fran Trutt, "a disturbed woman," and assisted Trutt in planting a bomb in U.S. Surgical's parking lot. Trutt was arrested and charged with attempted murder.[52] Stallwood calls U.S. Surgical's setup "sinister" and doubts that the bomb would ever have been planted without prompting from Sapone, who also attempted to infiltrate Earth First!.[53]

Anarchist Animal Liberators

As with Earth First!, anarchists are making their presence felt in the Animal Liberation movement, though their presence is not nearly so contentious. "Mel," a California anarchist, feels that Animal Liberators can generally be divided into "professionals" on the East Coast and anarchists on the West, although he acknowledges that this is not always the case. The East Coast/professionals often work in good-paying jobs and generally restrict their activities to liberating animals from research laboratories, relying heavily on the media coverage of their raids to increase public awareness about vivisection. Some of them feel that only scientific arguments should be used against vivisectors. They do not always destroy researchers' instruments, and during a raid they may not even remove all of the animals from a laboratory.

On the other hand, West Coast/anarchistic Animal Liberators are less well-educated and hold menial jobs or work only part-time, preferring instead to devote as much energy as possible to their cause. They not only remove all of the animals they can from laboratories, but they are prone to do more damage to the labs and attack a wider variety of targets than their East Coast counterparts, including factory farms and facilities where laboratory animals are bred. Their opinion is that animal research is one part of an oppressive system, all of which should be brought down by whatever means one can use short of injuring other living beings.

To achieve these ends, anarchists are more likely to use arson or other highly destructive means. Mel says that along with liberating animals and creating an atmosphere wherein animals' rights will be discussed in the media, the anarchists' purposes in carrying out any activity are to inflict economic damage on the target and to discourage people from entering into professions which involve the use of animals. By using arson against the livestock industry, furriers, researchers, and others, Mel says anarchists hope to "cost them [in] what they are more concerned with than animal life: money. If they refuse to see the immorality of their actions, we'll put it out there for them. We'll force their insurance rates to skyrocket and we'll put them out of business if we can. It has happened over and over again in the U.S. and in England. If you can smash windows in a butcher's shop, that much less money will be spent on animal carcasses and enlarging the business."[54]

He says a similar message awaits those who would become involved in the "business of animal exploitation"; they should be ready to put up with animal liberations and economic sabotage. "It's not very common to have a single-issue group go into Yuppieville and destroy a lawyer's work or an accountant's," Mel observes. "But it's becoming common for Animal Liberators to mess up that neat little world by rescuing animals and otherwise making it unappealing to pursue a career in psychology or biology or veterinary science that is based on animal experimentation."[55]

Mel and others say that the greatest threat to the Animal Liberation movement is not the crackdown from outside but the backbiting, gossiping, and separatism within the movement. Having designed their movement after the British version, activists have few effective means of communicating directly with one another or of increasing solidarity, as there are at the Earth First! Round River Rendezvous. The connections that do exist from group to group are tenuous, and as such have helped breed jealousies, complaints about methods, and a lack of trust, all of which have severed many of these links and further fragmented the movement. On the other hand, this may have benefitted the ALF and similar groups because infiltration is extremely difficult. Only three people other than Fran Trutt have been arrested for Animal Liberation activities—ironically, all of them were found with liberated rabbits in their possession. All received fines.

Mel's vision of the future of the Animal Liberation movement is certain to alarm many. "I think when the ALF acts over here, people—the authorities and breeders and researchers—learn from it really quickly," he says. "It wasn't like that in Britain—for some reason they were really slow in picking up on a lot of that stuff. [Animal Liberators] could get away with the same sort of attack over and over. The U.S. is bigger, but it's more sophisticated. So I think there are going to be fewer actions, but those that happen will be bigger. There are going to be a lot fewer butchers' windows broken and a lot more buildings getting torched."[56] That may reflect a trend in the overall radical environmental movement, although economically "small" actions, from pickets and civil disobedience to tree-spikings and monkeywrenchings, continue apace.

More and more Earth First!ers and Animal Liberators are acknowledging the close ties between ecosystems and individuals and between pain and suffering on the part of captive animals and environmental abuse in general. These activists are increasingly willing to cross the boundaries between their respective emphases, and as they do so, new directions may emerge in the movement. "Targets" of common concern, such as the Dixon Livestock Barn, may be attacked more frequently and more ferociously. Participation throughout the movement may also increase as connections within the movement are made.

A powerful countervailing trend may be at work as well: the preponderance of public and private intimidation and the investigation of radical environmentalists. Fear and suspicion of new adherents, even if they claim experience elsewhere within the movement, may curb the free flow of ideas and discourage alliances. A greater problem for potential spreading of the movement, however, is the intransigence of many within the movement. Activists often refuse to acknowledge the value of another "branch," much less the commonalities between them. Despite this, it appears that in the future the spirit and commitment of radical environmentalists will continue a blurring of the distinctions between activists' concerns.

CHAPTER 8

RADICAL ENVIRONMENTALISM'S INTERNATIONAL FACE

Far from having a lock on radical environmentalism, the protest methods used by activists in the U.S. actually have lagged behind those in some other nations. The Animal Liberation movement, for example, was well underway in Britain before it took hold in a serious way in North America. The union between loggers and environmentalists which Judi Bari and Darryl Cherney began forging in 1988 was anticipated by a dozen years in the Amazonian rainforest. And some clearly violent approaches to environmental preservation, still untried here, have been used elsewhere—elephant poachers are shot on sight in Kenya, and tribespeople in a remote Philippine valley took up arms to fight a dam proposed by former dictator Ferdinand Marcos. On the other hand, often what might be termed "radical" environmental protests in the Third World, in communist nations, and elsewhere in the developed world do not seem very dramatic or ambitious compared to events in the U.S. However, considering the political oppression under which eco-warriors in those other countries struggle, their actions are as radical as anything that has been attempted here.

Animal Activism in the British Commonwealth

Britain's Animal Liberators first made a name for themselves in the 1800s, when young people calling themselves the "Band of Mercy" began damaging hunters' weapons.[1] In 1977 the Band of Mercy re-emerged with a vengeance. Veteran hunt saboteur Ronnie Lee and others formed the core of a new and far more radical Band. Initially, they slashed the tires of hunters' vehicles and then moved on to arson, causing £45,000 worth of damage in two attacks on vivisection facilities. They hit "laboratory animal-breeding establishments, damaging and burning their vehicles" and destroyed a sealing boat, forcing the cancellation of a seal hunt that has not taken place since. Those first actions were "a tremendous initiative," says Kim Stallwood of People for the Ethical Treatment of Animals. "It really set the energy going." [2]

Stallwood joined PETA in 1987 following a dozen years as an Animal Liberation activist in Britain. He became a vegetarian in 1974 after working in a chicken processing plant, and made the step to veganism two years later. After working for a small anti-factory farming group, he became a radicalizing force in the British Union for the Abolition of Vivisection (BUAV), which was formed in 1898. In its first eighty years of existence, the BUAV swung between extremes of action and inaction; Stallwood and others felt it was time for some serious changes, and in the late 1970s a number of radicals won election to the BUAV board of directors. Soon thereafter, Stallwood says, "The BUAV adopted a policy of supporting illegal activities, providing they didn't cause any harm to any life." Foretelling PETA's relationship with the American Animal Liberation Front (ALF), Stallwood said the BUAV was "given information and we used that information. We acted as media representatives for [Animal Liberators] and we championed their raison d'etre and why they did what they did. The old guard were very hostile towards that, but we felt the circumstances and the climate had changed." [3]

After serving a prison sentence for some of their Band of Mercy activities, Ronnie Lee and thirty other British radicals founded the original ALF (similar groups exist in Canada, Holland, Germany, New Zealand, Australia, South Africa, and France, as well as in the U.S.). They did so because "nothing was happening" to stop vivisection and other animal abuses, Stallwood says. "It was a drastic situation and we needed a drastic course of action. No one was thinking about it, no one was concerned about it, no one knew anything about it. The illegal activity brought it out and gave it immediate attention....There had been centuries of legal activity that had come to nothing. I don't think it is that unusual, because when you look at any movement for social change there has always been this combination of legal and illegal activities." [4] A sea of change throughout Britain has ensued in the years following Band of Mercy's revival, Stallwood says. Over the last decade and a half, vegetarianism has become widely practiced and cruelty-free goods are carried by every major supermarket chain.

Still, the Animal Liberators see much left to accomplish, and they have set about pursuing the goal of a cruelty-free society by using a combination of peaceful and destructive campaigns aimed both at consumers and retailers. Efforts by anti-fur activists have led to dramatic reductions in sales of fur coats in Britain and West Germany; the famed Harrods department store decided to stop selling furs in April 1990 after sales dropped forty percent in four years and following several firebomb attacks at other stores owned by its parent company. [5] The Canadian Animal Liberation Front Support Group—one of numerous groups established by ALF sympathizers that publicize ALF actions and provide legal and financial assistance to activists accused of wrong-doing—reports that the Debenhams department store chain in England ceased fur sales after ALF members firebombed three of its outlets. The bombings reportedly cost the chain more than nine million pounds in actual damage and lost sales. The Canadian group said the "so-called 'bombs' were timed incendiary devices set to go off in the early hours of the morning when the stores would be deserted. The idea behind this kind of action is to start a very small fire with enough smoke to activate the store's sprinkler systems...and cause maximum damage through subsequent flooding throughout the store." One Debenhams store where the sprinklers were switched off for maintenance did receive extensive fire damage.[6]

It appears that the attacks were costly to the movement as well. Although the American ALF has been virtually untouched by the law, at times there have been a dozen or more Brits serving jail sentences for Animal Liberation-related activities. In June 1988 two ALF activists were arrested on charges of conspiring to commit arson and of possession of incendiary devices. They were convicted and received sentences of as long as four years, four months in prison. And ALF co-founder Ronnie Lee was sentenced to ten years in prison in February 1987 on three conspiracy charges; two others were convicted with him.[7] Australia and New Zealand are also hot spots for those determined to end cruelty to animals through destructive means. Window smashing and spray painting furs are frequent occurrences at furriers' shops in Australia, especially around Melbourne. Authorities there put the value of property damage between 1986 and 1988 at more than A$1 million. In New Zealand, animal experimentation laboratories, hog farms, meat trucks, and butcher shops have been targeted by radical environmentalists armed with firebombs, slingshots, and paint.

Europe's Fight for Its Environment

Ecology and Revolution

Elsewhere in the world, the environment and politics are more closely linked than in the U.S. Earth First!er Greg King sees ecological anxieties as driving the worldwide struggle for democracy that erupted at the end of the 1980s. "The snowballing environmental movement is actually a revolt," King says. "It's definitely a revolt in China, in Russia, in Poland. Those are very much environmental uprisings....It's not coming across to us in this country like that."[8] Some observers did perceive the existence of an ecological foundation as a basis for democratization in Eastern Europe before the stunning developments of 1989 and 1990. In 1986, *U.S. News and World Report* carried a story that noted, "For governments of the East bloc, contending with an ecology-minded citizenry is a new, disquieting prospect. Though the number of protestors is small, their issue is real, reinforced by the chemical disaster in the Rhine [which occurred at a Swiss pharmaceutical plant and wiped out life in the river] on the other side of Europe's ideological border. The companion plagues of modern manufacturing and nuclear energy have caught up with countries still playing catch-up."[9] One chronicler of the emergent grassroots revolution in environmentalism worldwide wrote, "In the industrial heartland of the Soviet Union and Eastern Europe, hundreds of localities have erupted in protest over the severely polluted conditions they endure, and a number of Soviet nuclear plants and Polish industrial facilities have been closed as a result."[10]

In a clear example of the relativity of radicalism, activists who were forbidden to protest in pre-democracy East Germany laid bed sheets on the rooftops of their homes to speak for them—air pollution dissolved the sheets. Although such an act would attract substantial attention in the U.S. if the results were the same, it would hardly be termed "radical" by anyone. What made the bed sheet protest—as well as other actions that are a common part of the political world in the West—radical was its context. It is difficult to draw parallels between the environmental sabotage occurring here and the gravity of comparatively innocuous protests that have taken place in Eastern Europe. The risks are—or until recently *were*—far greater in communist nations. Tree spikers or monkeywrenchers in the United States do not face decades of imprisonment at hard labor, or incarceration at mental institutions, as they would in Eastern block countries for far lesser acts. Even with the imposition of severe penalties for "crimes," environmental activism endured. When a Hungarian group, Danube Circle, demonstrated against construction of a hydroelectric dam on the Danube after it was told it could not do so, the protestors were dispersed by truncheon-wielding police. Eastern Europeans fought back however they could against their oppressors; in Poland, a mass for victims of the Chernobyl nuclear power plant disaster easily developed into an anti-government rally.

In at least one Warsaw Pact nation, Bulgaria, a dissident environmental group was credited with taking the first bold step of loosening the otherwise iron-fisted communist grip on political power before any others dared. Eco-Glasnost "emerged...as a dominant opposition force" in the last weeks of 1989, according to the *New York Times*. When the group attempted to register with the Bulgarian government as a dissident organization, it was rebuffed. Undeterred, the environmentalists took their case to the nation's supreme court, where the government's prosecutor admitted "that a lower court had erred in denying registration to Eco-Glasnost." Said one Eco-Glasnost member, "'If we are registered, we could bring about the start of a grass-roots democratic movement.'"[11] Ironically, earlier in the year the government had banished the founders of the Party of the Green Masses, the precursor to Eco-Glasnost who promoted environmental protection, political reform, and improved human rights.[12] After Vaclav Havel was elected president of Czechoslovakia, he said that a dirty environment was a source of shame to his nation and that ecological restoration would be of vital importance to the new government. "'Our country does not flourish,'" he said. "'We have the worst environment in Europe.'"[13] In public opinion polls taken after the peaceful overthrow of the Communists, the Czech "Green" political party appeared well-positioned to become the number two party after the nation's first free elections in forty years.[14]

As Western freedoms spread like wildfire through the East, even the Soviet Union was not immune to environmental protest and a growth in ecological consciousness. Nikolai Vorontsov, Soviet minister for the environment, says that his nation's ecological problems overshadow all others, "ahead of nationality conflicts and the economic crisis." More than ninety million Soviets live in areas where pollutant levels exceed permissible levels by *ten times* or more.[15] Increasingly, Soviet citizens are speaking out against the ruination of human health and nature which has proceeded almost without restraint for decades. In Siberia, far from the media centers and from those of power, people braved the cold and repression to march for the protection of Lake Baikal.[16] In 1988 the rebellious Baltic states witnessed the emergence of a Green Party that emphasized environmental issues.

That political parties arose among dissident environmentalists in the Soviet Union exemplifies the political power of ecological consciousness. It also speaks to the bravery of those in the movement that they would confront the once omnipotent and still dominant state in such a fashion. Echoing the media-savvy sentiments of Paul Watson and Mike Roselle, Estonia's Green Party leader Juhan Aare said, "The Green Movement...is not dependent [on the Communist Party]; it is an organization of people....We have various means of reaching the public: TV, newspapers, and radio."[17] In neighboring Lithuania and Latvia, too, "the Greens have gained enormous popular support and have served as major catalysts for the broader-based movements for national self-government."[18] Greens were among the leaders of Sajudis, the Lithuanian coalition which in February 1990 threw out the Communists in Eastern Europe's first free elections since the 1930s.

Two years earlier, 1,500 Balkan residents linked hands to form a human chain around a nuclear power plant to protest its planned expansion. And in an even larger show of unity by the people of the three tiny nations, thousands stood together in a human wall along hundreds of miles of Baltic coastline from Lithuania to Estonia to show their united support for remedying the heavily polluted Baltic Sea's environmental problems. Like the bedsheet protest, it was a quiet, simple act that spoke volumes about the love of a people who know and revere the land that nurtures them, and about the human will to live free—a will that radical environmentalists say should be respected in all else on the planet.

The Greens' Slow Gains

American-style radical environmentalism has been slow to take hold in Western Europe. Although Europeans have been quick to embrace radical causes, and sometimes to take to the streets to express their advocacy, they often are attracted more by philosophy than action. So it was logical that the political philosophy of environmental preservation was embraced there at the same time that radical environmentalism emerged elsewhere. In 1973, England became the first nation with a Green party, calling itself the "Ecology Party." Along with other social, military, and economic aspects, their platform stresses unilateral nuclear disarmament, taxing "waste, not work," self-sufficiency in agriculture for Britain, the banning of some pesticides immediately, and an end to vivisection. Although Greens in Britain have yet to win major elective offices, they attracted 2.3 million voters in the European Parliament elections in June 1989. Those same elections saw Greens from other nations take thirty-seven of the 518 seats in the Common Market's legislative arm. After that stunning showing, Socialist French President Francois Mitterrand and even Tory Margaret Thatcher in Britain took notice of environmental issues. A month earlier in Australia, the Greens won enough seats in the Tasmanian state parliament to establish themselves as the key party for any successful coalition government.[19] But the most successful Green Party to date sprouted in the early 1980s in West Germany. *Die Gruenen* soon won more than two dozen seats in the Bundestag and later took advantage of their grassroots support to win elections at the local and regional levels, joining ruling coalitions in the states of Hesse and West Berlin. Refusing to play by the mainstream's rules, the Greens take hard-line stances on environmental preservation and restoration and are responsible for the development of numerous innovative social programs, many with a socialistic flavor.

As for direct action, the number and extent of protests in Western Europe does not compare with that of the U.S. However, members of the West German group "Robin Wood" frequently hang banners illegally from buildings and conduct similar Greenpeace-like environmental protests. In Italy, generally years behind its neighbors in environmental legislation, citizens in the small port city of Manfredonia blocked roads leading into their town for three days in 1988 to protest the use of a factory in the city as a storage center for toxic wastes. Reaction against a government plan calling for the documentation and storage of toxins ran strong in other port cities as well, but nowhere like in this Adriatic city of 57,000, which had already been contaminated by hazardous substances from a local petro-chemical factory.[20] And in an act reminiscent of the Strawberry Liberation Front's destruction of genetically engineered plants in the U.S., in August 1989

Dutch activists calling themselves the "Seething Spuds" destroyed 400 genetically altered potato plants that were the subject of biotechnology research. The plants' biological coding was tampered with to make them more resistant to herbicides.[21]

Rainforest Radicals

"The rainforests," says Australian John Seed, "are the womb of life. They are home to half the world's species of plants and animals. They're responsible for the creation and maintenance of the atmosphere and of the hydrological cycle."[22] Incredibly, these places so vitally important to the world's ecology are being destroyed at an astounding rate; an area the size of South Carolina is cut from the Amazonian rainforest each year. And the pace of destruction is no slower in the tropical rainforests in Zaire, the Philippines, Borneo, Thailand, and elsewhere. Not only does the killing of the trees lead to numerous plant and non-human animal extinctions every day, but a slow genocide is taking place there as well. Every rainforest is, or until recently was, inhabited by indigenous people. "They are suffering from some of the worst malnutrition in the world," Seed says, "because their game animals and foods are being destroyed. They see this as the end of their world. For some, this all must be unimaginable."[23] Those same people fight a valiant, all but hopeless battle for their homes.

Largely at Seed's instigation, in recent years a second front has been established, this one by people in developed nations. Their involvement is crucial because the root of rainforest destruction is not the chain saw or the deliberately set forest fire to clear land for pastures. Rather, Seed says, "Rainforest destruction continues because people continue to eat beef, drink coffee, use timber, and the other unsustainable uses of the rain forests; because the Third World debt exists," and because of lusts for ever-greater profits, the resource mentality, the inability of people to see the personal connections with the planet, the lack of social systems capable of saving the forests in rainforest nations, corruption, and because of the whimsy of people like the environmental minister in Sarauak, Malaysia, who thinks a bit less rain, which he feels is brought on by the presence of the rainforests, would be good for his golf game.[24]

Chico Mendes: Rainforest Savior

The story of Francisco Mendes Filho shows the powerful human and ecological links that are the reality behind the struggle for rainforest preservation. In some photographs, Chico Mendes looks up from a desk covered in paper work: the union organizer and inadvertent environmental hero stares glumly at the camera with the baggy eyes and puffy cheeks of the miserably overworked. In others, he holds his two young children, they and he at ease and laughing at one of those little, meaningless things that means everything. For more than twelve years Mendes and the rubber tappers he organized into the Workers' Party blocked development in the Amazon rainforest. Actually a union, the Workers' Party claimed only 3,000 members but in fact represented 165,000 families, and Mendes was its most powerful spokesperson. In 1987 the United Nations Environmental Program honored him with its Global 500 Award for environmental protection. Then, on December 22, 1988, Mendes the unionist, environmentalist, and father became Mendes the martyr, gunned down at his home by the son of a cattle rancher who wanted to turn more of the rich palette of Brazilian rainforest into monochrome pasture.

Mendes was born in the Brazilian jungle in 1944. At the age of nine he began working with his father as a rubber tapper, moving through the jungle and finding rubber trees amongst other exotic flora. With a sharp knife the tapper carefully slits the tree's bark, collecting the milky latex sap in a cup. Later the tapper prepares the latex and sells it to the outside world. An estimated 300,000 Amazonians live from the proceeds of rubber tapping and from small subsistence food plots. They also collect and sell Brazilian nuts, cashews, bananas, and other produce of the forest at rates that are truly sustainable.

When Mendes was seventeen he met Euclides Fernando Tavora, a former army officer and leftist revolutionary who had escaped from prison after being jailed for his support of a 1935 uprising. Tavora taught Mendes to read and simultaneously imbued him with a powerful political consciousness. For three years Mendes trekked through the jungle every weekend to Tavora's home, a three hour walk each way. "I soon learned that he was not only interested in teaching me to read," Mendes wrote. "His greater interest was in teaching me other things that were very important for the future. We were being robbed and exploited by the patrons, the big landowners, and we could do nothing because we didn't know how to count or read."[25]

In 1965 Mendes' mentor became ill and left the jungle, never to return. For years Mendes felt lost, but he never forgot Tavora's admonition to join with others in a struggle against the landed classes. Almost simultaneously in 1975 the Brazilian National Confederation of Agriculture Workers and well-to-do farmers arrived in Mendes' home state of Xapuri. Invoking a federal law, both claimed huge chunks of the jungle as theirs to clear and to use however they wished. Within months, thousands of tapper families had been pushed off the land.

Mendes recalled Tavora's words and rose to the defense of the people. On March 1, 1976, he led sixty rubber tappers in a three day, non-violent siege of an encampment of workers who were surveying a huge section of forest for an absentee owner who planned to raze it. From then until his death, Mendes and his followers conducted a running direct action campaign that would be the envy of any radical environmentalist in the U.S.

In forty-five actions they sat in front of bulldozers and stood between chainsaw-wielding loggers to protect the rainforest. Fifteen times they won "partial victories," as Mendes called them, leading to the preservation of nearly 3 million acres of jungle.[26]

In 1986 Mendes and other rubber tapper union leaders joined with the native Amazonian Indians to fight development. Like the work of Earth First! union activists Judi Bari and Darryl Cherney with lumberjacks and saw mill workers on California's North Coast, this was a momentous development, as Mendes explained: "The Indians are the legitimate owners of Amazonia, and the rubber tappers were used [by the landed classes] to destroy them and their resources. It was a very big war for many years." After decades of continued animosity, the joint effort stunned many. "People were amazed," Mendes recalled, "saying, 'Indians and rubber tappers together. Didn't you fight before? Weren't you enemies? How is it that now you're united?' And we responded, 'We understand today that our fight is the same one.'"[27] The shared vision for Amazonia was one of "extractive reserves" granted to them by the state. The tappers and the Indians could take from the land as they needed, so long as they did no damage to it.

It was at this time, said Mendes, that international environmental groups "discovered" the rubber tappers. He credited them as being instrumental in propelling the Brazilian government to begin setting aside the reserves. Although some, including those from the very international environmental groups that Mendes said were so important to his cause, downplay the essentially socialistic thrust behind the extractive reserve concept, socio-political analysts see it as vital to the Indian-rubber tapper cause. "It is ridiculous to see the activities of the rubber tappers divorced from their union politics or the labor movement," write Susanna Hecht and Alexander Cockburn.[28] Mendes, who from his teens viewed Brazil's gentry as the enemy of his people, synthesized environmental preservation and political self-empowerment in a new movement. He died in that struggle.

But his life's work was not in vain. He played the central role in focusing the world's attention on the South American rainforests and showed the human side of what once was called the "green hell." To Chico Mendes it was a green heaven. He wrote, "People ask us, 'You don't want to destroy even one more tree in all of Amazonia?' No. We are conscious of the fact that down throughout the years the rubber tappers and Indians established their subsistence plots and never threatened the forest."[29] Mendes' dream was of a new tribalism, one in harmony with nature and sustainable for the people. His approach and his character were reminiscent of the century's greatest leaders. "Chico Mendes believed in systemic change, and that's his brilliance," says Randy Hayes of the Rainforest Action Network. "In my mind, he absolutely is a Gandhi, a Martin Luther King. He stood for building alliances between the rubber tappers and the indigenous peoples.

He built coalitions and camaraderie between groups that were once enemies, and he understood the flow of capital" out of the forests and into the pockets of the already-rich, a central issue in rainforest activism.[30] But Mendes' dream may never be realized, the forces causing rainforest destruction never harnessed. Twelve percent of the Amazonian rainforest, about 250,000 square miles, has been destroyed in the years since Mendes' first protest. And with Brazil owing $110 billion in foreign debt, the prospects of reforming the nation's land use policies to benefit the rainforest appear dim.

World Action for Rainforests

As John Seed implies, the rainforest preservation community's perspective is that the problem, the disease, infecting the rainforests does not exist in the forests which are being destroyed. The destruction is merely symptomatic of the Eco-Wall, an inability by those in developed nations to understand and act on their role in the decimation of rainforests. It also is systematic, a part of the world economic system led by the World Bank. Established under the Marshall Plan after World War II as the Bank of Reconstruction, the World Bank eventually found itself with a lot of cash and nowhere to spend it. So it set about "developing" the Third World to improve the "standard of living" of the world's poor. Funded completely by national governments—the U.S. is responsible for twenty percent of the deposits—the Bank made a $2 billion profit in 1988 yet was completely unaccountable to taxpayers in the U.S. or anywhere else.

Much of Brazil's towering debt is owed to the World Bank, which despite several years of protests has yet to re-direct itself from environmentally disastrous projects in Brazil and elsewhere. As less-developed nations find themselves owing more and more money to the World Bank and to other international development-oriented institutions (including the International Monetary Fund, the Inter-American Development Bank, and the Asian and African Development Bank), a vicious circle develops. Today, loans are often made for projects like the Xingu Dam on the Amazon, which, if built, would inundate thousands of square miles of rainforest. The electricity generated by the dam would go to power developments throughout the region, thereby wiping out more rainforest. But Brazilian leaders say that those dams are necessary to enable them to repay prior World Bank loans for other developments. It is worth noting that many of those same well-to-do Brazilians stand to profit from the debt-loan cycle, thereby feeding the destruction of their own nation and their people.[31]

At some point the cycle must stop, says Randy Hayes. The Bank had a chance to turn over a new leaf in May 1990 when the world's finance ministers were asked by France to adopt a $1.3 billion fund to protect the environment in Eastern Europe and the Third World. The U.S, Britain, and Japan all refused to endorse the plan, and it failed.[32] Hayes and others have gone much farther, proposing a reconstituted World Bank that earmarks half of its money for the protection of critical ecosystems, including tropical rainforests. The other half would be given to the establishment of buffer zones around those ecosystems for sustainable agriculture and other permanently self-supporting uses of the land. There would be no loans, only grants. "If we've subsidized nuclear power," asks Hayes, "why the hell shouldn't we subsidize ecologically-sound agriculture in certain parts of the Third World?"[33]

The quiet-spoken Hayes moved to California in 1973 "to get involved in environmental issues." He enrolled in an environmental planning program at San Francisco State University, and in 1983 co-produced an acclaimed documentary, *The Four Corners: A National Sacrifice Area*, about the spoilation of the Desert Southwest, for his Master's thesis. Hayes sees in rainforest issues the same forces at work as in the Four Corners region: fragile ecosystems, conflicting cultures, and insensitive governments and multinational corporations ruining the place. Following John Seed's tour of the U.S. in 1983 and 1984, during which he established thirty local rainforest action groups, Hayes and Earth First!er Mike Roselle decided to take on the role of coordinating the geographically disparate groups. They sat down with a set of press-on letters and created the Rainforest Action Network's (RAN) first stationery (the group was later formally incorporated as a non-profit organization, and the stationery is a bit fancier today). Four years of rapid growth in RAN membership—it now stands at 30,000—is reflected in the 150 Rainforest Action Groups across the U.S. that take a grass-roots approach to protests for the rainforest. Another 100 "RAGs" are spread throughout the world.

In 1985 RAN sponsored a three-day conference to consider the best means for bringing the international rainforest activism community together. Out of that came the World Rainforest Movement (WRM), an informal coalition made up of key contacts throughout the world who collaborate on global campaigns. There is substantial agreement in the WRM about the root causes of destruction. Echoing Seed, Hayes says, "When I look at the rainforest issue and I think of the areas that are most interesting in terms of trying to help resolve it, I think of Japan, Europe, and the United States. Those are the three areas where, if significant change can happen, we can save the rainforests." Hayes adds, "People make a mistake when they say, 'Oh, the tropical rainforest issue. The problem is down there, thus the solution must be down there.'...The question is, how do we get industrial society's foot off of the throat of the rainforest?"[34] For this reason, RAN's field projects are in places like Houston, where Conoco Oil is based; Philadelphia, home to Scott Paper Company; and Tokyo, where the insatiable Japanese appetite for timber is whetted.

This perspective on the problem of the developed world's role in rainforest destruction is somewhat radical. In late 1989 representatives of a

South American tribal people's coalition called COICA visited rainforest advocates in the United States, including the World Wildlife Fund and Conservation International. The Amazonians expressed resentment that these organizations were making deals with their governments concerning their homeland in a well-intentioned example of multi-national tinkering. Tribal peoples, says Hayes, do not need outsiders telling them how to preserve their places; rather, they need action on the part of the people best situated to end the external disease of rainforest destruction, remembering that forces within their nations play a role as well.

From RAN's first project—a boycott of Burger King restaurants that was called when Roselle uncovered evidence that the huge chain imported beef from cattle grazed in former rainforest—it embraced this approach. In 1989 RAN's activism took on a special importance when the ability of the U.S. to act effectively on rainforest issues was called into question as it was confronted with the destruction of its own tropical rainforests. A $1.5 billion geothermal plant was proposed for the Wao Kele O Puna rainforest on the island of Hawaii near the active Kilauea volcano. The 500 megawatts of electricity generated there would be sent by undersea cable to the booming islands of Oahu and Maui.[35] RAN took the lead in opposing the plant. "If we can lead by being ecologically sound ourselves, then that will have important reverberations," says Hayes. "If we can't stop the destruction of an American tropical rainforest in Hawaii, where there are indigenous peoples who feel that is a sacred area, how can we expect to have any influence in these other areas?"[36]

He is optimistic that WRM can effectively apply broad-based pressure on near-term struggles like the Puna geothermal plant. He also sees a need for more strategic, global campaigns on rainforest issues. But it is only through long-term, systemic change that rainforests and most of the world's other ecosystems will be preserved, Hayes says. Fundamentally restructuring the World Bank is but one example of what is needed. Far more ambitious is the advocacy by some WRM members of a retooling of the world's monetary system. Their plan would base a currency's value not on speculation or even gold, but on a nation's ability to produce food in an ecologically responsible and sustainable way. Each nation's currency would symbolize an ecologically sustainable relationship to Earth. "We need to recognize the nature of our wealth," Hayes says. "It's a tragic wealth. Our financial wealth in the United States has been produced by pillaging the planet and stressing the planet's life systems....We're taking the capital out of the bank, and not the interest."[37]

Industrialism and Tribal Peoples: The Environmental Link

Before humans settled in stationary farming communities, they practiced a nomadic or semi-nomadic hunter-gatherer way of life. The Penan people of the Sarawak state of Malaysia are among the last hunter-gatherers anywhere in the world, and their jungle home for untold thousands of years faces imminent destruction at the hands of loggers furnishing timber to Japan, the U.S., and Australia. Their struggle for the preservation of their ancestral forests began in 1987 when they blockaded logging roads into their home rainforests. Soon after, Malaysian Friends of the Earth representatives uncovered evidence that Sarawak Environment and Tourism Minister Datuk Amar James Wong owns more than 700,000 acres of Penan rainforest land. He also owned many of the firms cutting the trees. Wong has fiercely fought the Penan, taking out injunctions against them and ordering a police crackdown against the continuing Penan blockades.[38]

In the years since, neither Wong nor the blockaders have shown any indication of backing down, but it is Wong who is winning the battle. The destruction of the dense mahogany, teak, meranti, and Pacific maple forest continues unabated at a rate of seven square kilometers per day. The police have repeatedly brutalized blockaders, who, under virtual martial law, have had their rights totally ignored. They are sometimes jailed for months simply for sitting in a logging road. Other Sarawaki tribes have managed to keep their land free of loggers—the assertive Iban tribe blew up twenty-five bulldozers and logging trucks in 1982 after loggers refused to leave their lands. When the loggers returned in 1986, a similar incident occurred. But the pacific Penan are loathe to engage in property destruction, even though their homes and essential lands are being wiped out.

The Penans' protests have attracted worldwide publicity to their fight to preserve their forest home. Their efforts, and the general plight of rainforests everywhere, prompted the Rainforest Action Network to announce a boycott of all tropical hardwoods in November 1989.[39] Even the Penan's neighbors in North Borneo, one of the world's major exporters of tropical hardwoods, have risen up against loggers. They, too, blockaded roads and threatened to burn down logging bridges. But their efforts have direct and tragic consequences for the Penan; as log exports to Japan decreased in North Borneo by upwards of fifty percent between 1988 and 1989, exports from Sarawak increased by seventy-six percent. To meet this demand, around-the-clock logging was instituted in July 1989, a rate of cutting that would decimate the remainder of the Penans' rainforest in one year. The Penan feel helpless in the face of this onslaught. They have little to eat, and starvation has become commonplace. Yet they fight on. "It's such a literal life-and-death struggle for the Penan that their will power won't be easily broken," says Randy Hayes. "Certain parts of the Penan Rainforest are like the bombed-out cities of Europe, right now. Even within those areas the Penan live on."[40]

Like the Penan, numerous other indigenous peoples identify indelibly with the places where they and their ancestors have lived for generations. For them, ecological consciousness through a close identification with their place is as automatic as a heart beat. These peoples' very beings are a part of the ecology; they feel at one with the land in a way few Westerners know. One of the rare success stories of a native people's fight against industrialism is that of the Bontoc and Kalinga tribes of the Philippines. Their home is in the Chico River valley, nestled deep in the Gran-Cordillera mountains on the main island of Luzan several hundred miles north of Manila. In 1973 then President Ferdinand Marcos announced plans to locate the largest hydroelectric complex in a valley in Southeast Asia. The four electricity-producing dams and one diversion dam would flood 1,400 square kilometers in the Valley, displacing 85,000 people. Most of those left homeless would be Bontoc and Kalinga. "The people of the Chico River Valley, particularly the Kalinga, have a deep religious bond with their home," writes Chip Fay, a member of the human rights group Survival International U.S.A. "They believe that their well-being depends upon the ongoing collective efforts of the living and the dead....Should the living allow burial grounds, villages, and rice terraces to be submerged by the dams, the wrath of angry spirits would certainly bring further disaster."[41]

The hillside rice paddies farmed by the Valley's people show amazing productivity, despite the intensity of their use. The farmers do not use synthetic chemical additives or sophisticated equipment; they and the spirits see to each year's fruitful harvest. But Marcos planned to put an end to their idyllic lifestyle. Despite the people's protests, plans for the dams continued. The World Bank became interested in the project and approved money for studies. When talks with officials in Manila failed to quash the dam, 150 tribal leaders allied themselves with one another and soon began monkeywrenching at government work camps.

In 1976 the Kalinga started receiving aid from the communist New Peoples Army. This armed resistance drew Marcos' wrath, and he sent more than 700 soldiers to the Valley. Curfews were imposed, and late in the year 150 Kalinga and Bontoc leaders were arrested. Many were held for up to eight months. Four years later, after continued delays and protests against the dam, opposition leader Macli-ing Dulag, a Kalinga village official, was assassinated by members of the Philippine Army. This proved to be a breaking point in the struggle. The people rallied to the cause, and by 1981 the Chico River dams were placed on hold. Only with the accession of Corazon Aquino to the presidency in 1986 was the conflict finally ended.[42]

Africa: Women for Green Belts, Children for Elephants

Professor Wangari Maathai of Nairobi, Kenya, is an environmental renegade of the least expected kind. On a continent where women bear much of the responsibility for food production but benefit from few rights and little respect; where environmentalism is, charitably, in a nascent stage; and where the lust to catch up with the excesses of the West is deeply felt,

Maathai finds herself pushing against the very foundations of culture, economics, and politics. She heads Green Belt, a movement begun in 1977. Since then it has spread its unique program combining reforestation and women's self-help to more than thirty other African nations. Green Belt's goals in planting trees are to stop soil erosion, provide fuel, beautify landscapes, and to generate income for women. The several hundred tree nurseries supported by the movement provide seedlings for use on public and private lands as green belts, or wooded areas surrounding or separating developed areas. The women, who have little disposable income, earn the equivalent of 2.5 cents for each tree they plant that survives more than three months outside of the nursery; they have planted ten million.

In 1989, Maathai took the bold step of standing up to the Kenyan governing party and objecting to the planned construction of a 60-story skyscraper in a Nairobi park. Maathai, who like Chico Mendes was awarded a United Nations Environmental Program Global 500 award, fears that the government's harsh retaliation for her stubborn resistance to the development program will affect Green Belt's ability to function. In Kenya, a bad word from the authorities is the worst sort of rebuke. Once more, radical environmentalism has come under fire from the authorities. The poor who benefit from Green Belt's tree planting program hear secondhand that the government has declared "'that the movement is subversive,'" Maathai says. "'Then they are scared. They don't want to be seen as against the Government, which can lead you into a lot of trouble. And a lot of politicians know that is the way the people feel.'"[43]

Elsewhere in Kenya, and nearly everywhere else on the continent that elephants are found, pachyderms are being decimated. Between 1973 and 1989, Kenya's population of elephants dropped at an incredible rate, from 130,000 to a mere *17,000.* Almost all of the decline was due to poachers killing the leviathans of the land for their ivory tusks. The situation got to be so bad that in late 1988 Kenyan President Daniel arap Moi ordered that elephant poachers be shot on sight.

Only recently did the world community begin acting with one voice to halt the continued destruction of the largest living land animals. Yet even as the Convention in International Trade in Endangered Species (CITES), a treaty-making body comprised of more than 100 member nations, debated whether to ban the global trade in ivory, a unique radical protest was underway. On October 11, 1989, the third day of debate on the ivory trade issue at the conference in Lausanne, Switzerland, 400 schoolchildren stormed the session chanting, "Don't kill the elephants! Let the elephants live!"' Carrying banners demanding the end of ivory trading and wearing papier-mache elephant heads, the children marched into the middle of the heated discussion. The Swiss branch of the World-Wide Fund for Nature sponsored the action. Five days later, following the children's action and intensive lobbying by major environmental groups, seventy-six of the ninety-one nations in attendance voted to classify the African elephant as endangered and to ban the ivory trade.[44]

Asia: Thailand and Taiwan Fight Tin and Titanium

In 1986 the people of the picturesque island of Phuket, in the Andaman Sea off of Thailand's southern coast, rose in protest against yet another World Bank-sponsored project. This one was a refinery producing tantalum, a rare metal valued for its uses in high technology. Tantalum is a by-product of the manufacture of tin, the mining of which had long taken place on the island. Phuket's residents recognized the deleterious effects that tin mining and processing was having on their island and feared its impact on the growing tourist trade; they soon came to see tantalum as an even greater threat.

The Thailand Tantalum Industry Corporation used the World Bank money to construct the refinery near houses and a college. To oppose the refinery the islanders formed the Committee to Coordinate Action Against Pollution in early 1986. Soon thereafter, a videocassette of the Bhopal disaster was distributed throughout the island. One report on what followed said, "It would be hard to imagine a better organizing tool in Phuket, where videocassettes are passed hand-to-hand like good books...."[45] Fearful of the potential toxins and pollutants emitted by the factory, the people became agitated. Anxiety spread throughout the island of 200,000, and on June 1, one-fourth of the islanders rallied to call a halt to the plant's construction. They agreed on a boycott of Coca-Cola because its Thai bottlers owned stock in the tantalum company. The controversy quickly grew to a matter of nationwide importance. On June 23, 70,000 islanders marched to a meeting with the Thai industry minister, Chirayu Isarangkun na Ayuthaya. When he saw the crowd's angry mood, however, Chirayu fled to another province.

Not knowing he had left the island, thousands of angry residents combed Phuket. Hot, tired, and without answers from the government about how it would address their concerns, late in the day they turned on the nearly completed plant. By the next morning it lay in ruins, torched by some protestors while others literally "lifted fire trucks off the ground to prevent them from going to save the burning buildings. In the end, the plant suffered $25 million in damage and was essentially destroyed."[46] It was the most costly single act of ecological sabotage in history. The protest degenerated into a riot, which left a hotel with a $400,000 repair bill, one police officer injured, and more than fifty people arrested. The Phuket experience helped propel the Thai government to take a serious look at its environmental regulations and the role that local peoples play in plant sitings.

Similar results came from less destructive actions in Taiwan in opposition to a Du Pont chemical plant. In March 1987, Du Pont scratched plans to build a $168 million factory that would have produced 60,000 tons of titanium dioxide each year. Chlorine gas used in the manufacture of the paint and plastics additive was the object of scorn in the city of Lukang; not only is chlorine a fast-acting and deadly poison, but the process would have produced large amounts of acidic wastewater. At about the same time as the Phuket protests were shifting into high gear, the citizens of Lukang "broke through a police cordon and marched through the town," protesting against the plant. "A month later more than a score of them picketed government offices in Taipei."[47] In August residents again marched, this time wearing T-shirts reservedly proclaiming, "I love Taiwan but want no part of Du Pont." That action, radical for Taiwan, resulted in the detention by riot police of 270 activists for six hours and helped push Du Pont out of town.

The Lukang struggle had momentous importance for the nation as a whole. After reporting the government's intention to quadruple its environmental protection budget, Taipei's China Post, said, "The protests are seen as a warning that people are no longer prepared to put up with pollution, which spewed freely into rivers and the air during the island's rapid industrialization in the 1960s and 1970s....The government is now coming under pressure to improve the quality of life on the island."[48]

India and Ecological Gandhism

For years radical environmentalists have touted their heightened environmental consciousness and the Gandhist approach that comes with it. Those who claim non-violence is but a "tactic" simultaneously and paradoxically show their commitment to the cause and the shallowness of their rhetoric. *Ahisma* is a way of life or it is little else. In recent years that philosophy has returned to India in the form that the Mahatma intended: highly visible, outspoken, and innovative campaigns, but with an environmental twist.

The Gandhi name has been a factor in Indian politics since the Mahatma's time. The heir apparent to former Prime Minister Indira Gandhi was her youngest son, Sanjay, who was killed in a stunt plane crash in 1980. His wife, Maneka Gandhi, took it upon herself to break with her mother-in-law's politics. Since then, she has became a primary force for carrying on the non-violent tradition and for extending it to the environment. At thirty-two, Maneka is the leader of India's major opposition party, Janata Dal. Moreover, according to the *New York Times*, "Her consuming passion is ecology. Because her famous name brings opportunities her way, she is beginning to make a measurable dent in the public conscience. She has, for example, turned what was supposed to have been a political column into a space for ecology in a leading magazine."[49]

Among her projects, Gandhi is attempting to rehumanize a nation which has lost its love of animals. She operates her own animal shelter and is acutely aware of the tragedies of inner-city stray animals. One of her successes was the defeat of a proposal by the city of Calcutta to export stray dogs for meat. The battle won, she set about raising money for a canine birth control vaccine.

In a nation not known for environmental protection, even comparatively minor inroads are major steps. Gandhi is helping to develop a new kind of harness for bullocks, one-third of which die from neck cancer. And she is fighting for controls on transporting animals to slaughter and for the way they are killed; currently, most die a lingering death of up to forty minutes after being slit in the throat. Gandhi and her supporters have even endeavored to purchase all of the birds on sale at a bird market and release them into the wild. Hers is as ambitious a struggle as any in the environmental community. With India's burgeoning population pressuring ecosystems like nowhere else on the Earth, Gandhi remains philosophical, stating that one "in a panic has no time for other species, and we are all in a panic."[50]

Some are joining Gandhi and slowing down to help the environment. One focus of their efforts is an area in central India along the Narmada River unknown even to many Indians. As with Muir, Brower, and the Kalinga, the issue is dams. From now until well into the twenty-first century, the Indian government plans to spend $20 billion to construct thousands of dams of various sizes along the river for irrigation and hydroelectric power to serve the states of Gujarat, Madhya Pradesh, and Maharashtra. Tribal peoples will be the ones to suffer. The Narmada is sacred to the indigenous people of the region, who comprise a substantial portion of the more than 1.5 million Indians destined to lose their homes and livelihoods if the World Bank-funded project is successful. The two largest dams were already under construction when, according to one report, environmentalists "and public action groups from all over the country, along with a couple of Bombay film stars, opened their campaign against the Narmada project at Harsud with the first large national environmental demonstration in India. Organizers hope it will be the start of a 'green' movement in the subcontinent.'"[51]

Besides an unwillingness to leave their homelands, many along the Narmada do not trust the government's promises of compensation. They point to the example of Bhopal, where residents waited for years after the tragic chemical leak and have yet to receive promised relief. Support for a no compromise stand against the dam project is coming from the cities. With the Mahatma as an example, "Indian ecologists and development experts, armed with the best scientific education acquired at home and abroad, are beginning to move into villages like Harsud, trying to make millions of disadvantaged Indians aware of the issue." As in the Amazon, a struggle over ecological issues is being used as a unifying political tool to end the oppression both of the land and the people who depend upon it. Even if the effort fails, says a booklet, "'We will have shown that we are no longer willing to be taken for granted."[52]

Chipko: Tree-hugging for Earth and People

Mahatma Gandhi's spirit also resides in the Chipko Movement, India's tree huggers. Chipko literally means "to hug" or "to cling to,"[53] and the movement got its name in 1973 when Indians in the Himalayan foothills rose up to protect their forests from destruction by huge logging firms. Forest destruction had led to several disastrous floods—in 1970 the Alakhnada River rose sixty feet and killed 200 persons. Commercial logging and road building contributed to the severity of the deluges, although the native people, too, were partially to blame. They used wood as their primary source of fuel, but the Indian government gave them no formal rights to the land, and they paid little attention to its preservation.

In the years prior to the first Chipko protests in 1973, the region had seen growing dissatisfaction over the awarding of forestry contracts. Federal forestry officials consistently granted contracts to low land loggers, ignoring the poverty of the people of Uttarakhand. Another problem was that logging was permitted in crucial watersheds. Finally, villagers from Gopeshwar decided to fight back using only their bodies. At the first Chipko protest, following a meeting where villagers had agreed to take a firm stand against a logging operation by hugging the trees, the activists never got a chance to act—the loggers turned back when they encountered a peaceful but determined crowd of about 100 people just outside of the forest.

Chipko made its presence felt again a few months later. Incredibly, the government announced an auction of 2,500 trees from the Reni forest overlooking the Alakhnada River that had flooded so severely. Chandi Prasad, who originated the Chipko concept, visited towns near the Reni to promote this newest in Gandhian techniques. Many villagers were receptive to the idea, and two Chipko workers remained as organizers after Prasad left. Following the January 1974 auction of the trees, Prasad confronted the contractor and warned him that members of the Chipko Movement would be waiting when his loggers arrived in the forest. Months passed, and then the government surprised the people of the Reni by announcing that compensation for land confiscated for military purposes following the India-China war of 1962 would be paid in late March.

Early one morning the men of the area around the Reni forest left for the town of Chamoli to collect their money. Only when they arrived in Chamoli did they discover that the reimbursement scheme was a setup to allow the loggers into the forest. Back at a forest village, a little girl saw the sawyers heading for the trees and told an elder of the village, Gaura Devi, who gathered a group of thirty women and children and led them into the forest. They found the loggers, all men, preparing their lunch. Some of the men were drunk, and one approached the women with a gun. Gaura Devi stepped into his path, "bared her breast, and said, 'This forest is like your mother. You will have to shoot me before you can cut it down.'"[54] The stunned loggers left the forest, and the women's actions prompted an official state report on the forest. The report, released two years later, recommended protection not only for the Reni, but for an even larger section of the Alakhnada watershed as well.

In the years since, the Chipko Movement has spread throughout India. Today it not only emphasizes saving forests but restoring them as well, and to that end millions of trees have been planted. The movement has evolved into a struggle both for local autonomy and for the land. Prasad has said that Chipko "goes beyond the erosion of the land, to the erosion of human values." He adds, "If we are not in a good relationship with the environment, the environment will be destroyed, and we will lose our ground. But if you halt the erosion of humankind, humankind will halt the erosion of the soil."[55]

Learning from One Another

What emerges from this brief survey of radical environmentalism around the world is that national and international political and economic powers take much for granted. Axiomatic to the world view of Western governments and institutions is a belief that "development" can only flow from West to East and from North to South. Nothing, the arrogant believe, can be learned from people who earn a living tapping rubber trees or farming terraced rice fields, not even if those ways of living are immeasurably richer in meaning and more beneficial to the Earth.

Slowly, too slowly, the World Bank, national governments, and multinational corporations are beginning to reorient themselves from environmentally destructive practices, which so often decimate cultures, to those which support them. Creative methods of relieving the immense debt burden on nations like Brazil, the Philippines, and India are being proposed. Some dam projects are halted, some roads go unbuilt, occasional development projects are foregone because of international pressure. But how many animals, plants, and landscapes have been forever lost by misguided, occi-centric policies? And how many cultures have we obliterated? "Were the World Bank to consider the rights and wishes of tribal people," writes Chip Fay, "it would likely find that, like the Bontoc and Kalinga, most of them have nothing to sell."[56] Add the Amazonian Indians, rubber tappers, and the Penan to that list.

How plausible is it that U.S.-styled radical environmentalism will spread throughout the world? That answer can best be found in governments' actions. The environment is taking its rightful place at the center of the worldwide political arena, and in individual nations as well. Will Eastern Europe really clean up its environmental mess? Will it recreate wilderness? Will it only go part way, or will the push for Western ways of life prove so overwhelming that even the ecological basis for reform in those nations will be forgotten? Will Kenya listen to Wangari Maathai and will the Indian government hear the people of Harsud, who demand that the land be nurtured and protected for itself and for the preservation of its life-sustaining essence? Will the Eco-Wall be overcome through a new, Green politics? Some sort of grassroots action, certainly, is essential for environmental preservation. Without ecological wisdom, the will for ecological preservation and restoration does not exist. Radical environmental activism is only one means of calling attention to the need for a new human-Earth relationship. Other approaches will be tried as well, but the "something else" of direct action will always be lurking where all else has failed.

PART THREE

ENVIRONMENTAL ACTIVISM IN PRACTICE

CHAPTER 9

HANGING GEORGE WASHINGTON'S BIB

Mike Roselle is wilderness personified, a grizzly bear of a man behind wolf-grey eyes who revels in taking on all challengers to his territory—wild lands from rainforests to deserts.[1] The Kentucky native's manner and drawl are that of an amiable southerner, but Roselle sits nervously, squirming so much that by all appearances he has to get to an urgent appointment somewhere else *soon*. Very much a peripatetic, on call and with a calling, Roselle's experience in the first ever banner hanging from Mt. Rushmore proves the itinerant wilderness guardian's eagerness to go where the action is. His willingness to sacrifice dearly for his radicalism became the stuff of legend among radical environmentalists following this action, which demonstrates as well the differences between Greenpeace, the first well-known radicals, and today's vanguard of the radical environmental movement.

Roselle's invitation to join the 1987 Greenpeace protest on the batholith where the visages of presidents Washington, Jefferson, Theodore Roosevelt, and Lincoln gaze stolidly over the South Dakota hill country sounds like something out of a James Bond thriller, or perhaps an episode of "Mission Impossible" for the radical environmental set. Roselle recalls, "I got a call from a Washington, D.C., Greenpeace campaigner. He says, 'Mike, we got something for you to do. If you want to do it, I can't tell you about it over the phone, but I want you to be on the next plane to Rapid City.'" Roselle says with a smile, "Now, that's one of the reasons I don't work for Greenpeace anymore. I mean, it was exciting to get called out like that a lot. That's the way the whole bomb campaign, the nuclear test campaign, got started. 'Mike, want you to be in Las Vegas tomorrow.' And I figure, well, I'm your guy." Since the Mt. Rushmore action, though, Roselle has yet to work with Greenpeace.

Of Yippies and RARE II

Roselle's past reveals that he is far from the ideal Ian Fleming hero. The son of a painter who "worked on military bases quite a bit," Roselle spent most of his formative years on the tough streets of inner-city Louisville. His mother had him baptized a Catholic so that he could attend parochial school rather than decrepit public institutions. That didn't keep him off the streets, but the streets led him to the Cabbage Patch Settlement House, which was started by Louise Marshall, a descendant of the famous U.S. Supreme Court Chief Justice, John Marshall. "Miss Marshall," as she was known, was a social worker with a green conscience, committed as she was to taking children who lived far from nature out into parks and forests. "Even though it was a Christian organization, they thought that this was absolutely important," Roselle says, displaying the ambivalence—even contempt—that many radical environmentalists feel toward Christianity or any other organized faith. "So they had a program of day camps and week-long camps." The outings suited Roselle just fine. As a child he was always fascinated by the nature books he found in the library. "When I was eleven years old," Roselle says, "they took us on a two-week trip to Grand Canyon, Zion, and Bryce Canyon national parks." He was no choir boy, though: "I remember shoplifting in all the souvenir stores," he says with a playful grin.

At thirteen Roselle was already active in the Vietnam War protest movement. He was arrested for demonstrating in Los Angeles' Elysian Park, an incident that permanently tainted his view of authority and the law. "I was totally surprised that it was illegal to distribute literature in a public park," Roselle says. "The arrest destroyed my respect for government, what freedoms we have. I became very anti-social, opposed to almost everything. A lot of us were in that mode." He spent time with Abbie Hoffman's Youth International Party (the Yippies), joining a collective of anarchists outraged at what they saw as the moral bankruptcy of American society. Roselle learned the rudiments of organizing, radicalism, and confrontation from the Yippies at numerous protests, including uprisings at the Democratic and Republican national conventions in Miami in 1972. Months later he was there at the gloaming event of the anti-war movement, Richard Nixon's second swearing-in. "That was the last big demonstration against U.S. foreign policy for that era. The inauguration of Nixon was really demoralizing to the movement."

Like so many others, Roselle was burned out and needed some time to put years of protest against an intransigent government into perspective, to decide "whether I was an anarchist, a communist, a socialist, or just trying to reform the U.S. government." He headed to North Carolina's Great Smoky Mountains National Park. "I got so much out of this first hike that everything came together," he says. "I said if I can do this a couple of times a year, life will be worth living." It was in the Smokies that he first felt the spark of environmental consciousness. "I remember seeing a golden eagle flying over a pristine valley from the Appalachian Trail near New Found Gap. It just blew me away that there were still places like this."

Roselle wanted more. He toured the nation, travelling thousands of miles by Volkswagen bus in seemingly desultory wanderings, a peculiarly American twist to the time-consecrated "walkabout." And as happens in the Australian ritual, a new awareness grew in him. Its apotheosis came beside a pristine creek in a New Mexico wilderness area. Roselle remembers "looking into a stream and seeing a rainbow trout, just watching this fish, and for the first time in my life not thinking about grabbing a pole, just appreciating the fact that there was still this kind of scenery. It changed my life. I realized that relating to the wilderness meant more than just going backpacking a couple of times a year."

From New Mexico Roselle's trekking took him to Wyoming, where he got to know the state representative for Friends of the Earth, Howie Wolke, while both worked at a restaurant in Jackson; the friendship was sealed when each realized the other was stealing pastries from the establishment's fulsome bakery. It was 1975, and Wolke's Friends of the Earth salary was measly in light of the dozens of hours of work he put into the job each week on top of his restaurant chores. His strident advocacy piqued Roselle's interest. "He got me going to hearings to testify on behalf of wilderness," Roselle remembers. "I'd never met a conservationist before. The whole time I was in the anti-war movement, we pooh-poohed the environmental movement....After I made a connection with the wilderness, it seemed to me that all the other stuff—the political stuff—didn't matter. In some sense, it even went beyond what we consider the most sanctified thing in the world, which is human life, to make a deeper connection that mortality is part of living and that what's really important is that we preserve the ecosystems that produced us."

Roselle educated himself about the environment and environmental issues, gradually taking up causes on his own and getting others to follow. But money was tight, so on occasion he worked as a roughneck in the Wyoming oil fields. "I had a rule that I would work in the oil fields until I had a thousand dollars saved up, and then I would quit," Roselle explains. "Generally, I could do that in thirty or forty days. After I got known down there, I didn't even have to look for jobs. They'd call me up." Spending time around the newest, most expensive technology and "drilling through millions of years of geology" had its allure, he admits. For "even though I was a conservationist and I realized there were limitations to fossil fuel development, there was a certain excitement to being at a wellhead." Still, Roselle says, there was no excusing such un-ecological behavior. "I had my scruples: I'd never work in a roadless area that we were trying to save....Thinking back about that, it seems like a rationalization that I probably couldn't do now because I've learned a hell of a lot about natural resources."

By the late 1970s Roselle was committed to a life of environmental activism, perceiving as he did the need for a new twist to the old ways. "I was ready to reach back into my radical past," he says. "Conservationists had not been confrontational up to that point. They wanted to do things the easiest possible way, to work with people, to raise the fewest red flags as possible, to develop positions that other conservationists could support." Then came the RARE II process that catalyzed the radical environmental movement. Industry's steamrolling of the RARE II process confirmed Roselle's belief in the futility of compromise. His postmortem of the process is pointed. "We should have had an Earth First! proposal. The Wilderness Society should have been on its own, and so should the Audubon Society and the National Wildlife Federation, to show the diversity of perspectives. Then the Forest Service would have had to deal with each of these groups and their constituencies one-on-one instead of dismissing us all as a bunch of California hippie backpackers. . . ." With the sour taste of RARE II fresh in his mouth, Roselle helped establish Earth First! and began applying his radical tools to the machinery of environmental destruction.

George Washington's Bib

Radicals of the green stripe flocked to Earth First! to learn the active, non-violent confrontation methods from anti-war movement veterans like Roselle. He spent half a decade organizing increasingly visible protests against logging in the Pacific Northwest's old growth forests, getting arrested again and again in the process, and succeeding in spreading word of the urgency of the situation to a nation unaware that some of its grandest natural treasures, its green cathedrals, were falling to the chainsaw at an astounding rate.

While getting Earth First! off the ground, Roselle took a job as Greenpeace's first (and only) National Direct Action Coordinator. He pulled together a small team of activists with diverse backgrounds to provide expertise to local campaigns, their objective being to get Greenpeace's message on the evening news in the most effective way possible. The group consisted of climbers, boat drivers, media experts—people who knew how to liven up a "Clean up the River" or "No Nuclear Plant in Our Backyard" protest. Roselle left Greenpeace after a year, in large part because he was not allowed to help create the radical policy alternatives for which he was assigned to garner publicity. Nevertheless, he told them to call whenever they might need him.

A year later, in October 1987, the call came to fly to Rapid City. "They had been wanting to do an action at Mt. Rushmore for quite some time, but they didn't exactly know which issue to focus on," Roselle says. "When they did the Hiroshima Day action on the Statue of Liberty, it produced a really good photograph that went around the world.[2] That's the kind of thing that Greenpeace can do. To them a good photograph is worth more than a story." Once in South Dakota, Roselle was told that the mysterious action was to protest acid rain. A crucial vote was about to be taken in Congress on a key piece of acid rain legislation, and Greenpeace wanted a high-visibility effort to get a photo on front pages and film on the evening news in hopes of prompting citizens to contact their representatives.

The plan was to hike up the mountain under cover of darkness, then drape a banner like a bib beneath Washington's chin. The drape-like sign, reading "WE THE PEOPLE SAY NO TO ACID RAIN—GREENPEACE," was the largest of its kind ever made. Sewn by a sail maker in two parts and designed to be supported by an array of rock climbing ropes and clips, it measured sixty feet by 120 feet when fully unfurled. The banner was not the only component of the display, however. There was also a huge cloth "gas mask," which was to be placed over President Washington's face. Roselle thought the idea was cute but not necessary. "There was a big argument in the motel room," Roselle says. "Do we hang the banner first and then come back up and do the gas mask, or do the gas mask, then the banner? I said, 'This is what Greenpeace taught me: if it's not an action without the banner, then you do the banner first. You can do the gas mask, and it's no action. If you get caught right after you do the gas mask or if you drop the banner on the ground and don't have time to retrieve it, it's not an action. So common sense says you hang the banner first.'

"I had done a lot of actions in National Parks, and [park rangers are] very good at responding to things like this. I told them, 'Do not underestimate the ability of the Park Service to respond quickly....You get that thing hung and you get your photograph and then the action is an action. It doesn't matter if it's up there all day or if it's up there for fifteen minutes, as long as the UPI photographer down there in the parking lot gets the photograph and the news cameras get the video footage.' I was overruled." The gas mask would go up first. Roselle remembers the Greenpeacers saying, "'Oh, we'll have plenty of time.'" In the end, they didn't.

The action group made the arduous trip to George Washington's crown under miserable conditions. There were the three climbers who would do the actual banner hanging, two coordinators, the acid rain campaign director, two media people, and some "sherpas"—activists who carried supplies. Roselle made the trip, too, lugging a 100-pound backpack of equipment, no mean feat even for someone six-foot-four with muscles that start at the fingertips and extend as solid as granitic plutons up to broad shoulders.

Knowing that there were no formal trails to the top of Mt. Rushmore, the Greenpeace reconnaissance team had scouted a route leading up the back. They had not gone all the way up, though. On the night of the action, after hours of climbing in the pitch black forest, the party found that the trail, such as it was, petered out above the tree line among rocks covered in ice from a rain and snow storm earlier that evening. The route appeared hopeless; clearly it was extremely dangerous. The only alternative was a frontal assault up an equally non-existent trail. The trip took Roselle and the others across a massive, precipitous, unstable rubble heap, the detritus from the carving of the four presidents' heads. As he stumbled and slipped beneath the sixty-foot-tall sculptures Roselle remembers "quietly cussing my campaigner," the action leader. The action had taken on a depressing quality.

Finally, they made it to the top. The supplies were dropped, and all but the climbers and the rope watcher scrambled down to the parking lot to catch the show. At first light three tiny figures could be seen clamoring across Washington's face attempting to attach the "gas mask." It was only then that they discovered that Washington was not carved as a bust but as a relief, the face distorted to provide the correct perspective from the ground. When the climbers attempted to hang the mask, its symmetry made for trouble. "They spent two or three hours messing with that gas mask, and they didn't get it on," Roselle says. He was chagrined that no one had checked the site in person for quirks such as the Washington relief. In fact, the entire protest had been planned using a postcard purchased at the Mt. Rushmore Visitors' Center with the carvings' measurements printed on it. "I didn't do the recon on this," Roselle says, chafing at the memory. "It's like in the retail business. They say there are three factors to success: location, location, and location. Well in this kind of action the three keys are reconnaissance, reconnaissance, and reconnaissance. There's nothing that takes the place of good reconnaissance, and we did not have good reconnaissance when it came to the gas mask, and we did not have good reconnaissance when it came to the route up the mountain."

Roselle, surprised by the park rangers' lethargic response, watched as they finally make their way toward the climbers. Meanwhile, it was agonizingly slow going at the top. After two hours of wasting time, the decision was made to abandon the gas mask and to hang the banner as quickly as possible. The left half, reading

WE THE
SAY
ACID
GREEN

was to be hung first. As coordinator of the climb, Roselle was supposed to stay in radio contact with the lookout on top and with the support team at a nearby motel. The rope watcher on Washington's shoulder operated an FM transceiver to communicate with Roselle and a Citizens Band radio to relay messages to and from the climbers. The climbers wore sophisticated CB headphone sets costing more than $2,000 apiece that permitted them to talk with one another without yelling. But when the rangers and sundry other law enforcement personnel arrived on the scene, they quickly arrested the rope/radio man. Direct radio contact with the climbers was lost.

Then one climber, Steve Loper, went completely down the face to straighten out his tangled climbing ropes. "One of the things we decided on was that no one comes off the ropes," Roselle says. "Well, there had been a Park Service guy in the bushes at the bottom of the scree slope waiting for him to do that. When he saw Loper come off, he grabbed him." The remaining climbers realized that unfurling the second half of the banner would be difficult, perhaps impossible. Then Roselle saw the ranger who nabbed Loper pulling at Richard Harvey's ropes. Harvey was using a special climbing tool, a Jumar Ascender, to keep him in place on the rope. By pulling on the rope, the ranger could have deactivated the Jumar's holding mechanism, with tragic consequences. Certain that the rangers on top were monitoring his transmissions, Roselle told them to warn off their overly enthusiastic fellow lawman. By doing so, Roselle effectively "aided and abetted" the climbers, and he was promptly arrested. Soon after, the climbers quit the action. Sculptors working on the nearby Crazy Horse monument arrived on the scene later, rappelled down, and cut the half-banner's support ropes. The on-site action was over.

Trial by Trial

Roselle, Harvey, Loper, Ken Hollis, and Phillip Templeton were arrested, booked, and released; their equipment was confiscated. The trial, such as it was, was not held until January 25, 1988, three months after the activist's arrest. "This is another thing that I disagree with Greenpeace about," Roselle says. "With Greenpeace, the action is over when the arrests are made. They want to clean up after that—let's cut our losses." Greenpeace does not abandon its activists, but it does not use the trial to its advantage, either, Roselle says. Although not every trial can be a grand show, the press is always hungry for a sensational story with moral undertones (or, better yet, moral overtones). Roselle knows this well, and he recognizes the solidifying effects a sensational trial or a jail term of the proper length can have on the movement. "With Earth First!, the action's not over until the *action* is over. The trial and the jail part are just as important—jail solidarity, hunger strikes, media events, demonstrations outside the jailhouse. We've always done that. We learned this from the Livermore Action Group and countless other organizations that have worked on non-violent direct action, and we really believe in that."

But he was working with Greenpeace, which "wanted to hang banners on other monuments." Roselle grudgingly acceded to their wishes that he plead guilty and avoid a show. "I wanted to plead not guilty and use a necessity defense: I *had* to hang that banner. Acid rain is killing the forest. I had to do this action." He adds with a grin and a manic, growling voice, feigning possession by a tree-hugging demon, "My conscience wouldn't leave me alone if I didn't do it! And then of course you get convicted anyway. But you go through a trial." As it was, "if we plea bargained, they'd give us four months, they'd suspend three of them, and they wanted to keep our equipment. They loved our equipment. . . .We caucused and we said, 'No way, we're not going to give those guys our equipment. We're not going to accept a plea bargain, but we'll plead guilty.' We got the same sentence, except they didn't get the equipment."

The sentencing hearing was held on the spot. The other defendants made statements to the court about their characters in the hope of getting the lightest possible jail term. "My opinion is that you ask for the most serious sentence," Roselle says matter-of-factly, pushing the envelope of the no-compromise ethic farther than even the most committed might demand. He refused to plead with the judge for leniency and found the testimony of one defense witness, who lectured the judge about the values of the Mt. Rushmore presidents, "kind of demeaning, myself. I don't believe any of those assholes ever stood for anything except for making money. Those guys on that mountain are not exemplary human beings." He pauses to reconsider. "Well, some of Jefferson's writings are okay, and I've got a soft spot for Lincoln."

"A Question of Survival"

There were no soft spots in the county jail in Rapid City, where Roselle and the others were locked up as federal prisoners. They all signed up for a work release program, but the work bored and offended Roselle. "One Saturday they sent us out to clean up after a Knights of Columbus bingo game," recalls the recusant. "I came back and said, 'Look, I'm not going to work for the Pope. Besides, there are a lot of guys around here who could use a minimum wage job, and the Knights of Columbus are raking in the money.'" When he objected to cleaning up the bingo hall again the next day, Roselle was sent to solitary confinement for nine days. Later he discovered that, as a federal prisoner, he was prohibited from working off of the jail premises.

The afternoon before his thirty days were up, Roselle's life began to get strange. He was taken to see his probation officer, although he was not about to take probation—he could not accept the three years of limited liberties which went with the deal. The probation officer, who refused to shake Roselle's hand, started running down a list of the terms of his release, things like keep a "regular job," work "regular hours." Roselle, always one to give authority figures a difficult time since his Elysian Park arrest, interrupted. He asked what those directives meant: he was an environmentalist—was that a regular job? The probation officer growled at him, then read on. Finally, Roselle stopped him and announced what he knew all along, that he would not be signing the probation papers. Flabbergasted, the probation officer left the room with a curt "Very well!" Roselle was carted back to solitary.

Things got weirder that evening. Because the judge had *assigned* Roselle (and the others) to probation without asking if they accepted the terms, Roselle was set to be released the following morning along with the other Greenpeacers. He had not signed his probation papers, yet in the court's eyes he was to be released on probation. When his jailers realized this, they called in a federal marshall who arrested Roselle for violating the terms of a probation that he had never agreed to and that would not have gone into effect until the next day. Roselle was hauled back into court several days later on the charge of violating his non-existent, non-operable probation by exercising his right not to sign his probation report.

Recognizing this as an opportunity to make a public pronouncement about the action, Roselle smuggled to his lawyer a statement for the press. The local Sierra Club chapter rounded up a large audience, complete with media coverage, to witness what was supposed to be a pro forma probation violation hearing. Apparently stunned by the huge crowd, the judge quickly sentenced Roselle to serve the ninety days remaining on his four-month prison term and all but ran from the courtroom as Roselle's attorney hollered a request that his client be allowed to read the statement. Copies were distributed to the press, and Roselle held a number of jailhouse interviews. David Brower happened to be in the Greenpeace offices when a copy of Roselle's statement, sent for Greenpeace approval, came in by facsimile machine from Roselle's lawyer. A few days later Brower read the statement at an environmental conference in Oregon which Roselle had agreed to attend months before the Mt. Rushmore action. The statement's imprisoned author, half a continent away and having had his rights thoroughly trampled upon, received a standing ovation.

In the statement, Roselle said, "I'm afraid I must disagree with your Honor's claim that we violated a 'just' law by hanging a banner on Mt. Rushmore. The present federal statute making the climbing of Mt. Rushmore illegal was enacted in the aftermath of an American Indian Movement demonstration during the early seventies. . . .The intent. . .is obvious: to discourage further demonstrations at the monument. . . .This law is clearly designed to restrict freedom of political expression, and as a result it has a chilling effect on our First Amendment right to free speech." He went on to "say that, in all due respect to the cherished ideals that the carved heads of the four former presidents represent, the sculpture itself is a violation of the mountain into which they have been dynamited." And after invoking the Nuremberg Principles, which oblige citizens of the world to stop tyranny, Roselle added, "Conditions today are not really that different than they were in pre-war Germany, though the totalitarianism our society is experiencing has taken on a different form and its victims are different. Now it is the wildlife that suffers the threat of extinction. The whales, the wolves, the bears, and even the forests, lakes, rivers, and oceans, which have existed here since creation, are in grave danger. And if they go, human beings cannot be far behind. It has become a question of survival."

Jailhouse Radical

Back in jail, Roselle, who says his keepers were mad and embarrassed that he had quit the work release program and feared his bad example might spread, was confined to a solitary cell for another two weeks. He took advantage of the one hour each day he was allowed to mingle with the other prisioners to organize a movement to improve the food. Inmates were rarely given fresh fruit or vegetables, and constipation was as rampant and as hard as steel bars. But most of the prison population just wanted salt and pepper, Roselle says. He was told the condiments had been banned years before after a prisoner in leg irons attempted to escape by throwing salt in a guard's eyes.

Gleefully recalling his prison activism, Roselle says, "We had this petition for fresh fruit and vegetables—and salt and pepper! We got ninety-nine percent of the inmates to sign this thing and we sent it off. . . .Somehow, they pegged me as the troublemaker. So we had these meetings with the chief of police and the jail staff. They said, 'We have a licensed dietitian prepare these meals,' and I said, 'Okay, you're on. Let's see her license!' They never showed me her license." The diet soon improved, and Roselle was promptly shipped out to the Hughes County Jail at Pierre, where he had no complaints about the food and peaceably served out his time.

While in jail Roselle received enough letters of support from sympathizers nationwide to fill an orange crate. He answered every one, read ravenously, and mailed Earth First!'s annual Direct Action Fund solicitation letter. For maximum effect, he asked to use the jail's own envelopes for the fundraiser, but the sheriff refused. Roselle then asked a friend to have envelopes printed with the jail's return address. "It was the most successful mailing I ever did," he says.

Soon after, Roselle's four months were up. "I got out and I was white and pasty, and it took a while for me to get over it," Roselle says. "I wasn't bitter and I didn't feel like I had missed out or anything. To me it was part of the job. It re-emphasized to me that you're not taken out of the action when you're put in jail. I was able to communicate with a tremendous number of people. The statements that I wrote and the coverage of what I did and why I did it reached a lot of people, and it got the same message out as we try to get out when we do a direct action." Roselle adds matter-of-factly, "With Earth First!, no one is so important that they can't go to jail. When we have an action we say this is why we're doing it, we have these moral responsibilities, international law, etcetera. Everybody plays by those rules, regardless of who you are. If it's good for the goose, it's good for the gander. You gotta do it."

CHAPTER 10

NOT JUST TREE HUGGERS ANYMORE

Judging by the press accounts, the 1989 Earth First! Round River Rendezvous was a madhouse full of paranoid, anti-American environmental crazies. The tribe's press-chosen "leaders" were constantly talking about the FBI's crackdown on the "organization" (because that was all they were being asked about), and a group at the rendezvous burned an American flag. Totally ignored by the media, grassroots activism—the heart and soul of the movement—was alive and well, concocting the biggest public education/media event in the decade since Earth First!'s founding: one week of non-stop, nationwide tree sitting. For years the concept had fermented in the movement's collective unconsciousness until it overflowed at the Rendezvous like a too-full vat of its favorite ale.

Tree sitting holds an allure to eco-warriors for several reasons. The inherent drama of climbing trees in the Pacific Northwest, where the first branch on an ancient redwood or Douglas fir emerges 100 feet or more from the ground, and then staying there for days at a time is exciting for the climber and—nearly always a consideration—it makes for great press. When a tree sit looks out over a once dense forest that has been clear cut, the public education potential of the media event is all the more powerful. Also, sitters speak of the close relationship that develops with the trees— John Muir, an avid tree climber, wrote that these seemingly sedentary creatures journey farther than most humans, though they never take a step.

On an economic front, tree sitting attacks timber companies at the point of production and slows or even halts tree cutting. Logging operations often are marginal propositions, and any substantial delay can push those who prey on thousand-year-old trees out of business or at least out of an ancient forest. Further, because tree sits involve large numbers of support people for each climber, they build solidarity within the movement by bringing together large numbers of activists who must tend to one of their own for days at a time while everyone involved risks personal injury or arrest. And trees epitomize wilderness. Deserts and oceans are wild places, too, but their wildness is forbidding and foreign to most.

Danger is present at any tree sit. Angry loggers have cut nearby trees so that they crash onto sitter's perches, and trees have actually been cut from beneath activists, in some cases causing severe and even permanent injury. Although it would seem that such acts would be worthy of criminal investigation on suspicion of assault, attempted murder, or even violating sitters' rights to exercise their First Amendment liberties to free speech, no charges have ever been filed against loggers.

With the Earth First! preoccupation with wilderness, and given its increasing reliance on tree sitting as a form of protest, the momentum naturally built toward a unified week of outrage against timber interests. Earth First! had brought off smaller scale, widespread operations before. There was a "National Day of Outrage" on the anniversary of Muir's 150th birthday in 1988, and before that coordinated action days for redwoods and rainforests. But a week of activity was unprecedented. "It's a brand new concept: defending the planet," says Earth First! organizer-musician Darryl Cherney. "It has never been done before in the history of the world as a cause."[1] Unlike prior "aerial occupations" in the big tree country of Washington, Oregon, and Northern California, however, the emphasis for this action, dubbed "Save America's Forests," was on exactly that—all of the nation's timbered lands: not just the oldest and most majestic ones, but also "second-growth" and "third-growth" forests that had already been cut once or twice before. Accomplished tree climber and sitter Greg King explains, "We were trying to show that there are threatened forests here in this country, even on the East Coast, that need protection just as much as any tropical [rainforest] around the world. Although it is admirable and important that we pursue the preservation of tropical forests from this country, it is at least as important, if not more so, that we pursue preservation of the forests that are here better than we're doing that now."[2]

The primary threat to forests in the U.S. comes from the timber industry, Earth First!ers say. To these mega-corporations, trees are nothing more than another investment, not home to marbled murrelets, northern spotted owls, deer, and bear. Tree cutting is not controlled by the people who live in the shadows of the trees, but by Wall Street investors overshadowed by takeover bids and junk bond debt. All that matters to them is the bottom line. "Even though you're getting less per acre and less per tree" as the old trees are cut, says Earth First! organizer Judi Bari, "what the corporations are considering is not how much timber they're getting, but how much money and if they invest the money in a non-timber enterprise, would it produce more than if they left it in standing trees? So the criteria for cutting down trees have nothing to do with forests, nothing at all. That's the problem with having corporations making decisions about forestry."[3] And that's the problem that the tree sitters set out to warn the public about in the summer of 1989.

How to Sit in a Tree

Tree sitting became something more than child's play when anarchist-activist Mike Jakubal and several others sat in Oregon's Millennium Grove in 1985. Those first sitters went up the trees by nailing in pitons. Since then the techniques have changed considerably. As with any radical environmental protest action, the first essential step is reconnaissance. For tree sitting this typically entails locating areas of active cutting, finding the easiest and least conspicuous routes to those sites, and choosing trees that will make the right statement. For the most part, these are the tallest, most impressive flora possible, those clearly visible from a nearby road or those which overlook recently cut areas.

After the tree or trees are selected, the sitters volunteer, banners are made, equipment is collected, and an entourage numbering as many as twenty people for each tree sitter hikes in as far as ten miles to get to the site. The group may carry 250 pounds or more of gear and provisions per sitter—their backpacks contain food, water, clothing, climbing gear, banners, and everything else the sitters will need for the duration of their stay. Essential to the operation is the door-sized "platform" that is hauled in for each sitter; for days on end these two-and-one-half-foot by six-foot wooden shelves are a sitter's home.

Sitters and their support teams often enter the targeted area under cover of darkness. When possible, a base camp is established for the entire sit. However, because tree sits usually take place on private land or on public lands that are under a "closure order" that excludes all unauthorized persons from entry, base camps often are some distance away. The laborious process of actually putting a sitter up a tree may begin by moonlight, at dawn or dusk after loggers have gone home. The first step has a gutsy "spur climber" carrying up a rope and various equipment essential to setting up the platform. The spur climbers strap special tree climbing spurs onto heavy-heeled boots. Although the spurs do not hurt redwoods or Douglas fir, the most frequently sat-in trees requiring spur climbing, thinner-barked species would be severely damaged by the long, thick, sharp spikes, each of which weighs four to five pounds.

With spurs set, a climber straps on a heavy belt resembling those used by weight lifters, wraps a lanyard made of thick rope around the tree, and hooks each end into the belt. From there, it's straight up the tree trunk. The climber leans toward the tree, flips one side of the lanyard upward, then the other, leans back to increase the tension, dislodges one spur, steps up, stabs with the spur, then dislodges, steps, and stabs with the other.

This wearying form of vertical self-torture is repeated until the climber reaches the desired platform height, typically just below the tree's canopy of limbs, somewhere between eighty and 150 feet off the ground. Once there, the climber affixes a "girth hitch" around the trunk and prepares ropes that will secure the platform to the hitch. The climber raises the platform with the aid of a Jumar Ascender, a ratchetting climbing tool which holds the rope and whatever is attached to it in place even if the climber lets go. Then the guy ropes are attached to the platform's eye bolts using carabineers, another rock climbing tool. Greg King says this process is the most hazardous aspect of the operation. "Sometimes you have to pull the platform up with one arm and snap it in as you're dangling from the tree. That's the first thing you do, get the platform up. Then you can stand on the platform and haul the rest of the stuff up with the [Jumar] pulley system, and it's much easier." When all is ready, the climber rappels down and the sitter "Jumars" up to the platform. Amazingly, no Earth First!er has ever been severely injured at any of its several dozen tree sits.

From Collective Unconsciousness to the Trees

King calls tree sitting "a witnessing action," a quasi-religious act of devotion intended to draw attention to the horrors of modern forestry. The tactic is far from radical, at least in any pejorative use of the term. "I think what would be radical would be if they started cutting down our tree sitters," the brown-haired, engaging King says with uncharacteristic glumness. "But sitting up in a tree to keep it from being cut—that's not nearly as radical as the ancient civilization, I think it was near Lebanon, where the indigenous people stood in front of trees every day, and every day the woodsmen would come up and cut them in half. They'd take the bodies away and cut down the trees. Tribes would keep doing that and doing that. *That's* pretty radical, when you know it's going to happen and you do it anyway."

The concept for extending the sorts of tree sits that King had perfected in the Pacific Northwest to a nationwide level bubbled over amidst all the FBI and flag burning hullabaloo one afternoon at the 1989 Rendezvous. A crowd attending a workshop on forest protection was discussing how best to publicize Earth First!'s fight for the trees. Darryl Cherney recalls walking past the session when "somebody called out to me, 'Hey Darryl, we're doing a nationwide tree sit. You want to be the press coordinator?' I immediately said yes." The outspoken Cherney felt that no one in the movement was better qualified to effectively handle such an undertaking than he. Besides, it was a great way to get the struggle into the nation's living room, and it was an opportunity to highlight the plight of the ancient redwood forests so dear to his heart. He was right on all counts. The dates for the National Tree Sit Week were set for Sunday, August 13, through the following Saturday.

A former record company publicist, Cherney is the consummate hippie environmentalist, the sort that gets under the skin of backwoods loggers and fat-cat executives as soon as he walks through the doorway: self-assured, short, skinny, with jet black hair, a scraggly beard, darting eyes, and an unstoppable, pithy, Brooklyn mouth. In his four years of fighting for the redwoods, Cherney raised press cultivation to an art form, earning for himself a sobriquet only an Earth First!er could love: "Media Slut." To video and print journalists, who had so often misunderstood (and misrepresented) the movement, Cherney's ability and willingness to convey environmentalists' anger, and to succinctly state the radical environmental position, was a godsend.

In keeping with the decentralized approach that it takes to almost everything that it does—as well as because the tribe is inherently haphazard in its organizational efforts—this most complicated of Earth First! actions was initially handled more casually than the way most people would set up a lunch date with a friend. Only in the two weeks immediately before the National Tree Sit Week began did media coordinator Cherney and Jean Crawford, the overall national coordinator, begin planning the event in earnest. Fortunately for them, two countervailing Earth First! characteristics were at work: the independence and the commitment of the tribe's warriors. So the response was no surprise when Crawford and Cherney finally began telephoning those who had expressed an interest in the action at the Rendezvous. "Throughout the country, everybody intended to do the Tree Sit," Cherney says. "It was as though it was an idea whose time had come.... Everybody was going full-tilt boogie on it. At that point I quoted Gandhi: 'I must hurry to catch up with the masses, for I am their leader.'"

It is impossible to imagine a major environmental organization pulling off this operation in a matter of a fortnight. Their hierarchies, bureaucracies, concerns for safety and legality, and the lack of committed individuals willing to be there for an issue at short notice all work against such bold actions. The mainstream groups are best at working slowly and in situations where control and direction are necessitated. On the other hand, nowhere have Earth First!'s strengths—speed, flexibility, and dedication–been more clearly demonstrated than in the Tree Sit week. The only centralized aspects of the action were the information clearinghouse maintained by Crawford, Cherney's publicity mill, and an equipment bank that King created to assist sitters nationwide. "The sites, how the action was to happen, and the climbing—everything was taken care of on a local basis," King says. "Of course, that's the way we like to do it—keep it spread out and hard to pin down. One of the intentions of the Tree Sit... was to point out to the feds and whoever else is looking that this movement is not organized out of Arizona. It's organized out of the hearts of the people who are doing it." The Tree Sit week, then, was a show of strength and resolve by the grassroots.

Judi Bari, who was drafted to organize sits in Northern California, had laid the groundwork in redwood country by establishing or enlarging numerous local Earth First! groups since early the year before. Albion, Ukiah, Laytonville, the Pacific Coast, Sonoma County—her work was beginning to pay off throughout the vast, rural area. The witty, fast-talking union organizer was eager to take advantage of every opportunity afforded her. When the Tree Sit Week came along, she recognized it as the ideal chance to solidify individual groups and to get activists together from throughout the area.

In some ways Bari had been *too* successful in her organizing efforts. Her work had increased environmental consciousness to the point where the mere mention of a tree sit sparked rivalries, owing in large part to the close identification people had with the trees in their areas. Bari began scouting for possible tree sit locations in early August. She had all but decided on a site near the community of Albion when she went to Willits to meet with the Sherwood Forest Association, a group sympathetic to Earth First! but not fully aligned with it. The folks there wanted a sit in their neck of the woods, but they promised to support whatever decision Bari made. "After the meeting," Bari recalls, "one of the guys called me and said, 'I'd still like you to look at our trees.' So I said okay, and we arranged to go out. I go to his house, and the first thing he says is, 'I want you to know that I really support your work, and I wanted to give you this,' and he hands me a hundred dollar bill."

To shoestring operations like Bari's, a hundred dollars is a small fortune. "At that point, I decided I didn't care what his trees looked like," she says with a chuckle. "Hey, if you've seen one clear cut, you've seen 'em all! So he took me out on this road, and I have to admit it really blew me away. I was stunned by it. This road went through dramatically atrocious clear cuts. I thought that was good, and then they started giving us all these other offers of support to sway us to do it over there." When Bari urged the Albion group to do a logging road blockade of some sort and to help out with support for the Sherwood Forest action, they became upset. Faced with two stubborn groups, friendly bribe in hand, and enthusiasm from all quarters growing, Bari did the logical thing for an unstoppable activist—she created twice as much work for herself by agreeing to coordinate tree sits for both groups.

The Tree Sit Experience

Bari says that the action in her area "grew as it happened" into a tree-loving monster. When Pam Davis, a friend assisting Bari with the Northern

California sits, realized that no one had planned an action in Sonoma County, she called a group of friends together. Overnight they painted a banner and strung it above a freeway. The Albion group, which went ahead with plans for a road blockade, became unsettled about its tree sit. Then, in mid-week, it raised a platform. There were so many sitters that the Albion activists rotated in the trees to give as many people as possible a chance to make their statement.

Arcata: Hanging out at Hauser's

The monster grew to thirteen sits and numerous ancillary actions in eight states: California, Colorado, Illinois, Massachusetts, Montana, New Mexico, Oregon, and Washington. Undoubtedly the most audacious tree sit of the week, and probably of all time, took place in California Assemblymember Dan Hauser's front yard in Arcata. The legislator is unanimously reviled by Earth First!ers, and is generally disliked by many in the less radical niches of the environmental movement, for his anti-old growth timber stances. One of Hauser's largest campaign contributors is the infamous Pacific Lumber Company, or "Palco," the former family-owned timber giant that was scooped up in a junk bond deal and whose redwoods were being wiped out at twice the sustainable rate to pay off the debt.

Democrat Hauser also fought repeated attempts to strengthen the state's regulations governing forest practices, and he vehemently opposed any notion of a state purchase of even a portion of Palco's remaining virgin forests. So it was with an eye toward the ironic that a record for activistic tree sitting was set in front of Hauser's home. A party-like atmosphere enveloped the twenty people who adorned the massive oak tree-like mutant acorns. Accompanied by guitarists, thirty others circled beneath the spreading branches and sang songs during the two-hour demonstration. Someone spray painted a white band around the tree, signifying that it was to be cut. When loggers got wind of the demonstration and showed up with plastic bags of trash that they said had been left at a prior tree sit, the Earth First!ers turned the event to their own advantage by pointing out that the empty cans of diet soda and the plastic food wrappers had contained the sort of processed fare which no known tree sitter would consume.

Sherwood Forest: Women in the Redwoods

Transplanted New Yorker "Hellen Woods"[4] didn't know what she was getting into when she suggested an All-Women's Tree Sit to Judi Bari during a Humboldt County rock concert in July 1989. Woods says the idea came to her when she realized that most tree sitters are men and because "loggers tend to have a little more respect, may even listen to you more, when they see a woman do it as opposed to a man."[5] A month later her telephone rang. It was "Jenny Dalton," an experienced tree sitter. Since Woods came up with the idea, would she like to join Dalton and a friend for the sit? Within days, Woods found herself tying knots, wearing a climbing harness, and dangling at the side of huge trees as Greg King rushed her through a crash course in tree sitting.

With Woods was "Jenny Drum," also a neophyte climber and the third member of the trio. After several hours of strenuous climbing, rappelling, and more climbing, practice was almost over. Woods was up one redwood, while Drum hung fifty feet off the ground from the tree next to her. Drum was to lower herself first, then Woods, concluding the first meeting of Tree Sitting 101. It had been a long, exciting day for both women, and each was worn out. Everything appeared normal as Drum began what was to be the first of several short drops to the forest floor. Then something went wrong. A knot that was supposed to prevent a free fall failed, and a mechanical safety device to hold her rope fast didn't work. Drum found herself hurtling toward the ground. Instinctively, she grasped at a second nylon climbing rope secured to the tree. She slowed herself enough to prevent severe injury or death from the fall, but, tragically, she was not wearing gloves. The plastic rope charred her hands black.

Woods watched it all in horror, uncertain of exactly what had gone wrong. For ten minutes she waited, suspended high above the ground, scared of moving for fear that the same thing would happen to her. Finally, she summoned the courage to lower herself. Drum was rushed to the hospital—her hands were useless to her for weeks afterward. Woods, who had to get back home so she could go to work the next morning, faced a four hour drive alone back to Oakland and the prospect of embarking on the tree sit without Drum, with whom she had quickly developed a warm relationship. "At the time I didn't foresee me being able to go back up," Woods says, "but I'm so glad I did." Four days later she was back at it. This time Cherney worked with her to reinstill her self-confidence. The former English teacher imbued his lessons with a Zen-like quality, Woods says. She relaxed under Cherney's tutelage and found climbing's intuitive, innate flow within herself. It was enough to get beyond her anxieties about making mistakes. Climbing became a thrill.

Six more days and she was going up a tree for the sit. "The adrenaline rush of climbing! I was just shaking," she says. "It was intense, intense. When you're climbing you get tired, not because your body is tired but because you're so emotionally wrapped up in it. There's no talking, everyone is working. We were working by an almost full moon. It was beautiful." By 4:30 on the morning of Monday, August 14, Woods was in her open-air quarters. She and Dalton were joined by "Pam McMannus," a last-minute replacement who was in Oregon on vacation when she heard of the sit and showed up to volunteer with a ground crew. Bari urged her to become the third sitter: McMannus called her boss to say she would be a couple of days late returning to work from her vacation. Her only training was with Cherney and Woods on the Thursday before the action.

When dawn broke Monday morning, the scene was a decided disappointment. Beyond their skinny trees and the huge banner that read "Clearcutting is Eco-terrorism" strung between them, the women faced a barren landscape, ravaged years before by loggers, that dropped away to the sea below. The site was the one lobbied for by the Sherwood Forest Association—a spindly forest near Ft. Bragg whose second-growth trees had already been thinned once. From dawn to dusk winds blew in from the Pacific, at times spinning Woods and her platform 360 degrees around the tree and bending the young redwood at forty-five degree angles. She "felt like a palm tree in a hurricane." Even worse, from her point of view, was that there were no active logging operations anywhere near the sit. "To me," complains Woods, "there is no point in that. You want to be sitting in an active site. Granted, we got more publicity for this tree sit than any other that they've done.... [But] to me it's pointless to just be sitting up there. The president of Georgia Pacific came by in his helicopter the next morning to check it out. The newspapers quoted him as saying, 'Everybody's asking me what I'm going to do. I don't know.' There was no point to doing anything because we weren't interfering with his operations."

The press ate it up, though, and Woods knew that was essential to the exercise. Bringing to mind former Greenpeace media whiz Bob Hunter's remarks about the idiocy sometimes necessary to get the environmental message across, Woods says, "I think that radical environmentalism is important for the mere stupid reason that it's going to take scaling the Golden Gate Bridge or climbing a hundred feet up in a tree to get the media attention and to bring the problem back to the people." "The Today Show," "ABC News," *Time* magazine, and members of the local press trekked out to "Club Red," as the site became known, to interrupt Woods and the others as they read books and enjoyed the scenery as best they could. Some of the best journalists in the nation asked penetrating questions like, What are you wearing? (They each brought a range of clothing to deal with the unpredictable North Coast weather.) What are you eating? (Health food, beer, water, and pizza on the last night.) Do you go to the bathroom up there? (Sitters never leave their trees, and *everything* is carried out.) But even those asking such vacuous queries could not miss "the problem," staring them in the face as it was from the clear cut across the road. The media brought home the intended message to the rest of the nation.

Despite the disappointing location and the shallow questions, Woods' four days up a tree profoundly moved her. The thrill of protesting and the beauty of the place touched her deeply. And the camaraderie of the action brought the women closer. Woods and Dalton, especially, "were truly bonded in that sit.... It was hard to scream from tree to tree, but the energy was there," Woods says. "It was all oneness, positive," so positive that Woods couldn't wait to go back up—she proposed a "Community Tree Sit" of fifty or more people, a virtual village in the trees, after she climbed down.

Montana: Fighting Back in Big Sky Country

For John Lilburn and others in the Montana "Wild Rockies" Earth First! group, the tree sit in their state was a way of dealing with the stress of federal investigations into their activities. The FBI had hit hard, raiding the homes of several activists in Missoula in an effort that Lilburn and others feel was clearly intended to shut down radical environmental protest in Big Sky country. The Montana activists saw the tree sit as a way of "striking back, sticking to our high ground, saying, 'Fuck you! You're not going to intimidate me into not doing anything,'" Lilburn says.[6] He was one of several ground support people who planned to put three sitters in a forest where the trees had been sold to Plum Creek Lumber Company, Montana's version of California's Pacific Lumber Company. Their reconnaissance completed, the group of about a dozen felt they had found the perfect location. The site "was right next to Lindbergh Lake, which had these hoity-toity rich people hanging out there," Lilburn says. Designer Liz Claiborne reportedly owns a house at the lake worth millions, and her moneyed neighbors were as opposed to the sale as were the Earth First!ers, although probably for reasons other than ecocentrism.

It was two o'clock on Sunday morning, the wee hours of the Tree Sit Week, and Lilburn's gang was hanging out in a bar near the lake. Mary Beth Nearing, a veteran of numerous tree sits in her native Oregon and an expert at non-violent civil disobedience, had helped train spur climbers and sitters; the banners were ready—"Survival or Stumps," "Live Wild," and "Stop the Rape;" the trees were chosen and excitement grew among the sitters and support personnel as they drank to Montana's first-ever tree sit. Everyone was ready to go the next day. Then someone looked up glumly from the first edition of the Sunday newspaper: a report said that Plum Creek had cancelled its plans to cut next to Lindbergh Lake. "Poof!" Lilburn says. All that work for nothing—the activists were determined to disrupt an active logging site, and Plum Creek had effectively blockaded their plans. Lilburn chuckles and scratches his head of long, black hair. Dark, downcast eyes light up at an image: "It would have been really weird" to have the penniless activists working on the same side as the rich vacationers, he says with a shy smile. Alas, it was not to be.

The group scrambled to find an alternative location nearby. By late Sunday they decided to put the sitters up at the Bunyan Meadow timber sale in Lolo National Forest on the boundary of the Mission Mountain Wilderness, not far from Lindbergh Lake. The area was Situation I, prime, grizzly bear habitat, containing a mixture of mature spruce, larch, and fir trees. Adding to the sale's controversy was the environmental review that supported the supposed benignity of the sale. The document was ancient, thirteen years old and grossly out of date. On the down side was the logging firm affected by the action. One of the attractions of the Lindbergh Lake action was Plum Creek's massive size and its rotten environmental record. But by choosing to sit in the Bunyan Meadow trees, the activists attacked a "classic small mill," Lilburn says, the sort of operators Earth First!ers generally avoid confronting. He shakes his head as he describes the opposition. "It was amazing. I couldn't believe these two guys. It was a father and son team, Christian logger types, Olin and Ernie." They tried to make the sitters lament their action, saying, "'You're takin' our jobs away. This sale is gonna keep us in operation for another year and keep people employed.' So," Lilburn says, "we weren't very popular for sitting there."

The sitters went up on Monday and stayed until Friday night, with Olin and Ernie cutting around them as best they could for two days. Lilburn was at the site almost continuously, despite the closure of the area by the Forest Service almost as soon as the action was discovered. To avoid arrest, Lilburn was forced to hide behind or beneath logging debris whenever anyone came near. The press was allowed in, however, and the sit received substantial attention throughout Montana. It was also noticed by authorities. They reacted slowly, not arriving until Saturday morning to extricate the sitters. Lilburn was told that eight carloads of law enforcement personnel and three fully outfitted professional climbers arrived, only to find a forest devoid of humans—the sitters had abandoned the trees in the night. To avoid the hassle of what they were certain would be imminent arrest warrants, however, the three sitters turned themselves into authorities two weeks later. They were the only ones arrested in any of the week's tree sits.

Oregon: An Informant Leads to a Rest Stop

When Karen Wood is asked about the Southern Oregon tree sit, her initial reaction is, "Oh God!" For all of its twists and turns, the story exemplifies both the dedication of radical environmentalists and the lengths to which authorities are willing to go to thwart them. "Right before the National Tree Sit Week came up," Wood explains, "there was a situation in the Siuslaw National Forest. It was called the 'Table 503' timber sale. There were [northern] spotted owls there; it was a roadless area; it was a bad, bad, bad, bad timber sale. We went up there to try to do something about it. Five people went in. We had an informant, we've found out since." Security was unlike anything Wood and the hardened activists she was with had ever seen. "They had people patrolling the area constantly," she says. "They spent something like $15,000 a day on security. Every time we tried to go in, the car would get stopped. It was rough."

To top it off, the Forest Service created a massive closure area that followed the protestors around like a rain cloud. The closure was moving, periodic, and unscheduled—in other words, its sole purpose was to make it impossible for activists to gain lawful entry to the area. Finally, the five crept cross-country through the woods for hours on end, successfully avoiding the omnipresent security. "They got to the area where they were going to be building the road [to haul out timber]," Wood says, "and they walked right into Forest Service people. The District Ranger himself was there! They *knew* they were coming. They said, 'We're here to do a tree climbing workshop. We're here to protest legally.' The area wasn't sup-posed to be closed unless they saw a notice or they were so told. So as far as they knew it was legal."

A climber had set up the equipment and a sitter was preparing to go up a tree "when one of the Forest Service people snapped," Wood says. "He went over to the rope and put a knife to it and said, 'If you climb, I'll cut you down.' And then he said, 'This area's closed. You're all in a closure area. You have to leave.' They said, 'Okay!'" The quintet was ushered from the forest down a section of road which had already been cut. At one point in the long march back, they asked if they could stop to eat. A ranger okayed the break. Within minutes a paddy wagon pulled up. Stunned, each of the five was interrogated for four hours before being ticketed for entering a closed area. They were released, but only after all of their climbing gear was confiscated. Wood's expressive face tightens with anger, then breaks into a "what do we do now?" smile. "So, we had five people cited for being in a closure, no climbing gear, and the National Tree Sit was in, oh, one week! We had been thinking that the Siuslaw action, if it worked, might turn out to be the Nationwide Tree Sit action."

On to plan two. Wood urged that the sit be moved to the North Kalmiop-sis area of the Siskiyou National Forest, the Southern Oregon woods near where she and the other defendants in the "Sapphire Six" cases were arrested in that infamous action. Others agreed, and Wood went with a small reconnaissance group to find and prepare a site. "We assumed our informant was still with us, but there was nothing we could do about that," she says. "We kind of hoped we had left him behind. We figured it was probably a Siuslaw person." There were twenty people all told involved in the planning of the Siuslaw action, and the suspect was one out of a core group of twelve or fifteen. "We got down to the Kalmiopsis and our recon people couldn't find a place where they were cutting. It was this horribly ironic situation." In this ecologically complex and diverse area that epitomizes what is wrong with the world's approach to the environment and that focuses the Earth First! debate over strategies and tactics as nowhere else has, it appeared that the chain saws were quiet. Finally, after extensive reconnoitering, an active tree cutting site was discovered. "Some people went down there to do a last minute recon," Wood recalls, "and there were cops everywhere. They said, 'We know who you are, we know why you're here, we know what you're doing. If you or your friends show up here again, you're busted.' So I thought, 'Great! Our informant is still with us, obviously.'"

On to plan three. There was no plan three. There hadn't even been a plan two until they were forced to think of one. Oregon Earth First!ers found themselves making it all up as they went. Some busied themselves trying to scavenge as much climbing equipment as they could. In the meantime, at the north end of the state a lone sitter managed to get into the tree outside of the Portland office of Senator Mark Hatfield, a logging industry apologist. Not to be outdone, Wood and company devised a final, sure-fire sit. Wood looks away, seemingly embarrassed at the memory: "We went out and put a tree climber up in a rest stop on I-5! We were like, 'Damn it! We're going to climb a tree!' It amused everybody. The headline in one newspaper was, 'Earth First! Occupies Rest Stop.'" Near the timber town of Grants Pass, a lone sitter perched above a banner reading "Clearcutting: The Greenhouse Effect Starts Here," while a support crew distributed literature to travelers who had paused from their travels along the interstate highway that runs the length of the West Coast. Wood chuckles as she recalls the incident: When someone approached a couple in an RV to give them information on the greenhouse effect, the female passenger said, "'Oh, no thank you. We're not from this area.' We were all amazed and wanted to ask them, 'I didn't know Winnebagos could do that! What planet are you from?'"

The sitter wasn't up an old growth Douglas fir, only a pine tree; nor did the action take a lot of planning and coordination, just a quick drive down the Interstate. But Wood and the others managed to salvage some dignity from it, and unlike tree sits in the wilderness, the feedback was immediate. "The really great close of the day was when this older couple walked up to us and asked if we were the Earth First! people," Wood says. "I go, to myself, 'Oh shit!.' Then I said [in a timid voice], 'Yeah.' And they said, 'Oh, thank God we found you. We heard you were here and we wanted to give you some money.' They sat down and talked to us a long time and told us that a lot of people in Grants Pass were completely behind us and what we were doing and that we should not let ourselves get discouraged by all this Yellow Ribbon stuff (the timber industry's anti-environmentalist campaign). They told us that there were a lot of people that still back us all the way."

Reaching out to the Rest of Us

Elsewhere, things went well, but not perfectly. First-ever sits in Massachusetts and Illinois went off without a hitch, while actions in eastern and western Washington went smoothly as well. In Colorado, though, no one remembered to tell the press where the sitters were located. Eventually, the media arrived, but the coverage was not as extensive as it might have been. When no journalists showed up in New Mexico, the two tree sitters abandoned their effort. "'It was boring,'" was what Cherney was told. "The whole point to tree sitting," he says, "is that you have to be like a tree, you have to sit in the same place and be patient and you will watch the world pass in front of you. But there is still this American instant gratification syndrome." These aberrations were the exceptions, however, and they were made up for in other ways. In a takeoff of the Northern Oregon sit in the middle of Portland, a woman went up a tree in downtown Santa Fe as the two men left their unnoticed perch. She stayed up for five days. Cherney revels in the image. "Took her shits and everything right in the middle of downtown Santa Fe!" he says with glee.

Such crude realities aside, Earth First!'s National Tree Sit Week deserves recognition as a vital step for the movement. Following scores of local demonstrations and infrequent national protests, the seven days of loose-ly-coordinated, generally well-orchestrated actions served notice that the wilderness bums can hang in there for the long haul with the slickest of the Gang of Ten's three-piece suits. Advertising experts say that a potential consumer has to be exposed to a message a minimum of three times within a short period to remember a product. By pounding away day after day on network television, in nationwide magazines, and through local newspapers, the eco-warriors reached millions they had failed to touch through their isolated protests. The no compromise ethic had never before been marketed so effectively for so long.

CHAPTER 11

RAID ON REYKJAVIK

Rod Coronado watched in horror, tears streaming down his young face, as the huge man strode to the side of a yelping, terrified harp seal pup, knelt, and crushed its skull with one blow from his wooden club. The man showed no emotion as he moved to another of the ivory-colored baby seals and then another, striking ferociously each time. Then the image on the television screen shifted to another man, this one being dragged helplessly across the ice toward a nearby sealing ship. He had attached himself to a long cable that extended from the ship out over the brilliant white ice; behind him freshly-skinned pelts were pulled along as well. Those images of the seals, the sealers, and of iconoclast Paul Watson's attempt to stop the hunt, filmed during Watson's final days as a Greenpeace activist, became a guiding star for the young Coronado's life. "I immediately knew that that's what I had to do, those were the people I wanted to work with and that was the avenue that I wanted to take," Coronado says. "It was no bullshit, just getting out there and doing what had to be done."[1]

That was 1979 when Coronado was twelve years old. He pursued his star, and within seven years his life grew to almost mythical proportions, his name and that of compatriot David Howitt written alongside Watson's in the list of legends of the environmental movement.

In fact, though, Coronado insists he is nothing more than an ordinary person unafraid of living out his dreams and taking risks for what he loves. Not long after the broadcast of the documentary on sealing, he saw news reports on the ramming of the pirate whaling ship *Sierra*, and his interest became focused on Watson's no-holds-barred fight for marine mammals. Coronado tracked down the Sea Shepherds and wrote to their leader. "It was funny because at that young age I wrote tons of letters to organizations," Coronado recalls. "I figured I would join all these groups. So I sent all these great twelve-year-old kid's, totally naive letters to these people. The only personal reply I received was from Paul." The other organizations asked people to mark a box and send a check for the corresponding amount.

In contrast, Coronado paraphrases the Sea Shepherd literature: "Send us money to buy fuel for our ship so we can go out and sabotage the bastards." And that is exactly what he did. In 1983 he mailed 200 hard-earned dollars to the Sea Shepherds to help purchase fuel for an expedition to stop those same sealers who had terrorized the harp seals on his television.

Like many other radical environmentalists, Coronado seems to have been born with ecological consciousness, the wilderness gene, a sense of connectedness, a higher level of compassion than most—*something* that catapults him over the Eco-Wall so early in life that he has no recollection of when or how it all began. Coronado's early interest in activism on behalf of animals bears this out and takes on a deeper, more ironic quality when juxtaposed with Watson's entre into radical environmentalism. As a young boy, Watson, too, took up the cause of those who could not speak for themselves; he wrote to Cleveland Amory, founder of the Fund for Animals, and asked how to get involved. Amory welcomed him without hesitation and later purchased Watson's first ship for him, the *Sea Shepherd*, which the renegade Watson used to hunt down and cripple the *Sierra*.

Watson would display the same sort of unswerving support for Coronado and Howitt as Amory bestowed on him. Somehow, it seemed that it was all meant to be. "One thing that I've believed in all along is synchronicity, that a lot of things weren't coincidence but were fate," Coronado says. "The time when I got out of high school to when I met Paul was a matter of only a few months, yet all through school I had wanted to do that. So, when I came back, a lot of my friends were actually shocked that I had achieved what I wanted to do, or at least part of it." It was, as Coronado says, as if he "didn't have a choice, that these things were just happening to me."

It was on a high school graduation trip to Vancouver, British Columbia, with his parents in 1984 that Coronado met Watson for the first time. Watson was not supposed to be there, but rather out on an action. Amazingly, and to Coronado's joy, it had been delayed. "I told him, 'I'm out of school. I want to work with you.' They were working on the Whaling Walls educational murals. He said, 'You can start now.' I saw my parents that night and packed my bags and said 'I'm going off to work with the Sea Shepherds.'" Coronado's stunned mother and father bade him farewell.

When the *Sea Shepherd II* was returned to the Sea Shepherds by a Canadian court early the following year—it had been confiscated by the Canadian Navy during the harp seal campaign that Coronado had contributed to because of Watson's interference with the slaughter—he turned his energies to preparing the ship for its next voyage. After two years in mothballs the old cod boat was in rotten shape. Climbing aboard it for the first time was a decided disappointment, Coronado says glumly. "I spent three months in port aboard ship just trying to get the thing going again with no electricity, no heating, no hot water. It was hell. But we stuck it out." Then as now, the crew was all volunteer and paid nearly all of their own expenses. During those months Coronado was exposed to a rich mixture of idealism and practicality freely shared by the peace and environment activists who hung out with Watson. The Captain became the teenager's mentor, often advising Coronado in ways that benefitted the student and not the sage. Whenever Coronado's money ran out, he headed back home to work in his father's small steel materials firm, then returned to the ship.

With their vessel finally back in working order, the Sea Shepherds headed to the Atlantic that summer. On their way to protect pilot whales against the annual onslaught in the Faroe Islands, Watson issued an ultimatum during a *Sea Shepherd II* sojourn at Reykjavik, Iceland. The Sea Shepherds could not take action that summer, but he warned the Icelandic whalers that he expected compliance with the International Whaling Commission's (IWC) moratorium on whaling, scheduled to take effect the following January. "We told them that if they didn't [comply], we would come back and enforce the International Whaling Commission moratorium against them," Watson says.[2]

Coronado took advantage of the stopover to wander down to the docks and check out the whaling fleet. He noticed that there was a twenty-four-hour patrol, but other than that only one guard was on duty with the four ships. "I thought, 'I bet if we weren't here there would only be that one guard on those four ships,'" Coronado recalls. "I just buried that in my mind. I thought, 'You could sabotage those boats.' That was that. I didn't think much more about it because of the Faroes." (Chapters Four and Six examine the annual Faroe Island massacre of pilot whales).

Preparation

Nothing changed in the early months of 1986. Iceland continued to kill whales, stating the kill was for scientific purposes and that it would abide by the IWC's "research whaling" guidelines. Again Watson warned that he was prepared to act, delivering his message with the *Sea Shepherd II* parked in the Malmo, Sweden, harbor during the IWC's annual meeting there. Research whaling was a sham, nothing but a cover for continued commercial whaling despite the moratorium. With some of the hunted species' populations dangerously low, there was no excuse for more killing.

Then the Sea Shepherds waited for the United States to enforce amendments recently passed by Congress to the International Fishery Conservation and Management Act. Watson explains, "These amendments state that any nation that attempts to undermine the authority of the International Whaling Commission will lose the right to sell fish products in the U.S. and the right to fish in U.S. waters, which is the only teeth the IWC had for enforcing its regulations." President Reagan "chose to discriminate on the

application of the amendment," says Watson. He refused to invoke sanctions against NATO ally Iceland, probably because he did not want to risk
losing the strategically important Keflavik Air Force Base. In July the
Reagan appointee-dominated U.S. Supreme Court declared the amendments unconstitutional on a 5-4 vote. "And to add insult to injury," Watson
says disgustedly, Reagan "turned a blind eye to Iceland's increased sale of
whale meat to Japan in return for holding a summit with Mr. Gorbachev in
Reykjavik. So the price of that summit was an increased number of whales
being killed."

When Coronado heard of Iceland's intention to continue killing whales,
his mind immediately ran to the whaling ships lined up neatly in
Reykjavik's dark harbor. Following the Faroese campaign, he approached
David Howitt, a quiet spoken Brit and one of the *Sea Shepherd II* crew he
knew best. Coronado offered Howitt the chance to be constructive for
nature through destruction of humans' killing tools, asking if he would like
to help sink the Icelandic whaling ships. Howitt quickly accepted. "It was
mutual," Howitt says. "He talked about the situation with me and I asked
for details about what was happening. We both felt that we ought to do
something together, and the plan grew out of talking with each other about
the possibility of bringing attention to it."[3]

Howitt was a relative newcomer to the Sea Shepherds, having joined
them in March 1986 after some friends who were playing benefit concerts
for the group took him to see the ship in Plymouth. "At the time I was
looking for something more constructive to do in the way of environmental
protection," Howitt says. A year older than Coronado, he had been raised
in St. Ives, a small coastal town in Cornwall, and had long felt a kinship
with nature. "I trained as a natural history photographer....And at the sight
of the ship in Plymouth, I jumped at the chance to help put it to sea."
Although he had no prior activistic experience of the sort he knew he was
in for with the Sea Shepherds, he wanted to do more than take pictures.
Howitt spent two months working on the *Sea Shepherd II* to make it
seaworthy and then sailed as an engineer to the Faroes. "I was set to work
in environmental protection in whatever way might be most effective," says
Howitt. He adds, "After studying natural history you realize that the
situation worldwide is getting pretty critical. I wanted to get involved in
whatever way seemed most constructive."

Coronado and Howitt wasted little time in preparing for their expedition, one that would prove constructive for the whales but extremely
destructive to the whaling industry. To fund the effort, the Californian
found work refinishing furniture in London and Howitt went to Kent to
pick hops. When they could, they researched Iceland's sordid whaling
history, concentrating on its contemptuous attitude toward the IWC and
its agreements with Japan for selling the meat. The conspirators also found
that whaling was driven by anachronistic societal values wherein

Icelanders clung to their ancient Viking heritage even as they enjoyed Western lifestyles and affluence. Whaling held little real significance for the average Icelander, although seventy percent of the population expressed support for the industry in public opinion polls.

They also learned that the Icelandic whaling operation was the exclusive province of Christian Lofsson, a rich businessman who owned a supermarket chain and had ties to the nation's political elite. The proceeds of the whale kill in 1986 amounted to $40,000 per animal, all coming from Japan. "Eighty whales," Coronado says. "It doesn't sound like a lot, but take eighty times $40,000 and you're talking about a huge profit for a month of work."

Neither Coronado nor Howitt doubted the legitimacy or the need for their plan of sabotage for one second. "We never had the qualms that a lot of people might think we had, or that people do have, in regards to the destruction of property and whether that is a line that you are ready to cross," Coronado says. From years of writing letters, passing out petitions, and attending demonstrations, as well as his familiarity with the failed efforts of those who had tried through non-destructive means to end the killing of whales, Coronado felt strongly that direct, decisive action was the only recourse. Driven by an innate love of all beings, Coronado and Howitt identified with the whales as one human might with another. They lived by—and were willing to risk death for—ecocentric principles. "For us, it was as simple as somebody who might stand in the line of fire to prevent somebody else from being killed," says Coronado. "It was simple self-defense in the sense not of our self-defense, but of the defense of the animals that didn't have the power of self-defense, or that were so above us in terms of morality that they didn't have a sense of violence for the sake of violence. We had to deal with the humans because we were humans ourselves!"

When Coronado and Howitt told Watson of their plans, he agreed to speak for them if they could bring off the action; Coronado sensed some doubt in his mentor's voice. The only other people who knew of the plan were Coronado's sister in London and a British Sea Shepherd contact. The raiders arrived in Iceland on October 15, 1986. Coronado and Howitt spent "days and nights at the coffee shops across the way" from the docks where the four whaling ships tied up, watching and planning. They even hid in scrap yards around the Reykjavik harbor to note the comings and goings of the ships, the crew, and to gain whatever insight they could into the operation. "Before we went there, we didn't really know how much we would be able to do to draw attention to the illegal whaling," Howitt says. "We had talked about sinking a ship, about scuttling a ship, and ways of doing it. For instance, we researched the scuttling of *Sea Shepherd* and the elapsed time that it took. We thought about it, but we had no way of knowing if we could do that safely until we had gone through the reconnaissance and came up with the best plan." Early on in their stay they purchased a pair of bolt cutters and some heavy wrenches at a local hardware store in anticipation of their future needs.

Out of curiosity, Coronado and Howitt one afternoon hitchhiked up the coast about fifty miles to the whaling station where the carcasses were taken for butchering. "We heard they had tours there, so we went to go take a tour," says Coronado. "When we got there, no one was around. It was closed down for the year. So we just started walking around, and we realized there was a lot we could do there as well as damaging the ships." Following their self-guided tour, the whale processing center was added to their "little campaign."

After a couple of weeks, money got to be a little tight. Coronado landed a job through two Swedish women whom he and Howitt had met at the Salvation Army Hostel where they were staying. Coronado recalls it with a wry grin and a mixture of glee and revulsion: "There I was, the only dark-complexioned, non-Icelandic speaking vegetarian working at this Icelandic meat packing plant. And that didn't raise any suspicions!"

Had anyone bothered to ask, the queries would have been well-placed, for Coronado was not interested in the job for the money alone; he was searching for "Whale Meat Mountain." The Icelanders hid a huge and mysterious mound of whale meat somewhere, and a meat packing plant seemed a logical place for it. As part of their original plans, Coronado and Howitt wanted to find the mountain and ruin the meat. When they later discovered the "mountain" at the whale processing station, it turned out to be the offal, bones, and non-sellable parts of carcasses that supposedly constituted 50.1 percent of the "usable meat" from Icelandic whale kills. A bare majority of the usable portions of the whales had to be kept in-country under the IWC's "scientific research" regulations. Iceland was clearly violating even those lenient restrictions.

Only nine days before the scheduled action date, Icelandic immigration authorities found that Coronado was working without the necessary documents. This might not have been much of a concern except that his very presence in Iceland was a danger in itself. Coronado had been banned from the Faroe Islands, and all other Scandinavian nations as well, due to his arrest stemming from the confrontations with Faroe authorities earlier that year. No charges were ever filed, but the arrests made it impossible for him to obtain a special permit allowing him to work in the country. The discovery of his illegal work status would lead to an investigation which would bring his prior arrest to light. He would not only lose his job, but be expelled from the country as well, thereby ending the eco-warrior's mission. Fate, however, was on Coronado's side. In their background check the authorities somehow missed the arrest record. Coronado was out of a job but also out of jail and still in the country.

Just before Coronado had lost his job, Howitt had traveled north to investigate the booming Icelandic fur industry. He was looking for evidence to confirm his suspicions that Fin and Sei whale meat from the "research" whaling was being sent to fur farms, another violation of IWC regulations. Whale meat was probably a relatively inexpensive source of food for the animals, and the farms were a local market for the industry, so Howitt's theory had a certain logic to it. The best Howitt could do was find evidence that a number of pilot whales which had recently become stranded on shore had been killed and sent to the farms. But he could find no proof that meat from the whaling industry was used to feed the caged animals.

On Howitt's return, he and Coronado took two days off to rest and prepare for their mission. After more reconnaissance came the fateful day. Coronado and Howitt mailed all of their research materials—notes, photographs, and a description of the action—to Sarah Hambly, the United Kingdom contact person for Sea Shepherd, then said their good-byes to friends at the hostel, telling them that they were going sight-seeing and would leave for home the next day.

Whaling on the Whaling Station

It was Saturday, November 8. Their agenda was set: first, they would rent a car, then eat at Reykjavik's only vegetarian restaurant, trash the whaling station, sink the ships, and leave. After renting the car and checking in their luggage at the airport for an early morning flight the following day, Coronado and Howitt drove to the restaurant. They figured the odds were good that it would be their last meal outside of jail for some time, and they had been saving what little money they had for one final feast. When they arrived at the restaurant, however, it was closed. It was one of only two disappointments in an action that was rife with potential pitfalls.

They settled for buying some food at a grocery store and then drove toward the whaling station, parking short of the processing center and eating their dinner while listening to the radio. When they tried to start the car, the battery was dead. There they sat, months of preparation and weeks of intensive reconnaissance behind them, plane tickets in hand, and, because they had listened to a radio powered by a weak battery, they were going nowhere. Or so it seemed. Coronado recalls with a smile, "Sure enough, here comes a van load of young Icelandic kids who probably lived in the adjoining town and probably worked at the whaling station. They were very friendly. They gave us a push and we got the car going. We said, 'Thanks a lot.'" The saboteurs changed clothes and parked in a quarry a mile south of the whaling station.

Coronado and Howitt slipped on day packs containing little more than flashlights and the bolt cutters and wrenches they had purchased weeks earlier. The weather, which had been pleasant all day, turned nasty, and it was raining as they walked toward the whaling station. When they neared it, they noticed someone operating an excavator. "We immediately dropped to the ground," Coronado says. They lay on the grass for an hour, the storm now pouring over them. At about nine o'clock the worker finally left. Thoroughly soaked but eager to get on with their task, Coronado and Howitt circled beneath the mercury vapor lights bathing the huge facility to confirm that it was unguarded. Then, charged with adrenaline, they entered through an unlocked door, quickly located the main circuit box, and shut down the power. For the next four hours they methodically made their way by flashlight through the complex in a focused, intense rampage.

"In the corner of one warehouse we discovered this computer room," Coronado remembers. "They had all the machinery being run by computers in this small room, maybe eight by ten feet. The walls were nothing but computers, printout machines, and stuff. At first, I just grabbed a few little things and smashed them, because I was afraid of being electrocuted. David didn't care, apparently, 'cause he just went in there and started whacking everything. It was just like these movies you see with panels exploding and LEDs flashing." He laughs, then his countenance takes on a serious look. "I don't know. We were destroying something that we knew was worth so much money. But at the same time it was such a good feeling because we knew it was costing the industry so much money."

The storm outside made for good cover as they smashed and bashed from one room to another. Contrary to press reports, Coronado says they never used sledge hammers. Two million dollars of damage was done with brains, time, and comparatively lightweight tools. "At the time all we had was a big crescent wrench and a pair of bolt cutters....We did just as much damage as a sledge hammer probably would have done. There were eleven different rooms in the whaling station, and we tried to spend as much time as possible to cover all of them. They had six huge Caterpillar generators that they used to run the refrigeration units and stuff. We spent at least an hour and a half, probably longer, methodically taking them apart—bending valves, filling sumps with stuff, cutting gauges. It was taking forever and we were getting all sweaty. We realized that we could be there all night. A group of ten people could be there all night sabotaging that stuff."

Outside they found the sterile trailer where the "research" was undertaken. That the justification for this vast computerized world of centrifuges, refrigeration, and electricity generation was for *research* became all the more unbelievable when they broke into the small portable building. "They had a couple of microscopes and some whale tissue samples," Coronado says disgustedly. "It wasn't a laboratory....It was on the fringe of being a laboratory. They'd take a few samples to tell how old the whales were, whether they were females, male, how long they were. Basic statistics," a hush puppy to appease the pliant IWC.

At one point the saboteurs split up. Soon, Howitt discovered Whale Meat Mountain stored in several massive refrigerators. He tried to maneuver a fork lift to remove the "meat" and dump it down the slipway. When that didn't work, Coronado and Howitt settled for wedging open the freezer doors. "We cut off all the refrigeration, then we sabotaged all the refrigeration units," Coronado says. "That was dangerous because we started cutting lines without knowing what they were for. Freon started escaping and I started getting these visions of this environmental disaster occurring in this beautiful fiord, so we just shut it down and left it like that. We hoped to leave the meat like that long enough so that it would thaw and they wouldn't be able to re-freeze the meat without damaging it. In the end they claimed that it wasn't done at all." When Coronado heard that, he urged that word be sent to the Japanese that the meat sold to them might have become spoiled.

In the plant foreman's office the saboteurs found the "scientists'" notebooks and other records. They put them into their backpacks, then smashed an array of radios used to communicate with the whaling boats. "They had this stereo system for playing music for the employees while they were out cutting" up the whales, recalls Coronado. "We got this weird idea of leaving a tape of whale songs, or if somehow we could interfere while they were butchering and put on whale songs. It was just something we thought about. But we knew we couldn't do it, so we smashed that up, too." Before they returned to Reykjavik, they threw spare ship parts and flensing knives down the slipway and into the frigid water. And in their last act before leaving, the Sea Shepherds found gallon jugs of liquid in a laboratory and splashed their contents over desks and anything else they saw. The mysterious chemical smoked and foamed; it turned out to be cyanic acid, certain to etch deeply into whatever it touched.

Amazingly, neither of the whale warriors were ever scared during their four-hour raid. "I don't remember any fear at all," Howitt says. "We had a lot of adrenaline flowing. Excited, I guess, is the word. We knew what we were doing, we were careful, methodical, and we felt we were doing a good job. We were alert—that's the adrenaline that keeps you alert. We were working pretty hard." Their determination and the elation at inflicting so much damage on the reviled industry drove them. Says Coronado, "We had made the promise that if the other got caught, *continue*, try to go forward and do the job....Even if we get caught and jailed, we have to do what we can, even if it costs us our own freedom. We didn't put ourselves on any higher moral plane. We had decided to do this job." He adds, ".Yes, we did that at a great risk. But to me it was a greater risk had we not accomplished it. I don't know how I would have felt if we had been nailed before we got into the whaling station or onto those ships. I would have felt like I had failed the whales."

Sinking Half the Fleet

Coronado and Howitt arrived back at Reykjavik at 1:30 on Sunday morning, too early to sabotage the whaling ships unnoticed. They used the next hour or so to eat a bite and rest from the excitement at the whaling station. Composed, they pulled into the harbor parking lot. There was only one other car. Coronado and Howitt knew from their reconnaissance to expect only the night watchman to be around. The three seaworthy whaling ships—a fourth was in dry dock—were tied up side by side, and the watchman always spent the night on the nicer of the three, the one farthest from the dock. Masked by their common everyday wear for late fall in Iceland—balaklavas and hooded jackets—they dashed through the freezing night toward the lone whaler tied directly to the dock.

Coronado and Howitt knew that they would only be able to sink the *Hvalur 6* and the *Hvalur 7* because damaging the third ship would have risked the guard's life and thereby violated the Sea Shepherds' code of non-violence. They wasted no time in getting to their task. "There was nobody around," says Coronado. "We timed it so that the tide was out enough so that the gunnel of the first ship was level with the docks. All we had to do was hop over. The engine room hatch was open. All the lights were on. Dave checked to see that no one was on board, just ran around the cabins." Then they went to work below decks of the 140-foot vessel.

Most ships' engines are cooled using salt water circulated by a pump. A tightly sealed cover, called a "salt water cooling valve," can be opened in dry dock should the need arise to service the cooling system. Opening the vent when the ship is in the water, however, causes flooding and can sink a ship if the valve is not promptly closed. Coronado and Howitt lifted one after another of the heavy steel deck plates that made up the engine room's floor, searching beneath them for the manhole cover-sized valve. When they found it, they used the ship's tools to remove most of the bolts, then pried at the valve until water began seeping in. They tasted it: salty.

Together, the scuttlers moved on to the other ship without completely removing the first whaler's cooling valve; they feared that by doing so, the ship would sink before they could finish the job. The locked cabin door to the second ship was coaxed open with bolt cutters. After checking to see that no one else was aboard, they moved to the engine room and found the cooling system valve at the same location as on its twin ship. "We took off all the bolts but couldn't get the valve off," Coronado says. "So Dave ran to get a pry bar from the other boat. I was sitting on the valve, and just as he was leaving all of a sudden, spshshsh, spshshshsh, water started squirting everywhere. I said, 'Dave, we'd better split. This thing's gonna go right now.' We pulled at the valve a little bit, then 'pop, pop' and water started gurgling all over the deck plates. Me and Dave got soaked, and we said, 'Shit, let's get outta here! This boat's gonna sink.'" They returned to the other ship and applied a pry bar to the valve with the same results. Mission accomplished, they threw their tools into the harbor and scampered to their car. Looking back, Howitt saw the boats listing. Half the Icelandic whaling fleet was harmlessly sinking to the harbor floor.

Trouble with the First Rule

Actually, their mission was not fully accomplished. The universally understood first rule of eco-defense, Don't Get Caught, had yet to test the young raiders. It didn't wait any longer. All day Coronado and Howitt had run on adrenaline and purpose. Nothing had deterred them, not missing their last meal or a battery sapped from playing the radio or even a misplaced but quickly found car key at the quarry parking site. Then fate threw them one final adrenaline rush. Coronado, who was driving, tells the story in a calm voice. "Not two minutes after we got into the car—where we had the record books, and I was wet from the knees down and I had grease all over me from the whaling station, plus we were wearing dark clothes—boom! A cop pulls me over. "I didn't even worry about it. I thought, 'They can't be *that* quick, they can't be that good.' When I rented the car I read about a bunch of their laws, and they said they were really strict about drunk driving. I thought, 'Just play it cool.' Sure enough, the policeman comes to the driver's side and asks me to get out of the car. He asked me to get in the back of his car. I had a stupid grin on my face, just tried to act as innocent as possible. I showed him my California driver's license, then he and his partner started speaking Icelandic. Then he asked, 'Have you been drinking any alcohol?' I said, 'Of course not. I don't drink.' He said, 'Okay. Have a nice trip,' and sent me on my way.

"David couldn't believe it! There they had me in the back seat of their car. You know those guys got yelled at when someone put the stories together!" Howitt had remained cool but felt fearful for the first time that night. "We didn't really think it was possible that we would be caught at that stage," says Howitt. "An hour later—then it would have been a different story....I was left in the passenger seat wondering whether to make a run for it but obviously knowing that we first had to check." During their reconnoitering, Coronado and Howitt hit many of the high spots in Iceland—docks, the whaling station, the meat processing plant, and a zoo outside of Reykjavik where captured orca ("killer") whales, harbor seals, and birds were held before being sold to marine parks or other facilities. The two thought they might be able to release a number of the animals before going to the airport. But they ran out of time—the scuttling operation took an hour and a half, and it was well after four in the morning by the time the police released Coronado. It was the only aspect of the ambitious mission that might be considered a "failure," and only the missed restaurant meal could rival it as a disappointment.

Once they had cleared customs at the airport, Coronado and Howitt learned that the poor weather conditions had forced a delay in their flight's departure, which was scheduled for 7:30. Anxious hours of waiting ensued. "Little did we know at the time but that they had discovered the ships," Coronado says. "They had sunk in thirty minutes." Watson had told them that the *Sea Shepherd*, which had been scuttled by opening its cooling valve, took about three hours to go down. "We thought, 'Oh, we've got plenty of time,'" Coronado recalls. "But as it turns out, we didn't have plenty of time. The ships sunk right away. They discovered them right away, too. But the police dispatcher only sent one car to investigate because he didn't suspect sabotage. They knew about it forty-five minutes before the flight left, but they didn't have the sense to put out a general alarm and shut down the airport."

Coronado and Howitt escaped safely to Luxembourg, where Coronado called Sarah Hambly in England. "I just said, 'Everything's been done just like we wanted. Two went down and we got the station as well.' Then I hung up." Hambly called Paul Watson with the news. When the story got out, the press jumped on it. Coronado says, "A reporter called Paul to see if Sea Shepherd wanted to accept responsibility. Of course, if lightning struck a whaling ship, Paul would accept responsibility for it." Watson told the press that the Sea Shepherd agents were safely hidden in Europe. "They (the Icelandic authorities) believed us until they discovered the whaling station," says Coronado. "Then they thought we had done that *following* sinking the ships. They launched this big manhunt, looking for us, whoever they thought that might be. Of course, we were long gone by that time.

"It was great because we hitchhiked from Luxembourg through Belgium, got on a ferry to Dover, got a bus from Dover to London, got off the tube in London. We were going over to Plymouth to meet Sarah. I remember going up to a kiosk where they had a bunch of newspapers. Of course we went to look for our dirty work, and there, on the front pages, was the headline, 'Saboteurs Scuttle Whaling Ships, Photo Page 6.' At that point we didn't know whether they had possibly seen them and plugged up the valves or what. We bought the papers and sure enough, there was the photo of the two ships. Then we knew we had been effective. But it didn't say a word about the whaling station." Coronado was amazed that the authorities had not checked there, too, especially after the police found that the ships were sunk through deliberate tampering. "They didn't discover the whaling station until Monday morning," he says contemptuously. "They didn't even have enough sense to check it. It wasn't discovered until people showed up for work."

In Plymouth, a network of safe houses was established to harbor Coronado and Howitt. "I talked to Paul, and he felt the best thing was for me to be in my own home country," Coronado says. "I flew to New York and met him there." A press conference in Cleveland Amory's office began a hectic several weeks of interviews and travelling for Coronado. Meanwhile, Howitt flew to Greece to lay low and relax. Soon after the action, Greenpeace announced a boycott against Icelandic fish products that Coronado credits as the final blow to the tiny nation's whaling industry. Thus, for a time the "niches" of marine mammal oganizations and activists actually worked as a system, and they succeeded in focusing intense pressure on Iceland in particular and on whaling in general. However, Coronado noticed that it did not take long before every article about the action "had at least one paragraph where Greenpeace separated itself from it and condemned it. But at the same time I thought it was good because it showed that Greenpeace didn't support direct action against whalers." Within Iceland, public opinion turned from seventy percent of the population in favor of whaling to sharply divided in a matter of months after the action. Sea Shepherd membership there grew from none to 200, and one member founded the Whale Friends Society. Magnus Skarphedinsson, Sea Shepherd's leading advocate in Iceland, has spoken before nearly half of the nation's 20,000 teenagers and reports that their concerns are spreading to animal rights and ecology in general.[4]

Looking back on it, Coronado and Howitt see that they started an avalanche of publicity on whaling at a time that the whaling industry was hoping to quietly go on about its deadly business. "A lot of people thought that the moratorium was in effect and that whaling was over," Coronado says. "We showed that it was indeed continuing. The scientific and environmental communities started questioning why they were continuing to kill whales." All of the negative publicity placed the whaling industry on the defensive, making it appear guilty. In the public eye, Iceland was tried and convicted. Whale Meat Mountain was less meat than mess, and the "scientific research" whaling had only the most tenuous links to research. Although none of the documents that the Sea Shepherds absconded with were directly incriminating, oddities stood out. The sizes of many of the whales killed by the Icelanders were recorded as just over the legal minimum length established by the IWC. Without fail, females were always listed as "dry;" by regulation, lactating females are not supposed to be killed.

But the most damning evidence was that Iceland never charged Coronado and Howitt, or anyone else, for the destruction of the whaling station and the ship scuttlings. "I wrote to Iceland *three times* demanding to know what charges were going to be laid," Paul Watson says, "and Iceland wouldn't answer my letters. In January of 1988 I flew to Reykjavik to demand that charges be laid, and they refused to lay charges....What we proved through that campaign is that what we did was perfectly valid and legal." The whale processing facility eventually was repaired at enormous cost. The two sunken ships were raised from the bottom of Reykjavik harbor in unusable condition. They were eventually re-outfitted, but in 1989 Iceland discontinued its whaling operations until the International Whaling Commission could meet in 1990 to reconsider its moratorium on commercial whaling. Ultimately, "the commission refused to even consider a request from Iceland for an annual whaling quota of 200 minke whales."[5] The ban on whaling worldwide remains in effect.

In the three and a half years since the attack, Howitt has spent nearly all of his time aboard the *Sea Shepherd II* as its chief engineer. When not on board, he has travelled to Alaska and Morocco to help clean up the massive oil spills there. Coronado continued to sail with the Sea Shepherds, although he and partner Sue Rodriguez-Pastor decided to stop crewing with them in 1990. They established an environmental research and investigations service to expose ecologically damaging practices. Coronado is active in Earth First! and Animal Liberation causes as well. Following the Iceland action, the FBI visited him and has returned several times since with questions about everything from Animal Liberation activities to an alleged bomb planting at an Army recruiting center.

Perhaps more annoying than the FBI intrusions were the pitiful attempts by the American press after Iceland to decipher "what was so unique and strange about this kid that he would want to do this crazy thing," Coronado says. To the media "it wasn't a question of why did I do it, it was what *made* me do it." The honest answer to the former, "the whales," was never adequate. He adds, "I just want to tell people that they can do the same thing if they are committed enough, and if they believe in it enough. They should set their goals as high as they want and they can achieve them. Don't feel like there is only this one 'element' of people in the world who do these types of thing. It isn't that way. It's just that some people have reached a certain level and they just can't tolerate it any more." Once they have overcome the Eco-Wall within themselves they are "compelled to follow a higher law and to not follow the laws that are established by the power structure to protect themselves. Sometimes you have to not question whether it's right or wrong but how you're going to do it."

CHAPTER 12

CROWD ON A CRANE

When most Americans over the age of thirty-five hear the word "Berkeley," they immediately think of "radical." Perhaps no other place signifies dissent as well as this, the cradle of the Free Speech movement of the 1960s. Students at the University of California, Berkeley campus vehemently protested against the Vietnam War and against then-Governor Ronald Reagan's attempts to quell their protests. Much has changed since then; to some extent the college world turned upside down. A generation of business majors swept through the nation's universities, and Berkeley was no exception. Conservatism was "in" in the 1980s and radicalism became more memory than reality. Moreover, the *cause* was missing.

Or so it appeared. Periodically, issues arose which inflamed students' passions at Berkeley and those of the residual radicals who remained in the town across the Bay from San Francisco. One was the University's repeated threats to forcibly remove a large homeless community from its encampment at People's Park. When the University's administration went beyond threats to action, violent confrontations resulted. But People's Park was no Vietnam. However, in the late 1980s an issue arose which served to bridge Berkeley's traditional anti-war, pro-freedom concerns with those of radicalism's cutting edge. Called the Northwest Animal Facility (NAF), "it was," in the words of Animal Liberator Todd Patterson, "almost the perfect vehicle" for uniting the community's disparate philosophies.[1]

Germ Warfare in the Middle of Town

The idea behind the NAF was to place nearly all of the University's animal experimentation laboratories under one roof—actually, under one plot of ground. The NAF was classified as a "P3 facility," meaning it was designed to house experiments using some of the most dangerous viral agents and chemical substances known. Plans called for an underground facility, a $14.5 million windowless grave for the tens of thousands of animals which would be tortured and die there each year. That was more than enough to get Berkeley's substantial Animal Rights community up in arms. And when it was made known that many of the planned experiments were for military purposes, the NAF drew further opposition from the hardcore of the traditional radical movement, the peace activists. More detailed revelations of the purposes behind some of those experiments—germ warfare research—and the proximity of the NAF to the Hayward earthquake fault, brought mainstream environmentalists and those concerned with human health and safety to the opposition's camp. Ultimately, the NAF became a focal point for "a huge coalition of people with radically different viewpoints," Patterson says. Dark haired and mustachioed, Patterson speaks in the clear, deliberate manner of someone comfortable with his thoughts and actions. He was especially pleased with the emergence of the "coalition," a concept which fits snugly into his holistic philosophy on life and living, a vision that was refined in the mid 1980s when he spent six months among anarchist squatters in an abandoned West Berlin factory.

At thirteen, following his grandfather's death, Patterson took a hard look at the world around him. "Within a year I was a communist, an atheist," he explains. "I started to think about what I really wanted out of life, what my ideals were, and how I could change my lifestyle to reach those ideals. Did I really think that capitalism was okay?" By high school he was a vegetarian. It was heavy stuff for any teenager, but in the Pittsburgh suburbs there was hell to pay for doing anything outside the monotonous norm. "All of my classmates grew up to work in gas stations or in the department stores," Patterson recalls, "people who went out deer hunting on the weekends and who aspired to work in the mills. They were always questioning me about the things that I wanted to do, so I was getting all this practice in arguing and really figuring out what I meant. They thought it was bullshit. They'd throw it back in my face."

After two disappointing years at the University of California at San Diego, where he met other vegetarians for the first time, he left for Berlin. On his return Patterson eventually settled in Berkeley and became connected with what may be the nation's most active Animal Liberation network. He exemplifies the almost non stop drive of many within the radical environmental movement, having participated in banner hangings across the country, most of which have led to arrests. Unlike most in that line of work, Patterson gained the majority of his climbing experience scaling flag poles and the vertical faces of buildings, not by groping for handholds on granite outcroppings in the wilderness. This gives an added dimension to activist Rufus Cohen's observation that Animal Liberation activities are primarily an urban manifestation of environmental consciousness. The NAF allowed Patterson to add crane climbing to his list of structural ascendences, as well as his arrest record.

Things were not good for lab animals at UC-Berkeley before plans were announced for the NAF—not that they ever are—but Berkeley had acquired an especially reprehensible reputation for poorly run facilities. In the early 1980s the student newspaper exposed researchers' cruel treatment of their subjects and the filthy, overcrowded conditions in campus animal labs. Improperly anesthetized kittens awoke screaming during surgery; monkeys were reported to have gangrene, gigantic tumors, and fingers that had been chewed off by cage mates. Based on that information, the American Association for Accreditation of Laboratory Animal Care (AAALAC) in 1984 pulled its approval of Berkeley's facilities, and the U.S. Department of Agriculture, charged with enforcing federal animal care guidelines in laboratories, fined the University $12,000. Berkeley's former veterinarian for campus research said, "UCB research investigators and administrators, as a group, demonstrated consistent unwillingness to self-police when it came to maintaining humane conditions and humane practices in animal research."[2]

But University officials, adept at the political game, turned the poor lab conditions into a big selling point on the need for the NAF. They claimed that the University would be unable to again obtain AAALAC accreditation until it got more space. A lawsuit filed in 1987 by In Defense of Animals (IDA) against the University labeled such statements as false; cutting back on the numbers of experiments and keeping existing laboratories clean would remedy the roadblocks to re-accreditation, they retorted. That was an unlikely solution given the $12 million in grants that 200 Berkeley researchers receive each year. State legislators, who control the University's budget, ignored evidence that the Department of Psychology, which was to receive one-third of the space in the 33,000 square-foot NAF, conducted numerous experiments "of no value" that constituted "pseudo-science, revealing nothing of value to justify their cost and the cruel experimental techniques involved."[3] In October 1987 the Department was the primary focus of a two-week series of demonstrations sponsored by IDA. The protests culminated in the arrest of forty activists who blocked entrances to buildings housing animal experimentation laboratories.[4] Dr. Elliot Katz, IDA's founder and a long time foe of animal research at Berkeley, says, "I think that most people who are sensitive would look at (the justifications given for the NAF) and say, 'That's crazy.' But most people, unfortunately, just don't want to be bothered."[5]

Activists, on the other hand, were not about to buy the University's public relations line that things would get better for the animals once they were moved to the NAF. "That's bullshit," says Patterson. "When you're being tortured all day, who cares if you return to a clean cage at night? It's like it's a better jail." This was a jail intended to prevent any breakouts or *break-ins.* "The Bay Area has been one of the most active in terms of Animal Liberation activities," Patterson says. "The University definitely picked up on that. This thing was going to be underground, it was going to have unbelievable kinds of security measures. Basically it was going to consolidate a lot of the research into this fortress-like structure." The NAF was to be funded in increments, with yearly outlays appropriated by the Legislature for architectural drawings, engineering, construction, and so forth. Initially, there was only a low profile movement against the NAF. Animal Rightists wrote to state legislators urging them to vote against funding for the initial stages of the facility. But the massive University lobby steamrolled all opposition with its assurances of security, better animal care, and prestige. It was that very lobby that became the target of the activists' opening salvo in their direct action campaign against the facility. On May 17, 1988, only months before the planned ground breaking for the NAF and prior to final legislative approval of construction funds, Patterson and a small group of others lobbied in their own way. They took over the office of the University's chief lobbyist in Sacramento and held a press conference on the spot, one block from the state Capitol. Across the street a group of protestors unfurled a banner from a building. All were arrested and fined, but their takeover served notice that the fight was on.

Commandeering the Crane

A short while later, funding for the initial construction of the facility was appropriated by the Legislature. On the day that the University started to cut trees and clear land for the NAF, IDA's Katz led a protest at the site and was roughed up by campus police; another protestor had her thumb fractured. A short time later, a coalition of Berkeley radicals met for the first time to discuss what could be done to stall the project and energize the community against the facility. A takeover of the huge construction crane on the site was the immediate choice. "It was the perfect symbol because it was very high, very visible throughout Berkeley," Patterson says. The protestors saw in the crane "a perfect symbol of conquest over this huge University....We knew it would be a media gold mine in terms of being the perfect visual image....And it would be something that the University couldn't forget."

Crane sits were not a new phenomenon to Animal Liberation protestors in the Bay Area. In the spring of 1988 seven activists occupied a construction derrick at an animal experimentation laboratory under construction at the University of California campus in Santa Cruz. They lasted only a day because they were completely unprepared—they took no warm clothing or food. But they succeeded in coercing the University to allow outside observers into the laboratories and permit them to videotape what they saw.

The Berkeley group called itself the "Coalition against Militarism and Animal Research." They took two months to plan the action, during which time they observed the construction site from adjacent buildings to assess which would be the likely problem spots and how to gain entrance. One obvious, literal barrier was the tall perimeter fence and the shorter one around the base of the crane. However, neither was topped with barbed wire or appeared much more of an obstacle than the average enclosure around someone's backyard. Another concern was the two security guards who maintained a constant presence. Fortunately for the activists, the reconnaissance revealed that the guards spent most of their time watching television inside their portable trailer, not roaming the site looking for mischief-makers. At four o'clock on the morning of February 21, 1989, the crew of six crane commandeers, three men and three women, approached the site. Each carried their own provisions, including two backpacks bulging with additional burdens—huge banners to be lowered off of the crane's long boom.

Lee Dessauxxx, widely respected as the pre-eminent banner hanger and building scaler in the radical environmental movement, was among the six. A veteran of the Santa Cruz takeover as well, Dessauxxx (it rhymes with "guess so") is a standout in a movement full of quirky characters. In outer appearance he is doubtless one of the most radical of the radicals, shaving his hair and eyebrows in eccentric styles. His habiliments come in two styles—punkish all-black and punkish all-camouflage. Of average height and build, the thirty-five-year-old Dessauxxx is one of the best-humored of activists, his friendly laugh flowing freely throughout a conversation; he even admits that his creative hair cuts are a joke of sorts, a way to tease people into believing that they are code signs of the latest radical fringe or that they hold some other sort of bizarre significance.

But what distinguishes Dessauxxx as an eco-warrior is his amazing talent for climbing almost anything. A mountaineer for twenty years, Dessauxxx's first banner hanging was co-sponsored by David Brower's Earth Island Institute, Earth First!, and local Animal Liberation activists in St. Louis. A protest of the Ralston-Purina company's continued purchase of tuna from fleets that set their nets on dolphins, the action took place at the company's January 1988 stockholders' meeting. Dessauxxx climbed what he calls, in casual rock climber parlance, "a fairly exposed, semi-dangerous route up the outside of the old railroad station," now a hotel, where the meeting was being held. Truth is, he went 100 feet up a sheer wall without using any sort of climbing aides to assist him or to prevent his death in case of a fall. Once at the top of the building, Dessauxxx secured himself with a rope and climbing tools. Then he lowered himself to the edge of a gable and struggled to set up the banner, which "was a complicated affair—it had a lot of PVC piping and ropes and stuff."[6] A stiff wind was blowing, making the experience "like wrestling with a giant kite." Eventually, he unfurled it successfully. St. Louis officials had never before seen such an exploit. They reacted by calling several hook and ladder trucks and dozens of police officers to the scene. Dessauxxx, who says he would probably not attempt the same action in the same way again, safely rap- pelled down the face of the building. He was promptly carted off to jail, the first of a dozen arrests he has endured in the course of fifteen or so banner hangings.

Dessauxxx says he and others "planning the Berkeley stunt felt we had maybe a twenty-five percent chance or less of actually pulling it off. This was a $15 million building site, and the chances of a half dozen people scrambling up a giant crane with supplies just seemed fairly remote. But we wanted to give it a try." He and Patterson each laugh about how they brought off the first phase of the action. When the group reached the perimeter fence they tried throwing their forty-pound backpacks over the barrier. "It was quite comical," recalls Dessauxxx. "Here we were, six of us trying to throw our packs and they just kept bouncing back. It was like rebounding a basketball." Patterson confesses, "I was the first one to get to the fence, and I was trying to climb in. I got caught up in it and was trying to get free. Others went over to the main gate and just pushed it open. It wasn't even locked! They get over to the crane and I was still trying to get off of this fence.

"Climbing the crane was a bitch with all of this stuff on your back. It took a long time to get up. Then, when we got to the base of the cab we knew we'd have a problem." As expected, the cab door located at the top of the ladder and overhead was locked, necessitating a breathtaking maneuver by Dessauxxx. To perform the feat, he climbed onto a small platform attached to the vertical support structure. He tied himself into a belay with Patterson bracing himself at the other end of the fifteen foot rope in the case of a fall. Dessauxxx stepped out onto an exhaust pipe, stood on his tiptoes, then leaned out into space, 160 feet above the ground, while simultaneously reaching up to grab hold of anything he could feel in the overhanging cab. Stretching to his full five feet, ten inches, Dessauxxx managed to grasp the edge of the cab's metal flooring. From there "it was a grunt move of pulling myself up" says the dexterous Dessauxxx. "But it was hairy. I remember that feeling of one's butt hanging out into space." The experience was unlike any of his previous climbs, including the one in St. Louis. "It's one thing to be 160 feet up on a building or a cliff or something. But with the crane, and I think we noticed this not only on the initial climb but throughout the eight days we were up there, there was this very airy feeling about it. Sometimes the crane swayed in the wind a bit. With the exception of when you're on the vertical part, you just have 160 feet of dead air below you in a vertical drop."

Once in the cab, Dessauxxx dropped an etrier. "Originally we were going to have everyone come up that way, but it was really fucking hairy going up this rope ladder, unbelievably hairy," says Patterson, who was the only one who actually used the flimsy contraption. "It was the scariest thing I've ever done." In lieu of asking the rest of the group to risk the same trip, and aware that it had been more than two hours since they had entered the site, Patterson worked fast at removing the hinges to the doorway while Tanya Cizewski pried at it from beneath. Finally, they succeeded in removing the door, and the weary crew climbed into the cab. As yet unnoticed, they took time to rest and enjoy the view of Berkeley, the Bay, and San Francisco beyond as dawn broke. Then they climbed out onto the crane's long arm, or jib, and unfurled the two massive banners, which they had finished sewing in a factory in lower Berkeley only shortly before they went up. The banners read "STOP GERM WARFARE LAB" and "NO TOXIC ANIMAL LAB." They each measured approximately fifteen feet by thirty feet, the largest one weighing fifteen pounds.

Construction workers arriving on the job were the first to sound the alarm that something was amiss. Soon the site was swarming with Berkeley city police and campus security. Using a bullhorn they called upon the protestors to quit the action. Then an officer climbed up the stairs and issued a similar demand. It was not until then that the occupying force recognized the need to secure the hatchway, which they did by placing the crane operator's refrigerator, heavy electrical cables, tools, and whatever else substantial they could find on top of the door. The six answered that they were not budging. They had brought a five-day supply of food and enough determination to hold out until they were satisfied that people had gotten the message about what was happening on the site.

The media quickly caught wind of the action and congregated around the crane. One innovative television news crew interviewed the protestors by hollering questions from a building near the crane. Although the sitters were generally pleased at the quality of the press coverage (they were ecstatic at the extent of attention—the story dominated the local news for more than a week), Patterson recalls reporters asking, "'Why couldn't these people take the legal route?'" Such questions are frustratingly typical, Patterson says. "They weren't looking at the history of it. We had tried to oppose it on legal grounds for a long time. Finally, when that failed we saw no other recourse."

With some success the University attempted to convince the press that the protestors had climbed the wrong crane, that it was being used only for construction of a plant genetics building next door. In fact, says Patterson, it was used for both. "The press picked up on this and gave us hell for it. As always, they like to paint you as hot-headed idiots who are just so anxious to do an action that you do something rash and don't think about the consequences. It's unfortunate because all of us were against the genetic experiments as well, the whole designing nature thing. Plus, they were going to be doing animal research in the genetics building as well. The press never picked up on that, of course."

Far below, negotiations to end the occupation lasted for just one day. Unlike the officials at the Santa Cruz campus, those at Berkeley wanted the protestors off the crane, period. They found the activists' demands, like ending all animal experimentation and refusing to accept any more Department of Defense money, completely untenable. Dessauxxx says no one held any delusions that the demands actually would be met. It was the statement that mattered, drawing attention to an issue that the press and many in the community had studiously avoided.

As a show of solidarity with the sitters, dozens of Berkeley radicals maintained a constant vigil in the shadow of the crane on a traffic island in the middle of Oxford Street. While most of those on the structure were animal rightists, Patterson says, "A lot of the people on the ground were activists against militarism. That's a point we kept hammering home, that this was just part of the military-industrial complex. This thing was evil on so many fronts. It was the perfect melting pot for so many activists." The middle-of-the-road radicals sometimes swelled to more than 100 in number. They shouted "We love you!" "You're doing a great job!" and similar messages of support to the crane sitters. From their "nest," the protestors used a powerful megaphone to call down to their supporters and to goad their detractors. Dessauxxx recalls, "There's a certain feeling about the comedy of the situation....We would yell stuff like, 'All you workers and all you cops: It's never too late to turn in your tools and weapons and join the revolution!' There was a real feeling of power both by being on the crane and being vocal using the bullhorn." Two pre-planned demonstrations on the ground drew large crowds, and at one point a huge mob attempted to break down the central gates to the site, resulting in numerous arrests.

When they were not granting interviews or taunting the authorities from above, the protestors spent time reading and talking in the cab or hanging out on the counter-jib, the short balancing arm which was exposed to the open air and had a four-foot-wide wire mesh floor. There they made a makeshift house out of dark plastic tarpaulins and foam mattresses they found in the cab. It was difficult to get much rest, however. "Cops would be fucking with us continuously," Patterson says. Using tactics similar to those employed against tree sitters, "at three in the morning they'd ring loud bells or shout at us with bullhorns, 'Wake up, wake up!' They'd throw stones at the crane, turn on floodlights, just to give us shit so that we couldn't sleep." But the protestors' spirits were high. They traded insults with construction workers on an adjacent building who wrote signs like "Nuke the Kittens and Puppies." The sitters joked about a bull's eye that construction workers painted on the ground beneath the jib. Although most in the group did not know the others very well initially, as they talked with one another and endured the hardship of living for days in cramped quarters their solidarity grew.

Viking to the Rescue

On the first day of the action, before a strong police presence could be established, a supply team sent up the last of the group's water. In a pre-arranged maneuver, only hours after the occupation began the sitters threw a line to supporters who had snuck onto the roof of an adjacent building. The supply crew escaped moments before a police squad rushed onto the roof. Water was one thing; food was another. The protestors' stocks were exhausted much faster than they had originally expected; what was thought to be five days of food had to be stretched to make it three. By the fourth day, with their food gone and intimidated by a restraining order prohibiting further crane sitting, Patterson and three others climbed down the crane and into the waiting arms of the police, satisfied that their point had been made.

Dessauxxx and Cizewski remained on the crane, determined to delay the project as much as possible. Patterson flashed a signal to their support team on his way down the ladder, letting them know that Dessauxxx and Cizewski needed more food. That evening, supporters signaled the pair that they should be prepared for a food pickup at four o'clock the next morning. Emergency resupply points had been selected as part of the reconnaissance. The plan was similar to that used for the water pickup on the first day: the sitters would drop a line and a member of the support team would clip on a bag of food and dash away before the authorities could react. Dessauxxx recalls, "At about three in the morning I woke up and was very silently working my way out onto the jib. It sticks way out there, probably 150 feet. Of course the crane was all lit up at night, but I was trying to do this all very secretly. I didn't make any noise and I was moving very slowly. We had noticed that by three or four in the morning the cops were just sitting there drinking coffee. They were pretty sedated."

Dessauxxx, who "was probably halfway out on the jib," says that "all of a sudden I heard all this wild yelling. I looked back and thought, 'Oh my God, what's happening?' What I saw was a person running for the crane and maybe a dozen cops all converging on the base of the crane. This wild maniac flew over the chain-link fence—of course, the gate was locked by then—and started scrambling up the crane. He eluded a dozen cops, and some of them were so pissed they were throwing rocks at him." The crane rang with the pinging of missed projectiles as the rucksack-laden daredevil raced up the ladder. With no walkway on the jib to allow him to rush back to the cab, Dessauxxx could only hold on tight and watch. From her vantage point on the counter-jib, Cizewski saw what was happening and quickly removed the heavy materials covering the door. She later told Dessauxxx that she briefly opened the door and then became alarmed that the person climbing the ladder might be a police officer. She closed it and rushed to take another look from the counter-jib. She told Dessauxxx that she thought, "'No, it can't be a cop; he's got two-foot-long hair and looks like a Viking.' He was screaming at us to open the door, so Tanya pulled back the door."

The Viking turned out to be Jeff Miller, a friend of Dessauxxx's from Berkeley, carrying twenty-five pounds of food in his backpack. Miller had volunteered to take the food to the emergency pickup site, but when he approached the area beneath the end of the jib he spied a police officer sitting nearby. Miller's only options were to leave his fellow activists to starve or to make a dash for the crane. When he was safely in the cab a celebration ensued, and Dessauxxx and Cizewski convinced him to stay for the duration.

Throughout the action the protestors were anxious about a possible air assault by a SWAT team or a maneuver like the one Dessauxxx had used to swing into the cab. But later on the fifth day the police chose a more direct attack route. Apparently embarrassed by the lax security early that morning, officers climbed to the top of the ladder and ripped apart the doorway to the cab. "It was like a war up there," says Dessauxxx of the vicious pounding. "Our supporters and the spectators down below were just going crazy. We were advertising over the bullhorn, 'They're trying to get us!'" The cab takeover proved but a minor inconvenience to the sitters because the only access to their quarters on the counter-jib and the jib was through a second door on the roof of the cab. They secured that opening from the outside about a half-hour before the police broke through. Negotiations began again, but when they failed the next morning the police assaulted the top door and entered the crane. That forced the sitters out onto the precarious jib. To ward off any further encroachment, they warned the police that they would not be taken off the crane. To demonstrate how serious they were, Dessauxxx rappelled twenty feet beneath the jib and suspended himself in mid-air. Cizewski was prepared to use a lock and chain to secure herself onto the crane structure in a precarious position. Miller crawled to the end of the long arm. The police never chanced an excursion onto the jib.

Two days later, eight days into the action, the sitters were worn out. Attorneys from the Animal Legal Defense Fund negotiated a settlement with the University, which agreed to drop criminal charges. Later that day Cizewski, Dessauxxx, and Miller abandoned the crane. In the end they and the other protestors were each sentenced to eighty hours of community service in lieu of jail time or fines.

Aftermath

In addition to their misdemeanor convictions, the University attempted to extract $200,000 in restitution from the protestors. "They claimed we cost them hundreds of thousands of excess dollars, which we did," says Patterson. "The main thing was lost construction time—workers sitting on their asses doing nothing. Every day it was costing them fifty grand." However, because the protestors were propertyless, penniless, and without steady jobs outside of environmental activism, lawsuits to recover the damages were little more than a formality.

Patterson was pleased to see that grassroots resistance to the NAF grew dramatically in the weeks following the crane takeover, as he had hoped it would. "We raised the public's consciousness about it," he says. "People in Berkeley know about it now, what a danger it is. We let the University know that it's not a thing that they can just bulldoze past the people without a fight." But it is doubtful that a grassroots movement, the city council's long-stated objections, or even a successful court challenge by IDA will stop the facility. Although an appeals court directed that the University develop a new environmental impact report, its ruling said the report satisfactorily addressed the risks associated with animal research.

Elliot Katz of IDA argues that only non-animal methods of experimentation should be used at the NAF, and he counts as a Pyrrhic victory the state university system's decision to establish a center for alternative methods of research. The stated purpose of such research centers is to minimize or eliminate the use of animals in research. "But," Katz says, "the center for alternatives will once again likely be used to placate the public, as a public relations tool [allowing the University] to say, 'Look, we have a center for alternatives. Give us money for the center.'" Katz adds, "Part of the AMA Action Plan states that they want to create a companion health funding base to take money away from the Animal Rights movement," referring to the American Medical Association's "Animal Research Action Plan" that outlines its counter-attack against the movement. The demand for a benign facility was again pressed in lawsuits filed in March 1990 that attacked the revised environmental assessment. IDA joined Berkeley Citizens for a Toxic Free Environment to further contend that the accreditation argument was "false and misleading," while in its own lawsuit the City of Berkeley said the NAF "could release 'toxic, infectious, and radioactive agents into the environment.'"[7]

But how successful were the crane sit, the other civil disobedience actions, and the lawsuits against the Northwest Animal Facility? Pyrrhic victories do little to free animals. The view of many Animal Liberators is that frustrating efforts like those in Berkeley, where protests occur in the open in an attempt to directly engage the public, are basically failures. These "defeats," say some, vindicate those who would go farther to act on behalf of animals by liberating them from laboratories or even burning-down the labs. Yet Patterson does see in the Northwest Animal Facility struggle an important lesson for other communities. "It's important to remember that people really do possess the power," he says. "You don't realize how much power you do have until you go in and try to stop it." He adds, "It's very important to get the community involved. That was fairly successful in this action. Of course, they had a vested interest in watching out for their own safety." Still, making the connection to animals, even in a city full of cutting-edge radicals, remains a difficult task. "If this hadn't been a P3 laboratory, where people's health was at risk, it would have been a lot harder," Patterson admits. "That's a perennial problem with the Animal Rights movement—people look out for themselves and not for the animals."

CHAPTER 13

ON THE WARPATH WITH ANNA, MEL, AND LIB

In April 1987, Animal Liberationists carried out one of the most costly and most controversial acts of environmental sabotage in the United States. One of the ALF members responsible for that action tells her reasons for burning down an animal research laboratory in the last part of this chapter. Another member of her "cell" describes the liberation of several dogs used by the surgeon who performed the famous "Baby Fae" gorilla-to-human heart transplant. The chapter begins with the story of one of the first Animal Liberators in the U.S., a woman driven by conscience and philosophy to, as she says, "act for those who cannot act for themselves."

Anna: Middle-Class Liberator

Like so many radical environmentalists, little in Animal Liberator "Anna's" background would lead one to suspect that she would go to the extremes or take the chances she does on behalf of non-human animals.[1] Born and raised in a middle-class neighborhood in Minneapolis, she says she always loved animals, recalling that she once berated her brother for taunting a menacing dog that a neighbor kept in a fenced-in yard. She was a good student in high school and attended a large state university in the Midwest, where she majored in political science and for a time intended to pursue a law degree "because it seemed like a good way to have a positive impact on the world." Rather than immediately go to law school, Anna decided to take some time off after college. She moved to New York City and took a job as a researcher in a large law firm.

While shopping for Christmas gifts she took a leaflet from one of a small group of anti-fur activists outside of a large department store. "Something in that handout really moved me," Anna says. "It made me think about these issues for the first time, wearing fur and leather, especially. And the more I thought about them, the more curious I got." She telephoned a number listed on the brochure and was placed on the group's mailing list. Eventually, she took the next step and attended an anti-fur rally. "I had never done anything like that," Anna says, "and it was really uncomfortable to walk up to a bunch of people I didn't even know and say, 'Hi, I'm here to help.' But the people there, especially the women, really made me feel welcome. I still didn't do much chanting, just passed out literature." An energetic woman in her sixties, "Jane," befriended Anna at that first rally. Jane had been involved in anti-fur and anti-vivisection activities for years, since well before they become widely noticed. Through her, Anna began to learn about the more radical side of the movement. "Jane isn't interested in the philosophical or academic questions," Anna says, "the kinds of things I always enjoyed. All she wants is action *now*, and she only looks at the practical consequences—whether something she does is going to reduce animal suffering. To the extent that there is a philosophical side to her, she despises oppression."

Anna's first illegal act for animals came "after an anti-fur demo at a fashion show," Anna says. "I had known Jane for a month or two when she asked me out for coffee. We were talking about how great the demonstration had been—at least fifty or seventy-five people showed up, most of them women—and she asked how I was with a spray can! I didn't know what she was talking about." In a city full of graffiti artists, Anna and Jane soon developed their own style to the point where they could work on two lines at once outside of a research center or corporate headquarters, the paint bright red, symbolizing the blood of animals that had been spilled for human greed and gain. Their slogans usually involved phrases like "NYU = Death and Suffering" and "Repression of Animals is Repression of All." In the intervening years Anna and Jane have even attacked grocery stores, hitting the meat counter before the morning rush, "to make people think," Anna says, "to remind them of the suffering the cows and pigs and chickens go through to become a meal for people, the excruciating pain and the fear. We want to end the blank images of nothing but a piece of meat there. Hey! That was once an animal just as much alive as you or me."

Bringing Peace, Freedom, and Hope to the Real World

Anna says she overcomes her fears in carrying out such actions through the strength of her emotions about the "inhumanity" inflicted on the animals. Ironically, in the first and perhaps most dangerous action she has undertaken, Anna says she had too little time to be scared. "Jane and I had done several of these spray paint attacks," she says, "and we started signing them 'ALF.' But we felt a little insincere because to us using the Animal Liberation Front name meant freeing animals." Over a vegetarian dinner one evening, Jane revealed that she had a contact at a university laboratory in a city several hours away. It was their chance to become full-fledged

Animal Liberators. "I just said 'That's great! Let's do it.' She said, 'Good, we go in a week.'"

This was in the early days, Anna says, before extensive reconnaissance was necessitated by surveillance cameras, squadrons of guards, and "modern labs that are designed knowing that people want to get into them." Because Jane was retired and living on a pension, she had time to travel and "to scope the place out" to the extent it was necessary. The "inside" contact was a person with access to the lab whom Jane had befriended for just that purpose. "You can't ask for better information than what comes from someone inside the place," Anna says. "They know who will be around working late and when security patrols check the area." Anna is hesitant to divulge the details of the experiments which she and Jane knew they would ruin by taking the animals, saying only that they were "physiological in nature" and that the researcher was "well-known to the Animal Rights community for his cruelty. His prior experiments were even worse than needless. They just replicated experiments that people had done five or ten years before. We wanted to ruin his experiments and to make him and others think long and hard the next time they hurt an animal. But most important for us was to save lives."

On the afternoon of the liberation, Anna and Jane drove to the city where the lab was located. During the ride Jane filled Anna in on the plan. The actual liberation, like the rest of the operation, was straightforward considering the apparent danger inherent in what they were doing. "We parked as near to the building where the animals were kept as we could get," Anna recalls. "It was just after midnight, late in the fall term, and the library had just closed. To look like students we dressed in jeans and light jackets, and we both had backpacks on. We also wore gloves; it wasn't really cold enough for them, but we didn't want to leave fingerprints." Inside their daypacks they carried pillowcases for the animals. By prior arrangement, Jane's contact had unlocked a side door to the building just before the two liberators were expected to arrive. "The room where the animals were kept was actually a converted closet on the third floor of this old classroom building," Anna says. "We knew exactly what to do: in the door, up the stairs. Our contact had also left the closet door unlocked. The contact was somewhere in the building, but we did the whole thing so that the person could honestly say they had seen no one. I guess that mattered to them."

Anna opened the door to the large walk-in closet and found the light switch. Three sets of eyes, two kittens and a cat, blinked at them. The adult had an electrode protruding from her skull to allow measurement of her brain wave patterns. Anna remembers thinking "it was unbelievable that an animal could live its life in a cage that small—they looked to be a foot or foot and a-half on each side. The cats started running around frantically when we stepped into the closet, but they calmed down and took to us very quickly. To me their tameness made the experimenter's work even more tragic. These cats could have been somebody's pets." Before leaving that morning, Anna and Jane used a borrowed typewriter to compose a message to the researcher. The note condemned society's abuse of animals and wished the researcher "Peace on Earth" from the cats, which Anna and Jane named Peace, Freedom, and Hope. "Our purpose in choosing those names was to make people realize it was an act of liberation in a profound sense of the word," Anna says solemnly, "that we were taking the cats to a freedom they had never known before and that the act was done with the best of intentions to allow them to live in peace and free from violence." They inserted the note in a copy of Peter Singer's *Animal Liberation* and left it atop one of the empty cages. While Jane removed the three cats and placed them in the pillowcases, Anna photographed the cages. The pictures, developed by a friend in the movement, were delivered to the major newspaper in the university city with a copy of the note for the researcher.

From a telephone outside of the city, Jane called a veterinarian who knew of the planned liberation and had agreed to examine the cats. In the early morning hours they met him at his clinic. He found the kittens to be in good shape, but it was obvious that the older cat suffered from a number of physical, and perhaps psychological, traumas that would make her life miserable. The vet decided to put Peace to sleep. "Peace was so sad," Anna says in a quiet voice. "One pupil was dilated more than the other, and she seemed to be so lethargic. I rode with her on my lap from the lab to the veterinarian's office, and she started purring. I wonder if she knew that she was being freed? I think just those last few hours of love were very important to her." Anna says that was the purpose behind the action, "to have done something concrete to help the animals—like Jane says, 'Right now and not later.' That's the feeling I have. Experiments on animals have to stop now, not some time in the future. I knew that by taking those cats I was saving them from ultimately being killed." Through their contacts in the movement, Jane and Anna had arranged for the kittens to be placed together in a loving home.

Anna continues to work with Jane and others on their spray paint campaigns and surreptitiously marks fur coats with red lipstick whenever she sees them being worn, a "mark of shame" monkeywrench of sorts which is costly to remove. She views these and other actions as part of the larger process that will inevitably lead to an end to humans' exploitation of animals.

Anarchy for the Animals

"Mel" is one of many California Animal Liberators who agrees with the generalization that the ALF in the eastern U.S. emphasizes the importance of liberating animals and getting good, positive press out of it. West Coast liberationists, in contrast, practice the anarchy which they see as an ideal future for society by actively engaging in a spectrum of endeavors using a variety of means to free non-human animals—as well as humans—from oppression. Mel and others of his ALF "cell" spend substantial amounts of time away from their home bases living out of their backpacks and working with others in a small but close-knit network of like-feeling Animal Liberators.

Now in his early thirties, Mel refuses to say much about his background or what, if anything, prompted him to become interested in Animal Liberation. He does admit to having been strongly influenced by events that occurred during a stay in Britain in 1985 with a friend. The trip was a turning point for Mel in two important, interrelated ways. After talking with a friend of his host about vegetarianism and factory farming, Mel entirely eliminated meat from his diet within two months, and eighteen months later was a vegan. The other important event was an underground newspaper interview he read where a British ALF member said that one "joined" the ALF simply by participating in actions.

Mel and his British friend, "Reed," whom he got to know while the Brit stayed at Mel's home in Colorado as part of a high school foreign exchange program, both felt strong connections to the Earth. They had spent many weekends backpacking together in the Rocky Mountains and discussing the world's problems. "After we read that interview we stayed up all night talking," recalls Mel. "We took it really seriously, the idea that we could do something. Not just could, but *should*. It was on our shoulders. It was time to pay our dues to the animals. Vegetarianism was one thing, but it was so passive. We began to look for ways to get actively involved in the struggle."

While touring throughout Britain, Mel noticed several former fur shops where signs hung over boarded-up store fronts. He remembered film clips from news broadcasts documenting attacks on furriers. One fur shop in Bristol was attacked sixty times in one year and was finally put out of business. Neither Mel nor Reed had ever been involved in even so much as toilet papering someone's home as a birthday gag, but a combination of anger at the cruelty of the fur industry and the evidence that the attacks actually worked spurred them to try such things themselves.

Late one night they skulked through town toward a fur shop. Nervously, they approached it, looked at one another, and then had at it. First, they sprayed the exterior of the building with red paint, like Anna and Jane, to draw attention to their acts and to symbolize the animals' blood spilled in making the furs. Then they threw two rocks through the front window and leaped into the shop to paint the furs as well. Exhilarated, they ran and shouted back home. During the ensuing nights, Mel and Reed went out repeatedly on these "smash attacks." The enormity of the destruction he helped cause and the fact that it was being perpetrated in a foreign country did not sink in until Mel went out alone for the first time, shortly before he left for the States. It was a double blow of culture shock, both in the sense of being in a foreign land whose justice system he knew even less about than his own and of becoming involved in a sub-culture that revolves around illegal acts. But Mel didn't stop. His solution was to force himself to do more. He and Reed were gratified to see that their efforts were appreciated by many Brits. The newspaper accounts quoted conservative Animal Welfare officials as voicing support for the attacks. "That's the best thing over there—the above-ground welcomes you as a part of the movement," Mel says. "Like with lab break-ins: you never see the mainstream shun evidence that is illegally obtained." In contrast, Animal Welfare groups in the U.S. want no association with the radicals.

After he returned home, Mel decided to start his own ALF "cell." In Britain there are several such cells—the Southern, Central, and Northern are the best known of them. Each is established by activists like Mel who heed ALF's call to organize one's own group and not to depend on others to do the work for them or to attempt to contact those in existing groups. The terminology is important as well, for "cell" implies revolutionary tendencies, an appropriate label in Mel's view. When he approached two long time friends about joining him, neither hesitated. It was near Thanksgiving, and when newspapers reported that a turkey farm had been broken into, the cell became inspired. They picked up where Mel had left off in Britain, smashing windows and spraying blood-red paint on fur and butcher shops. The following Easter they continued another British tradition, liberating rabbits. The cell, now located in California so that it could choose from a wider range of targets, heard through casual conversations with members of the Animal Welfare movement of a rabbit breeder in the southern part of the state who supplied animals to universities and research centers. As part of their reconnaissance they entered the dingy metal shed one evening. They were shocked to find dead rabbits on the concrete floor, filthy conditions, and a nauseating smell. When they raided the facility a week before Easter, the trio took 115 rabbits with them in a utility van. Their press release was delivered to a group which had agreed to serve as a media contact for the liberators, and the sally reaped a substantial amount of what Mel feels was balanced publicity. Tragically, twenty of the rabbits died outside of captivity because of diseases already infecting them.

It was the first animal liberation for all of the cell members. Since then, Mel admits to having been involved in ten similar actions at suppliers, factory farms, and research labs. He says that it is more difficult to free animals from laboratories than from factory farms because reconnaissance at a lab requires a "student look" and because a substantial amount of stealth is needed to avoid the ever present police patrols and security systems. In contrast, factory farms can be scouted from across a field. Animal breeders, however, are on a level by themselves because the breeding facility is usually on the fancier's property.

Liberating Loma Linda

Mel and his cohorts have pulled-off a number of dramatic actions which reaped substantial publicity, much of it negative, for the movement and saved hundreds of animals' lives. Among their attacks was one at a kennel housing animals used by Dr. Leonard L. Bailey, who conducted the sensational transplant of the heart of a baboon into an infant named "Baby Fae" in 1984. The raid took place on August 15, 1988, near Loma Linda University, east of Los Angeles. Early reconnaissance by the group revealed that Bailey's office on the Loma Linda campus was heavily guarded. Through continued observations they discovered the kennel site, known as the "farm," just off of campus. There, larger animals, such as goats and dogs, were kept prior to and following experiments. It was the target they had been looking for. "Countless" nights spent watching the building followed to ensure that the cell members knew the timing of the guard checks and other particulars. Eventually, it became clear that they had a two-hour time frame with which to work. "Before we actually freed any animals, we entered the lab several times to locate documents that might shed light on the experiments," Mel says. "We also wanted to get to know the animals. It was kind of neat because after the first time, the dogs never barked again."

Mel will not say how he and the others repeatedly gained such easy access to the building, but in so doing they uncovered numerous research files. Press reports following the break-in said that the perpetrators cut through a fence and entered the building through a side door. The dogs were Labrador retrievers, apparently Bailey's breed of choice because of their "substantial stamina," says Mel. The group also found photographs of Bailey's test subject animals, including one of a baboon with a shaved chest and a button reading "Just Say No to Drugs," which Mel calls "a bizarre, callous joke." (Making fun of their subjects is not uncommon among animal researchers—John Orem at Texas Tech filmed a movie apparently depicting a "mad scientist" at work.)

Mel says the plan was to take two dogs and a like number of goats. Ironically, despite their extensive reconnaissance the group found it could not take the goats because on the evening of the liberation farmers were harvesting alfalfa in a field next to the goats' pen. They would almost certainly have noticed the activists in the area. The raiders were thrilled, however, to discover five puppies which had just been brought to the kennel from an Arizona operation calling itself an "animal shelter," Mel says. "We got all five of them out before the bastards had even touched them. The adults were really ecstatic when we let them out of their cages, but they freaked out when we tried to put them on a leash. That was when it really hit us that these were honest-to-God laboratory dogs." They were "purpose-bred" for research, meaning they lived their entire lives in sterile laboratory surroundings.

Hidden from the farmers by the building, Mel and the others carried all of the dogs to their van. When the dogs were safe, the cell members returned to the offices and doused them with crimson paint. Later that evening they transferred the dogs to another van, and an intermediary drove them to another state. Initially, the adults dogs were separated for security reasons, but they were re-united later in the home of "a childless couple that likes to go camping. They have no idea where the dogs came from," according to Mel, who has not seen any of the dogs since the night of the liberation. The adult dogs, which Loma Linda officials told the press were used for breeding, "had to be taught how to play and to be shown what it was like to run in a field," Mel says with a sigh. "That makes the sort of loving home they eventually found even more important. The dogs found out that not all humans are bad and that life is not the living hell that it seems to be in a laboratory setting." The puppies, not yet scarred from years in a cage, were placed in good homes and easily adjusted to their new freedom.

Along with various photographs obtained by the liberators, documents they stole purportedly showed that "Dr. Bailey had full prior knowledge that Baby Fae could never survive and, in fact, did not expect her to do so based on his prior research," according to the group's press release. Those papers evinced that fewer than one percent of the animals which received organ transplants from other species survived for more than three months. The cell also alleged that the baboon whose heart was given to Baby Fae was awake when its heart was removed but unable to move because it had been injected with a muscle relaxant. Damage caused by the raid was estimated to be $10,000.[2]

Mel says he and his fellow cell members act "to save lives, the only lives those animals have. They have been spared, whereas before they were destined to live horrible lives. They've gotten a reprieve." However, he does acknowledge a tension between logic and compassion when acting as an Animal Liberator. "The animals don't cost much, maybe ten or fifteen dollars each for a rabbit and a couple of hundred dollars each for dogs," he explains. These sorts of liberations are emblematic, he says, of the larger struggle for freedom for all animals, which often do not have even a minimal monetary value placed on their lives. Although Animal Liberators' impact on a particular experiment may be tremendous, Mel says in a system that kills hundreds of millions of animals each year, the direct impact on the overall research establishment is minuscule. "What's really exciting is when you get the feeling that the people out there are getting the hint," Mel says. "Every little bit helps. When you see that people are not afraid to sign their name to a letter to the editor supporting these illegal acts, it is affirmation that what you're doing is having an effect. I think the industry realizes it too. Every time we bring out evidence like we did at Loma Linda, they lose not just in dollars but in face, too. There's a little more truth that comes to the surface."

Torching the "Torture Chamber"

"Lib" joined Mel's ALF cell when the other members realized they needed more help in order to accomplish all they had planned. She and Mel were reluctant to say how they met, but she did offer that she had known one or more members of the cell "for some time" before she became involved. Like Mel, she declines to give any information about her personal background. Lib admits to participating "in a couple of minor actions—window smashings and paintings, that sort of thing" before she and others undertook the largest single act of environmental monkeywrenching in U.S. history and one of the largest in the world: the arson attack on a veterinary building under construction at the University of California at Davis, in April 1987.

The attack was the first U.S. ALF action against an unfinished building, says Lib, and the first involving arson. The idea was hatched after Animal Liberationists read of plans for the Thurman Veterinary Diagnostic Laboratory (VDL) in campus publications. "Word got around about what it was for, and our cell discussed it a lot," Lib says. State officials saw the VDL as the core facility in a five-site "diagnostic center." The purpose of the labs, alleges Lib, would be "to stop diseases occurring because of intensive confinement on factory farms. Their aim was to develop the ultimate farm animal—the ultimate cow, the ultimate chicken, the ultimate pig." Lib says that the researchers hoped to create, using means including genetic engineering, animals which would not maim themselves or others, would grow rapidly or otherwise produce in high volumes, would process food with minimal waste, and which would have strong defenses against disease. The research would take place in "the ultimate torture chamber," as Lib calls the VDL, "a huge, almost totally windowless building where everything that happens—like every other vivisector's laboratory—would be hidden from the public. All the public gets are the 'benefits,'" she says sarcastically, "less shit, more genetically tinkered animal products, and the satisfaction that we have warped nature even worse than before."

Following unsuccessful, non-destructive protests by others against the VDL, the Animal Liberators decided their only option was to burn down the laboratory before it was completed. The target was almost perfect from the perspective of safety—it was far from any other human or non-human animals, meaning it was unlikely that anyone would be accidentally injured. The building's remoteness also offered the perpetrators substantial insurance against being seen by passersby. While a building of its sort would have made a tempting target anywhere in the U.S., says Lib, the VDL was all the more enticing because animal experimentation at UC-Davis "is the epitome of scholastic research. The Veterinary Department is world renowned. What's ironic is that people think vets are supposed to help animals. But most of what goes on at UC-Davis is government-sponsored and funded research tied to the development of agribusiness. Animal agriculture is a multi-*billion* dollar a year industry in California, and the government and business are in cahoots trying to protect it and enlarge it." Lib says the public health arguments put forth as part of the justification for the VDL are specious, and that the animals would be healthier for meat-eating humans and for themselves if allowed to live their lives naturally. To undertake its "life-destructive" experiments "designed to fuel America's hunger for meat, milk, and eggs," Lib says animal experimentation will be essential, although officials denied in published reports that any animal experiments would take place at the VDL. Regardless of those assertions, Lib says the attack on the VDL was a "chance to hit them on two fronts: farm animals and vivisection."

Activists were called in from other parts of the country to assist with the reconnaissance and the planning of the action. They were also needed because some in the cell had chosen to limit themselves to non-destructive Animal Liberation activities, like raiding factory farms or researchers' laboratories. Although these others in the cell were supportive of the plan to raze the VDL, they felt uncomfortable participating in an arson. "That's a real societal hang-up," says Lib, "and there are some even in the ALF who have this fear that people will be turned off by arson. That's a possibility that is really troubling to most of us, I think. We're not a bunch of pyromaniacs." She equates burning down an animal testing laboratory or a fur shop with the torching of cotton gins in the antebellum South by slaves, only in this instance the enslaved are not able to act on their own. "We see arson for animals as the ultimate non-violent tactic because you're stopping vivisection before it can begin. They can't operate until they have remedied the problem of finding a location where they can work." She adds, "Even if they won't all participate, I know that every person in every ALF cell in America believes that every animal experimentation lab in the country should be burned down."

As at Loma Linda, the long nights of reconnaissance were spent ascertaining the timing of security patrols and gleaning information about the building that would help make the action more successful. An additional concern was the presence of on-site guards or guard dogs. "We took an extra long time to recon at Davis," Lib says. "Fire is incredibly dangerous, and we weren't about to risk anybody's life. So we just kept an eye on the building until we were confident that we could act without hurting anyone." Once patterns began to develop and it was clear the building was without a nighttime guard, Lib and the others set about determining how best to set fire to the structure while ensuring that they could get off campus before the flames were noticed. In the end they used "a slow but effective incendiary device" of an uncertain type, although Lib says it was "small enough to be stamped out with one's foot and minimally combustible," a description that sounds much like a cigarette-and-matches setup popular in Britain that was once pictured in the *Liberator*, the newspaper of the U.S.

Animal Liberation Front Support Group.[3] Lib says the device used at the VDL was timed so that when it ignited no one would be in the building.

At about three o'clock on the morning of April 16, the group scaled the chain-link fence surrounding the VDL. Unexpectedly, they found gallons of red primer paint outside of the building, and one person splashed "ALF" on the exterior wall while others were inside preparing the flammable device. Once it was set the group quickly left. They then raided a University motor pool a half mile away, vandalizing seventeen state-owned vehicles by puncturing their tires and spray-painting "Animal Liberation Front" and "Stop the Torture" on them.

"The fire was discovered by a researcher working late who saw his new lab going up in flames," Lib says gleefully. "They said that the fire was so hot that the steel structure was damaged." Half the building was destroyed in the three alarm blaze, which set back the completion date for nearly a year. There were no reports of injuries to firefighters or to anyone else as a result of the action. The FBI was called in to investigate the fire because of the "terroristic" nature of the attack. No arrests were made despite a total of $11,500 in rewards offered for the capture and conviction of anyone involved in the assault. Damage to the building and the vehicles was originally set at $2.5 million; the final figure was $4.6 million.

Lib remains unaffected by society's taboos against arson or any other type of property destruction. "My way of looking at it is that any opportunity for the public to see government sponsoring research on animals is good for us," she says emphatically. "It's important for the public to know that the people mutilating animals are not just a bunch of mad scientists working after hours in their garages. It's people in laboratories built with our tax dollars who are doing experiments which are useless, also financed with our tax dollars." She is unfazed by Animal Welfare groups' condemnation of the deliberately set conflagration. "Did they stop this thing or shut it down for even one day?" she asks rhetorically. "How did they use that lab to raise the public's awareness about factory farming or animal experimentation? For me it's simple: short of hurting some other person or another living thing, I'll do whatever it takes to get that message over to people and to cost the vivisectors every penny I can."

CHAPTER 14

IN THE WILD WITH
"THE TOWN CRIER OF THE GLOBAL VILLAGE"

John Seed, an Australian whom the *Christian Science Monitor* has called "the town crier of the global village," doesn't remember exactly how he came to environmental activism. Like many early Earth First!ers in the United States, he protested against the Vietnam War as a teenager, and there were one or two environmental preservation marches that he vaguely recalls as well. When he eventually allowed himself to be swept away by a swell of environmental consciousness, it came with ambivalence and even guilt. He was a talented artist, a committed Buddhist, and a farmer. "For some time after I got involved," he says in a soft accent with mixed Australian and British tones (he lived for a time in Britain), "I remember wondering if I was just trying to escape from meditation or life back on the farm, looking for something more exciting to do. I didn't really trust that strong impulse that got me involved in environmentalism....I just found that more and more I was going out there, doing actions and (spending time) on the road."[1]

Since then, the late 1970s, Seed has yet to stop traveling. Co-founder of a wildly popular environmental awareness workshop called the Council of All Beings, Seed spends less than half of his time at home in Lismore, New South Wales. His journeys usually take him to the U.S. for several months each spring, and from there he may travel to Eastern Europe, or wherever else he is called. The heart and soul of Seed's activism, however, are the world's rainforests. In the early 1980s he began publishing the *World Rainforest Report* "out of a shack that had a solar panel that powered his computer," says Randy Hayes, co-founder of the Rainforest Action Network. "He put out this simple rag with this lofty title, and people like [noted biologist] Paul Ehrlich thought this was one of the most useful documents out there in the early days before rainforests became 'chic.'"[2] With the *Report* known worldwide today, and having seen his Rainforest Information Center, after which Hayes' group in the U.S. is patterned, grow to stand on its own, the forty-four year old Seed has all but traded in office work for a lap-top computer and a permanent plane ticket.

Spirit and Action

Why, Seed wonders, should he sit talking for a book that is going to "waste paper" when he could be out fighting for the Earth? Like Mike Roselle, he is both loathe to stay for long and a great talker when he can be pinned down. And like Roselle, there is no doubt that his heart is in *action*. Talking into a tape recorder is excruciating. Discomfort endured for the Earth, on the other hand bothers Seed but little. "I've got no problem, like I did a couple of weeks ago, chaining myself by the neck to the suspension of a vehicle to stop that vehicle from being moved from the path of logging crews wanting to get in and log the forest," Seed says. It took a long time before the police realized that their saws were no match for the Kryptonite bicycle lock. Their only option was to dismantle the vehicle's suspension. That done, Seed was arrested and driven two hours to the nearest police station for booking. "Then as soon as they let me go I took the lock off so it was ready for the next action. I've got no trouble with that. It's not that I'm brave. It's just that's what I'm into, that's what I like to do. But as far as answering questions, I'm just not into it!"

Yet the amiable Aussie talks on. Looking back on it, Seed locates the roots of his environmental addiction in the varied and visually stunning places around his childhood home: the sandstone country, dense eucalyptus forests, and the rocks and surf of the coastline around Sydney. "I think I was completely unconscious of it when I was growing up, but it had a profound effect in retrospect," Seed says. "I used to go surfing on the weekends when I was in school. There's something totally natural about it—you couldn't cheat or lie. You either caught the wave or got dumped." In that sort of natural honesty Seed found both the other-worldly and the basic. "I feel very spiritual about nature," he says. "That's where I have my spiritual experiences. That's the touchstone against which everything else has got to ring true." Indeed, nature's *truth* is what drives him to fight for the Earth in a variety of creative ways, the object of all of them being the elimination of the Eco-Wall through individual enlightenment and action. "It seems to me that unless there is a radical, thoroughgoing, *unprecedented* change in consciousness sweeping throughout the human race within a decade or so, we can kiss complex life good-bye," he says imploringly.

To help inculcate others to the need for such change, he and environmental activist Joanna Macy created the Council of All Beings. A Council is a workshop, a fluid, flexible process involving people who make a conscious decision at the beginning to work to heal the planet. From there, a Council sometimes involves a series of exercises designed to enable participants to feel their part in nature. Everyone disperses to the surrounding ecosystem to discover, and then to *become,* some aspect of the local non-human natural world. At the Council, these beings vent their anger and frustration at the stand-ins for the human population, then share a gift of some sort, and later dance and celebrate their oneness. Seed figures he has conducted some-where between sixty and 100 Councils and has become so inundated with them that he no longer leads them in North America, but instead devotes his time training workshop facilitators. No one may make a profit from a Council; it is all tilled back into the Earth, going to fund a variety of environmental projects. The process seeks to motivate people like no other tool at their disposal to live and act in ways contrary to the Eco-Wall; in Seed's words, the Council of All Beings moves people "from having ecologi-cal ideas to having ecological identity, ecological self....In the end, what we want to do is to turn people into activists."

The Fight for the Nightcap

Seed's own serious environmental activism began in the rainforests of the Nightcap National Park in New South Wales in 1979. There, 300 protestors demanded an environmental impact study of proposed logging in the Park, which resembled a U.S. National Forest in its lack of protection from development. The Park's huge trees were a remnant of a rain forest that covered Australia as long as 100 million years ago, and it included Aboriginal initiation and burial sites. The activists undertook civil dis-obedience in the virgin rainforest near Terania Creek by camping among the trees and walking slowly in front of bulldozers cutting a road into the area. This, the first full-scale environmental protest in Australian history, occurred nearly four years before the first comparable Earth First! action in the United States.

Two ministers of Parliament supported the activists' demands, and the study was undertaken. When the inquiry wholly ignored the protestors' proposal for a 247,000-acre National Park and instead allowed logging of portions of the rainforest, the activists again took up their struggle. It continued for three years. Near the end, in July 1982, the Nightcap Action Group (NAG), including Seed, set up camp on Mt. Nardi in a last-ditch effort to save what forest they could from the unremitting logging. Hundreds of people joined them, and seventy were arrested under a new, stricter trespassing law passed in reaction to their efforts. Seed and others soon discovered logging in Griers Scrub, an area that none of them had ever visited because it was on the opposite side of the range from their protests. From their camp atop the mountain, however, they could hear the chain saws hundreds of feet below. Rather than wait for the logging to come up the mountain, they went down to confront the loggers.

It took several tries to negotiate the steep canyon. "Eventually," Seed says, "we got down there, and when we did we discovered the most beautiful flooded gum trees, *Eucalyptus grandis,* that we'd ever seen. *Massive,* mighty trees, and these were the ones being logged." In the ensuing fight, both sides employed intensive psychological warfare. The protestors' strength was their non-violent approach, their mere presence in the forest. The loggers, who were paid three to four times what they normally would receive to stay at the site despite the protestors, answered by spiting the protestors, cutting the biggest of the trees. The 250 to 300 foot tall sentinels of the forest, Seed says, "would smash to pieces when they hit the ground––they were hollow up the guts. The loggers knew that, and they were doing that because they knew the amount of pain it caused us. They were saying that our presence there was worse than useless, that because we were there, they were feeling annoyed. And when they felt annoyed, they cut the old trees down."

When the activists attempted to alert the authorities to logging irregularities at Griers Scrub, such as cutting on slopes as steep as fifty degrees, ignoring erosion mitigation steps, and "harvesting" of unmarked trees, they were arrested. They followed with more direct civil disobedience actions, steeling themselves against the day that the loggers would attack Mt. Nardi itself. Public sentiment for permanent preservation of the Park was running upwards of seventy percent. The protestors had the people on their side. What they needed was time.

Time ran out early one September morning. The NAG activists maintained a constant vigil along the lone road to Mt. Nardi. To slow the onslaught they felt was certain, they sabotaged the roadway, removing steel cattle guards at several crossings and blocking the road with cars. They also prepared the makings of a bonfire in the middle of the road. At three-thirty the radio crackled with the news that trucks were rolling up the mountain. Those in the base camp scrambled down the slope, set fire to the huge mound of debris, and gathered behind it as the police-escorted bulldozers trundled up the road. Cars and cattle guards were easily negotiated. Then the NAG protestors took their places in the middle of the road in a last-ditch effort to halt the column, but to no avail. A bulldozer casually dispensed with every obstacle, eventually pushing the blazing fire into some of the road sitters and over the edge. Police carted off the road sitters. By dawn the way was clear.

Swatted away like flies, within a matter of days the activists saw the lush mountain begin to fall. They continued their blockades in hopes of slowing the cutting of thousand year-old brushbox trees, a companion of eucalyptus and rainforest species. Tensions on the part of the authorities began to rise, and things got especially nasty on October 1, 1982, when police cleared protestors from the path of the logging trucks using their cars and even the trucks, running over and injuring some. Forty more activists were arrested. But the end was at hand. Non-violent, largely non-destructive protest won out. Later that same day, a court injunction was granted, halting the logging on Mt. Nardi. Protestors turned their blockade headquarters into a tree-planting camp while they awaited the outcome of the legal action seeking a permanent stay on logging in the Nightcap. On October 26 the New South Wales government bowed to increasing public pressure and officially set aside the entire 247,000 acres as the protected Nightcap National Park.[3]

Struggle for a Wild River

During the latter stages of the Nightcap protests, three members of the Tasmanian Wilderness Society (TWS) visited Mt. Nardi and were arrested for participating in a blockade. Their mission was to ascertain whether blockading might work in their struggle to save the Franklin and Gordon rivers from the first of what would be many huge dams. The Franklin was Australia's lone remaining wild river, running as it did free from the boulders left by the last glaciers through verdant rainforests to the confluence with the Gordon, and thence to the Indian Ocean on Tasmania's southwest coast. Its path was called the Franklin-Lower Gordon Wild Rivers National Park; as in New South Wales, the "park" designation held little meaning if some "higher purpose," in this case electricity production, could be invoked. The dam the TWS fought against was without a use. The Hydro-Electric Commission built dams to spur development, not to serve an immediate or emergent need.

As the river's protagonist, the TWS took a no compromise approach to its defense of the Franklin. The Tasmanian government recognized the strength of sentiment for the river, and it backed off of its big dam proposal. Instead, in 1980 it proposed a smaller one on the Gordon above its junction with the Franklin. When the upper house of the state Parliament insisted on damming the Franklin, a legislative battle ensued that stalled the project for two years. In the midst of this political battle, the matter was put to a referendum. The people were given the option of selecting the smaller dam on the upper Gordon or one which would flood much of the densely wooded watersheds of both rivers. In a stunning act of electoral defiance, one-third of the voters wrote "No Dams" on their ballots.[4] Still, in May 1982 voters elected a pro-dam Liberal Party majority to head the provincial government, and the TWS knew its only alternative was to fight to swing public opinion their way.

The three TWS activists who were arrested with the Nightcap Action Group reported enthusiastically about the blockade strategy. Seed's group had already been invited to the island to join TWS's effort when the Nightcap victory was announced. Flush with their success, Seed and two carloads of Nightcap protestors headed toward Tasmania. They stopped at an anti-American military bases action in Victoria along the way, eventually arriving in Hobart on Tasmania's south coast. They were about to engage in a monumental struggle, one of the greatest environmental victories by a citizens group ever achieved using direct action.

In sheer numbers, no similar environmental protest has come close: more than 2,600 people participated in the action, with 1,272 arrests. Their sacrifice was for a river on which travelers could go for days without seeing another person, meandering with the water through tree-studded gorges and amongst a temperate rainforest of exquisite beauty and delicateness, comprised primarily of myrtle beech and Big Billy and asparagus pine. Seed remembers the literal tenderness of the land well, like the still-visible ruts left by logs dragged across the ground by horse teams eighty years before. "In the sub-tropical rain forests it's not like that," Seed says, "and up in the tropics, a mark like that would be gulped up by the forest in a matter of months. But down there it's so fragile that no matter where you walk, no matter how lightly you walk, you sink *inches* into the moss. The softness of the place!" He was so troubled by the damage that a simple footstep caused that he walked as little as possible. "I felt very much like an intruder. The place wasn't built for large, heavy things like me."

Summer Camp

Activists demanded that the government halt all dam construction by December 14 or else they would act en masse. Aware that they had little chance of stopping the "march of progress" by mere threats, TWS was hard at work in the ensuing weeks. The Nightcappers were put to work establishing a food buying co-operative for the blockaders and setting up a kitchen at a site donated to the TWS by local sympathizers. Everyone involved in the long-term operation, between fifty and sixty volunteers, contributed twenty or thirty dollars a week out of their $100 unemployment checks for food, and a crew drove to Hobart to get the best buys. "Greenie Acres," as the final base camp was called (the first was a city park that health inspectors said was unsuited for the purpose), was two miles outside of the port city of Strahan, about twenty-five miles down river from the dam site. At any one time after the blockade began, 150 or more people from throughout Australia were there, most of whom were blockaders preparing to go up river. They ate meals served in a large tent, with bread baked in an oven made entirely of materials found around town. The place had the feel of an open-air commune.

With the Strahan camp in good shape, Seed and others went up river and established a collective, called the River Base Camp, to keep an eye on the Hydrology Commission's activities and to map the area for the activists who would follow. Along the way the Nightcap Action Group had been renamed the Nomadic Action Group, but a friend sharing Seed's tent awoke one night with what became his favorite name of all for the group. She sat bolt upright in her sleep and called out, "Nightmare Action Group!"

"I've always thought of it like that ever since," Seed says. "We were a bit of a nightmare for the environmental movement, a bit like Earth First! is in the United States. They (the TWS) were freaked out because they thought we would get them in trouble or give them a bad name or something."

The NAG's reputation for stunts like removing cattle guards was widely known. When the blockades began—the government totally ignored the December 14 deadline—they took periodic two week turns at River Base Camp assisting soon-to-be arrestees. There were always two assistance groups at the camp, and before NAG arrived for its first stint, rumors spread through the camp that they might be "too radical" and generally irresponsible. Sure enough, on the first day Ian Cohen and a friend named "Annie" wandered into the bush. (Cohen seems to be a dyed-in-the-wool trouble maker: to this day he has a habit of riding the bows of nuclear-armed warships arriving in Australian ports, protesting their presence by literally holding onto the leading edge of the ship after catching up with it on his surfboard.) The two were out all night, and although Seed and the other NAG members were not alarmed, the other group was. The next morning a group took a boat up the river and found the two miscreants waiting for what they knew was an inevitable pick up, totally unrepentant after a night of hiking and otherwise enjoying themselves beneath a full moon.

River Base Camp was a bit like summer camp, with NAG and the other support people acting as counselors for a constantly changing bunch of charges. As many as 100 people each day came up on the *J-Lee-M*, a tourist boat that was loaned by the operator as a troop and supply transport ship for the duration of the blockade. All of the protestors were trained in non-violent civil disobedience in Strahan. The training included role playing exercises, where protestors acted the parts of police officers or loggers; workshops on consensus decision-making; and opportunities for the activists to get to know one another before the action. Seed, who learned civil disobedience from Quaker Peter Jones, rebelled at the training's heavy-handed and "authoritarian" bent. In fact, none of the non-violence trainers had ever participated in a non-violent protest. Seed admits, however, that the training was effective.

By the time the activists arrived at the River Base Camp, they were prepared to be arrested. When they disembarked from the *J-Lee-M* they were welcomed to the camp and then briefed on the menu of arrest choices available to them. The camp-like air of the place was added to by the expectation of the soon-to-be arrestees. These people were fully prepared to bash away at a very tangible and growing block in the Eco-Wall in the gentlest, yet most profound, way possible. Dams, those curtains of concrete and steel, do more damage to the environment in a single stroke than any other single incursion into wilderness. Even clearcuts can, over centuries, patch themselves. But dams drown habitat permanently, the protestors knew.

To liven the mood, there were campfire sing-alongs each evening. The next morning, Seed says, "we'd act as guides to take them out to wherever they were going to get arrested....They'd get arrested and away they'd go. They'd get taken away on a big police boat, owned by another tourist operator, and then another hundred people would come up and do the same thing." Day after day the process was repeated in time, taking on an almost ritualistic quality: from Strahan up the steam to River Base Camp, the next day to the damsite for arrest, from there back downriver to jail in Strahan, thence to a quick trial and release.

Inexorably, the list of arrestees grew, clogging the jails and the courts, attracting more and more publicity. The protests actually took many forms, nearly all of them blockades of one sort or another. Some of the first to be arrested were people in "duckies," bright-yellow, inflatable, non-motorized dinghies; they strung themselves out across the river, connected by a single rope in human booms to halt the transportation of equipment to the dam site. During the second week of 1983, less than a month after the blockade began, the first bulldozer for use in clearing trees and constructing the dam's foundation arrived in Strahan. In the early morning hours telephone communication in the city was cut off by the authorities and eighty police officers escorted the behemoth earth mover to its barge along the river. As it was towed up river, swimmers and scuba divers attempted to halt the barge's progress. But rather than stop for the activists in the water and a bevy of duckie paddlers on the river, the tug boat literally ran them over. In the face of such hostility the Greenies kept up their struggle as they had from the start: unremittingly and non-violently. On land they chained themselves to bulldozers and other equipment, pitched tent cities in the middle of roads, and occupied the crane in Strahan used for loading equipment onto the barges.

On the rare occasions when monkeywrenching replaced civil disobedience, it was met with a chilly reception from the TWS. "The Tasmanian Wilderness Society has never had a very Earth First! approach about the destruction of property or machinery, things like that," says Seed, whose initial introduction to Earth First! came during a visit to Australia by poet Gary Snyder in the early 1980s. "I remember that there was a huge problem when people went out and painted the windscreens of some of the machinery with yellow paint so that they were unable to work for several hours while they scraped it off. That was seen as violence by TWS."

The media, of course, was of crucial importance in the struggle for the Franklin and Gordon. An information center in Strahan relayed the latest happenings to journalists, and as the weeks went on the blockade attracted world-wide attention. By February, six weeks after the start of the blockade, rallies in support of the TWS were attracting massive crowds by

Australian standards. Alerted by the press coverage, 20,000 people attended a demonstration in Hobart on the fourth of the month; in Devonport, population 15,000, nearly 2,000 came out in support of the TWS on the nineteenth; the next day 4,500 rallied in Sydney; a week later crowds of between 5,000 and 6,000 attended anti-dam rallies in Melbourne and Adelaide.

Sensing the mounting public pressure against dam construction, the federal government desperately looked for ways of breaking the blockade. Every day the controversy dragged on, the government lost ground. On January 19 it offered Tasmania $500 million to stop the dam. Two weeks later, then Prime Minister Frasier announced a federal election for March 5—his government was slipping away with each arrest. Then the Tasmanians formally rejected the federal government's bribe. "At that point," Seed says, "two weeks before the federal elections, once this issue had displaced even all of the economic issues from the front pages of the newspapers, the Australian Labor Party announced they would stop the dam" if elected. The dam would decide the entire election. For the first time in recorded history, an environmental issue became the central point in a government's fight for survival.

Back at the blockade, strategy quickly changed. The Tasmanian government banned camping along the Franklin in late February and evicted seventy-seven people from the River Base Camp. With their essential front-line encampment dismantled and the elections so near, the TWS decided to close down all but a small part of its presence on the river and to fan out across the nation to work for Labor Party candidates. They concentrated on eleven marginal Parliament districts around the country. "These were electorates where less than a couple of percentage points separated the two major political parties," Seed explains. "I was at an electorate in Brisbane, and we went from door to door handing out literature and talking with people. I think in our electorate we went to every door twice, asking people to vote for the environment." Each of the eleven close districts went to the Labor candidate, putting the Labor Party over the top. Bob Hawke, the new Prime Minister, began his victory speech by saying, "The Dam will not be built."

Everyone's Role in Saving the Rainforests

Unwilling to let the rest of the nation tell it what it ought to do, the Tasmanian government took Hawke's decision to the Australian Supreme Court. On July 1, 1983, by a 4-3 vote, the Court upheld the Labor government's decision. The Dam let go its dying breath; the River breathed anew. That the final victory came by the slimmest of margins was appropriate, Seed says. "I like to think that maybe if any one person had been less committed among the thousands that took part, that it might have gone the other way. It felt like that a lot of the time. I don't think people were ever really confident that we could pull it off." The bulldozers left, and the river was free.

When the first of the Franklin and Gordon blockade arrestees were off-loaded from the police boat in Strahan, the officers formed a human wall to prevent anyone from escaping. Although some protestors later received rough treatment at the hands of the authorities, as the police grew to understand the gentle, cooperative attitude of their captives a congenial relationship slowly developed. It lasts even today; at one of Seed's recent arrests, a police officer proudly listed the other environmental actions where she had served. "They really like it. It's like their picnic—they get a day in the bush," Seed says. "Nowadays, they don't resent any longer, as they used to, being a part of the theater of social change." The police recognize the importance of saving the forests and their crucial role in making that possible, "that without their blue uniforms things could get violent. They're the referees, part of the process of media and social change. I think they're secretly pleased by that role." They also represent an aspect of the Eco-Wall, that of anti-environmental repression and laws, that in Australia is slowly crumbling. Seed notes with glee that the Melbourne Port Authority recently ordered 500 "Police for Rainforest" bumper stickers from the local Rainforest Action Group.

From the Franklin, Seed and the NAG went to the other side of the continent, Cape Tribulation and the Daintree region of Queensland, to engage in another prolonged struggle for rainforests. The provincial government there was determined to push a road from Cape Tribulation to Bloomfield, "cutting the tropical rain forest wilderness of that area, containing the world's oldest plants, the angiosperms, in half," says Seed. "Although a tiny area—one quarter of one percent of Australia's land area—it contains fully one-third of our species of plants and animals." In 1984 a score of people shut down construction of the road. The action was all the more noteworthy because it was there that activist Doug Ferguson invented the technique of stopping machinery by burying oneself in a mound of dirt in the middle of the bulldozer's path, a tactic used throughout the world since.

Early the following year, Seed and others purchased a bus and painted it as a rainbow. They drove 1,500 miles from Lismore to the Cape to join the struggle for the Daintree once more. After two months, the authorities turned dogs on the protestors and broke through their road blockade. Such brutality made little difference, Seed says. That same Australian spirit which went unbroken despite rough treatment at the hands of the police in Tasmania remained alive. And like the Franklin and Gordon struggle, the federal government stepped in to stop the road. A Labor government soon came to power in Queensland and halted the state's court challenge to the federal action. The Daintree rainforest, like those of the Franklin and

Gordon and in New South Wales, was subsequently listed by the United Nations as a World Heritage preserve because of its unique ecosystem.

"The Last Generation"

Seed's struggles, not only for Australian rainforests but for those in Southeast Asia and South America as well, leave him with an appreciation of the enormous burden on the shoulders of everyone on the planet today. "We are inextricably imbedded in the biology of this planet," he says in a passionate voice. "That biology is being torn to shreds before our very eyes, and we're the last human generation that's going to have the chance to do anything about it." He advocates widespread direct action on the part of people in developed nations to force the essential changes. "Greenpeace is not going to save the planet, Rainforest Action Network isn't going to save the planet. It's going to be small, non-hierarchical groups of people beginning in the so-called developed countries. If enough of these get serious enough, who knows?"

Such action can only occur if there is a watershed change in the way humans interact with their world. Without scaling the Eco-Wall, humans, the rainforests, and all else will not long survive. "What are the chances of this miraculous revolution in human consciousness? I haven't got a clue!" Seed says. "All I know is that I still feel highly motivated to spend my life doing things which would seem quite futile and stupid unless there were some chance of all of this happening. I guess there's a part of me that still feels it's all possible."

PART FOUR

INSPIRATION AND THE FUTURE

CHAPTER 15

STIRRING THE POT:
RADICAL ENVIRONMENTAL LITERATURE, MUSIC,
ART, AND THEATER

Social movements crave inspiration to keep them alive and vibrant. The American Revolution had more than its share of these engage 'em and enrage 'em types—Patrick Henry demanding liberty or death, Thomas Paine who stirred the Minute Men to victory at Trenton with his tract that began, "These are the times that try men's souls." So too with the abolitionist, women's suffrage, unionist, civil rights, and anti-Vietnam War movements. Self-evidently, movements also need something to move against: the oppressiveness of George III, of slavery, of men, of whites. When these two forces come together—the inspiration responding to the instigation—a movement is born. This chapter examines the work of a few of the artists, essayists, poets, musicians, and actors whom radical environmentalists look to for insight, support, and humor, whose works reflect the fear and hope embodied in the movement.

Literature

Edward Abbey: Spark to the Movement

Edward Abbey called himself a "literary bum." He wrote to "share," to "record the truth, to unfold the folded lie" and, "most importantly, to defend the diversity and freedom of humankind from those forces in our modern techno-industrial culture that would reduce us all, if we let them, to the status of things, objects, raw material, personnel; to the rank of subjects."[1] He despised anything heavy-handed, controlling, pretentious, or that abused the land. Authority, growth, progress, civilization—these were his enemies. The spirit of Jefferson, Whitman, the eagle, coyote, sandstone, and river came to rest in one "lean and hungry beatnik bard with notebook and ballpoint pen (his 'software')," as he described himself disguised as the lone chronicler of an Earth First! action in his last novel, *Hayduke Lives!*.[2]

In that volume Abbey closes a circle that he began with *The Monkey Wrench Gang*, his comical, profane, overdrawn, and readable novel published in 1975. Earth First! came about through circumstances that Abbey could not have foreseen, but many of its strategies, tactics, and attitudes reflect those found in *The Monkey Wrench Gang*. The book follows a motley crew of four as they set out to halt whatever destruction they find in the American Southwest. There is A.K. "Doc" Sarvis, M.D.; his lover/nurse, Bonnie Abzug; George W. Hayduke, Vietnam Vet (Green Berets) and explosives technician extraordinnaire; and Seldom Seen Smith, nervous jack Mormon (relative of the recusant) and river runner. They meet on a Seldom Seen-guided rafting trip. From there they embark on a neo-Luddite rampage, pursued all the while over dusty roads and steep cliffs by Mormon Bishop and Utah lawman J. Dudley Love. This rollicking tour of the canyon country of southern Utah and northern Arizona predates *Ecodefense*, by more than a decade, as a how-to guide to the most technologically ruinous of ecological defense methods. The Gang burns billboards; disables bulldozers—or drives them off cliffs; tosses caltrops, twisted metal spikes, into the road to puncture Bishop Love's pursuit; ruins oil well drilling equipment; blows up railroads over which mining trains run; pulls up survey stakes plotting new highways; and vandalizes Smokey the Bear signs with impunity. They drink, curse, fear for their lives, get shot at—all in defense of Mother Earth.

The book, as with most of Abbey's work, succeeds in maligning numerous customs, beliefs, outlooks, and lifestyles. He once wrote, "If there's anyone still present whom I've failed to insult, I apologize."[3] The characters who flail the offenses are chock full of contradictions, many of which are reflected in the radical environmental movement but which are overlooked by those quick with the "ideologue" and "dogmatist" labels. They are willing to die for the wilderness but see nothing wrong with throwing beer cans out of the car window along any highway that has been constructed without their say-so. After a time in the outback the Gang longs for hot showers and Holiday Inn pie and coffee. Mechanical artifacts are the objects of unremitting attack, yet Hayduke is deeply attached to his Jeep. Abbey's Gang wastes none of its time resolving individual or group inconsistencies, however, any more than most of us do. For them to do so would get in the way of a rip-roaring story and obscure one of the truths about each of us which Abbey surreptitiously exposes.

In *Hayduke Lives!*, which Abbey completed shortly before his death in March of 1989, Hayduke brings the Gang together for one final, massive monkeywrench, while Earth First!ers spike trees and undergo brutal treatment at the hands of Bishop Love and other authorities. Meanwhile, Abbey keeps popping up. The physically detached but emotionally involved journalist watches with amusement from the sidelines as the movement he inspired takes its lickings and keeps on kicking.

Many give *The Monkey Wrench Gang* a disproportionate amount of credit for inspiring the foundation of Earth First!. Its primary importance was probably in forming the ideas and values that Earth First! espouses, including the ethics of machine breaking, as Mike Roselle notes. Rarely, he says, did he come upon a copy in the late '70s that was not dog-eared from being passed from person to person and being read countless times. "You could discuss things with your friends after reading this book that for some reason you may not have discussed with them before," Roselle says. "I noticed that when I was living in Wyoming, amongst our circle of friends when we found somebody who hadn't read the book, we'd say, 'Here! You gotta read this book!' They'd read it, and when we asked, 'What did you think?' they'd say, 'Aw, it was great! Let's go cut down a billboard.' It had that kind of effect."[4] Earth First! activist Darryl Cherney, after re-reading *The Monkey Wrench Gang* for the first time in several years, was struck by Abbey's clearly ecocentric perspective and by how the Gang set the stage for the movement. "Our principles have changed very little since Edward Abbey wrote *The Monkey Wrench Gang*," says Cherney. "I was astounded at how many casual remarks Abbey might make that have become an integral part of Earth First! philosophy."[5]

From *The Monkey Wrench Gang*, Ed Abbey

In the midst of the Monkey Wrench Gang's first outing, a nighttime raid on a road construction site at Comb Wash in southeastern Utah, a security guard suddenly arrives in a pickup truck. Doc Sarvis hoots an owl-like warning call, sending the other three Gang members scurrying down a steep embankment. Now they listen as the guard drives back toward the main highway.

Hayduke slipped his revolver back into his rucksack, blew his nose through his fingers and scrambled up the talus to the top of the roadway. Smith and Abbzug emerged from the dark.

"Next time dogs," says Hayduke. "Then gunners in helicopters. Then the napalm. Then the B-52s."

They walked through the dark, up the long grade into the eastern cut. Listening for the bearded goggled great bald owl to sound.

"I don't think it's quite like that," Smith was saying. "They're people too, like us. We got to remember that, George. If we forget we'll get just like them and then where are we?"

"They're not like us," Hayduke said. "They're different. They come from the moon. They'll spend a million dollars to burn one gook to death."

"Well, I got a brother-in-law in the U.S. Air Force. And he's a sergeant. I took a general's family down the river once. Them folks are more or less human, George, just like us."

"Did you meet the general?"

"No, but his wife, she was sweet as country pie."

Hayduke was silent, smiling grimly in the dark. The heavy pack on his back, overloaded with water and weapons and hardware, felt good, solid, real, meant business. He felt potent as a pistol, dangerous as dynamite, tough and mean and hard and full of love for his fellow man.[6]

In his numerous essays, Abbey's eloquence shines even brighter than it does through the eyes and voices of his fictional characters. In books such as *Desert Solitaire*, *Abbey's Road*, and *One Life at a Time, Please*, Abbey develops his favorite themes of freedom, love of all things wild, and our obligation to defend them. The best of his pieces constantly bring forth new wonders. Canyon walls glow with an almost blinding palpability. The reader rides rolling river rapids and twists, bobs, weaves, and winds with two gopher snakes locked in a mating ritual. Abbey tears apart the evils of "industrial tourism," and then tells how to resolve them. He dismantles modern literature for its sycophantic ways and probes the earliest incarnations of the novel and the essay in an attempt to unearth the political, argumentative, and inventive qualities that are necessary to make them valuable once more.

By no means is Abbey the only essayist or fiction writer that radical environmentalists turn to when they seek a literary mentor. Abbey provided a list of some of the others: Edward Hoagland, Joseph Wood Krutch, Wendell Berry, Annie Dillard, John McPheee, Ann Zwinger, and Peter Matthiessen. Farley Mowatt should be added, as should Wallace Stegner, Rachel Carson, Loren Eiseley, John Muir, and the many other "nature writers" who espouse a ecocentric point of view in their writings. None of these are as consistently explicit as Abbey in their advocacy of the destruction of the Eco-Wall. Rather, they are political in the sense of offering alternatives. They also revere landscapes and deplore the destruction of wild lands at human hands. The impact of their writings is measured on individuals and in a personal way, not on Earth First! or any other aspect of the movement as a whole in the same way that Abbey's writings give voice to some of the core values commonly held by eco-warriors. On the other hand, none of these others caused so much anger among potential friends of the movement as did Abbey. His honest yet insensitive remarks and character portrayals offended many, and to the extent that he was seen as Earth First!'s literary embodiment he doubtless cost the movement numerous supporters; he may well have won over many more.

From *Desert Solitaire*, Ed Abbey

While a seasonal ranger at Arches National Monument, Abbey was called to join in a search party looking for a man who had been reported missing. The man was found, dead, sitting beneath a juniper only steps from a dropoff that plunges to the Colorado River.

Looking out on this panorama of light, space, rock and silence I am inclined to congratulate the dead man on his choice of jumping-off place; he had good taste. He had good luck—I envy him the manner of his going: to die alone, on rock under sun at the brink of the unknown, like a wolf, like a great bird, seems to me very good fortune indeed. To die in the open, under the sky, far from the insolent interference of leech and priest, before this desert vastness opening like a window onto eternity— that surely was an overwhelming stroke of rare good luck.

It would be unforgivably presumptuous to pretend to speak for the dead man on these matters; he may not have agreed with a word of it, not at all. On the other hand, except for those minutes of panic in the ravine when he realized that he was lost, it seems possible that in the end he yielded with good grace. We see him staggering through the fearful heat and glare, across the tilted ledge toward the juniper, the only tree in sight. We see him reach it, at great cost, and there, on the brink of nothing and everything, he lies down in the shade to rest. He would not have suffered much after that; he may have died in his sleep, dreaming of the edge of things, of flight into space, of soaring.[7]

The Poets: Jeffers, Snyder, and Others with Vision

While Abbey, and to a lesser extent some other prose and fiction writers, helped inspire the radical environmental movement to action, poetry's role in the movement is more difficult to discern. In general, poetry serves two functions: to give voice to ecocentric philosophy and to serve as a medium of expression for activists. Of the philosophical poets, Robinson Jeffers and Gary Snyder probably are the best known. Jeffers labelled the philosophy inherent in his poetry "inhumanism" but had the term existed he might well have called it "ecocentrism." His explicitly non-human centered world view was promptly labeled "misanthropic" by critics. Misanthropy, of course, is common among radical environmentalists. In the post-war 1940s, however, utterances such as Jeffers' "I'd sooner, except the penalties, kill a man than a hawk," became the object of immediate condemnation. Muir got away with a similar statement forty years earlier, writing, "Well, I have precious little sympathy for the selfish propriety of civilized man, and if a war of races should occur between the wild beasts and Lord Man, I would be tempted to sympathize with the bears."[8] Abbey expressed an analogous sentiment thirty years after Jeffers' lines were published: "...I have personal convictions to uphold. Ideals, you might say. I prefer not to kill animals. I'm a humanist; I'd rather kill a *man* than a snake."[9]

This is not the stuff of human-haters, however. Labelling Jeffers a misanthrope is little more than a quick way out the back door to avoid confronting the profound truths in his poetry. He was angry at humans, not hateful of them. And what of it? Jeffers saw in non-human nature the continuance of evolution and of hope; he saw humans struggling to snuff out immense possibilities through continued mindless technological development. Like Abbey, Jeffers argued for the replacement of politics within his genre. He waged war on the war-makers, arguing tirelessly through his verse against U.S. involvement in World War II, which he was convinced would only lead to other, greater conflagrations. His objection to war-making further belies the "misanthrope" label, for surely a human-hater would not miss a chance to kill off a chunk of the species.

In Jeffers' original preface to his lengthy poem "The Double Axe," he defines inhumanism as "the devaluation of human-centered illusions, the turning outward from man to what is boundlessly greater." He said inhumanism "is a step in human development,"[10] mirroring the arguments used in favor of ecocentric ethics. Jeffers wrote that inhumanism "is based on a recognition of the astonishing beauty of things, and on a rational acceptance of the fact that mankind is neither central nor important in the universe; our vices and abilities are as insignificant as our happiness."[11] He explained the purpose of that detachment in a decidedly *humane* passage, writing, "Turn outward from each other, so far as need and kindness permit, to the vast life and inexhaustible beauty beyond humanity. This is not a slight matter, but an essential condition of freedom, and of moral and vital sanity."[12] Such love of the non-human world led him to revel in the thrill of a vulture circling as he played dead on a hillside, the huge bird descending in an ever-narrowing spiral, eager to test the quickness of the flesh:

> *To be eaten by that beak*
> *and become part of him, to share those wings*
> *and those eyes—*
> *What a sublime end of one's body, what an enskyment;*
> *What a life after death*[13]

and to write, in "The Beauty of Things," that humanity, "you might say, is nature dreaming, but rock / And water and sky are constant...."[14]

"Hurt Hawks," Robinson Jeffers

I

The broken pillar of the wing jags from the clotted shoulder,

The wing trails like a banner in defeat,
No more to use the sky forever but live with famine
And pain a few days: cat nor coyote
Will shorten the week of waiting for death, there is game without talons.
He stands under the oak-bush and waits
The lame feet of salvation; at night he remembers freedom
And flies in a dream, the dawns ruin it.
He is strong and pain is worse to the strong, incapacity is worse.
The curs of the day come and torment him
At distance, no one but death the redeemer will humble that head,
The intrepid readiness, the terrible eyes.
The wild God of the world is sometimes merciful to those
That ask mercy, not often to the arrogant.
You do not know him, you communal people, or you have forgotten him;
Intemperate and savage, the hawk remembers him;
Beautiful and wild, the hawks, and men that are dying, remember him.

II

I'd sooner, except the penalties, kill a man than a hawk; but the great redtail
Had nothing left but unable misery
From the bone too shattered for mending, the wing that trailed under his talons
when he moved.
We had fed him six weeks, I gave him freedom,
He wandered over the foreland hill and returned in the evening, asking for death,
Not like a beggar, still eyed with the old
Implacable arrogance. I gave him the lead gift in the twilight. What fell was
relaxed.
Owl-downy, soft feminine feathers; but what
Soared: the fierce rush: the night-herons by the flooded river cried fear at its rising
Before it was quite unsheathed from reality.[15]

In the years since Jeffers' death in 1962, environmental concerns have increasingly come to the fore in the American consciousness. So it is a bit odd that those like Gary Snyder who choose to explore ecocentrism through their poetry are shunted by many of the literati. But Abbey warned that today's critics and readers want to escape from politics and the issues of the day, not to gain insight into them. Snyder persists, however. He embraced Earth First! in its earliest days and spread the word about the new environmentalism to activists like John Seed in Australia. He once told an interviewer, "...I suppose that 'Gary Snyder, eco-poet' is a current enough description. I see my role as trying to present some alternatives, and to tell people what the normal world was or could be like if we took on the job of reknitting our connections with each other and with the natural world."[16]

Snyder was awarded a Pulitzer Prize for his 1974 book of verse and prose, *Turtle Island*. Like Jeffers, Snyder revels in life—all life. The life-affirming celebrations of the beat poet cum environmental muse are just as deep as Jeffers' but with occasional smatterings of humor. Snyder's "Smokey the Bear Sutra" combines Zen terminology with Western environmental themes to create a grinning assault on the forestry industry's lone public relations tool. In another poem, "Bear," a marauding ursine breaks into a neighbor's house, scares one of Snyder's sons, and wanders down the hill to wreck the poet's apiary and steal all of the honey. Angry? Snyder's verse never shows it, but rather thrills at the thought of the huge omnivore wandering in the woods near his home. Something else is here, with us, occasionally invading our world and wrecking it as we have so thoughtlessly, carelessly invaded the wild.

"Bear," Gary Snyder

Kai was alone by the pond in the dusk. He heard
a grunt and felt, he said, his hair tingle.
He jumped on a bike and high-tailed it down
the trail, to some friends.

Scott stood alone in the dark by the window. Clicked
on his flashlight and there out the window, six
inches away, were the eyes of the bear.

Stefanie found her summer kitchen all torn up.

I went down the hill to the beehives next morning—
the supers were off and destroyed, chewed comb
all around, the whole thing tipped over, no
honey, no larvae, no bees,

But somewhere, a bear.[17]

Jeffers and Snyder are well-known poets, widely recognized and the topics of extensive critical evaluation. Virtually unknown outside of the movement are those who publish on occasion in a variety of small-scale periodicals and environmental newsletters. Eco-warriors' poetry reflects their love of wild places and wild beings, their fights to save what they can, and their angry reactions to the onslaught of techno-society. Kathy Minott, a California ecofeminist and Animal Liberator, writes of spirit, land, and animals. In addressing these multiple themes, Minott exemplifies the emerging unity of concerns among eco-warriors who observe no boundaries in the movement. The verse of another poet, Michael Robinson, is inspired by his experiences in the wild and in defense of wild places. In "Cutting Fence" he writes of climbing "down the steep ridge with no nails left," an apparent allusion to tree spiking, and of ruining a rancher's wire barriers, presumably to allow wildlife to move freely.

"Holy Cow," Kathy Minott

Barefoot,
pregnant,
and soon to be in the kitchen
of your captors

You stand,
confined,
designed
to sustain your jailor
with your precious milk
and meaty flesh

For you,
sunshine
is a hint of light
through the crack above your
head,
wind
is but a noise against the
walls that surround you

The only bee
that stings
is the syringe
that shoots chemical nectar
through your veins
to sweeten
your price at market

Soon, you will give birth
to a calf
that will be taken away
by your executioner
after he wipes his face
from a feast

of flesh and potatoes

When your body is tired
and can produce no more,
you will die at the mercy of those
you have served so well,

Never knowing that the grass
was greener
along the horizon.[18]

"The Dying Mouse in the North Cascades," Michael Robinson

She wears an undergarment of cold.
Her legs twitch when I touch her.
Her belly is moist, she blinks.
But I see no wound, no crimson flare on the tawny fur.
She lies on her side in the mud of the trail,
overtowered by the green loudness of fronds and ferns
enclosing her tiny core of silence,
as a mountain mothers its inner-most granite.
Such a place to die! Fresh bear shit behind,
and the beguiling blue stream I waded which nearly swept me away.
Whether by hawk or ferret interrupted by my tread
before the kill was complete,
or whether a slow-biting disease is taking the mouse
I do not know and she will not disclose.
It is getting cold and dark, and soon I must make camp.
The mouse is slowing down when I touch her.
The grand electronics of life
uncoil in her as her nerves dull.
This evening's relentless darkness, death at the tail-tip of life…
This breath of the mountain in the wind and strange scents…
Someday we all must tread that shimmering path, sinking into the dark
water,
circling back into this hot-seed planet
from which that undying urge will pluck us again.[19]

Music

Singer/songwriter Darryl Cherney succinctly sums up the subversive power of radical environmentalism's music: "I think the importance of music is that it greases the skids, allowing us to get a political message across that normally might be grating on the general public's nerves. You can say very radical things and, if it's accompanied by a sweet melody, it helps the listener understand." Within the movement music functions in important ways as well. In fact, no aspect of radical environmental art more directly and profoundly affects activists than the movement's music. This crucial role for music is hardly unique to this movement. "If you look at music historically," Cherney notes, "from the American Revolution to the radical labor movement, to the Civil Rights Movement, right up to the '60s with the longhair rock and roll that emerged to inspire people to rebel, music has consistently performed an important function."[20] Wisconsin Earth First! activist Bob Kaspar, who hosts a weekly folk music radio show, concurs. "What Earth First! has done is to invite these musicians into the movement. That's something that hasn't happened since the anti-war days of the late '60s and early '70s and the civil rights movement of the mid-'60s."[21]

Road Shows

Bart Koehler, one of Earth First!'s founding fathers, calls his musical self, "Johnny Sagebrush," the movement's original "outlaw singer."[22] The son of a music teacher, Koehler has been an on-again, off-again professional musician since the age of ten. His musical acumen was known to a Wyoming state senator with whom Koehler hatched the "concept" of Johnny Sagebrush. Both were angered over the threat of James Watt's Sagebrush Rebellion to wild country in the West, and it dawned on them that they could fight the Rebellion with song. They combined "Johnny Horizon," the mascot of the much reviled Bureau of Land Management, and the Sagebrush Rebellion to get Johnny Sagebrush. Originally, Johnny was to sing pro-Sagebrush Rebellion songs. Confident that Johnny's popularity would skyrocket, Koehler and his senator friend fantasized that the day would come when Johnny—a recluse who would record but not perform on stage—would agree to sing before a joint session of the Utah Legislature at the Mormon Tabernacle in Salt Lake City. Just before the show, Johnny's cover would be blown when a vicious rumor would be circulated that he had funneled all of his millions to the Sierra Club.[23]

The "real" Johnny that actually emerged sang against the Sagebrush Rebellion and James Watt from the start. He was also half of the original Earth First! Road Show, a two-man minstrel troupe that made forty-four stops from coast to coast from September through November 1981. Dave Foreman joined Koehler, convinced as they were that an "environmental revival" featuring Johnny Sagebrush's guitar and Foreman's fire and brimstone ravings were the best way to spread the word about Earth First!. Koehler would warm up the crowd, then Foreman would whip them into a frenzy by recounting the evils that had been perpetrated on public lands and how the Earth First! missionaries were out to vanquish the wilderness-destroying zealots. Then Johnny would come on again to send them out the door singing. With luck, they would sell enough T-shirts each evening to buy gas to the next town.

The next year they did a miniature version of the same tour—sixteen shows in fifteen days. Audiences varied from six people in a living room during the first road show to 1,000 at a performance in Berkeley the next year. It was during the second Road Show, Koehler says, that he learned "why Hank Williams and Janis Joplin died young"—the constant traveling, partying, and singing exhausted him, and that was the end of the road (show) for him.[24]

"Bad Wolf," B.N. Koehler

I like my caribou juicy
Like my moose steaks thick
But you know those ecologists are right
I only take the weak and the sick

Chorus:
But I'm a bad wolf baby—chasin' caribou'
  I'm a bad wolf baby—look out
  I'm comin' after you

Caribou is tasty—Sitka deer are nice
But my bread and butter meal—is fresh caught mice

Chorus

They're chasin' me with rifles
Shootin' from fast flying planes
Huntin' me down from snowmobiles—
  It's drivin' me insane

Chorus

They want to fit me with a radio-collar
To help them track down my own pack!
I think it's time we drew the line
It's time to start shootin' back

Chorus (Howl for the wolves)[25]

Since the founding of Earth First!, touring musicians have become a primary means of spreading the Earth First! gospel. Several separate tours may be making the rounds at funky coffee houses and Unitarian Churches at any one time during the spring and summer. Roger Featherstone, whose slide show narration is interspersed between Dakota Sid Clifford's songs, has organized major tours around a variety of themes. In 1986 it was acid rain; rainforests in 1987; he did two road show exposes on uranium mining in 1988, and two others in 1989.

It all started when he saw a 1984 road show. Featherstone, a music therapist, became convinced he needed to get involved in Earth First! through its music. While road shows are never highly profitable, Featherstone is convinced that he will be able to make a living from them. "The tours that lose money are the ones that aren't done well, that aren't organized or promoted well," Featherstone says. "There's no reason that a tour should lose money. On the other hand, nobody's going to make enough money to retire." Encouraged by shows like the one in the spring of 1989 at the University of North Carolina at Asheville that outdrew a Greenpeace speaker who had been paid five times as much to give a talk, Featherstone says, "I think our tours are at a point now where they can really and truly hit the mainstream. That's always been one of my ambitions for the tour is to get out of playing to the choir and start playing to Joe Average."[26]

Music's Roles

Featherstone sees Earth First! music serving several roles. "I like to say there are three purposes: education, entertainment, and inspiration. I think all three are vitally important." He adds, "You're never going to reach somebody completely through intellect. You can speak to somebody until you're blue in the face and you're not going to get anywhere if there's not something to steer their heart....We've always had the Emma Goldman approach: If I can't dance, I don't want to be part of your revolution. It's always been real clear to me that you need to give them something more than just a lot of talk. A powerful song goes a lot farther than a few words. I've never considered doing it any other way."[27] Music also helps soothe frazzled nerves. At the height of a demonstration or at some other critical moment, an Earth First! musician or an assembled group of activists is likely to break into song to release tension. Many credit guitarist Dana Lyons for averting a riot by doing just that at a tense demonstration at the Okanagan National Forest headquarters building in eastern Washington in 1988.

To disseminate its music, Earth First! publishes the *Lil' Green Songbook*, the eco-warrior version of the International Workers of the World's book of radical union songs from the early 1900s. The *Earth First! Journal* also sells tapes produced by a dozen or more artists. Their styles vary tremendously. Darryl Cherney's two albums include tunes sung in his beloved country and western style, rock and roll, and folk and polka-style ballads. Bob Kaspar says Cherney's music is in a class by itself. "Darryl is not only an environmental activist, he's a union activist," he says. "He has a broad view of social problems, including environmental....He's a topical artist who tries to make songs that not only deal with the issues but that are entertaining to the audience. He'll play something in a country western style and something else in a reggae style. He will try to cater to the audience very consciously."[28] An Earth First! favorite from Cherney's repertoire is "You Can't Clearcut Your Way to Heaven." Its lyrics react both to the pervasive religious fundamentalism found amongst many redwood country logging families and to the destruction of ancient forests. The music twangs folksy and with a heavy heaping from a hymnal.

"You Can't Clearcut Your Way To Heaven," Darryl Cherney

Now the lord made the world in just six days
A wonder to behold when it was done
Deep oceans and blue skies, forests green and mountains high
With animals that crawl and fly and run.
But one of God's creatures wasn't pleased.
It wanted to create with its own hand
So it clearcut all the trees, carved the mountains, spoiled the seas
Proclaiming it the way that God had planned.

Chorus:
But you can't clearcut your way to heaven
No, strip mines don't make it with the Lord
Bulldozing the creation won't win God's admiration
And the pearly gates may close forevermore.

Now my mama used to read the family Bible
And it said thou shalt not covet, steal, or kill
But I coveted the forests and the mountains
Then I stole my Mother Nature's gems at will
And I killed off many critters to extinction
But I'm sure God must have made them by mistake
'Cause I had to keep my job, where I plunder, rape, and rob
But I swear to you its for my children's sake.

Chorus

Now today I heard they mined the Rock of Ages
'Cause they thought it had a chunk of gold inside.
And they're dumping PCBs into the Sea of Galilee
And they've milled the cross on which our savior died.
And they've leveled old Jerusalem for condos

Done put a shopping mall where Jesus did his thing
And as I looked on our success at creating such a mess
I swore I heard a band of angels sing...[29]

With Cherney, movement favorites include Cecilia Ostrow's melodious, deeply evocative songs. Ostrow shares Cherney's activism, having fought for the preservation of ancient forests in Oregon. But her music emphasizes more the spirit of a place than the struggles occurring there. Greg Keeler, a college English professor when he is not writing and recording, turns out occasionally bizarre tunes that haze society for its unbridled and manifold environmental destruction. His song "Manly Men," from an album called Nuclear Dioxin Queen, spoofs hunting on land and sea while a Marlboro Man melody carries the lyrics.

Someone once wrote that Earth First! songster Dakota Sid Clifford sounded like he had a corncob in his throat. More charitably, the veteran of the club scene at Lake Tahoe and of years of scratching out a living with his music, sounds like an older Jimmy Buffet. At times his music almost lopes along, but his grizzled voice adds a primeval edge to songs like "Greenfire," which borrows its title from Aldo Leopold's story about killing one of the last of the wolves in the Southwestern U.S., while "Bullshit" calls everyone's bluff, including Dakota Sid's own. Another "Earth First!" musician, Bill Oliver, regularly regales school children and groups including the Sierra Club and the Audubon Society with ditties like "Pretty Paper, Pretty Trees" (a plea for recycling), and his "Habitat" is a regular cheer at Earth First! demonstrations ("Habitat, habitat, have to have a habitat, have to have a habitat to carry on....Better to love it while we still have it or rat-ta-tat-tat, our habitat's gone").[30]

Kaspar senses that as their music and the movement matures, more Earth First! musicians are turning their attention to the bedrock of the movement, ecological consciousness. "They aren't just reflecting the superficial problems—the manifestations of environmental problems like the destruction of the ozone layer, acid rain, and rainforest issues," he says. "Some people are getting deeper into the philosophy, the underlying problem in the human psyche that is driving all of the industrialism which results in the destruction that manifests itself in a myriad of ways. I think as more of these musicians get to know one another better, there will be growth and the songs will become deeper and more meaningful in terms of the spiritual side of humanity."[31]

Animal Liberators have their own sources of musical inspiration. Many have became involved in the movement through punk rock bands which have taken up the cause of freeing non-human animals from oppression as a theme in their music. Hunt saboteur Rufus Cohen credits British punk rockers with profoundly influencing American activists, revealing yet another aspect of Animal Liberation that has its roots in England. These groups "put out a lot of information in their albums," Cohen says. "Some of their songs are about hunt sabotage and others about Animal Rights in general. One of the earlier bands was called 'Crass.' They didn't sing about Animal Rights so much, but they did put out the information for people who wanted it. Out of them came a band called 'Conflict,' which had an ALF song and some hunt saboteur songs. They did a lot of benefits" to raise money for the movement.[32]

Punk music is known, primarily by rumor, for its chaotic, discordant sounds and unintelligible lyrics. While there is a blaring quality to some of the music, the lyrics of the Animal Liberation songs resound with humor, bitterness, and pain. Musical form follows content much more so here than in any other environmental protest music. The pointed words and jabbing, needle-like guitars of the most provocative punk-Animal Liberation music call to mind the torment which fills the days of laboratory animals. Song titles include "Wall of Fur" and "The Bushes Scream while Daddy Prunes" by The Very Things, "This Is the ALF" by Conflict, and the Crucifucks' "Earth by Invitation Only" and "Cut down the Trees and Build Another Factory." The group Chumbawamba even recorded "Knit Your Own Balaklava," giving (unusable) directions for creating the sort of full-face covering worn by Animal Liberators during their raids.

People for the Ethical Treatment of Animals followed the lead of British Animal Liberation organizations by holding three large concerts to benefit the movement and several smaller ones. They also released an album, *Animal Liberation*, in 1987. Between songs the innovative set includes dialogue from videotapes captured by the Animal Liberation Front and brief narrative segments explaining the uses of civil disobedience, urging creation of a "life community," and noting the staggering numbers of animals which die for human consumption each year.

Art

Graphics

Animal Liberators also produce shocking and innovative works of art, many in advertisements for their organizations. One billboard campaign sponsored by the British group Lynx Educational Fund for Animal Welfare, Inc., shows a high-heeled woman dragging a bleeding fur coat behind her. The caption reads, "It takes up to 40 dumb animals to make a fur coat. But only one to wear it." PETA placed a full page advertisement in the New York Times picturing a fork and knife-wielding *Tyrannosaurs rex* and offering suggestions on "How to win an argument with a meat eater." It was spare on excess copy, devoting the entirety of the ad space below the T-Rex to statistics supporting vegetarianism. Another of PETA's ad agency-produced pieces reads, "Imagine having your body left to science...while you're still in it." A photograph accompanying the copy shows a small monkey taped and clamped to what can only be described as a torture device.

Whaling Walls

No doubt the most ambitious art project sponsored by a radical environmental group were the Sea Shepherds' "Whaling Walls." The sites included buildings in Honolulu, Seattle, and two locations in British Columbia—Vancouver and White Rock. The White Rock wall was dedicated to seven gray whales that had died because of pollution. "Ironically enough," says Rod Coronado, who helped paint several of the walls, the deaths resulted "from a paint plant chemical that had been released by vandals into the bay. They think that sediment settled and the gray whales, because they are sifters and they feed along the bottom, picked it up. They had extensive liver deterioration, and they think that contributed to their deaths." The same paint company donated the paint for the wall. The project's paramount concern was teaching local residents about the environmental destruction occurring in their own backyards and about the whales and other ocean dwellers affected by humanity's thoughtlessness. "So many people have stereotypes about what whales are, the stereotypical sperm whale spouting water," says Coronado. "One of the things I noticed was the number of people who were awestruck at seeing what they *really* looked like and how big they really were. All of the paintings were cutaways of the water and showed the whales full-sized and anatomically to scale."[33] Each wall pictured indigenous whales in their local ecosystem—along with the grays there were orcas in White Rock, and in Hawaii the Sea Shepherds painted humpbacks like those that migrate annually past the islands.

Coronado feels that the educational impact of the walls was profound, given the large numbers of people who queried him at each location. Most of the whales were painted on the sides of hotels or other large buildings with blank walls. In exchange for the "canvas" and helping with accommodations for the artists, the buildings' owners were mentioned in all publicity. The Hawaii wall was the largest, at twenty-two stories tall. Coronado recalls the scene from a helicopter ride he took after finishing the wall: "There was the total concrete jungle of downtown Honolulu, and sticking out of the middle of it was this huge blue humpback whale breaching (leaping out of the water)....We put all of the local Hawaiian fishes, the endangered monk seal, and a lot of different things in it." The project was short-lived, at least in terms of Sea Shepherd involvement. At the outset the plan was to paint 100 Whaling Walls world wide, but the agreement with the artist broke down after only six walls had been painted with Sea Shepherd assistance.[34]

The Sea Shepherds may soon find themselves back in the art business, if Paul Watson has his way. He hopes to capture a forty mile long drift net from a Japanese fishing boat in the North Pacific and create a massive sculpture with it. Watson says, "We've been talking to some artists like Christo, who did the

"Running Fence," about turning over a forty mile net to him for an art project. We would like to string this thing up in the Nevada desert and have children do cutouts of dolphins and whales and things and stick them on the net."[35]

T-Shirts

As with nearly everyone who has something to say, T-shirts have become a popular mode of expression among eco-warriors. It would seem that there is nothing particularly radical about wearing a T-shirt. But T-shirts can be a means of self-expression and may even be an important means of iden-tification (recall that the ubiquitous "clenched fist" T-shirt is as close as Earth First!ers come to a membership card). The message makes all the dif-ference. PETA's shirts feature several bright, cheery designs which invite questions about their content, giving activists a friendly way to spread the word. Others are more direct. A black square over the heart on one shirt frames the words "FUR IS" in a sharp typeface; "DEAD," in a spray painter's blood-red scrawl, completes the thought. A PETA sweat shirt, modeled in advertisements by television actress Rue McClanahan, pictures Sara, one of the Silver Spring Monkeys, looking forlornly through a wire cage.

Earth First!'s T-shirts run the gamut from bold to beautiful to humorous. Along with the standard clenched fist shirt, one favorite shows the image of a crossed monkey wrench and stone club, signifying past (stone club), present (monkey wrench), and future (stone club). A mother grizzly and her cub amble across a meadow before a brilliant sun in another shirt that proclaims, "American Wilderness—Love It or Leave It Alone."

Colorado artist Roger Candee is responsible for the popular Earth First! T-shirt design called "Canyon Frog." The idea came to him on a backpacking trip into Grand Canyon when frogs started croaking around the edge of camp. Listening to their booming calls, Candee and a friend became con-vinced the frogs had a firm message for the travelers. "They were telling us that we were in their place and we'd better not mess around or there'll be some hell to pay," Candee says. A draftsperson by trade, "Canyon Frog" Candee is one of several artists who regularly contributes to the *Earth First! Journal.* He is best known for his humorous portrayals of friends and foes alike. The good-natured fifty year-old is concerned that the movement is losing its light touch. "There are too many black things that happen in the world," says Candee. "We need to get those into the forefront but also inject some humor into them, make them somewhat more palatable."[36]

Perhaps none of Candee's drawings are as humorous or as haunting as his portrayal of "Freddy" the Forest Service Ranger for the official poster/T-shirt for the National Day of Outrage against the Forest Service on the sesquicentennial of John Muir's birth in 1988. The concept emerged during a meeting between Candee and Earth First! direct action coordinator Mike Roselle. Candee says that after discussing several ideas "all the factors came together—the somewhat derogatory name 'Freddy' that we call the Forest Rangers..., then we've got this horrible character in the 'Nightmare on Elm Street' movies. I've never even seen one of the films, but the promotions show this deranged character with these long arms. I thought it would be great to have him running a bulldozer with a Ranger's hat on, tearing up the countryside. I think the point got across."[37] In the T-shirt/poster, Freddy simultaneously bulldozes, clearcuts, and pollutes his way across the drawing, smashing and slashing through an environmentalist's B-movie nightmare.

Theater

Peter Steinhart, the *Audubon* magazine columnist and observer of the overall environmental movement, feels that "show"—theater—can be extremely effective in attacking someone who "isn't playing by the rules." Indeed, the movement's common-sense concern with attracting the media's attention testifies to its preoccupation with show. Greenpeace's famous skydive off a power plant smokestack was one of the earliest and best examples of the explicitly theatrical, dramatic side of activism. As with the Cracking of Glen Canyon Damn, when "you want to show how stupid they are, one of the best ways is through humor," Steinhart says.

A bit closer to what is more commonly considered "theater" are the guerilla theater skits commonplace in the movement, most notably at Earth First! demonstrations. Steinhart says that skits can educate, entertain, and they avoid negative backlash inherent in many other of the movement's tactics. He prefers that people "win with wit rather than brawn. The best way to win is to play within our desire for good character. If you can be funnier, wittier, smarter, more understanding, and win through that, then you win it all," the moral victory included.[38]

Most guerilla theater productions are haphazard affairs. Scripts often are written only hours before an action takes place, and there is little or no time to hone lines or stage directions. When there is time to do it well, theater can be an especially powerful tool. PETA Executive Director Kim Stallwood recalls an Animal Liberation protest at Trafalgar Square in London, the traditional end point of protest routes. "We did a demonstration there which involved 9,000 people," Stallwood says. "We had a slogan, 'Every Six Seconds an Animal Dies in a British Laboratory.' At the base of the plinth of Nelson's column we made a mock laboratory. We got a tape loop playing that struck a bell every six seconds and a sign with big numbers on it that turned over every time the bell struck. Two people dressed as scientists took people from the audience at the demonstration and symbolically killed them. They would lie on the ground. At the end of the hour we had 600 people lying down. While this was going on we had a rally. It was very effective. I even got a letter from New Scotland

Yard, from the police whom I organized the demonstration with, saying how effective it was. It was startling. It got the message over that in that hour 600 animals had died."[39]

Guerilla theater serves vital purposes both for viewers and for the actors. "The attraction of it is that everybody is interested in spectacle, everybody is interested in costume and some disguise of oneself to present a larger image in life," says actor Lee Stetson. "It's a human condition and has been since the first story teller put on a feather and danced around the fire....People need a larger perspective on issues and sometimes a simpler perspective." Stetson remembers performing sidewalk theater during the Vietnam War days, when guerilla theater allowed him and others "to get out there and shock people, to titillate them in some way so that they begin to find another way of looking at things."[40]

That new perspective is, in fact, central to all aspects of radical environmental art. From the philosophically complex messages of Jeffers' poetry to the blaring, shocking, and sometimes funny themes in music and on T-shirts, artistic expression reflects radical environmentalism's concerns and empowers activists with creative means of expressing themselves. Music and theater, especially, allow these people, apparent misfits embracing views so foreign to most in society, to convey their concerns in less threatening, more understandable ways than the usual lecturing, picketing, or destroying equipment. Their audience, though, remains restricted to those in the movement and perhaps passersby on a busy street. As with their philosophy and overall perspective, radical environmentalists await a broader following for their art as well.

CHAPTER 16

CONCLUSION: OF CHANGE AND CONSTANCY

What is the nation's foremost domestic terror threat? White suprema-
cists, whose legacy of murder and torture goes back more than a century? Radical separatists who have killed FBI agents and declared pockets
of the U.S. their own sovereign territory? Think again. Each year in their
reports to Congress, the FBI and the Bureau of Alcohol, Tobacco, and Firearms name "ecoterrorism" as the nation's foremost home-grown danger.
No longer limited to tree spiking and break-ins at university laboratories,
radical environmentalism's destructive side is portrayed as the functional
equivalent of Al Quaeda, though activists have yet to injure, much less kill,
anyone in their attacks.

How did a poor, uncoordinated, seemingly unsophisticated, band of
ecoteurs come to such infamy? Moreover, with all the attention devoted to
so-called ecoterrorism, is sabotage and subversion all there is to the movement today?

I will attempt to answer those questions in the pages that follow, but be
forewarned that this new concluding chapter—which replaces the original written in 1990—is necessarily incomplete. Some might say it would
be better to write an entirely new book than to attempt to summarize fifteen years of radical environmental history in a few pages, and they have a
point. Protests are a daily occurrence, making it impossible to summarize
radical environmentalism's goals and tactics compactly. The movement
has evolved and divided. New issues to tackle—externally and internally—have emerged. New faces have entered the scene and old ones have
departed. The government has cracked down, and other opponents have
lashed back in new ways.

Fair enough. None of those points, however, make the foregoing chapters less relevant for understanding the movement today. The movement's
current concerns and challenges—in both broad and, for the most part,
fine strokes—are the same or quite similar to those of fifteen years ago.
Where they differ and where new ones have arisen, I think an update of

the old material and the introduction of the new can be accomplished in this chapter.

So I begin not so much with summaries of the recent histories of the major radical environmental groups that were introduced earlier in the book, as by noting exemplary "actions"—some of which took place in an hour, others after years-long struggles—that were undertaken in the final decade of the twentieth century and the first years of the twenty-first. I also introduce the Earth Liberation Front, which has become a lightning rod for the "terrorism" charges leveled against the movement. Finally, I will discuss a number of themes that characterize radical environmentalism today.

A note on sources: In keeping with the book's original methods—which drew from the movement's own outlook rather than from external interpreters of it—I once again have sought out activists' words for most of the information presented here. I disproportionately rely on the *Earth First! Journal* because it remains a crossroads vehicle for communication within the movement generally. In any given issue of the *Journal*, one is likely to read not only about Earth First! actions but those by the Animal Liberation Front (ALF), the Earth Liberation Front (ELF), the Sea Shepherds, and by grassroots environmental activists around the planet. Given the movement's Luddism, it may come as a surprise that the internet has been a boon for those seeking to get out the word about their actions; it, too, was an important source of material for this chapter. In contrast, I have only minimally relied upon mainstream newspaper articles and scholarly publications, since they often obscure what is happening in the movement and overly manipulate activists' perspectives.

Admittedly, the movement's self-reportage is not always reliable. Some writers in the movement have been known to be highly selective in the facts they report, though the same is certainly the case for journalists, who typically write briefer stories than those that appear in the movement's publications. Moreover, journalists often are constrained to write in ways that editors will approve of, and they seldom take the time to obtain the in-depth knowledge necessary to grasp the issues that activists advocate—and the reasons for their advocacy.

I encourage readers to keep in mind that this book's original and lasting emphasis is on *understanding* the radical environmental movement. I see no better way to obtain that understanding than by allowing the activists to speak for themselves. From there we can praise them or berate them. But, first, we need to listen.

Earth First!: The Struggle for Headwaters Forest

Headwaters Forest entered the environmental consciousness in 1986, when Earth First! activists "discovered" a huge grove of ancient old growth redwoods and Douglas firs on Pacific Lumber Company (Palco) land. Though Headwaters was ultimately a victory for Earth First!, it was a bittersweet one—in some senses one not yet ended.

Early-on, repeated lawsuits filed by the Environmental Protection Information Center and the Sierra Club Legal Defense Fund successfully protected Headwaters against Palco's efforts to "liquidate" its holdings there— the largest grove of privately owned coastal redwoods in the world. In the meantime, Earth First! and others advocated a debt-for-nature exchange of the sort commonly used between developed and developing nations that would protect Headwaters and wipe out the $1.6 billion debt owed to the U.S. government by Pacific Lumber's parent company, Maxxam Corp. The debt was the result of the bailout of another of Maxxam's holdings, a failed Texas savings and loan.[1]

By 1995, a climax to the decade-old struggle seemed near. Palco signed an agreement to delay logging Headwaters while it worked out a deal to cut trees on federal land in exchange for preserving the redwoods, but not before Earth First! had turned up the heat. In response to an exemption from logging rules granted Palco by the state of California, organizers attracted 500 people to a rally—on only six days' notice. Earth First! dug in its heels. Judi Bari observed, "[T]his time, the defense of Headwaters was accomplished in the political arena. Next time, we must be ready to defend it on the ground."[2] Or in the trees.

The renewed civil disobedience campaign for Headwaters began with a rush. On September 15, 1995, 264 people were arrested for trespassing when they crossed a spray-painted line from a state highway onto Palco land, in the process setting a new Earth First! single-day arrest record. That same day, the California Senate overwhelmingly approved legislation directing the State Resources Agency to negotiate a deal to purchase 3,000 acres in and around Headwaters.[3]

What appeared to be *the* deal for Headwaters came more than a year later. It gave Charles Hurwitz and Maxxam $380 million and failed to protect groves that were home to marbled murrelets, an old growth-dependent sea bird listed as a threatened species.[4] The supposed deal was preceeded by intense activism, signaling the public's support for a no compromise approach to Headwaters. An astounding 1,033 activists were cited for trespassing on Palco land on September 15, 1996—nearly four times the record number arrested exactly a year earlier—all for civil disobedience.[5] Among the last activists nabbed in the Headwaters campaign that year was actor Woody Harrelson, arrested for hanging a banner from Golden Gate Bridge.[6]

Amidst the Headwaters activism, Judi Bari died on March 2, 1997. Diagnosed with breast cancer the previous year, she struggled mightily to the end, refusing hospitalization and chemotherapy and giving a moving deposition in her lawsuit against the FBI and the Oakland Police Depart-ment only weeks before her death (see "Who Bombed Judi Bari?," below). The most powerful female activist the movement had seen—and one of the most courageous of a band of brave folk—was gone, but the struggle for Headwaters, and for an environmentalist-worker alliance, continued.

Of the latter, probably the most notable is the Alliance for Sustainable Jobs and the Environment. Beginning with the United Steelworkers of America, who were on strike against the Maxxam-controlled Kaiser Alu-minum Corporation, and now extending to unions across the nation, ASJE advocates "blue-green" unity along several fronts: jobs, restoring damaged lands, halting Maxxam and other "rogue corporations," fighting corporate globalization, and producing clean energy.[7] Among ASJE's board members is Karen Pickett, long-time Earth First! activist and close friend of Bari's. In many ways, ASJE is Judi Bari's vision realized.

September 25, 1997, saw the first of three almost identical, harrowing as-saults on Headwaters activists that occurred over less than a month's span and that tell us much about radical environmentalism's place in California's timber country. In each of the incidents—at Palco headquarters in Scotia, at the Bear Creek logging site (on October 3), and at Rep. Frank Riggs's local offices in Eureka (on October 16)—local police swabbed or squirted pepper spray directly into nonviolent protestors' eyes, causing them unimaginable anguish.

At the Palco headquarters action, the police never bothered to negoti-ate with the Earth First!ers. Rather, they informed the seven activists who had chained themselves together and were sitting on an office floor that in five minutes they were going to use "chemical agents" on them. Three pro-testors, including one with asthma, unlocked themselves from their steel-linked human chain. Those left were in pairs, no longer such a large mass that they could not have been carried from the building—something police often do. Instead, the authorities proceeded as planned, almost robotically.

A juvenile in the group, "Spring" Lundberg, told what happened to her: "I heard people start screaming out and cries coming. It was so awful and they were just going along with it and then they came to me. I was kind of, as I said, in the fetal position and they forcefully wrenched my head up and held my forehead and pressed my face back so that they could ap-ply this liquid pepper spray to my eyes." The police used a cotton swab. Spring continued, "They ran it along the bottom of my eyes and the crack so it would seep in. And as they were applying it I was saying, 'I am your daughter. I am your daughter, I am your daughter. . . .'"[8]

At Rep. Riggs's office, a similarly brutal scene was filmed by the police. When the footage was broadcast nationwide following release of the video in court,[9] it prompted California's attorney general to call the police actions "'un-precedented' and in violation of 'acceptable police community practices.'"[10]

Later that year, a wandering activist named Julia "Butterfly" Hill arrived at the Headwaters base camp. Despite having been told repeatedly that her help wasn't needed—a rare refrain in the movement—Julia Butterfly managed to make it to camp. She did a short treesit in "Luna," a thousand year-old redwood, and a few days later Julia Butterfly took to her perch again when loggers were threatening the majestic tree. It was December 10. "Two weeks turned into three," she wrote in an article presciently headlined "Treesitting without Limits," "and after three I thought, 'I'm so close to a month I might as well stay.'"[11] Julia Butterfly continued her sit for longer than anyone might have imagined.

A second human tragedy befell the Headwaters protest eighteen months after Judi Bari's death. On September 17, 1998, David "Gypsy" Chain, a popular and experienced activist, joined others in nonviolently confronting a logger in the woods, questioning his role in destroying marbled murrelet habitat. The logger chased the protestors, then went back to work, eventually cutting down a tree that fell on Chain, killing him instantly. No criminal charges were filed.[12]

Even as the human carnage was added to the ecological, the struggle for Headwaters continued far away from the woods in cities like Sacramento and Washington, D.C. In early 1999, a deal finally was struck for Headwaters, with mainstream environmental organizations and politicians taking the credit. Of the 60,000 acres in Headwaters *Forest,* Palco sold 10,000 acres—including the 3,000 acre Headwaters *grove*—to the U.S. and California for nearly $500 million; 210,000 Palco-owned acres were placed in a habitat conservation/sustained yield plan that allows Palco to avoid provisions of the Endangered Species Act, though other provisos were included to protect trees and animal species like the marbled murrelet that nest in them.

The bargain permanently preserved only 10 percent of Headwaters. About 9,000 acres of nearby old-growth Douglas fir stands were left vulnerable to cutting, though some other areas were placed off limits to logging for 50 years, and Julia Butterfly's Luna went unprotected—with her still in it. Earth First! vowed to oppose the deal through the courts, led by the activists and attorneys at the Environmental Protection Information Center, and to continue its fight to secure a debt-for-nature swap for the land, though its efforts ultimately proved fruitless. Compromise won out.[13]

Julia Butterfly remained in Luna until she and her supporters made a special deal with Palco for Luna and three acres around it. She finally quit her sit on December 18, 1999, having gone 738 days, more than two years, without her feet touching the ground—a world record treesit that garnered the redwood preservation movement untold publicity.[14] The deal Julia Butterfly and her supporters cut had them paying $50,000 to Palco, which donated the same sum to the forestry studies program at Humboldt State University.

In 1999 Gypsy Chain's parents filed a wrongful death lawsuit against Palco, the logger who felled the tree on him, and others. The suit was settled out of court, and while the financial settlement was not disclosed, Pacific Lumber was required to leave the tree that killed Chain where it lay, to erect a memorial marker nearby, and to convene a community roundtable to discuss logging protests.[15]

Eight of the pepper-spray victims filed a federal civil rights suit against Humboldt County and the City of Eureka in October 1997. Three trials ensued before the plaintiffs were each awarded nominal damages of $1 in April 2005. However, the activists pressed a judge to force the defendants to cover the activists' legal fees, an ordeal that continued through late 2005.[16]

And still the struggle for the redwoods continues in the woods, as it no doubt will until the last of the grand trees is cut or preserved. In 2003 nearly 100 protestors were arrested for attempting to enforce a judge's order prohibiting Palco from logging one old-growth tract after the company allegedly ignored the judge's ruling. One of those jailed was grandmother and Earth First!er Naomi Wagner, whose violation was hugging a tree.[17] In 2005, activist Willow began the second year of his Humboldt County treesit, and others created the "Persistent Resistance for the Forest" campaign, intended to expose "the hidden forces that perpetuate local deforestation" in Northern California.[18]

Earth First! Coast-to-Coast

Headwaters was not the only long-running Earth First! campaign of the last fifteen years. Among the notable struggles was Cove/Mallard, the defense of a 76,000 acre *de facto* wilderness in central Idaho that began in 1992. Home to endangered salmon, and to elk, moose, cougars, lynx, and numerous other animal and plant species, the Cove/Mallard area was a crucial wildlife corridor joining the Gospel Hump and River of No Return wilderness areas. Activists labeled the complex of timber sales and roads a "poster child of the misguided land use policies in the West."[19]

Scores of protestors were arrested at Cove/Mallard, and the backlash against Earth First! in Idaho was severe. Not only were protestors repeatedly attacked, they were also sued by logging companies, and a patently unconstitutional law prohibiting "solicitation to halt or impede lawful forest practices" was placed on the books in an effort to halt confrontations in the forests and speed up the logging.[20] It didn't work. On-site activism and legal challenges in the Cove/Mallard region were ultimately successful, with only three of the nine timber sales logged. However, attention shifted to the adjacent Otter Wing timber sale in 1998; it was spiked in 2002.[21]

Montana witnessed an eight-year struggle to halt the slaughter of bison leaving Yellowstone National Park during the winter in search of food.

The state's politically powerful ranching community feared that the bison might bring *brucellosis* with them—a disease that may cause cows to abort their calves, although no documented case of such interspecies infection exists. Lawsuits by mainstream environmental organizations and Native Americans failed to halt a slaughter that began in 1985,[22] and in 1997 a coalition of Native Americans and non-Native environmentalists formed Buffalo Nations,[23] later renamed the Buffalo Field Campaign, and took to the brutal Montana winter, interfering with the slaughter year after year. Activists also took their protests inside, at one point dumping "rotting buffalo entrails on a table . . . , splattering Sen. Conrad Burns and U.S. Agriculture Secretary Dan Glickman"[24] to dramatize the horror of the slaughter.[25]

In 2005 Montana's new governor appeared more sensitive to the buffalo issue—or at least the bad press it had garnered for the state—and replaced enough members of the state Fish, Wildlife, and Parks Commission to halt the slaughter.[26] Activists were pessimistic that the moratorium would last long, however.

Oregon continues to be a hotbed of Earth First! activism. At the Sugarloaf protest in the mid-1990s in the Siskiyou National Forest, dozens of activists were arrested.[27] The Warner Creek fire in 1991 opened a new front in the timber wars, as Earth First!ers began protesting "salvage logging" operations there and the Forest Service's ecologically and economically nonsensical fire-suppression policy. Earth First!ers and others calling themselves Cascadia Forest Defenders mounted the largest, longest road blockade in environmental history to keep out the loggers. In 1996 the struggle for Warner Creek ended with an Earth First! victory—one that sociologist Douglas Bevington calls "one of the most significant Earth First! success stories of the past fifteen years."[28] Salvage logging would not go away, however, and the "Biscuit Fire Recovery Project," proposed by the U.S. Forest Service in 2003, opened up the hard won North Kalmiopsis roadless area to cutting— indeed, to the largest timber sale in history: 1 *billion* board feet.[29]

Elsewhere, Earth First! fights on with continued vigor. In Arizona, the long-running protests against the observatory on Mt. Graham continued. Despite Apache and environmentalist efforts, the telescopes were mounted, sacred sites were desecrated, and the Mt. Graham red squirrel's habitat was partially destroyed.[30] North Carolina and Tennesse's Katúah Earth First!ers advocate for ancient forests, against coal mining, and alongside groups opposing the Ku Klux Klan.[31] Indiana saw its first-ever treesits in 2001,[32] and in 2003 Massachusetts Earth First!ers fought to defend thirteen acres of old growth red oaks from cutting—a speck by west coast standards, but ecologically priceless and politically symbolic.[33]

Less geographically focused, Earth First!ers have joined activists in all three of the terrestrial prongs of the radical environmental movement to protest, in various ways, genetic engineering. What began in California in 1987 with the "Strawberry Liberation Front" protest[34] has grown into a string of articles[35] and actions. Similarly, among those taking action against nanotechnology has been "THONG"—Topless Humans Organized for Natural Genetics—which saw female and male activists run naked in one protest, and, in another, interrupt a cocktail party for nanotech executives in Chicago by stripping down to their thongs. Another 2004 protest, this one in Leeds, England, showed less skin and more stink as protestors "deployed rotten comfrey and fish-bait stinkbombs" at a nanotech tradeshow. No one was arrested in the protests.[36]

The Sea Shepherds: Norway Declares War

The most disturbing in a litany of assaults endured by the Sea Shepherds occurred on July 6, 1994. The Norwegian Coast Guard attacked the Sea Shepherd vessel *Whales Forever*, which went to Norway to interfere with that nation's plans to resume whale hunting in spite of the eight-year ban by the International Whaling Commission. In the annals of high seas environmental protest, only the French government's murderous sinking of the *Rainbow Warrior* in 1985 (see Chapter 4) exceeds Norway's callous overreaction to nonviolent confrontation.

On the second of July, a U.S. Navy vessel that refused to identify itself shadowed the *Whales Forever* until it reached Norway's 200-mile fishing zone, where it broke off contact and radioed the Sea Shepherds' position to the Norwegian authorities.[37] The Norwegians conducted naval exercises within a mile of the *Whales Forever* on July 5. The following day, while seventeen miles off the coast—five miles from Norwegian jurisdiction—the captain of the Coast Guard ship *Andenes* radioed *Whales Forever's* Paul Watson of his intention to arrest the Sea Shepherd captain for violating Norway's territorial waters. Watson insisted that he was in international waters, but to no avail.

Using the only weapon at their disposal, the *Whales Forever*, the Sea Shepherds fought off harassment by a Norwegian military helicopter and the *Andenes's* repeated efforts to stop their ship, but they could not outrun the Norwegians. When the *Andenes* rushed *Whales Forever* with the intention of ramming it amidships, "Watson threw the wheel hard to starboard to avoid the ram. The *Andenes* struck the bow of the *Whales Forever* just back of the Coast Guard ship's prow. The bow of the Sea Shepherd ship peeled backward and down in two sections, 'like a pair of giant thumbs was peeling the skin off an orange,' a crew member said. The *Andenes* put a 30-foot gash down its own side."[38]

The drama was only beginning. Norwegian Commander Erik Blom informed Watson he was authorized to "'use whatever means we need to take your ship under arrest.'"[39] Watson refused to stop, whereupon Blom lobbed a shell at the *Whales Forever*. The Sea Shepherds were under a full-blown attack by a sovereign government's navy. It was as if the Scandana-vians had declared war.

Watson altered course and transmitted a Mayday call. Members of the crew rushed to the bow of the boat, despite Watson's orders to stay away from the front of the ship after Blom radioed that he planned to fire a sec-ond shell precisely there. The crewmembers were risking their lives to keep the *Whales Forever* and its captain out of Norway's hands. On reaching the bow, the crew smelled diesel fumes and looked over the edge to see that the earlier collision had opened a fuel tank. The second shell sailed over the bow.

As the *Andenes* followed closely behind the *Whales Forever*, eleven jour-nalists sailing with the activist ship began to get word out to the world about what was happening. When Norway's national radio network requested an interview with Watson later that day, the Captain replied, "That's fine, but you may want to tape something now, as we are under attack and I don't know if we will still be afloat or alive by 6 o'clock."[40]

They were. Even after commandoes in Zodiacs (ironically, the same type of inflatable vessels Watson used against whalers when he shipped with Greenpeace) attempted to depth charge the *Whales Forever*, Watson did not halt. Two days later the *Whales Forever* limped into port for extensive re-pairs.

In a somewhat less dangerous venture, starting in December 2000 the Sea Shepherds began patrolling the Galapagos Islands, under a contract with the Ecuadorian government, to halt fish poaching. The Sea Shepherds's vigilance has resulted in numerous arrests and a variety of other actions such as drift net confiscations near the famous national park.[41]

After a six-year hiatus, in 2004 and 2005 the Sea Shepherds returned to the Labrador and Newfoundland coasts in Canada to pursue one of their signature causes, opposing the harp and hood seal slaughter. Subsidized by the Canadian government, the sealers planned to kill more than a million juvenile seals between 2003 and 2005.[42] On March 31, 2005, in the St. Law-rence Gulf, fifteen Sea Shepherd activists were assaulted by sealers wield-ing the "hakapiks" and clubs used to kill seals—this after both the Cana-dian Coast Guard ship *Amundsen* and a sealing boat took runs at ramming the Sea Shepherds' *Farley Mowat*. Both missed, and so did a sealer firing a rifle in the activists' direction. Sailing with the activists were Canadian journalists, who made the incident national news.[43]

Eleven protestors were arrested that day for entering the seal hunt area without a permit, but no charges were laid against the sealers who attempt-ed to treat their antagonists as if they, too, were seals. The activists were released without bail a day later, and the sealers killed their full quota of 320,000 seals in the St. Lawrence and on the Labrador Front.[44]

The Animal Liberation Front: SHAC Attack

At a time when the U.S. is at war with terrorists following attacks on the nation's mainland, destructive tactics have made the Animal Liberation Front the focus of intense investigations, resulting in the ALF being labeled one of the two top domestic terror threats.

Since 1990, ALF cells have caused millions of dollars in damages, stepping up their attacks on university and private research facilities that experiment on animals, freeing thousands of animals from fur farms, and going after corporations like never before.[45] The latter efforts, particularly against Britain's Huntingdon Life Sciences—a massive contract animal testing company primarily serving European nations—demonstrate the group's ability not only to sustain a campaign, but to do so internationally.

ALF activists across Europe and in the U.S. have gone after not only HLS, but corporations that use its services and that supply it with everything from trucking to money. In 2000, 1,500 activists in the UK in support of SHAC—Stop Huntingdon Animal Cruelty—protested at the sites of several of HLS's largest clients, and "U.S. activists flooded the phone lines, email systems, and offices of Stephens, Inc.," an investment banking firm that loaned HLS tens of millions of dollars.[46]

According to the ALF, Huntington uses 180,000 animals in its labs annually and experiments on 70,000 daily. In the UK, SHAC protestors confront Huntingdon employees every day outside of HLS's main research lab. In concert with those public confrontations, the ALF "has waged a series of car bombings [of unoccupied vehicles] and attacks on workers' homes."[47] Such tactics are among the most controversial of any pursued by radical environmentalists (see "More CD, More PD . . . More 'Terrorists'?" below).

The Earth Liberation Front: Freedom through Fire

Animal liberators comprise but one radical environmental group atop the U.S. government's list of domestic terror threats. The other, the Earth Liberation Front, did not exist until 1992 and did not make an appearance in the U.S. until 1996. The ELF's approach is as brutally straightforward as the ALF's: Destroy the tools of environmental destruction *and do nothing else.* There is no such thing as ELF street theater or an ELF treesit. "Burn baby, burn" is its de facto motto.

In the first *Earth First! Journal* article on the ELF, "Sea Elf" wrote, "The ELF solidified in 1992 at the first UK Earth First! gathering in Brighton, England. Earth First! had begun to impact the environmental movement in Britain . . . [and] had threatened sabotage when necessary, but up until April '92 very few actions had been publicized."[48] When a £500,000 attack on peat harvesting equipment brought intense focus on the British Earth

First!ers, the "movement was not ready for it."[49] Activists who embraced ecotage then created the ELF so that "Earth First! could continue its public nonviolent activities."[50]

But the split among British Earth First!ers wasn't just about civil disobedience versus destructive environmental advocacy. ELF sought to advance a broader social agenda, distancing itself from the misanthropy that characterized Earth First!'s early years. Sea Elf wrote, "ELF dumped the American baggage that had followed Earth First! to Britain, especially the macho, male-oriented 'eco-warrior image,' which was in American pioneering culture. ELF also disavowed the reactionary, apolitical rantings about population controls and immigration that some Earth First!ers in the U.S. were voicing.

"Instead, ELF looked to Europe for its history of radical change . . ., giving a social as well as an ecological flavor to how people. . .pursued their lives and their actions."[51] Thus, the ELF sounded almost scholarly in its tone and in its deliberate linking of environmental issues with social justice concerns. "ELF is not a 'radical environmental group,'" wrote Sea Elf. "[I]t is an ecological resistance movement that embraces eco-feminism, animal, earth, and human liberation. . . . [T]argets should be not only the vivisection labs, but also the very foundation of capitalism: the sources of profit."[52] In theory, at least, ELF would be avowedly revolutionary and unashamedly anarchistic: egalitarian, anti-authority (of all types), and utterly opposed to Western economics.

Before ELF arrived in the US, it had spread to the Netherlands and Germany, and the sister group Earth Liberation Army was active in Canada. Finally, in 1996 U.S. ELF announced its presence with authority, torching a Willamette National Forest truck and, in 1997, a Bureau of Land Management wild horse corral in Burns, Oregon. In 1998 ELF activists claimed credit for the $12 million arson of a half-completed ski resort in Vail, Colorado, that allegedly was constructed in prime habitat for endangered lynx. For five years it was the costliest example of pro-environment property destruction on record. Then, on August 1, 2003, ELF firebombed an unfinished San Diego condominium complex valued at $50 million.[53] Since then, activists have torched housing complexes and genetics research laboratories, among scores of other actions, and—in a throwback to ecotage's days of yore—have even claimed credit for tree spiking.

But the ELF may have received more publicity for its torching of sport utility vehicles than anything else. The popular gas-guzzling global greenhouse-makers have been burned by ELF activists in many states and several countries. In turn, the authorities have come down hard on captured activists,[54] and some are receiving extraordinary sentences for their crimes. In June 2000 Jeffrey "Free" Luers and Craig "Critter" Marshall set fire to three SUVs in a Chevrolet dealer's lot in Eugene, Oregon. Luers was found guilty and sentenced to 22 years and eight months in prison.

Ruckus Society: Raising a Fuss the Old Fashioned Way

Around the same time that the ELF arrived in the U.S., Mike Roselle and former Greenpeace ship captain Howard Cannon created the "Ruckus Society" to teach the fundamentals of nondestructive direct action after Greenpeace shut down its weeklong camps, which had long been integral to teaching activists the basics of civil disobedience tactics and strategy.

Ruckus has grown to become an important bridge between U.S. and international CD activists. In 1996, its first full year of existence, Ruckus contributed to protests in the U.S. aimed at Japan's Mitsubishi Corp., Brazil's mahogany logging, and UNOCAL's destruction of rain forests and cultures in Burma.[55] Yet as global as Ruckus's view was, training director Mojgone Azemun noted that "'what was constantly not addressed in the organization [in the late '90s] was, what about indigenous people and people of color from this continent? Where's the space and where's the attention focused on their struggles?'"[56] As a result of such reflection, Ruckus training camps are richly diverse and full of activists asking difficult questions of themselves, their home organizations, and of Ruckus. It typically organizes two to three week-long "Action Camps" each year and several more "microRuckus" camps.[57]

International Radical Environmentalism: Unifying Disparate Movements

Impossible as it is to summarize the North American radical environmental scene in a handful of pages, any attempt to more than hint at the wide range of issues and tactics found elsewhere around the planet is doomed to failure. Suffice it to say that daily resistance to the forces of environmental destruction is now the norm on every continent but Antarctica. Outside of the (over-) developed nations, activists take their lives into their own hands to protest what is typically not simply environmental destruction, but the destruction of livelihoods, ways of life, and entire cultures.

Indeed, what is narrowly "environmental" in places like the U.S., Europe, and Japan is essential elsewhere. Such a realization opens the door to alliances across movements, a fact that many activists were slow to recognize until what is likely to be seen in retrospect as the signal event of our times for worldwide activism generally: the Seattle WTO protests in 1999.

Established in 1995, the World Trade Organization sets standards that its 148 member nations must follow to trade with others. Conflicting standards—including environmental laws—may be appealed to secret panels that decide whether a nation's laws are out of line with WTO agreements; if so, the WTO rules stand, and any nation that resists them risks trade sanctions. As the watchdog group Public Citizen damningly notes, "The WTO [functions] principally to pry open markets for the benefit of transnational corporations at the expense of national and local economies; workers, farmers, indigenous peoples, women, and other social groups; health and safety; the environment; and animal welfare. In addition, the WTO system, rules, and procedures are undemocratic, un-transparent and nonaccountable and have operated to marginalize the majority of the world's people."[58]

The WTO's powers include ultimate authority over "intellectual property" questions, a growing topic as multinational corporations practice "bioexploration," which involves patenting potentially useful substances, especially those from plants (as for medical purposes). Often, the bioexplorers are working for major corporations outside of the nation where the plants are found. The corporations receive massive economic benefits from plant substances they could not have created on their own, while local peoples and distant governments receive little or nothing in return. Activists call the practice "biopiracy."[59]

And so the stage was set for massive resistance at the 1999 WTO meetings in Seattle. The *Earth First! Journal* ran a four-page insert inviting activists to join in the protests,[60] and invitations like it were accepted by thousands from around the world.

When they arrived, all hell broke loose. Banners were hung from huge cranes at the port, "tripods" and lockdowns of the sort usually only seen in forest road protests emerged in the middle of downtown. The "Black Bloc" (or Block)—black-clad, brick-throwing, disaffected young anarchists—smashed the windows of McDonald's restaurants, GAP clothing stores, Niketown, and other companies implicated in some of the worst of globalization practices. The WTO opening ceremonies were delayed.[61] And that was just day one.

The anarchists shouted "Fuck shit up" and threw teargas canisters back at the police. Marchers were indiscriminately shot by rubber bullets. Some took over a dump truck for use as a "bunker." Driven by the police, the protestors—numbering between 50,000 and 100,000—extended their presence throughout town. A civil emergency was declared. One protestor wrote, "Gas stations are instructed not to sell gas in containers," doubtless due to concerns about Molotov cocktail making, but none were ever thrown.[62] For five days the protests went on. More than 500 were arrested, most of them for acts of civil disobedience; the Ruckus Society had prepared many CD activists for the experience. In the end, the WTO talks collapsed. Many delegates seemed convinced by the protests that the WTO might harm people in their countries. "The talks have ended in failure," the *Earth First! Journal* correspondent wrote. "The world will never be the same."[63]

As the University of Washington's WTO History Project notes, "The protests against the World Trade Organization that rocked Seattle, Washington, in late 1999 were an incredibly significant moment in the history of popular protests. Not only did the protestors succeed in disrupting the meetings of the world's most influential trade-governing bodies, but the event drew together incredibly diverse constituencies that represented a wide range of interests, many of which would seem to be incompatible at first [glance]."[64] The *Journal's* post-Seattle analysis similarly observed, "Unlike the antiwar protests of the '60s, this time we have the added leverage of finally focusing on the overarching system causing all the problems, not just a single issue. Now diverse movements are acting together. . . .We need to reach across color and cultural barriers . . . by getting involved in each other's causes."[65]

In the years since, activists have made regular pilgrimages to protest international trade meetings wherever they occur. The *Earth First! Journal* regularly features not only international actions—something it had done for years—but articles advocating bridge-building between peoples and causes have increased in number. And the overarching phenomenon that the WTO activists were protesting—"globalization," the homogenization of everything from what people plant in their fields to what they see in their media, a process that benefits the powerful and ignores the powerless, including the environment—has become a fundamental part of radical environmental discourse.

Major Themes within the Movement

In the last decade and a half, the radical environmental movement has continued to grapple with old demons even as new ones have emerged, and this section identifies the major trends, continuing and new. I have ordered these topics on a rough continuum from those of primary concern to society—or societies—at large to those that tend not to be noticed outside of the movement but that are of considerable importance inside of it.

Globalization's Backlash

Radical environmentalists' concern with global issues is a fundamental part of their cause, and the movement has long been interested in—and supportive of—global environmental activism. Increasingly, however, activists are realizing in ways that go beyond the old "Think Globally, Act Locally" bumper sticker that there are no exclusively "local" environmental problems. Nor are there any narrowly "environmental" problems, at least not according to some experienced ecocentric activists. From species extinction to global climate change to indigenous people's rights, the planet—all of it, humans included—is most properly seen as one entity (though not everyone in the movement shares that perspective[66]).

What brought about this new mindset on the part of some in the movement? First, Seattle drew together incredibly diverse movements. Radical environmentalists found themselves planning protests and marching alongside labor union members, farm workers, indigenous peoples, human rights advocates, and others from grassroots movements around the nation and around the world—even disgruntled French dairy farmers! Opposition to corporate globalization, already a powerful movement outside of North America, united them all. Many were probably surprised by the company they were keeping on the streets of Seattle, but since then they have worked to overcome past differences and unite against a common foe.[67]

Second, activists who were present and those who watched from afar came to understand the results that direct action can achieve. Seattle legitimized direct action as a powerful tactic that could produce results where classical mainstream political lobbying failed. Direct action unified movements, attracted media attention, showed activists around the world that they could fight back against globalization's onslaught, and it even appeared to convince some government ministers to re-think their support of corporate globalization.

After Seattle, globalization was everyone's problem—and alliances employing direct action were central to the solution. Together, activists recognized that the multinational corporations' massive power can only be turned back through a long-term, coordinated effort taking place on multiple fronts. The alliances that have lasted and grown now for years show no signs of weakening or retreating, and the organizational and tactical techniques used in Seattle and elsewhere since are the tools of a new, unifying (if not entirely unified) global movement.

More CD, More PD . . . More "Terrorists"?

Outside of the "alternative media," we do not hear much about the conflicts between development and those who would protect nonhumans. One senses the major news media hardly know what to make of tree sitters and animal liberators—Julia Butterfly's protest stands as a noteworthy exception. Publishers, editors, and broadcasters seem to think if they ignore things they don't like, those things will disappear.

But this movement isn't going away soon. If anything, it is picking up steam. Consider the Ruckus Society's training of activists not only from North America, but from around the world, in CD techniques. Activists flock to its camps. Then they return to far-flung places where such activities have never been attempted before and they go about peacefully confronting the forces bent on destroying ecological and human communities in remote locations like Costa Rica, Burma, Tibet—and Indiana and Massachusetts!

Thousands have been jailed in recent years in the U.S. alone for openly protesting timber cutting and animal experimentation. While no count of actions or arrests exists (although one anti-environmental website helpfully lists the names of those arrested at a number of actions), the numbers held for CD are on the increase, judging from the pages of the *Earth First! Journal*.

So, too, has PD (property destruction), which, for our purposes and for the moment, includes ecotage and monkeywrenching—been on the increase. No less an authority than the FBI has accumulated data indicating an upsurge in PD, and in its 2002 report to Congress, the FBI said it "estimates that ALF/ELF have committed approximately 600 criminal acts in the United States since 1996, resulting in damages in excess of 42 million dollars." By May 2004 the total was "more than 1,100 criminal acts in the United States since 1976, resulting in damages conservatively estimated at approximately $110 million." The Bureau sees no end in sight: "It is believed these trends will persist, as extremists within the environmental movement continue to fight what they perceive as greater encroachment of human society on the natural world."[68]

Continued Tactical Debates

Even as the pace and impact of environmental protest quickens and grows, old questions over tactics remain. Is the movement, and, more important to activists, the planet, best served by civil disobedience or by property destruction? It is probably not correct to say that most activists embrace one or the other as the sole acceptable tactic. The prevailing rhetoric—at least within Earth First! as reflected on the *Journal's* pages—is to advocate both CD and ecotage, as it always has. Given the *Journal's* democratic ethos, it is safe to say that most activists accept destructive tactics as an important option, even if they do not engage in PD themselves.

Yet the counter-arguments by the CD "dogmatists"[69] expressing anxiety about PD remain, as they have since Tolstoy and Gandhi. A cornerstone of the CD response is that the moral force of a worthy position is lost when violence (or destruction) is used against violence. None other than occasional ecoteur and Earth First! co-founder Howie Wolke has said, "I think that civil disobedience has always occupied an essential role in American politics—and I fear the day where it no longer does so. We should all fear that day, even people who may vehemently disagree with the goals of a particular nonviolent civil disobedience protest."[70] More colorfully, Judi Bari wrote, "Earth First! has treated monkeywrenching like a boy scout panty raid. Our failure to recognize the seriousness of the tactic has helped to endanger public Earth First!ers, isolate and discredit our movement, and drive away some of our best activists."[71]

Philosophically, monkeywrenching never meshed with CD, but at least it fit into a protest strategy that was enunciated early in Earth First!'s existance. ALF and ELF activists, guided by an understanding of anarchy that condemns corporatist-state power in any form as oppression, enact a vicious morality of their own that denies capitalism and representative government any moral standing at all. They conceive environmental activism largely in those abstract terms, not as local struggles that are played out in front of a larger public that might be convinced to join the cause.

Karen Pickett has remarked, "'Our motto is 'No Compromise in Defense of Mother Earth!' not 'Fuck Shit Up!'""[72] With so much economic and political power behind the creation of planet-killing and animal-torturing technologies, can any acts of destruction match, much less exceed, corporations' and governments' ability to wreak havoc? Is a war versus the corporate-state winnable through PD? Is there any choice other than CD?

There's another dimension to this debate, a semantic one of more importance to activists than anyone, but insightful for its illumination of the broader movement's fissures: Some CD advocates within the movement who envision a place for environmental sabotage also ask if a distinction shouldn't be made between "PD" and "ecotage/monkeywrenching." Key to the logic of the latter is that it is a last-ditch tactic to preserve wild places, one that is employed only when all other avenues are closed off. PD is different. It seems almost vengeful, these activists say, and its point is primarily political and economic, not ecological: it raises the price of doing business but otherwise fits poorly within the traditional CD-ecotage strategy. Few buildings or SUVs, once burned, go unreplaced. Few experiments, once destroyed by animal liberators, go uncompleted. "Free" Luers will not be free for more than 22 years—what might he have been able to achieve in that time through nondestructive means had he taken that path?

These fundamental divisions over tactical issues within the movement are substantial enough that one author wrote, "While there is considerable room for varying lifestyles and personal philosophies within the Earth First! movement, Earth First!ers need seriously consider whether there is enough room to accommodate individuals whose revolutionary angst overshadows their love of the wilderness to the point that they become a liability to its preservation."[73] Of course, ELF activists see the issue quite differently. One told a British newspaper, "'Violence to property . . . [is] a form of liberation.'"[74]

PD advocates don't make it easy on themselves. They continuously challenge boundaries, and the latest tactical developments in the ALF and the ELF are as ominous as they get. If activists' threatening rhetoric is to be believed, it appears that it will not be long before the terrorist label is supplanted by "assassin." The objects of direct activists' ire have long feared for their persons. As far back as 1988, threats were being made against animal researchers' lives.[75] Is such rhetoric verging on reality today?

The Powerful Respond

Corporations Say, "SLAPP 'Em Around"

Corporations have used a host of insidious weapons against environmental activists. They have sent—or allowed—toughs to beat up protesters, created fake press releases, and defamed individuals and groups through the media while Web pages created by industry front groups distort facts without addressing allegations against corporations.

But no corporate attack on activists is quite like "strategic lawsuits against public participation," or SLAPPs. George Pring and Penelope Canan, both of the University of Denver, coined the term in 1988 to mean, roughly, lawsuits filed with the intention of stifling legitimate "speech"—including oral and written communication and protest actions—where that speech is aimed at effecting some governmental or corporate behavior. Pring and Canan wrote that SLAPP-like litigation was not uncommon immediately after the American Revolution, but it was largely nonexistent for a century and a half until it reemerged in the 1960s as a way to quell protest.[76]

Contemplating the uses of SLAPPs, one observer wrote, "Citizens have been sued for testifying before their city councils and county commissions about building permit and zoning change applications, for expressing concerns to school board members, and for reporting violations of environmental laws to regulatory agencies, to give just three of thousands of examples. In short, these citizens were sued for doing exactly what the Constitution allows and encourages them to do. . . . In a representative democracy, public participation is the cornerstone of the system; it is a bedrock principle that connects government to the governed. It legitimizes the system and helps to make government accountable."[77] SLAPPs, then, are nothing less than assaults on the foundations of democracy.

SLAPPs are a tool of the powerful used against those who question them. SLAPPs sap movements and activists of their meager resources of time and money and cause them enormous anxiety.

None other than Pacific Lumber Company went after California activists using a SLAPP as its weapon in 1996, and it has returned to that tool repeatedly—in mid-2005 it had *five* active SLAPPs against activists. One protest group, the Mattole Forest Defenders, was engaged in a range of activism, from civil disobedience to petitioning governmental agencies to challenging Palco's right to log along sensitive salmon spawning grounds in the Mattole watershed. After Palco SLAPPed the Mattole Defenders, Karen Pickett wrote, "This action is clearly designed to quash dissent and protest against PL. . . . This is a company that has no qualms about flouting the law. . . . They seek to chill dissent, but they forget that tens of thousands of people have showed up to protest their logging activities. They can't silence that many voices."[78] Other Earth First!ers participating in nondestructive protests have been sued as well, sometimes successfully.[79]

Palco also has engaged in smear campaigns over the airways—one such effort prompted "more than 60 doctors, lawyers, city council members, clergy and local residents" in timber country, California, to demand that Palco "'stop producing media material claiming that civil disobedience is an act of terrorism."[80] Since the 9/11 attacks, "terrorism," always an emotion-filled label, is increasingly used indiscriminately to brand resistance of various types. Its use is often a hollow but persuasive rhetorical strategy, one quick to attract uncritical media attention. Corporations have found in *terrorism* a useful harassment technique without having to physically bully activists.

Of course, corporations often do not have to do the dirty work of stifling liberties on their own—they have legislators available to take care of that kind of thing. One example occurred in Oregon, where, in 2001, the state legislature passed a measure classifying attacks on corporate property as "hate crimes," a designation previously reserved only for human beings.[81] And, as noted above, Idaho's lawmakers responded to the Cove/Mallard protests by placing a patently unconstitutional measure on the books prohibiting "solicitation to halt or impede lawful forest practices."[82]

Battling the Grand Inquisition

Probably the most valuable tool government possesses to probe into any resistance movement, radical environmentalism included, is the grand jury. It's a frightening process and one that I know well, for it was my refusal to answer all of a grand jury's questions into my research on the movement that led to my jailing for more than five months in 1993.

As *Eco-Warriors* was first published in 1990, I had just begun my Ph.D. studies in sociology at Washington State University. I planned a dissertation that would build on my knowledge of radical environmentalism developed through researching and writing my book, and I maintained contact with several of the activists I got to know over the previous years. One of them was Rod Coronado, who ended up housesitting for my family while we traveled to the East Coast in 1991.

We returned to find that the ALF had broken into a research facility at WSU, freeing some coyotes and making away with several mink and mice. Computers were destroyed, and the damage totaled $100,000. Months later, Coronado was named a suspect in the raid, and in May 1992 I was subpoenaed to appear before a federal grand jury. Believing I had spoken with those involved in the break-in, the government wanted me to testify about what it thought I knew.

Eventually I ended up in a federal courtroom, where I insisted to the judge that if I had spoken with the activists involved in the WSU raid, everything they told me was protected by a promise of confidentiality that I, as a researcher akin to a journalist, would not reveal the names of those with whom I spoke or what they said to me. My interviews, if any (I never admitted to that point), were protected under the Constitution's free press clause. The government was equally adamant that Coronado was only my friend, that it was impossible for us to have a professional, researcher-subject relationship. Ultimately, two federal courts ruled that I had to testify. My only option was to go to jail.

Years later, my grand jury experience seems surreal. The only people in the room besides me were one or more prosecutors, twenty-three grand jurors, and a court reporter. No judge. No attorney representing me. It was a grand inquisition. But for the fact that the grand jury is mentioned in the Constitution, you would think it would be outlawed as antithetical to the U.S. justice system.

When the prosecutors began asking questions, I answered a number of them because doing so wouldn't make me divulge my sources. But it was my sources the government was after, and I ultimately refused to answer more than 30 of its questions. My sealed lips prompted the judge to find me in "contempt of court." Contempt is its own class of crime, neither felony nor misdemeanor. I was never read my Miranda rights. Never arrested, tried, or convicted, when I still refused to answer those questions, the judge jailed me. For 159 days. Only when the judge gave up hope that I would testify further to the grand jury was I released, and I never did answer the prosecutors' questions.[83]

Ultimately, no one was prosecuted for the WSU break-in, though three others besides me were also held in contempt. The FBI listed Coronado as among its "most wanted." He was finally captured in 1994 and sentenced to 57 months in federal prison for crimes including involvement in an arson attack at Michigan State University—the first-ever federal ALF prisoner.

Grand juries are a fact of life for the radical environmental movement. Activists, their family, friends, and coworkers, are regularly subpoenaed to appear in those star chambers. Hearsay and illegally-obtained evidence can be admitted in grand juries, and, like me, witnesses can see their Constitutional right to remain silent wiped away by a judge's pen stroke. From there, activists face immediate jailing if they refuse to cooperate fully. Yet, amazingly few of them do cooperate, so steadfast is their commitment to their cause.

Of course, the government also goes after movements more directly than through the grand jury process, as it did in its "sting" operation against the Arizona Five (Ilse Asplund was added to the original Four). The case ended with Dave Foreman being placed on probation for giving the others $100; everyone else took plea bargains, and Mark Davis and Peg Millett each went to prison for years.[84] The FBI's intention in the Arizona Five sting was to "'send a message'" to Earth First!.[85] The message appears not to have gotten through.

Who Bombed Judi Bari? Don't Ask the FBI

On the other hand, the FBI *was* sent a message—by none other than Judi Bari and Darryl Cherney. As I wrote in Chapter 5, immediately after the car bombing that nearly killed them, the FBI and the Oakland police implicated Bari and Cherney in their own bombing and even arrested them. But soon they were freed as the FBI continued what would prove to be, charitably, a woefully botched investigation and, more appropriately, a deliberate effort to frame the activists.

The bomb, it turned out, was a sophisticated killing machine. It was "time-delayed, motion-triggered, nail studded" and meant to kill Bari (the nails did not match any in her home or car, as erroneously reported after the blast).[86] Even though the FBI's chief explosives expert had written that the bomb was placed out of view beneath the driver's (Bari's) seat, the agents on the scene steadfastly insisted that Bari and Cherney were the only suspects in the attack—or what the victims, given their public and political personas, called the "assassination attempt."

The bombing followed months-long efforts by their opponents to discredit Northern California Earth First!. Using Earth First!'s name, an unknown group distributed "phony press releases calling for violence; fake terrorism manuals; false media stories," and activists received "continuous death threats [and] harassment."[87] Once more, Earth First! was under attack.

But in 1991 the activists turned the tables, suing the FBI and the Oakland Police Department. As the plaintiffs' web page notes, the suit alleged that the FBI and OPD

- falsified, fabricated, and manipulated evidence,

- perjured themselves under oath to get search warrants and high bail,

- conducted a sustained media smear campaign to fool the public,

- blamed the victims, despite clear evidence of their innocence,

- conspired to frame and demonize Judi Bari and Earth First! for political reasons,

- spied on nonviolent environmentalists in a phony investigation of the bombing,

- failed to investigate fingerprints and other evidence pointing to the real bombers, and

- covered up their own wrongdoing and obstruction of justice.[88]

Delay after delay ensued. But finally, on June 11, 2002, following a six-week trial and seventeen days of jury deliberations, the victims became the victors when Bari's estate and Cherney were awarded $4.4 million. As reporter Nicholas Wilson wrote for the pair's hometown online newspaper, "Eighty percent of the damages were for violation of free speech rights under the First Amendment, validating Bari and Cherney's longstanding claim that they were targeted for false charges because of their political activism for the redwoods. The balance of the damages was for the Fourth Amendment violations of false arrest and unlawful search."[89] Both sides appealed the verdict on multiple grounds, and it was not until May 7, 2004, that the case was resolved; all of the appeals were dropped, and the FBI and the city of Oakland paid the plaintiffs $4 million.

The victims were vindicated and, in a too rare moment in the history of U.S. radicalism, justice was served. Immediately after the verdict in 2002, Cherney said, "The American public needs to understand that the FBI can't be trusted. Ten jurors got a good, hard look at the FBI and they didn't like what they saw. Earth First! is known for blockading things like clearcuts. Today we blockaded the FBI from clearcutting the Constitution."[90]

No clear answers emerged from the trial regarding who bombed Bari and Cherney, and we are unlikely ever to know. But the question of why they were attacked may be a bit clearer: When the bombing occurred in 1990, Earth First! was bringing substantial pressure to bear against Northern California timber firms through its massive Redwood Summer protests. Together with an initiative to more strongly regulate timber cutting in the state, Redwood Summer's rallies, marches, and civil disobedience actions threatened timber companies' comfortable, and largely hidden, existence. Go after the leaders, the bombers must have reasoned, and the pressure will be off. They were wrong, as the protests at Headwaters Forest and elsewhere in redwood country demonstrate to this day.

As speculative as any answers to the who and why questions must be, some chilling facts did emerge from the trial. In particular, "the FBI infiltrated and spied on Earth First! almost from its beginning in 1980, with the earliest known FBI report on it dated 1981. Heavily censored FBI documents obtained through [the] suit indicate weekly meetings in spring 1990 between an FBI agent and a secret informant in Northern California. Deposition testimony by Oakland Police Department officers and FBI agents states the FBI had an informant on EF! leaders, and the FBI told OPD that Darryl and Judi were already 'the subjects of an investigation in the terrorist field' when they were bombed. Were they under surveillance when the bomb was placed?"[91]

Radicalizing the Mainstream

One of the most surprising developments in all of environmentalism in recent years was the success of radicals not simply in gaining the mainstream's attention for their causes, as happened at Headwaters and elsewhere, but in actually entering the power elite of the best known of them all, the Sierra Club. Paul Watson, David Brower, and Dave Foreman all have sat on the Club's board of directors since 1995. Moreover, the radicals have managed to encourage bolder positions by the mainstream. For example, in 1996 the Sierra Club membership responded to a nationwide effort by Club rebels Chad Hanson and David Orr by approving a "Zero Cut" policy by a 2-1 vote. Hanson, who was elected to the Board the following year, wrote, "The Sierra Club now joins Earth First!, the Native Forest Council, and many other environmental groups who support ending all logging on public lands nationwide."[92]

On the other hand, when the Sierra Club's members were presented with a referendum that would advocate severe reductions in immigration into the U.S., something Ed Abbey surely would have liked, they voted it down. For once, a Sierra Club fight riled Earth First!ers. Those attending a 1998 activist conference opposed the proposal as "flagrantly racist." However, others found that analysis simplistic, insisting that the issue was not simply immigration or the nation's increasing population, but also Americans' propensity for mass consumption, the nation's policies on free trade, and its support of repressive foreign governments. Earth First! dissenters insisted that effective coalitions with social justice groups would be possible even as it supported reduced immigration, but only if the group took a broader view of the issue.[93]

Gender: No Longer Cowboys and Cowgirls, But . . .

At times, the mere mention of conflict has produced conflict in the movement. Consider gender. Catia Juliana, a member of the editorial collective in 1994, wrote, "On occasion I have heard Earth First!ers doubt whether we should be discussing social issues (such as feminism). After all, aren't we all about saving the wild? What does feminism have to do with ecocentrism? How do these issues fit together, and why should you care?" She answered these questions, and anticipated the post-Seattle activist world, writing, "The problems we deal with as Earth First!ers are inextricably tied to the other ideological pathogens [patriarchy, hierarchy, capitalism, globalization, racism, and anthropocentrism] that are destroying the wild and free peoples throughout the globe."[94]

Seven years later an occasional *Earth First! Journal* contributor using the name of Ed Abbey's heroine in *The Monkeywrench Gang*, Bonnie Abbzug, wrote in a similar vein: "EF! loves quoting, photographing, and fervently following white, financially secure, college-educated men. These boys aren't on the top of the list of who Earth First! needs to be listening to. . . . EF! and the larger environmental movement have some skeletons in the closet that need to be thrown out. Wilderness preservation often meets skepticism from those working for social justice because most environmentalism is very white and middle class. . . ."[95]

More recently still, James John Bell wrote in the *Journal* that Earth First!'s continued grappling with sexism in the movement was essential. "Understanding gender dynamics inside and out of movements for social change is a critical first step for all activists," he insisted.[96] Earth First! is by no means a "boys club." Indeed, in the 1990s it underwent a "feminization," as Douglas Bevington terms it.[97] So today's gender struggles are less about cowboys and women—fundamental gender issues, such as do women have a place on the front lines of environmental resistance movements—and more about the elimination of the last vestiges of inequalities of all kinds among radical activists.

Race: A Continuing Hurdle

Among those inequalities is one that has dogged the movement from its earliest years, and like never before, the radical environmental community finds itself grappling with its lack of racial diversity. Even as its activists work with others from across the oceans to fight corporate globalization, they struggle to attract nonwhites to the cause.

No point of tension between whites in the movement and nonwhites outside of it attracted more attention than the Makah whale hunt. In 1998, after the Makah, a Native American tribe in Washington State, received permission to reinstitute its gray whale hunt after 70 years, Paul Watson pledged to do everything within the Sea Shepherds's ability to halt it.

On the pages of the *Earth First! Journal*, author Jim Page accused Watson of misanthropy and implied that Watson and several of his supporters were racists. In response, the Sea Shepherds wrote, "The view of the Makah whale hunt as strictly a native rights issue and a clash of 'ideologies that pit nature against humanity' is simplistic in the extreme," and they implied that the Makah hoped to sell whale meat to Japanese corporations.[98] Former Sea Shepherd crewmember Rod Coronado, a vegan and a member of the Pasqua Yaqui nation, replied, "The predominantly Anglo environmental and animal rights movements also fail to address the 'eco-imperialism' issue, whereby indigenous peoples are denied the right to self-determination. . . .The *Earth First! Journal* believes that all parties in the Makah whaling issue need to be heard."[99]

The Makah whale hunt debate raged, but it was not the first of its kind. For instance, in 1994 Canadian David Orton wrote, "Environmentalists and organizations who have come forward as promoting alliances with aboriginal peoples . . . seem to present an 'alliance' as merely a blanket endorsement of stated aboriginal positions. One cannot ignore obvious environmental (or social) contradictions within native communities, just as one cannot ignore

contradictions held by non-native environmentalists. . . . Traditional natives and radical environmentalists are working shoulder-to-shoulder on a
number of environmental issues. Yet generally ignored in non-native mainstream (and most of the radical) environmental circles are such contradictions as" First Nations' cooperation with logging and other development,
support for fur trapping and wolf kills, invitations to site nuclear waste
facilities on one Canadian reservation, and advocacy for open dumping of
toxic wastes into oceans.[100]

Those who responded to Orton's article observed that he "focuses only on
native collaborators and mentions indigenous responses to collaboration as
an aside," noting that "indigenous resistance is current and widespread."[101]
Another respondent, noted social ecologist Brian Tokar, observed that First
Nations live the same sort of awkward, sometimes contradictory relationship with the land that many environmentalists enjoy: "Native people are
neither 'model environmentalists' nor are they blind participants in environmental destruction. . . . Native people fighting to protect the land . . . need to
be supported. Those who make compromises with the system, often under
conditions of extreme coercion, need to be approached cautiously and with
understanding of their own precarious situation."[102]

Tensions between Earth First!, in particular, and members of other racial
groups persist as well. "Puck," a former member of the *Earth First! Journal* collective, wrote that in a two-year span "most of the people of color
I know who were once in the Earth First! movement have left—all citing
reasons of racism within the scene." She argued that native peoples are not
the only ones to whom the movement should look for alliances: "We have
allegiances to build in many of the most polluted, oppressive environments
in the U.S. and beyond. . . .

"It's insulting as hell when white people talk about ecological issues like
they're Great White Secrets that people of color don't care about and can't
understand. . . . We would also do well to destroy the stereotype of all environmentalists being white and middle class—because we aren't." Puck
suggested that Earth First! "create a space where marginalized people who
call out shitty, oppressive behavior don't have to deal with a defensive and
reactionary majority. . . . [Y]ou should change things so that people of color
don't keep leaving."[103]

Sentiments like Puck's have dogged Earth First! for years. In the mid-
1990s I met an environmental justice scholar who had read *Eco-Warriors*.
Over lunch, she asked, "Why are Earth First!ers so racist? Why don't they
care about what's going on in the inner cities or with people of color?" I
imagine there is less racism in the movement than in most corners of our
society, but critiques like these point to a fundamental contradiction in
the movement, one that the activists themselves have been attempting to
address over the years, with little success. It probably emerges from the

biocentric perspective and the misanthropy that can easily result from it: If the land matters most, the needs of people—even potential allies—matter little.

On the other hand, some Earth First!ers insist that the movement is deeply concerned with the ways that society's divisions are replicated in the movement. Activist John Johnson wrote that "there is *a lot of work still needed* in EF!, the ecology movement, broader social movements, and society as a whole when it comes to racism, sexism, classism, and the lot." He also noted that in recent years there have been frequent articles in the *Earth First! Journal* "challenging racism and other -isms within and/or outside of the EF! movement."[104]

Indeed, the movement has made halting attempts to reach out to, or at least to understand the needs of, potential allies of color who live in urban areas. In 1999 the *Journal* published an interview with Robert Bullard, who coined the term "environmental justice." Bullard observed, "The EJ movement is an anti-racist movement, and I don't think you can get any more radical than fighting racism. Because when you talk about fighting racism, you make a lot of enemies because racism permeates everything. I think Earth First! can really embrace a lot of the environmental justice principles that we have and see that there are a lot of things that environmental justice groups are advocating and trying to implement that cut across some of the issues that you're addressing."[105] The same year as Seattle, this leader of a vibrant and growing segment of the environmental movement that emphasizes the needs of persons of color and the poor was inviting collaboration with radical environmentalists. It does not appear that his openness was reciprocated.

Also in 1999, one writer encouraged the movement to build on protests in Minnesota declaring a "Minnehaha Free State" near Minneapolis, arguing that doing so "symbolizes a necessary turn off from the forest road Earth First! has been following for nearly two decades." The enemy of wilderness, the writer said, is also the enemy of the working poor: "the multinational corporations who exploit all life and the rich that own them."[106] Of course, Judi Bari's critique—and, increasingly in the 1990s, that of Earth First! and the radical environmental movement generally—centered on the role of corporations, and their supporters in government, in the destruction both of ecological systems and human social systems.

Our Final Hope

Things have only gotten worse for the planet since 1990, when *Eco-Warriors* was first published. Today, we lose species at the rate of 50,000 *per year*, nearly double the estimates of 15 years ago. Global climate change's effects are seen in glaciers that melt at record rates and hurricane seasons that are the worst on record. Mercury from acid deposition, the result of burning coal to generate electricity, contaminates fish in remote lakes. Rainforests continue to be cut down, and the indigenous tribes within them are lost forever. Suburbanization marches zombie-like, unabated. Genetically modified crops—and, soon, animals—dominate food supplies. More and more nations openly violate the international ban on whaling. The litany of environmental wrongs goes on and on.

In contrast, the list of victories for the planet is briefer, but a surprising number of them are attributable to direct action environmentalism. In the course of fifteen years, Headwaters, Warner Creek, Cove/Mallard, and other wild places—large and small, from coast to coast and around the globe—were at least partially saved from saws and development, and illegal fishing around one of the planet's most important ecological centers, the Galapagos Islands, is being curbed. Some of those victories were aided by the mainstream, but few were initially identified by it. Pressured by activists of varying stripes, colleges and universities supervise animal testing laboratories as never before, on occasion sanctioning unethical researchers but often looking for ways to avoid animal testing altogether. Waangari Maathai, mentioned in Chapter 8, won the 2004 Nobel Peace Prize for her struggles for women and the environment in Kenya.

Encouraging as the victories are, the overall picture isn't pretty. Radical environmentalists battle foes who possess everything the insurgents are bereft of: money, influence, and the power they buy. Activists counter with tenacity, daring, creativity, and love. And one other thing, increasingly: numbers. We in the West contribute relatively little to those numbers, though our participation in movements that are a part of the umbrella anticorporate globalization movement is crucial to its success.

It is that latter movement, I suspect, that is the planet's best and final hope. It took the exquisitely organized chaos of Seattle for activists to realize their collective future. It is a future born of globalization's own contradictions, for there are only so many lands, oceans, and cultures that can be destroyed before people resist en masse and on behalf of themselves, their places, one another, and the planet. If the planet, and humanity, are to be saved, it will be through governmental politics—but the governments will be dragged to that point by activists united and willing to sacrifice for, and to make real, a new and harmonious world.

GETTING INVOLVED

Radical environmentalism—and its opposition—has an extensive presence on the internet. Below are sites for a number of the groups mentioned throughout this book or that were helpful to me as I developed the revised concluding chapter. I have also included web addresses for sites that can otherwise help interested readers deepen their understanding of the movement.

ABOVE THE FOLD
Worldwide environmental news articles; mainstream but informative:
http://www.environmentalhealthnews.org/

ANIMAL LIBERATION FRONT
http://www.animalliberationfront.com/
Press Office: http://animalliberationpressoffice.org/

JUDI BARI AND DARRYL CHERNEY LAWSUIT
http://www.judibari.org/

BITE BACK MAGAZINE
Chronicles Animal Liberation Front activities: http://www.directaction.info/index.htms

BUFFALO FIELD CAMPAIGN
http://buffalofieldcampaign.org/

EARTH FIRST!
Includes links to a number of local groups and information about a variety of issues: http://www.earthfirst.org/
Site for the Earth First! Journal: http://www.earthfirstjournal.org/

ENVIRONMENTAL ETHICS
http://www.cep.unt.edu/

EARTH LIBERATION FRONT
http://www.earthliberationfront.com/

GREEN THEORY AND PRAXIS
On-line, interdisciplinary scholarly journal: http://greentheoryandpraxis.
csufresno.edu/main.asp

HEADWATERS FOREST
Each of these sites highlights the struggle for California's ancient forests:
Bay Area Coalition for Headwaters Forest: http://headwaterspreserve.org/
Jail Hurwitz: http://www.jailhurwitz.com/
Sacred Redwood: http://www.sacredredwood.org/

IN DEFENSE OF ANIMALS
http://www.idausa.org/

LAST CHANCE FOR ANIMALS
http://www.lcanimal.org/

LOWBAGGER
Mike Roselle and cohorts' site for commentary and exhortation:
http://lowbagger.org/

MUSIC
*This page from Darryl Cherney's website includes links to other activist
musicians' own sites*: http://darrylcherney.com/links.htm

PEOPLE FOR THE ETHICAL TREATMENT OF ANIMALS
http://www.peta.org/

RAINFOREST ACTION NETWORK
http://www.ran.org/

RAINFOREST INFORMATION CENTRE
http://www.rainforestinfo.org.au/

REWILDING INSTITUTE
Created by Dave Foreman: http://rewilding.org/

RUCKUS SOCIETY
http://www.ruckus.org/

SEA SHEPHERD CONSERVATION SOCIETY
http://seashepherd.org/

STOP HUNTINGTON ANIMAL CRUELTY
http://www.shac.net/

WESTERN FIRE ECOLOGY CENTER
*Created by an Earth First! activist, it includes a number of scholarly papers on
fire ecology*: http://www.fire-ecology.org/

ERRATA

Page 19—Glen Canyon Dam was the result of a compromise that saved Dinosaur National Monument and was constructed before the Grand Canyon Dam fight.

Page 24—Most of the acreage proposed by Earth First! for wilderness designation in Arizona was not part of RARE II; it was under the control of agencies other than the Forest Service.

Page 38—Typically, the minimum size for wilderness designation is 5,000 acres (though some smaller wilderness areas have been designated).

Page 69—Foreman's birth city was Albuquerque; his birth year was 1945.

Page 62—The first Round River Rendezvous was in 1980 at T-Cross Ranch in Wyoming. The second, also the first Sagebrush Patriots' Rally, was in 1981 in Moab.

Page 65—At the Little Granite Creek Rendezvous, the 300 people in attendance marched roughly a quarter mile and symbolically blockaded the road; they did not remove all of the survey stakes.

Page 74—By 1991, *Ecodefense* had sold 25,000 copies.

Page 86—Ilse Asplund's last name is misspelled.

Page 86—One person who heard the FBI tapes of Fain's conversations with the Earth First!ers on May 30 has told me that Fain did not object to Davis's practice run with the blowtorch—the FBI agent encouraged it.

Page 89—The "puke-in" occurred in Bellingham, Washington.

Page 90—Nancy Zierenberg's last name is misspelled.

Page 90—I have been informed that Bari's claim of being only the second woman to receive a grant from the Earth First! Foundation is incorrect.

Pages 205–210—Lee Dessaux has been correctly spelled as Lee Dessauxxx, per his preference at the time.

NOTES

Chapter 1.   GANDHI MEETS THE LUDDITES

1. Interview with Myra Finkelstein, Palo Alto, California, January 29, 1990.
2. For the story of Watson's attempts to stop the B.C. wolf hunt, see: Robert Hunter and Paul Watson, *Cry Wolf!* (Vancouver, Canada: Shepherds of the Earth, 1985).
3. Interview with John Lilburn, Missoula, Montana, November 14, 1989.
4. Finkelstein interview.
5. Interview with Sue Rodriguez-Pastor, Davis, California, February 2, 1990.
6. Genesis 1:28, translated in *The New English Bible* (New York: Oxford University, 1970), p. 2.
7. Roderick Frazier Nash, *The Rights of Nature* (Madison, Wisconsin: University of Wisconsin, 1989), p. 113.
8. Comment by Michael Robinson on a draft of this chapter.
9. Interview with Jamie Sayen, Asheville, North Carolina, October 27, 1989.
10. M.K. Gandhi, *Non-Violent Resistance* (New York: Schocken Books, 1951), p. 379.
11. Ibid., p. 3.
12. Interview with Roger Featherstone, Tucson, Arizona, November 7, 1989.
13. Interview with John Seed, Lismore, New South Wales, Australia, taped answers to the author's questions in March 1990.
14. Stephen Fox, *The American Conservation Movement: John Muir and His Legacy* (Madison, Wisconsin: University of Wisconsin, 1985), p. 352.
15. Malcolm I. Thomis, *The Luddites: Machine-Breaking in Regency England* (Hamden, Connecticut: Archon Books, 1970), p. 159.
16. Interview with Darryl Cherney, Piercy, California, August 29, 1989.
17. Jon Stewart, "The Enforcer," *San Francisco Chronicle*, July 7, 1989, p. B3.
18. Keith Schneider, "Old and New Worlds Collide over Spray Plan," *New York Times*, August 18, 1989, p. A7.
19. "Bulgaria's First Mass Protest Under Communism," *San Francisco Chronicle*, November 4, 1989, p. A12.
20. Bill McKibben, *The End of Nature* (New York: Random House, 1989), p. 210.

Chapter 2.   A QUESTION OF COMPROMISE

1. Interview with Michael McCloskey, San Francisco, California, December 14, 1989.
2. Interview with Ben Beach, Washington, D.C., October 30, 1989.
3. John Muir, *The Yosemite* (San Francisco: Sierra Club, 1988), p. 191.
4. Ibid., pp. 196-197.
5. Stephen Fox, *The American Conservation Movement: John Muir and His Legacy* (Madison, Wisconsin: University of Wisconsin, 1985), p. 279.
6. David R. Brower, *For Earth's Sake: The Life and Times of David Brower* (Salt Lake City: Gibbs Smith, 1990), p. 365.
7. David Brower, Letter to Doug Scott, Conservation Director, Sierra Club, July 13, 1989 This letter is published in full in the first volume of Brower's autobiography, *For Earth's*

Sake, pp. 436-443.

8. Fox, *The American Conservation Movement*, p. 322.
9. Brower, Letter to Doug Scott.
10. Interview with David Brower, Visalia, California, October 20, 1989.
11. Ibid.
12. McCloskey interview.
13. Interview with Mike Roselle, San Francisco, California, July 28, 1989.
14. Beach interview.
15. Aldo Leopold, "The Land Ethic," in *A Sand County Almanac* (New York: Ballantine, 1966), p. 246.
16. Interview with Howie Wolke, Darby, Montana, November 13, 1989.
17. Interview with John Lilburn, Missoula, Montana, November 14, 1989.
18. Roselle interview.
19. Interview with Peter Steinhart, Palo Alto, California, January 8, 1990.
20. McCloskey interview.
21. Interview with Dave Foreman, Visalia, California, October 20, 1989.
22. Interview with Jim Norton, Phoenix, Arizona, November 8, 1989.
23. McCloskey interview.
24. Norton interview.
25. Foreman interview.
26. Norton interview.
27. McCloskey interview.
28. Roselle interview.
29. McCloskey interview.
30. Ibid.
31. Ibid.

Chapter 3.   ECOLOGY MEETS PHILOSOPHY

1. Interview with Darryl Cherney, Piercy, California, August 29, 1989.
2. Ibid.
3. Interview with Nancy Burnet, Riverside, California, November 6, 1989.
4. Roderick Frazier Nash, *The Rights of Nature* (Madison, Wisconsin: University of Wisconsin,1989), pp. 16-17.
5. Charles Petit, "Amazon Forest Is Shockingly Fragile," in *San Francisco Chronicle,* September 28, 1989, p. A1ff.
6. John Muir, *My First Summer in the Sierra* (Boston: Houghton Mifflin, 1911), p. 157.
7. Bill Devall and George Sessions, *Deep Ecology* (Layton, Utah: Gibbs M. Smith, 1985), p. 48.
8. Quoted in Aldo Leopold, *A Sand County Almanac* (New York: Ballantine, 1966), p. 197.
9. Devall and Sessions, *Deep Ecology*, p. 66.
10. See diagram, Devall and Sessions, *Deep Ecology*, p. 227.
11. Ibid., p. 14.
12. Poster in the Sequoia National Park Visitors' Center.
13. Bill Devall, letter to the author, October 30, 1989.
14. Devall and Sessions, *Deep Ecology*, p. 69.
15. This is the working definition used by Dave Foreman and Howie Wolke in *The Big Outside: A Descriptive Inventory of the Big Wilderness Areas of the U.S.* (Tucson, Arizona: Ned Ludd, 1989), p. 17.
16. Quoted in Devall and Sessions, *Deep Ecology*, p. 73.
17. Bill Devall, *Simple in Means, Rich in Ends* (Layton, Utah: Gibbs Smith, 1988), p. 156.
18. Ibid., p. 128.
19. Devall and Sessions, *Deep Ecology*, p. 17.
20. Interview with Dave Foreman, Visalia, California, October 20, 1989.
21. Devall and Sessions, *Deep Ecology*, p. 76.
22. Interview with Bill Devall, Trinidad, California, August 31, 1989.

23. Devall, *Simple in Means, Rich in Ends*, pp. 197-198.
24. Karen J. Warren, "The Power and the Promise of Ecological Feminism," *Environmental Ethics* 12:2 (Summer 1990), p. 125-126.
25. Ibid., p. 132.
26. Ynestra King, "The Ecology of Feminism and the Feminism of Ecology" in Judith Plant, ed., *Healing the Wounds: The Promise of Ecofeminism* (Philadelphia: New Society, 1989), p. 23.
27. Ibid., p. 18.
28. Marti Kheel, "Ecofeminism and Deep Ecology: Reflections on Identity and Difference," unpublished manuscript, p. 7.
29. Ibid., p. 15.
30. Ibid., p. 29.
31. Janet Biehl, "It's Deep, But Is It Broad? An Eco-Feminist Looks at Deep Ecology," *Kick It Over* (special supplement, date unknown), p. 2A.
32. Warren, "The Power and the Promise," p. 138.
33. Marti Kheel, "Animal Liberation and Environmental Ethics: Can Ecofeminism Bridge The Gap?" p. 17.
34. Interview with Marti Kheel, Oakland, California, April 6, 1990.
35. Kheel, "Animal Liberation and Environmental Ethics," p. 14. Kheel is citing Harriet Schleiffer, "Images of Death and Life: Food Production and the Vegetarian Option" in Peter Singer, ed., *In Defense of Animals* (New York: Basil Blackwell, 1985), pp. 63-73.
36. Kheel, "Animal Liberation and Environmental Philosophy," p. 15.
37. Kheel, "Ecofeminism and Deep Ecology," p. 30.
38. Kheel interview.

Chapter 4.   GREENPEACE: Bridge To Radicalism

1. Much of the background information about Greenpeace in this chapter comes from Robert Hunter's thorough history of the group's early years, *Warriors of the Rainbow : A Chronicle of the Greenpeace Movement* (New York: Holt, Rinehart, and Winston, 1979).
2. David Day, *The Whale War* (San Francisco: Sierra Club, 1987), pp. 124-126. In May 1990 a French tribunal admitted that France broke its agreement with New Zealand when it brought home two commandos who were convicted in the bombing from their prison on a Pacific island before their sentences were served. However, because the time frame for the three-year sentences arranged for by the United Nations had already passed, the two were not required to return to jail. See: "Tribunal Faults France for Freeing Bomber-Spies," *San Francisco Chronicle*, May 8, 1990, p. A20.
3. Hunter, *Warriors of the Rainbow*, p. 123.
4. Telephone interview with Peter Bahouth, March 7, 1990.
5. Ibid.
6. Ibid.
7. Telephone interview with Peter Dykstra, March 8, 1990.
8. Interview with Michael Robinson, Boulder, Colorado, November 11, 1989.
9. Dykstra interview.
10. Bahouth interview.
11. Interview with Paul Watson, Poulsbo, Washington, November 24, 1989.
12. Roderick Frazier Nash, *The Rights of Nature* (Madison, Wisconsin: University of Wisconsin, 1989), p. 191.

Chapter 5.   EARTH FIRST!: Cracking the Mold

1. Earth Image Films, *The Cracking of Glen Canyon Damn*.
2. Ibid.
3. Ibid.
4. Interview with Dave Foreman, Visalia, California, October 2, 1989.

5. Telephone interview with Ron Kezar, March 31, 1990.
6. Interview with Mike Roselle, San Francisco, California, July 28, 1989.
7. Interview with Howie Wolke, Darby, Montana, November, 13, 1989.
8. Ibid.
9. Ibid.
10. Roselle interview.
11. Foreman interview.
12. Dave Foreman's October 1981 article in *Progressive* was reprinted in *Earth First! Journal* 2:3 (February 2, 1982), pp. 4-5.
13. Roselle interview.
14. Ibid.
15. Ibid.
16. Ibid.
17. "Wilderness Preserve System," *Earth First! Journal* 3:5 (June 21, 1983), p.9.
18. Interview with "Diamondback" (location withheld at interviewee's request), January 31, 1990.
19. Jamie Sayen, "Taking Steps Toward a Restoration Ethic," *Earth First! Journal* 9:5 (May 1, 1989), p. 16.
20. Dave Foreman and Howie Wolke, *The Big Outside: A Descriptive Inventory of the Big Wilderness Areas of the U.S.* (Tucson, Arizona: Ned Ludd, 1989), p. 71.
21. Interview with Karen Wood, Eugene, Oregon, January 31, 1990.
22. Ibid.
23. Foreman interview.
24. Wood interview.
25. Roselle interview.
26. Dave Foreman, "Editorial," *Earth First! Journal* 2:5 (May 1, 1982), p. 2.
27. Foreman interview.
28. Interview with Karen Pickett, Berkeley, California, September 28, 1989.
29. Interview with Greg King, Visalia, California, October 20, 1989.
30. Interview with Leslie Sellgrin, Phoenix, Arizona, November 8, 1989.
31. Roselle interview.
32. Pete Dustrud in *Earth First! Journal* 2:7 (August 1, 1982), p. 2.
33. "The Open Page," *Earth First! Journal* 2:2 (December 21, 1981), p. 6.
34. Foreman interview.
35. Ibid.
36. Ibid.
37. Leroy Watson, in "The Open Page," *Earth First! Journal* 2:2 (December 21, 1981), p. 6.
38. Raging Bull Avengers, "Attention Responsible Officials and Editors!" *Portland Free Press* 1:8 (February 1990), p. 3.
39. Mike Roselle, "Meares Island: Canada's Old Growth Struggle," *Earth First! Journal* 5:3 (February 2, 1985), p. 1ff; Dear Ned Ludd, "Spike Those Trees!" *Earth First Journal* 5:5 (May 1, 1985), p. 31.
40. Michael Robinson, unpublished letter, April 1990.
41. Michael A. Kerrick, Forest Supervisor, Willamette National Forest, "Ecotage from Our Perspective: An Explanation of The Willamette National Forest's Policy on Environmental Sabotage Known as 'Ecotage,'" mimeograph, Willamette National Forest, September 1985.
42. Roselle interview.
43. Ibid.
44. Dave Foreman and Bill Haywood, eds., *Ecodefense: A Field Guide to Monkeywrenching*, 2nd ed. (Tucson, Arizona: Ned Ludd, 1987), p. 34.
45. Eric Brazil, "Tree Spiking in Mendocino Splinters All Sides," *San Francisco Examiner*, June 21, 1987, p. B-1.
46. Peter Steinhart, "Respecting the Law: There Must Be Limits to Environmental Protest," *Audubon* 89:6 (November 1987), p. 12.
47. Ibid., p. 13.

48. Roselle interview.
49. Ibid.
50. Pickett interview.
51. Ibid.
52. Ibid.
53. Ibid.
54. Sellgrin interview.
55. Ibid.
56. Green Ribbon Coalition, "Don't Be Fooled by Corporations," mimeograph.
57. Interview with Judi Bari, San Francisco, California, September 1, 1989.
58. Ibid.
59. Paul Grabowicz and Harry Harris, "Lab Tests Fail to Link Bomb with Items at Bari's Home," *Oakland Tribune*, July 18, 1990, p.A10.
60. Much of the information regarding the investigation and arrests of Earth First!ers was drawn from the following sources, most of which are redundant: Dale S. Turner, "FBI Attacks Earth First! Foreman, Millett, 2 Others Arrested," *Earth First! Journal* Special Edition (June 16, 1989), p. 1ff; Dean Kuipers, "Razing Arizona: Earth First! Last Roundup," *Spin* 5:6 (September 1989), pp. 32-38; Susan Zakin, "Earth First!," *Smart* 5 (September-October 1989), pp. 88-94; Nancy Schute, "Dave Foreman Meets the Feds," *Outside* (September 1989), pp. 15-16.
61. Kuipers, "Razing Arizona," p. 38.
62. Interview with John Lilburn, Missoula, Montana, November 14, 1989.
63. "Arizona 4 Update," *Earth First! Journal* 10:1 (November 1, 1989), p. 1.
64. Foreman interview.
65. Robinson letter.
66. Edward Abbey, "A Response to Schmookler on Anarchy," *Earth First! Journal* 6:7 (August 1, 1986), p. 22. The anarchy debate within Earth First! took off after a review of Andrew Bard Schmookler's book, *The Parable of the Tribes*. Other especially valuable essays in this series include: Andrew Bard Schmookler, "Schmookler on Anarchy," *Earth First! Journal* 6:5 (May 1, 1986), p. 22; Jamie Sayen, "'Anarchy' is Baggage," *Earth First! Journal* 7:4 (March 20, 1987), p. 36; Robert Goodrich, "Government and Anarchy," *Earth First! Journal* 7:8 (September 23, 1987), p. 24; and Christoph Manes, "An Anarchist Replies to Schmookler's Reply to the Anarchists," *Earth First! Journal* 7:8 (September 23, 1987), p. 25.
67. Mike Jakubal, "Why I Did It, Why I'll Never Do It Again...," *Live Wild or Die* 1 (February 1989), p. 2.
68. Chaco, "My Anti-Editorial," *Live Wild or Die* 1 (February 1989), p. 2.
69. Feral Faun, "Beyond Earth First!: Toward a Feral Revolution of Desire," *Live Wild or Die* 1 (February 1989), p. 16.
70. Ibid.
71. Foreman interview.
72. Bari interview.
73. Foreman interview.
74. Interview with Rick Bernardi, Palo Alto, California, October 1, 1989.
75. Interview with Nancy Zirenberg, Tucson, Arizona, November 7, 1989.
76. Bari interview.
77. Pickett interview.
78. Miss Ann Thropy, "Population and AIDS," *Earth First! Journal* 7:5 (May 1, 1987), p. 32.
79. Ibid.
80. Ibid.
81. Miss Ann Thropy, "Miss Ann Thropy Responds to 'Alien-Nation,'" *Earth First! Journal* 8:2 (December 22, 1987), p. 17.
82. Quoted in a draft chapter furnished by Foreman from his forthcoming book, *Confessions of an Eco-Brute*.
83. Edward Abbey, "Immigration and Liberal Taboos," in *One Life at a Time, Please* (New York: Henry Holt, 1988), p. 42.
84. Ibid., p. 44.

85. Ramon G. McLeod, "Earth's Population to Hit 8.2 Billion by Year 2020," *San Francisco Chronicle*, December 8, 1989, p. A2. This article notes, "The spread of AIDS, especially in Africa, is having virtually no effect on [world] population growth." Even with programs like the controversial one-child-per-marriage efforts of the Chinese, world population is growing at 1.8 percent per year. It now stands at 5.2 billion and is predicted to increase 3 billion over the next thirty years.

86. William R. Catton, *Overshoot: The Ecological Basis for Revolutionary Change* (Urbana, Illinois: University of Illinois, 1980).

87. Foreman, draft of *Confessions of an Eco-Brute*.

88. Richard N. Gardner, "Bush, the U.N. and Too Many People," *New York Times*, September 22, 1989, p. A19. Abbey mentions contraception in his immigration article in passing but makes no effort to consider the benefits of its widespread use.

89. Foreman interview.

90. Interview with Roger Featherstone, Tucson, Arizona, November 7, 1989.

91. Bari interview.

92. Roselle interview.

93. Charles Bowden, "Dave Foreman! In the Face of Reality," *Buzzworm* 2:2 (March/April 1990), p. 51.

Chapter 6.   THE SEA SHEPHERDS: Bringing Justice to the High Seas

1. Paul Watson, *Sea Shepherd* (New York: W.W. Norton, 1982), p. 70.

2. Interview with Paul Watson, Poulsbo, Washington, November 26, 1989.

3. Watson, *Sea Shepherd*, p. 214-215.

4. Ibid., p. 11.

5. Ibid., p. 212.

6. Watson interview.

7. Watson, *Sea Shepherd*, pp. 225-251.

8. Ibid., p. 250.

9. Robert Hunter, *Warriors of the Rainbow: A Chronicle of the Greenpeace Movement* (New York: Holt, Rinehart and Winston, 1979), p. 11.

10. Ibid., pp. 376-377.

11. Ibid., pp. 387-388.

12. Watson interview.

13. Ibid.

14. Telephone interview with Peter Dykstra, March 8, 1990.

15. Watson interview.

16. Ibid.

17. Ibid.

18. Ibid.

19. Ibid.

20. Interview with Scott Trimingham, Redondo Beach, California, November 6, 1989.

21. Interview with Rod Coronado, Davis, California, February 2, 1990.

22. Watson, *Sea Shepherd*, p. 153.

23. Watson interview.

24. Ibid.

25. M.K. Gandhi, *Non-Violent Resistance* (New York: Schocken, 1951), p. 161.

26. For more on Gandhi's philosophy and praxis, including vegetarianism, see Geoffrey Ashe's comprehensive biography of the Mahatma: *Gandhi* (New York: Stein and Day, 1980).

27. Watson interview.

28. Trimingham interview.

29. Coronado interview.

30. Interview with Myra Finkelstein, Palo Alto, California, January 28, 1990.

31. Trimingham interview.

32. Finkelstein interview.
33. Ibid.
34. Coronado interview.
35. Interview with Sue Rodriguez-Pastor, Davis, California, February 2, 1990.
36. Kenneth Brower, "The Destruction of Dolphins," *The Atlantic Monthly*, July 1989, pp. 35-58.
37. Finkelstein interview.
38. Rodriguez-Pastor interview.
39. Ibid.
40. Finkelstein interview.
41. Watson interview.
42. Ibid.

Chapter 7.   ANIMAL LIBERATION: From Labs to Hunt Sabs

1. Interview with Rufus Cohen, Clearlake, California, October 22, 1989.
2. Interview with Rick Bernardi, Palo Alto, California, October 10, 1989.
3. For the most widely-read statement of this position, see Peter Singer, *Animal Liberation*, second edition, (New York: Random House, 1990). Although this newest edition is a fully-revised version of his original book, published in 1975, and is quite thought-provoking, Animal Liberation philosophy has progressed far beyond the arguments that Singer continues to espouse.
4. Cohen interview.
5. See the last two chapters in: John Robbins, *Diet for a New America* (Walpole, New Hampshire: Stillpoint, 1987).
6. See comment, note 3.
7. Henry Spira, "Fighting to Win," in Peter Singer, ed., *In Defense of Animals* (New York: Basil Blackwell, 1985), p. 196.
8. Ibid., p. 199.
9. Physicians Committee for Responsible Medicine, "Beyond the Draize Test: World War II-Era Test is Cruel, Obsolete," pamphlet.
10. Douglas Starr quoted in Roderick Frazier Nash, *The Rights of Nature* (Madison, Wisconsin: University of Wisconsin, 1989), p. 188.
11. Alex Pacheco, "The Silver Spring Monkeys" in Singer, ed., *In Defense of Animals*, pp. 135-147.
12. Interview with Elliot Katz, Corte Madera, California, March 1, 1990.
13. Ibid.
14. People for the Ethical Treatment of Animals, "History of American Animal Liberation Actions," mimeograph, Revised July 6, 1989; and "Animal Liberation," *PETA News* 4:4 (July/August 1989), p. 13.
15. Nash, *The Rights of Nature*, pp. 17-18.
16. Interview with Marti Kheel, Oakland, California, April 6, 1990.
17. Ibid.
18. Interview with Rod Coronado, Davis, California, February 2, 1990.
19. Interview with Kim Stallwood, Rockville, Maryland, October 30, 1989.
20. People for the Ethical Treatment of Animals, "History of American Animal Liberation Actions."
21. "Vet School Deans May be Targets," *San Francisco Chronicle*, February 26, 1990, p. A8.
22. Jack Rosenberger, "Animal Rites," *Village Voice* 35:10 (March 6, 1990), p. 32.
23. "Texas Tech Exposed," *PETA News* 4:6 (November/December 1989), p. 16.
24. "ALF Talks," *PETA News* 4:6 (November/December 1989), p. 17.
25. "The 'Terrorist' Label: How to Neutralize It," *Animals' Agenda* 9:7 (September 1989), pp. 39-42.
26. Katz interview.
27. Bernardi interview.

28. Kheel interview.
29. Stallwood interview.
30. See: Robbins, *Diet for a New America*, pp. 112-121.
31. Ibid., p. 352.
32. Ibid., p. 367.
33. "Fur Facts: How They Live" and "Fur Facts: How They Die," *PETA News* 4:3 (May/June 1989), pp. 8-9.
34. "Montana Beavers," *PETA News* 4:1 (January/February 1989), pp. 14-15; and "Montana Beavers Win Round 2," *PETA News* 4:4 (July/August 1989), p. 6.
35. Anne-Marie Schiro, "Fake Furs are Saving Skins," *New York Times*, October 5, 1989, p. B1.
36. Dave Foreman and Howie Wolke, *The Big Outside: A Descriptive Inventory of the Big Wilderness Areas of the U.S.* (Tucson, Arizona: Ned Ludd, 1989), p.40.
37. Dave Foreman and Bill Haywood, eds., *Ecodefense: A Field Guide to Monkeywrenching*, 2nd ed. (Tucson, Arizona: Ned Ludd, 1987), pp. 165-169.
38. Interview with Nancy Burnet, Riverside, California, November 6, 1989.
39. Ibid.
40. "Paws for Thought," *PETA News* 4:4 (July/August 1989), p. 12.
41. Burnet interview.
42. "Berosini Busted!" *PETA News* 4:6 (November/December 1989), pp. 3-7.
43. Jim Mason, "A Trip to the World's Largest Exotic Animal Auction," *Animals' Agenda* 9:5 (June 1989), pp. 46-47.
44. *60 Minutes* broadcast, January 21, 1990.
45. Burnet interview.
46. "AMA Animal Research Action Plan," June 1989. Supplied by People for the Ethical Treatment of Animals.
47. Charlotte R. Otto, Director, Issues Management, Proctor & Gamble Company, "Animal Testing Coalition," Memorandum and Attachments, June 9, 1989. Supplied by People for the Ethical Treatment of Animals.
48. E. Edward Kavanaugh, President, Cosmetic, Toiletry, and Fragrance Association, Letter to Membership, June 27, 1989. Supplied by People for the Ethical Treatment of Animals.
49. Frederick K. Goodwin, Director of Intramural Research, National Institute of Mental Health, Memorandum to Lowell T. Harmison, Deputy Assistant Secretary for Health, "Reflections Following the 9/28/87 Meeting on the Animal Rights' Movement," September 29, 1987. Supplied by People for the Ethical Treatment of Animals.
50. Stallwood interview.
51. Ibid.
52. Diane Alters, "Private Eyes Are Watching Activists, Monitoring Issues," *San Francisco Examiner*, July 16, 1989, p. A2.
53. Merritt Clifton, "Earth First! Founder Busted in Possible Set-Up," *Animals' Agenda* 9:7 (September 1989), p. 20.
54. Interview with "Mel," place and date withheld at interviewee's request.
55. Ibid.
56. Ibid.

Chapter 8.   RADICAL ENVIRONMENTALISM'S INTERNATIONAL FACE

1. Philip Windeatt, "'They Clearly Now See the Link,'" in Peter Singer, ed., *In Defense of Animals* (New York: Basil Blackwell, 1985), p. 190.
2. Interview with Kim Stallwood, Rockville, Maryland, October 30, 1989.
3. Ibid.
4. Ibid.
5. "Harrods to Quit Selling Furs—Few Buyers," *San Francisco Chronicle*, February 15, 1990, p. A23.
6. Supplement to *Front Line News* 4 (Spring 1988).
7. Ibid.

8. Interview with Greg King, Visalia, California, October 20, 1989.
9. Douglas Stanglin, "Seizing the Politics of Pollution," *U.S. News and World Report* 101:23 (December 8, 1986), p. 45.
10 Alan B. Durning, "Worldwide Drive to Save the Earth," *San Francisco Chronicle*, June 6, 1989, p. A27.
11. Clyde Haberman, "Hearing Cheers Bulgaria's Dissidents," *New York Times*, November 14, 1989, p. A9.
12. "Bulgaria Expels Environmentalists," *San Francisco Chronicle*, April 11, 1989, p. A18.
13. "Havel: Communists Ruined Economy, Environment," *Peninsula Times Tribune*, January 2, 1990, p. A3.
14. "Czechoslovakia Turning Green," *San Francisco Chronicle*, March 19, 1990, p. A13.
15. Murray Feshbach and Ann Rubin, "Environmental Crises Join Soviet List of Headaches," *San Francisco Chronicle*, February 14, 1990, p. Briefing-4.
16. Photograph and caption, *Environment* 30:10 (December 1988), p. 4.
17. Dimitri Devyatkin, "Report from Estonia: An Interview with a Leader of the Green Movement," *Environment* 30:10 (December 1988), p. 15.
18. Rasa Gustaitis, "Greens Spearhead Baltic Movement," *San Francisco Chronicle*, July 26, 1989, p. Briefing-1.
19. "Greens Do Well in Tasmania Election," *San Francisco Chronicle*, May 15, 1989, p. A17.
20. Roberto Suro, "Suddenly, Italians Express Anger over Pollution," *New York Times*, November 18, 1988, p. A3.
21. "'Seething Spuds' Irate, So They Mash Potatoes," *Peninsula Times Tribune*, August 13, 1989, p. A2.
22. Interview with John Seed, Lismore, New South Wales, Australia, taped answers to the author's questions in March 1990.
23. Ibid.
24. Ibid.
25. Francisco "Chico" Mendes Filho, "Antihero," *Spin* 5:6 (September 1989), p. 76.
26. Ibid., p. 78.
27. Ibid.
28. Susanna Hecht and Alexander Cockburn, "Hecht and Cockburn's Reply," *The Nation* 249:8 (September 18, 1989), p. 292.
29. Mendes, "Antihero," p. 78.
30. Interview with Randy Hayes, San Francisco, California, March 16, 1990.
31. Susanna Hecht and Alexander Cockburn, "Fire Fighters," *Metro* 5:52 1/2, p. 12.
32. "'Green Fund' Fails," *Peninsula Times Tribune*, May 9, 1990, p. A-5.
33. Hayes interview.
34. Ibid.
35. Chris Vaughan, "Hawaii Natives Steamed at Geothermal Project," *San Francisco Chronicle*, April 3, 1990, p. B6.
36. Hayes interview.
37. Ibid.
38. The primary source for information regarding the Penan was numerous issues of the *World Rainforest Report*, published by the Rainforest Information Centre, P.O. Box 368, Lismore, 2480, Australia.
39. Charles Petit, "Rain Forest Group Urges Wood Boycott," *San Francisco Chronicle*, November 3, 1989, p. A17.
40. Hayes interview.
41. Chip Fay, "One for the Spirits," *Sierra* 72:2 (March/April 1987), p. 22.
42. Ibid., pp. 23-24.
43. Jane Perlez, "Skyscraper's Foe Draws Daily Scorn," *New York Times*, December 6, 1989, p. A6.
44. "Kids Storm Talks on Elephants To Demand Ban on Ivory Trade," *San Francisco Chronicle*, October 12, 1989, p. A26.
45. Dana Sachs, "Local Heroes," *Sierra* 73:5 (September/October 1988), p. 80.
46. Ibid.
47. Joan Hamilton, "A Grassroots Rebuff for Du Pont," *Sierra* 72:3 (May/June 1987), p. 68.

48. Ibid., p. 69.
49. Barbara Crossette, "A Gandhi Whose Cause is Animals," *New York Times*, April 24, 1989, p. A4.
50. Ibid.
51. Barbara Crossette, "Water, Water Everywhere? Many Now Say 'No!'" *New York Times*, October 7, 1989, p. 4.
52. Ibid.
53. Information for this section comes from Mark Shepard's book *Gandhi Today* (Cabin John, Maryland: Seven Locks, 1987), pp. 63-80.
54. Ibid., p. 75.
55. Ibid., p. 80.
56. Fay, "One for the Spirits," p. 24.

Chapter 9. HANGING GEORGE WASHINGTON'S BIB

1. Mike Roselle was interviewed in San Francisco, California, on July 28, August 3, August 25, and August 29, 1989. These are the sources of all quotes attributed to him.
2. On August 6, 1986, Greenpeace activists climbed the scaffolding supporting the Statue of Liberty during its restoration. They hung an American flag and a banner reading "GIVE ME LIBERTY FROM NUCLEAR WEAPONS TESTING, GREENPEACE." Four were arrested. The photo appeared the next day on page one of the *New York Times'* second section. *New York Times*, photograph, August 7, 1986, page B1.

Chapter 10.   NOT JUST TREE HUGGERS ANYMORE

1. Interview with Darryl Cherney, San Francisco, California, September 1, 1989. This is the source of all other statements attributed to Cherney.
2. Interview with Greg King, Visalia, California, October 20, 1989. This is the source of all other statements attributed to King.
3. Interview with Judi Bari, San Francisco, California, September 1, 1989. This is the source of all other statements attributed to Bari.
4. All of the women taking part in this action used pseudonyms to avoid prosecution.
5. Interview with Hellen Woods, Berkeley, California, February 8, 1990. This is the source of all other statements attributed to Woods.
6. Interview with John Lilburn, Missoula, Montana, November 14, 1989. This is the source of all other statements attributed to Lilburn.
7. Interview with Karen Wood, Eugene, Oregon, January 31, 1990. This is the source of all other statements attributed to Wood.

Chapter 11.   RAID ON REYKJAVIK

1. All quotations and comments attributed to Rod Coronado are from an interview with him that took place at Davis, California, on February 2, 1990.
2. Interview with Paul Watson, Poulsbo, Washington, November 24, 1989. This is the source of all other quotations and comments attributed to him.
3. Telephone interview with David Howitt, February 12, 1990. All other quotations and comments attributed to Howitt took place during this conversation. This is the source of all other quotations and comments attributed to him.
4. Interview with Scott Trimingham, Redondo Beach, California, November 6, 1989.
5. "Whaling Commission Refuses to Lift Ban on Hunting," *San Francisco Chronicle*, July 6, 1990, p. A19.

Chapter 12. A CROWD ON A CRANE

1. Interview with Todd Patterson, Clearlake, California, October 22, 1989. This is the source of all other statements attributed to Patterson.
2. International Society for Animal Rights, "Underground Animal Research Laboratory Proposed at UCB: Lab To Be Built with Your Tax Dollars!," mimeograph, January 1987.
3. Murry J. Cohen, M.D., Director of the Medical Research Modernization Committee and Associate Psychiatrist, Lenox Hill Hospital, New York City, in a letter to Douglas R. Blaine, February 19, 1987. Document supplied by In Defense of Animals.
4. Betsy Swart, "Direct Action for Animals Coast-to-Coast: U.C. Berkeley," *Perspective: The In Defense of Animals Quarterly Newsletter* 2:4 (Fall 1987), p. 1.
5. Interview with Dr. Elliot Katz, Corte Madera, California, March 1, 1990. This is the source of all other statements attributed to Katz.
6. Telephone interview with Lee Dessauxxx, March 10, 1990. This is the source of all other statements attributed to Dessauxxx.
7. Debra Levi Holtz, "New Challenges to Animal Lab at UC Berkeley," *San Francisco Chronicle*, March 17, 1990, p. A5.

Chapter 13. ON THE WARPATH WITH ANNA, MEL, AND LIB

1. The names of the Animal Liberators described in this chapter have been changed and information about them has also been altered. In some instances, the locations of their actions were felt to be so sensitive that they asked that certain details be withheld or altered prior to publication.
2. "'Gotcha' Loma Linda," *Liberator* 1988 (compendium of newspaper clippings and original articles published by the Animal Liberation Front Support Group), p. 1ff.
3. "Interviews with Animal Liberation Front Activists, *Liberator*, 1988, p. 12.

Chapter 14. IN THE WILD WITH "THE TOWN CRIER OF THE GLOBAL VILLAGE"

1. All quotations and comments attributed to John Seed are from an interview recorded by him in answer to written questions from the author, Lismore, New South Wales, Australia, March 1990.
2. Interview with Randy Hayes, San Francisco, California, March 16, 1990.
3. Some information for this section came from the Rainforest Information Centre's cassette tape *Nightcap Rainforest: Thinking Globally—Acting Locally* (Lismore, New South Wales, Australia: Rainforest Information Centre, 1982).
4. *The Franklin Blockade* (Hobart, Tasmania, Australia: The Wilderness Society, 1983), p. 4. This book, written by the blockaders, is a fascinating in-depth look at the joys and failures of radical environmentalism. Much of the background information regarding the blockade used here is drawn from this volume.

Chapter 15. STIRRING THE POT: Radical Environmental Literature, Music, Art, and Theater.

1. Edward Abbey, *Abbey's Road* (New York: E.P. Dutton, 1979), pp. xxii-xxiii.
2. Edward Abbey, *Hayduke Lives!* (Boston: Little, Brown and Company, 1990), p. 239.
3. Edward Abbey, *One Life at a Time, Please* (New York: Henry Holt, 1988), p. 5.
4. Interview with Mike Roselle, San Francisco, California, August 29, 1989.
5. Interview with Darryl Cherney, San Francisco, California, September 1, 1989.
6. Edward Abbey, *The Monkey Wrench Gang* (New York: Avon, 1975), pp. 90-91. Reprinted by permission of Don Congdon Associates, Inc.. Copyright © 1975 by Edward Abbey.

7. Edward Abbey, *Desert Solitaire* (New York: Ballantine, 1968), p. 240. Reprinted with permission of Don Congdon Associates, Inc. Copyright ©1968 by Edward Abbey.
8. John Muir, *A Thousand Mile Walk to the Gulf* (Boston: Houghton Mifflin, 1916), p. 122.
9. Edward Abbey, *Desert Solitaire*, p. 20
10. Robinson Jeffers, *The Double Axe and Other Poems* (New York, Liveright, 1977), p. 171.
11. Ibid., p. 172.
12. Ibid., p. 174.
13. From Robinson Jeffers, "Vulture," *Selected Poems* (New York: Vintage, 1965), p. 107.
14. From Robinson Jeffers, "The Beauty of Things," *Selected Poems*, p. 94.
15. Robinson Jeffers, "Hurt Hawks," from *The Double Axe and Other Poems* (New York, Liveright, 1977), pp. 45–46. Reprinted by permission of Liveright Publishing Corporation. Copyright © 1965 by Robinson Jeffers.
16. Burr Snider, "The Sage of the Sierra," in *Image*, September 17, 1989, p. 16.
17. Gary Snyder, "Bear," from *Left Out in the Rain* (San Francisco: North Point Press, 1986) p. 140. Reprinted by permission of North Point Press. Copyright ©1986 by Gary Snyder.
18. Kathy Minott, "Holy Cow." Reprinted with permission.
19. Michael Robinson, "The Dying Mouse in the North Cascades." Reprinted with permission.
20. Cherney interview.
21. Telephone interview with Bob Kaspar, February 3, 1990.
22. Telephone interview with Bart Koehler, April 27, 1990.
23. Ibid.
24. Ibid.
25. B.N. Koeler, "Bad Wolf." Reprinted with permission.
26. Interview with Roger Featherstone, Tucson, Arizona, November 7, 1989.
27. Ibid.
28. Kaspar interview.
29. Darryl Cherney, "You Can't Clearcut Your Way to Heaven." Reprinted by permission.
30. Bill Oliver, "Habitat," in Johnny Sagebrush, ed., *Little Green Songbook* (Tucson, Arizona: Ned Ludd, 1986), p. 43.
31. Kaspar interview.
32. Interview with Rufus Cohen, Clearlake,, California, October 22, 1989.
33. Interview with Rod Coronado, Davis, California, February2, 1990.
34. Ibid.
35. Interview with Paul Watson, Poulsbo, Washington, November 24, 1989.
36. Telephone interview with Roger Candee, February 3, 1990.
37. Ibid.
38. Interview with Peter Steinhart, Palo Alto, California, January 8, 1990.
39. Interview with Kim Stallwood, Rockwood, Maryland, October 30, 1989.
40. Interview with Lee Stetson, El Portal, California, December 11, 1989.

Chapter 16: CONCLUSION: Of Change and Constancy

1. Marble C. Byrd, "Pacific Lumber Threatens Headwaters," *Earth First! Journal* 15:4 (March 21, 1995), p. 1.
2. Judi Bari, "Headwaters Forest Still Stands," *Earth First! Journal* 15:5 (May 1, 1995), p. 6.
3. Randy Ghent, "Mass Action for Headwaters," *Earth First! Journal* 15:8 (September 23, 1995), pp. 1ff.
4. Josh Brown, Timber Wolf, and Rober Parker, "Headwaters 'Deal' Rejected," *Earth First! Journal* 17:2 (December 21, 1996), pp. 1ff.
5. Ibid., p. 21.
6. Sorrel and Squat, "The People vs. Woody Harrelson," *Earth First! Journal* 17:3 (February 2, 1997), p. 1.
7. Online: http://www.asje.org/.

8. Alicia Littletree, "Pepper Spray and Nonviolent Protestors," *Redwood Nation Earth First!* Winter 1997/1998, pp. 5, 8.

9. Anne Arkee, "Headwaters Pepper Mace Fallout," *Earth First! Journal* 18:2 (December 21, 1998), p.25.

10. Online: http://www.nopepperspray.org/factsheet.htm.

11. Julia Butterfly Hill, "Treesitting without Limits," *Earth First! Journal* 18:3 (March 20, 1998), p. 4; also see: Julia Hill, *The Legacy of Luna: The Story of a Tree, a Woman and the Struggle to Save the Redwoods* (HarperSanFrancisco, 2001).

12. Anonymous, "Death Is Not the Punishment for Trespass," *Earth First! Journal* 20:1 (November 1, 1999), p. 32.

13. Karen Pickett, "Headwaters Deal," *Earth First! Journal* 19:5 (May 1, 1999), p. 5.

14. Online: http://www.circleoflife.org/inspiration/julia/.

15. Almond, "David Chain v. Goliath Maxxam: Wrongful Death Settlement Reached," *Earth First! Journal* 22:1 (November 1, 2001), p. 19.

16. Online: http://www.nopepperspray.org/factsheet.htm.

17. Nutchatch, "Redwood Activists Fighting on Every Front," *Earth First! Journal* 23:3 (March 1, 2003), pp. 25-25; Anonymous, "Grandmother Goes to Jail, Begins Fast," online: http://www.contrast.org/treesit/archives/000066.html (March 24, 2004).

18. Verbena and Half-Hitch, "Defending the Redwoods with North Coast EF!," *Earth First! Journal* 25:3 (March 1, 2005), p. 26.

19. Billy Stern, "The Next to Last Stand: A Brief History of Cove/Mallard," online: http://www.wildrockies.org/cove/about/Next_to_Last_Stand.html, October 4, 1997.

20. Idaho Statutes 18§2005.

21. "Wild Rockies Earth First!," insert, *Earth First! Journal* 21:7 (August 1, 2001); Anonymous, "ELF Spikes Trees in Idaho," *Earth First! Journal* 22:2 (December 21, 2001), p. 26.

22. A counter of the current slaughter total—by 2005 it had reached 3,922—is available on the Buffalo Field Campaign's web page: http://www.buffalofieldcampaign.org/index.html.

23. James Barnes, "Last Wild Bison Herd at Risk in Yellowstone," *Earth First! Journal* 17:3 (February 2, 1997), p. 25.

24. Anonymous, "Delyla Sentenced," *Earth First! Journal* 18:3 (February 2, 1998), p. 28.

25. Anonymous, "Yellowstone Slaughter Disrupted: Bison Beats State 34-25," *Earth First! Journal* 18:3 (February 2, 1998), pp. 1ff.

26. Jonah Clarke, "Buffalo Hunt Canceled," *Earth First! Journal* 25:3 (March 1, 2005), p. 25.

27. Karen Wood, "91 Arrested in Sugarloaf Protest," *Earth First! Journal* 16:2 (December 22, 1995), p. 4.

28. John Green, "Warner Creek and the Sour Grapes Raid," *Earth First! Journal* 16:7 (September 21, 1996), p. 24. Douglas Bevington's comments were in a personal communication with the author.

29. Rolf Skar, "'Shock and Awe' Logging Proposed for the Siskiyou," *Earth First Journal* 24:2 (January 1, 2004), p. 36.

30. Evelyn Horne and Roger Beatty, "Mount Graham Desecration Continues: Judge Rules against Apaches," *Earth First! Journal* 21:6 (June 21, 2001), p. 6.

31. John Conner, "See You in the Mountains: Katúah Earth First! Confronts Mountaintop Removal," *Earth First! Journal* 25:1 (November 1, 2004), pp. 6-7; John Conner, "Tips for Taking on the Ku Klux Klan," *Earth First! Journal* 24:4 (May 1, 2004), pp. 22-24; Jonathan Crowell, "Earth First! Confronts the Aryan Nations," *Earth First! Journal* 19:8 (September 21, 1999), p. 10.

32. Wildfire, "Indiana's First Treesit in Its Third Month," *Earth First! Journal* 21:6 (June 21, 2001), p. 10.

33. Amy Thoreau, "Mass EF! Takes to the Trees," *Earth First! Journal* 20:6 (September 1, 2003), p. 25.

34. Anonymous, "The Strawberry Liberation Front," *Earth First! Journal* 7:6 (June 21 1987), p. 1.

35. See: Brian Tokar, "Genetic Engineering in the US: Bringing It Home," *Earth First! Journal* 19:4 (March 20, 1999), pp. 1ff.

36. Vic, "Resistance to Nanotech Grows," *Earth First! Journal* 25: 2 (January 1, 2005), p. 3.

37. Andrew Christie, "Norway Attacks Sea Shepherd," *Earth First! Journal* August 1, 1995, p. 5.

38. Ibid.

39. Ibid.

40. Ibid.

41. Paul Watson, "Report for the Galapagos," *Earth First! Journal* 24:1 (November 1, 2003), p. 38.

42. Paul Watson, "Return to the Seals: The Largest Marine Mammal Slaughter in the World," *Earth First! Journal* 24:3 (March 1, 2004), pp. 16-17.

43. Turtle, "Confronting the Slaughter: On the Frontlines of Canada's Seal Hunt," *Earth First! Journal* 25:5 (July 1, 2005), pp. 10-13.

44. Ibid.

45. A synopsis of some of the ALF's major actions through 1997 may be found in the "Animal Liberation Front: Past and Present" insert that appeared in the *Earth First! Journal* 18:3 (February 2, 1998).

46. Anonymous, "Born to Die at Huntingdon Life Sciences," *Earth First! Journal* 21:6 (June 21, 2001), p. 25.

47. Ibid.

48. Tara the Sea Elf, "The Earth Liberation Front," *Earth First! Journal* 16:7 (September 21, 1996), p. 18.

49. Ibid.

50. Ibid.

51. Ibid.

52. Ibid.

53. Rod Coronado, "Burn Baby, Burn," *Earth First! Journal* 23:6 (September 1, 2003), p. 3.

54. Fan, "A Stab in the Dark: The Feds' Frantic Search for the ELF and ALF," *Earth First! Journal* 24:3 (March 1, 2004), pp. 22-23.

55. Mike Roselle, "Dear Friends," *Louder than Words* (Ruckus Society newsletter, April 1997), p. 3.

56. Joseph Plaster, "Go forth and Process—The Ruckus Society Rethinks the U.S. Anti-Globalization Movement," *Earth First! Journal* 24:4 (May 1, 2004), p. 37.

57. Online: http://ruckus.org/index.php/training.

58. Online: http://www.citizen.org/trade/wto/.

59. Martin Khor, "Growing Opposition to Biopiracy, Life Patents," online: http://www.sunsonline.org/trade/areas/intellec/10260095.htm (October 25, 1995).

60. "Shut Down the World Trade Organization," insert, *Earth First! Journal* 19:8 (September 21, 1999).

61. Anonymous, "Hell No to the WTO: Kicking Corporate Butt in Seattle," *Earth First! Journal* 20:2 (December 21, 1999), pp. 6-7.

62. Ibid., p. 7.

63. Ibid.

64. Online: http://depts.washington.edu/wtohist/index.htm.

65. Woverine, "Where to Next? A Post-WTO Analysis," *Earth First! Journal* 20:3 (February 1, 2000), p. 3.

66. Jim Flynn, "Dear Shit fer Brains Letters to the Editors," *Earth First! Journal* 25:3 (March 1, 2005), p. 3.

67. For examples of some of the groups that have been created, see the web pages for The Alliance for Sustainable Jobs and the Environment (http://www.asje.org/), Global Exchange (http://www.globalexchange.org/), and the Global Justice Ecology Project (http://globaljusticeecology.org/).

68. Online: http://www.fbi.gov/congress/congress04/lewis051804.htm; also see: Marie McCullough, "Biotech Fights back on Animal Rights," (Wilkes Barre, Pennsylvania)

Times Leader, June 21, 2005, online: http://www.timesleader.com/mld/timesleader/living/health/11943841.htm.

69. Jeffrey "Free" Luers, "How I became an Ecowarrior: Part II," *Earth First! Journal* 24:4 (May 1, 2004), p. 40.

70. Dan Whipple, "Blue Planet: Ecoterrorism Redefined," United Press International (September 13, 2002), online: http://www.upi.com/view.cfm?StoryID=20020911-115335-8099r.

71. Judi Bari, "Monkeywrenching," *Earth First! Journal* 14:3 (February 2, 1994), p. 8.

72. Christopher Baer, "Thoughtful Radicalism Revisited: Because Sometimes *#%ing Shit Up Just Isn't Enough," *Earth First! Journal* 19:3 (February 1, 1999), p. 3.

73. Ibid., p. 29.

74. John Vidal, "Explode a Condom, Save the World," (London, UK) *Guardian*, July 10, 1993, p. 27.

75. Janet Wells, "Animal Researchers Feel Hunted," *San Francisco Chronicle*, January 1, 1993, p. A1.

76. George W. Pring and Penelope Canan, *SLAPPs: Getting Sued for Speaking Out* (Philadelphia: Temple University Press, 1996). I have attempted to simplify their complex definition of SLAPP.

77. Lori Potter, online: http://www.firstamendmentcenter.org/petition/topic.aspx?topic=slap.

78. Karen Pickett, "Maxxam SLAPPs Mattole Defenders," *Earth First! Journal* 21:5 (May 1, 2001), p. 7.

79. Erik Ryberg, "The Strange and Wonderful Tale of How I Got 11 Million Dollars Richer in Just One Single Day," *Earth First! Journal* 17:2 (December 21, 1996), p. 5.

80. Anonymous, "Eric Schatz and Pacific Lumber vs. EF!, the People, and the Forest," *Earth First! Journal* 23:5 (July 1, 2003), p. 7.

81. Anonymous, "'Eco-terrorist' Hysteria Sweeps Several States," *Earth First! Journal* 21:6 (June 21, 2001), p. 18.

82. Idaho statutes 18§2005.

83. Rik Scarce, *Contempt of Court: A Scholar's Battle for Free Speech from Behind Bars* (Walnut Creek, California: AltaMira Press, 2005).

84. Online: http://www.albionmonitor.com/9905a/jbrevisited.html.

85. Karen Pickett, "Earth First! Takes the FBI to Court: Judi Bari and Darryl Cherney's Case Heard after 12 Years," *Earth First! Journal* 22:6 (June 21, 2002), p. 6.

86. Ibid.

87. Ibid.; also see: Judi Bari, *Timber Wars* (Monroe, Maine: Common Courage Press, 1994).

88. Online: http://www.judibari.org/index.html.

89. Nicholas Wilson, "Jury Awards $4.4 Million Damages to Bari and Cherney," Albion (CA) *Monitor*, June 11, 2002, online: http://www.albionmonitor.com:16080/0205a/judibaritrial12.html).

90. Ibid.

91. Online: http://www.albionmonitor.com/9905a/jbrevisited.html.

92. Chad Hanson, "Sierra Club Goes Zero Cut," *Earth First! Journal* 16:5 (May 1, 1996), p. 1.

93. Garth Kahl, "Rethinking the Border," *Earth First! Journal* 18:5 (May 1, 1998), pp. 3ff.

94. Catia Juliana, "Say What?" *Earth First! Journal* 15:1 (November 1, 1994), p. 2.

95. Bonnie Abbzug, "Shouldering Earth First!'s Baggage: Wilderness, Privilege, and Immigration," *Earth First! Journal* 21:5 (May 1, 2001), pp. 21ff.

96. James John Bell, "Hayduke, Ecofeminism, and Monkeywrenching: The Fighting Words of Earth First!," *Earth First! Journal* 23:6 (September 1, 2003), p. 9.

97. Personal communication with the author.

98. Jim Page, "Tieing [sic] the Knot: Hug a Racist, Save a Whale—An Opinion," *Earth First! Journal* 19:4 (March 20, 1999), p. 6.

99. Rod Coronado, "The Issue at Hand," *Earth First! Journal* 19:6 (June 21, 1999), p. 7.

100. David Orton, "Rethinking Environmental–First Nations Relationships," *Earth First! Journal* 15:2 (December 21, 1994), pp. 3ff.

101. Mira Goldberg, "Toward Stronger Alliances: A Response to 'Rethinking Environmental–First Nations Relationships,'" *Earth First! Journal* 15:3 (February 2, 1995), p. 3.
102. Brian Tokar, "Respect Native Struggles," *Earth First! Journal* 15:3 (February 2, 1995), p. 26.
103. Puck, "Facing off the Radical Environmental Lynch Mob," *Earth First! Journal* 24:6 (September 1, 2004), pp. 30-33.
104. John Johnson, "Stupidity and Critics of the Ecology Movement," *Earth First! Journal* 25:4 (May 1, 2005), p. 12.
105. Errol Schweizer, "Environmental Justice: An Interview with Robert Bullard," *Earth First! Journal* 19:7 (August 1, 1999), p. 8.
106. Bob Greenberg, "The Urbanization of Earth First!: New Directions for the Movement," *Earth First! Journal* 19:5 (May 1, 1999), p. 3.

Index

Boldface numbers indicate the main discussion of the subject.

ABOUT THE AUTHOR

Rik Scarce is an assistant professor of sociology at Skidmore College. He received his Ph.D. in sociology from Washington State University in 1995. His M.A. is from the University of Hawaii (1984) and his B.A. is from Stetson University in Florida (1981); both are in political science. He is the author of *Contempt of Court: A Scholar's Battle for Free Speech from Behind Bars* (AltaMira Press, 2005), *Fishy Business: Salmon, Biology, and the Social Construction of Nature* (Temple University Press, 2000), as well as numerous book chapters and scholarly journal articles.